This Copy of

Source Records

of

The Great War

is registered in the name of

and dedicated to the

BOYS

of

COLBY ACADEMY

New London, New Hampshire

who gave their lives

in the service of their country

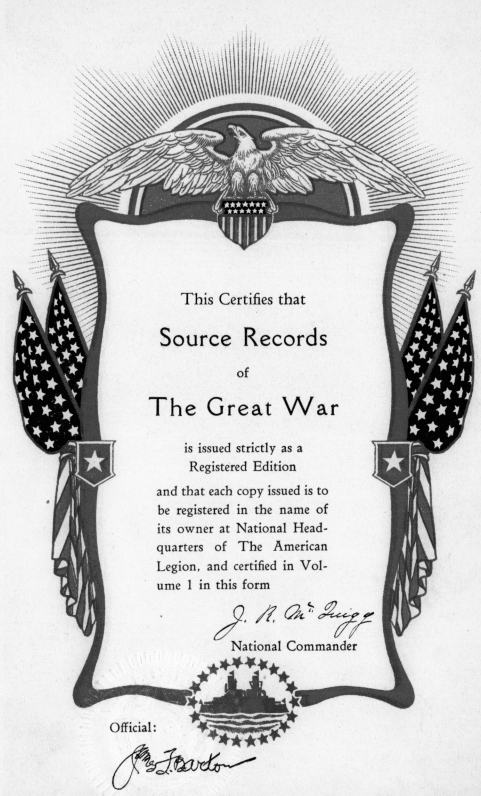

This Certifies that

Source Records

of

The Great War

is issued strictly as a
Registered Edition

and that each copy issued is to
be registered in the name of
its owner at National Headquarters of The American
Legion, and certified in Volume 1 in this form

J. R. Mᶜ Quigg

National Commander

Official:

Jas. F. Barton

National Adjutant

BINDING
Vol. I

The binding design on this volume is an authorized facsimile of the original art binding on the official French copy of the Versailles Peace Treaty, which was signed by President Poincaré and Foreign Minister S. Pichon, and deposited in the Archives of the French Government.

SOURCE RECORDS

OF

THE GREAT WAR

A COMPREHENSIVE AND READABLE SOURCE RECORD OF THE
WORLD'S GREAT WAR, EMPHASIZING THE MORE IMPORTANT
EVENTS, AND PRESENTING THESE AS COMPLETE NARRATIVES
IN THE ACTUAL WORDS OF THE CHIEF OFFICIALS AND MOST
EMINENT LEADERS

NON-PARTISAN NON-SECTIONAL NON-SECTARIAN

PRESENTING DOCUMENTS FROM GOVERNMENT ARCHIVES AND
OTHER AUTHORITATIVE SOURCES, WITH OUTLINE NARRATIVES,
INDICES, CHRONOLOGIES, AND COURSES OF READING ON SOCIO-
LOGICAL MOVEMENTS AND INDIVIDUAL NATIONAL ACTIVITIES

EDITOR-IN-CHIEF

CHARLES F. HORNE, Ph.D.

DIRECTING EDITOR

WALTER F. AUSTIN, LL.M.

With a staff of specialists

VOLUME I

COPYRIGHT, 1923, NATIONAL ALUMNI
Printed in U.S.A.

Some have keen wits to know THE TRUTH;
Some have strong hearts to tell THE TRUTH;
But how few know to tell it so
That all men see it is THE TRUTH.
                    —SIR THOMAS BROWNE.

TO THE READER

These volumes are an earnest effort to give the reader, in practical form, such frank and full information as will enable him to comprehend clearly this greatest of all wars. To follow the volumes most readily and pleasantly, to gather their knowedge most surely and simply, the reader is urged to approach them by the method here suggested.

Turn first to the Outline Narrative which opens each volume. It gives the general picture of the period covered, sketching briefly each Great Event, and showing how each crisis led onward to the next. This series of seven Outline Narratives in the seven volumes thus constitutes in itself a complete story of the War.

In addition to this, as each Great Event is described in the Outline Narratives, it is further emphasized by a footnote directing the reader to its more extended treatment in the body of the volume. For each event upon which the reader wishes fuller knowledge, he should next turn, as directed, to its special section. There he will find, first, a brief introduction giving the details of the event, pointing out its relation to other affairs, and explaining the real value and authoritative source of the articles which follow.

These articles include government statements, individual narratives, or historic documents, covering both sides of each large issue. The articles have been carefully selected from whatever authorities seem, in each particular case, to have best understood what really happened, and to have depicted it most vividly. They are the true "sources" from which future generations will build their knowledge of each event. Only, instead of leaving these "sources" for chance to confuse or to destroy, we are presenting them now, accompanied by the living comment of their own day as to their weight and truthfulness.

From these sections the reader can now and at once form his own accurate judgments about the War and its coming consequences. For example, on the German Chancellor's noted phrase declaring the Belgian treaty merely a "scrap of paper," this first volume gives the Chancellor's own explanation of what he said, and meant; it supplements this with the statement of the British Ambassador to whom the words were said, and the official comments of the rival governments. The volumes thus present a succession of dramatic antitheses, conflicts of statement as sharp and striking as the armed clashes on the field.

That every speaker may be given absolutely "fair play," we have even, as far as possible, had the translation of foreign documents made by writers in sympathy with the originals, pro-Germans for the German texts, pro-Russians for the Russian, and so on. Moreover the translations have been carefully followed by our editors to make sure that the atmosphere of the original is preserved.

As to the originals themselves, they are of course often violently one-sided. Hence the reader is urged, in weighing them, to accept the help of our explanatory introductions, and also of our footnotes. The latter give warning against any statements which the world can now positively declare to be mistaken—or worse. Thus forewarned, one may read the words of truth's worst enemies, may know the wiles of every foe, yet be misled by none of them.

In some such fashion, surely, will all histories be one day written. Only from such will later generations consent to read. So shall clear-headed men of the Future look back upon our Present with keener vision, and gather rich wisdom from the blunders of the Past.

For the scholar who seeks rather to consult our work for occasional reference, or to read fully upon some one nation or topic, we have given to the series a most thorough index. In the final volume will be found not only a complete General Index but also, as supplement to it, a Subject Index pointing out every mention of the more important themes. The reader is guided to outside books by a bibliography.

The editors ardently hope that the value of their work may prove equal to the earnestness of their effort. They have tried to serve you well.

THE EDITORS.

CONTENTS

VOLUME I—How the Great War Arose

ILLUSTRATIONS

VOLUME I

xv

VOLUME I
HOW THE GREAT WAR AROSE

AN OUTLINE NARRATIVE OF

THE CAUSES OF THE WAR

BY CHARLES F. HORNE

NEITHER you nor I nor any man has the right to-day to express doubt as to the true origin of the Great War. Such doubt may once have indicated keen and cautious thought. To-day it indicates either idle ignorance or obstinate falsity. If you do not know the facts, which are open for all the world to know, read them here.

The Great War could no more have been avoided than an earthquake or any other cataclysm of Nature's unknown forces. On the one side loomed the German character of strength and patience, of selfish caution in adversity, and vain and reckless arrogance in power. On the other, glowed the sunlight of democratic civilization, which encourages all peoples to aspire toward equality, and to prefer death to slavery. Given these opposing forces, and their clash was inevitable. The marvel now is only that we were all so slow to see the ominous approach of the disaster.

To say that a war arises from this or that individual event is folly. Such empty phrases were part of the old blind statecraft which we have outgrown. War springs from human nature. In the old, old days of kings, it may have sprung at times from some such petty growth of human nature as the ambition or ill-temper of a single monarch; but in this broader age, only some broader passion widespread among many men, such as that eagerness for supremacy toward which the German mind continued developing during two hundred years, only some such race-wide trait of nature can produce a war.[1]

[1] See § I, "The Opposing Forces," by Bergson, Lamprecht, etc.

"The war that shall end all war!" Has the human race really passed through that stupendous final experience of the great tragedy, the terror and the splendor and despair of destruction and devotion? We may all hope so, but mere hope will do little to change the future. Until the great majority of mankind have been educated into the true Democracy, until each one has grown to say in his heart, "I want the same rights and opportunities as my neighbor, *and no more,*" until that altruistic day arrives, strong and selfish men will still somewhere continue banding together in ever broader and craftier conspiracies to snatch the pleasant richness of life from those who seem too feeble or too ignorant to resist.[1]

The Great War sprang directly from such a conspiracy. Can we so educate the masses of our brothers that never again will any large portion of them be lured to be the servants and victims of another war-plot? At least we can make the effort by spreading to every corner of the earth some definite understanding of the meaning and the causes of the Great War. A later section of these volumes will speak of all the War's dreadful costs and agonies, and also of its heroes and their glorious service. Here we look only for its source.

THE SERAJEVO TRAGEDY

The Great War, then, began nominally because on June 28, 1914, an Austrian lordling bearing the stately title of Crown Prince, was slain at Serajevo, the chief city of Bosnia, a Slavic province held in subjection by Austria. The prince was shot by one of his own Slavic subjects, a young student named Princip, a mere boy of eighteen. A world war because a boy's hand on a revolver had held steady to its purpose, wherein older men had failed more than once before? Obviously not! The death of the Austrian prince was only seized as a fitting opportunity for starting projects which crafty conspirators, who called themselves diplomats, had been preparing and perfecting during many years.

[1] See § III, "The Culture of Democracy," by McElroy and Ruysse

The world does not even know—and as young Princip is since dead in prison we presumably never shall know—what really drove him to his sudden desperate deed. As for what the Austrian government afterward announced concerning his aims and course, there is not the slightest reason for accepting any word of it. Immediately on his arrest, Princip was turned over to police authorities of well established dishonesty and dishonor and was by them tried secretly. Austria might have made his trial open so that all the world could know the truth; or she might at least have entrusted it to Austrian judges of international repute whose word would have carried weight. She did neither. She left the investigation in the hands of an Under-Secretary of State already convicted of having forged documents for similar state trials and of seeking thus foully to destroy the government's leading Slavic subjects who were its political opponents. Under this criminal and utterly untrustworthy control, the Serajevo court took almost a month to deliberate, and then announced that its secret trial had established that Princip's attack was directed by Serbian government officials, inspired by the Serbian government. In all the international negotiations that followed, both Austria and Germany proved their own essential dishonesty by haughtily assuming that Serbia's guilt was neither to be questioned nor further investigated; it must be accepted as established on the mere word of these corrupt investigators in this travesty on justice.[1]

Our real knowledge of the affair, therefore, is limited to the fact that on that tragic day at Serajevo there were two attempts upon the life of the Crown Prince. The first was made in the morning by a man who had been a spy in the employ of the Austrian police; it failed. The second, made in the afternoon by the frenzied Bosnian student, succeeded. The Austrian judges grouped these two assaults together as a single plot. More probably they were separate. The first looks like a calculated deed, one instigated by the Austrian or German antagonists of the prince, and carried out by a hired assassin who thought mainly of his own safety—and

[1] See § XIII, "Assassination of the Crown Prince," Magistrates' Report, etc.

so bungled the attack.   The second seems individual, the
desperate recklessness of a young Slav maddened by the
weight of all the oppression laid upon him and upon his
race.

Viewed in this way, the two deeds lead us to an examination of their differing sources.   The one opens the German
causes of the War; the other the Austrian.   Austria wanted
war that she might fix more firmly her dubious power over
the Slavic people around her, that she might rule them with
more profit and more safety.   The German leaders wanted
war that they might dominate the world.   Germany, the
shrewder, stronger conspirator, needing aid in her vast plans,
dragged her feeble partner into a war far more tremendous
than Austria had ever dreamed of rousing.   To accomplish
this, Germany encouraged Austria—who scarcely needed
urging—to make the death of the Crown Prince a pretext
for what Austria hoped would be a brief and successful war
against two or three unready and half-hearted foes.

The proofs that this was the real origin of the Great War
lie all around us.   To see the whole upheaval clearly, however, and with broader vision, we must look beyond these
immediate impulses, to examine the older, broader, race-wide
causes which had lured Austrian arrogance and stupidity
into this snare, and which had created in Germany the yet
higher arrogance and perhaps equal though less obvious
blindness that tempted her to grasp at world dominion.[1]

AUSTRIAN SOURCES OF THE WAR

Let us take Austria first.   For her, the Great War was
born of the Dark Ages, a thousand years ago.   Then she was
the *Oestereich* or East kingdom, the frontier region of the
old Teutonic empire.   Her dukes were the frontier guards
of western civilization, defending it valiantly against horde
after horde of the wild Huns and Slavs who surged west-
ward against the sturdy Oestereich barrier.   In those days
the duty of every Austrian stood out clear and strong, to
fight these barbarians to the death in protecting his own
home.   So important indeed was the defense of the Oeste-

[1] See § V, "Germany's Dream of Empire," Von Bülow, Harden, etc.

reich that by degrees its dukes, the Hapsburg family, became the most powerful among the Teuton lords, and then emperors of all that was left of the old Teutonic empire. "Austria over all" was the proud Hapsburg motto in those days; and the Hapsburg "Archdukes" gave little heed to the younger upstart family of Hohenzollern dukes who were one day to change that motto somewhat sharply.

The one unfortunate side to the Austrians' heroic defense of civilization was that their idea that they must fight all eastern peoples, that Slavs were meant to be slaves, became so fixed in the minds of Austrians that they could neither forget this nor learn anything else. But in the course of centuries the Slavs and Hungarians settled down and in some sections, such as Bohemia, became as civilized as the Austrians themselves. A new barbaric race from further east, the Turks, became the menace of the frontier, and Slavs and Hungarians were in their turn its defenders. But Austria did not change. The Hapsburg family had acquired a fixed creed which taught their own "Divine Right," taught them that they were appointed by God to rule over just as many lands and peoples as they could clutch. Their Austrian subjects found equal profit in this faith, and trampled savagely upon any of the subject races, Slavs, Hungarians or Italians, who dared resist it.

When the French Revolution opened for Europe the great new "People's Era" of equal rights, the ancient Austrian power was first broken by Napoleon, that strangely confusing and unwitting champion of Democracy. Then followed a bright century of Democracy's triumphs over this oldest and most reactionary of modern autocracies. In 1848 the Hungarians fought Austria to exhaustion, and ultimately won equal rights within her empire. In 1859 the Italians fought her, and most of them escaped her thrall. In 1866 Prussia wrenched from her the lordship over Germany. After that, of all Austria's subject races, only the Slavs and a few kindred folk remained helpless in her grip.

Yet despite all these disasters, the immovable Hapsburgs, incapable as ever of either learning or forgetting, continued on their ancient course. To them the ideal world would have been one that never moved, that rested unchanged forever under their universal rule, a world wherein the good were rewarded by being allowed to hold a Hapsburg's horse, or serve at his meals, or even perchance to visit in the royal bed-chamber. As for the wicked—that is, the unsubmissive —they were to be punished by open war, or judicial murder in the courts, or secret assassination. Indeed, there is much of that grimmest humor which is said to rouse the laughter of the gods, in the spectacle of a Hapsburg objecting to assassination—and even in his holy horror of it summoning the world to war. Only as a weapon in the hands of their enemies have the Hapsburgs ever protested against murder.

By the beginning of this twentieth century, affairs were going badly in this medieval Austrian court. Democracy had roused from slumber even the patient and submissive Slavs. The Slavic folk of Serbia had become independent, self-governing, vigorous and happy in their freedom, and they encouraged the Austrian Slavs to seek a similar release. The great Slavic state of Russia was also feeling her "blood brotherhood" with these Austrian subjects. Even the Hapsburgs saw that the old autocratic despotism was no longer practical.[1] Or at least one Hapsburg saw it; that was the Archduke Franz Ferdinand, the victim of Serajevo. He had already advocated, not giving the Slavs their freedom, that would have been too wholly Democratic, it would have been admitting that a Slav had as much right in the universe as a Hapsburg prince—but the Archduke had suggested giving the Slavs equal political rights with the Austrians and Hungarians, and making a threefold instead of a dual empire.

Against a man so radical as this, and one who must very soon succeed to the throne of the aged Austrian emperor, there was bitter opposition among the Austrian aristocracy and among their Teutonic relatives across the German border. This may well have been the cause of the first Serajevo assault upon him. But whatever the ultimate plans of Franz Ferdinand, he had not yet relieved the subject Slavs from any of the thousand forms of oppression which made them

[1] See § IX, "Austria's Danger in the Balkans," by Ambassador Dumba, etc.

hate the whole Austrian race. The frenzied lad Princip was but the voice of a million of his fellows. They saw no way to freedom from the Hapsburgs except by using the Hapsburg method of force and fraud and secrecy. Franz Ferdinand, who sought to be the mediator between these hostile forces, was antagonized by both, was caught between the millstones.[1]

In opposition to him, the entire Hapsburg family had decided on employing once more the long tried methods of despotism to suppress the Slavic dream. Serbia, the home of the independent Balkan Slavs, was to be crushed out of existence. All the "Southern Slavs" were to be made Austrian subjects. Russia, the great eastern Slavic state, was to be tricked or frightened into abandoning them, or if she refused to yield was to be destroyed by Germany.

The righteousness of letting loose massacre and destruction on such a scale, troubled the Hapsburg councils not at all. Was it not to be done for the noblest of all purposes, the extension of the Hapsburg rule! But the feasibility of their purpose was less clear. Twice at least within the half dozen years immediately before 1914, Austria tried to induce her allies, Germany and Italy, to support her savage plan. Occasion for a war on Serbia could always be manufactured. But Italy refused the proposal flatly; and Germany held back.

In 1914 Germany's attitude changed. She was ready for war at last, ready to the last detail. So, when once more Austria urged on her the Serbian assault, with its included defiance of unready Russia, the answer was no longer "Wait!" but "Strike!" Poor, foolish, purblind Hapsburgs who could not see that they were being used as the catspaw in plans as broad and shrewd and fully up to date as their own were narrow and obstinate and medievally impossible!

So the fatal word for war sped from Berlin to Vienna early in July and the death of the unhappy anachronism Franz Ferdinand, a Hapsburg who had caught some half-glimmering of modern thought, was taken out of the dustbin of forgotten tragedies and suddenly staged as a hideous

[1] See § XIV, "Whose Victim and Whose Opportunity," Münz, etc.

Serbian plot. This cold, stern duke whose plans of mediation had made him most heartily disliked and watchfully
distrusted by his whole Hapsburg circle, was now proclaimed
its gallant martyr and pathetic hero. In the first days after
Serajevo the aged Emperor Franz Josef had said publicly
that the murder must not be used to incite racial antagonisms,
must not be treated as a national event but as a personal
Hapsburg sorrow. Now, no words of execration and incitement could be found too strong against the whole Serbian
race. Austrian public resentment was to be fully roused.
Western Europe was to be horrified by the outrage and prevented from coming to Serbia's aid.

GERMAN SOURCES OF THE WAR

Turn now to the German purpose in the War, a project
so much vaster, so much deeper of origin and broader of
meaning, that it seems scarce to belong in the same universe
with the Austrian futile obstinacy. The one was the last
relic of an outworn medieval system of despotism which
could not possibly have lasted many generations longer. The
other was a new and vigorous outgrowth from despotism,
an autocracy revised, modernized, made practical and terrible almost beyond belief. Moreover, this German autocracy
had gradually built up such a system of militarism as no
earlier tyrant had conceived, a foul and hideous Minotaur—
a Minotaur no longer a mere fantasy of ancient legend but
an actual living horror, a monster devouring all the virtue
and all the young manhood of its own land.[1]

To understand the German autocracy and this monster
it had created, we need not go back to very ancient days, but
only to that King Frederick II. of Prussia commonly called
"the Great." He closed his long and triumphant reign in
1786, just before the French Revolution struck the first great
blow against the ancient régime of kingship by divine authority—of which Frederick was perhaps the most grotesque
illustration. We often say, and justly, of some great man
that he lived a century ahead of his times, because though
we find him at odds with the common thought of his day,

[1] See § VI, "Militarism," by Bernhardi, Prince Frederick, etc.

later generations accept his doctrines and learn to treasure his every word. In that sense, Frederick II. surely deserved his otherwise dubious title of "the Great"; for we might almost call the Germany of 1914 the mirror of his mind. It quoted his maxims constantly, worshiped his deeds devoutly, and studied his military campaigns as models of perfection.

This chief national hero of Prussia had plunged his people into war solely because he possessed a larger, better-trained army than his neighbors and had found his soldiers too expensive to support in peace. Battle was to him an exact matter of business, though in his earlier days he was much impelled also by vanity and the desire for "glory." The cost of his campaigns in human life and human misery scarce touched him, so long as it was to be paid by other folk. His callousness and craft were not, however, the traits that made him great; in these he differed little from many another despot both before and since. There is, for example, no such wholesale murder to be charged against Frederick as the ravaging of the Rhine lands by Louis XIV. of France, half a century before. The soldiers of Louis by his orders laid these populous lands utterly waste, slaying or driving out all the inhabitants, so that the land should lie as a desert between him and his German foes. No, we can by no means rank Frederick first among the wholesale butchers of human kind. His claim to an evil preëminence is intellectual.

Frederick was absolutely indifferent to the mighty spiritual forces sometimes called the "Imponderables," self-sacrifice, equal justice, and eternal verity. He denied their existence; he challenged them to prove themselves against him. He saw exactly his own selfish motives of action, and he stated them with dogmatic frankness. There was for him none of that hiding behind veils of stately words and muddled thought wherewith other despots, like the Hapsburgs and later Hohenzollerns, have obscured their own intellects and salved their consciences. "Necessities of State," "Inherited obligations," "Evil done that good may come," "The upholding of a coronation oath to extend the realm"! All of these ancient shibboleths with which weak tyrants have hidden from themselves the horrors of their savagery, Frederick tossed aside. He had reached that scientific clearness of vision which has become the idol of our own age, wherein every thinker strives to dissociate himself from all inherited prejudice and to examine facts exactly as they are.

Therein lay Frederick's greatness. His range of vision was of the very smallest and meanest. He denied religion and denied morality; that is, he believed neither in human virtue nor in superhuman guidance, recognized the value of nothing but strength, wit, and earthly beauty. But such as his vision was, he had the courage to abide by it. Amid a whole world of pose and pretense, he was so cynically frank that his foes never quite believed him. His truth proved a deeper mask than falsehood.

Few Prussians of Frederick's day were so clear-minded as their master; but they gloried in his success. As for later generations, the more the Prussian aristocrats grasped the teaching of his strong, hard character, the more they worshiped him. His doctrines were so logical, so consistent, so satisfying to those who lived in wealth and high position, that many grew to be like him—in all but his frankness of self-revelation. Thus the soil was fully ready for the fierce pagan doctrine of Nietzsche, widely adopted by the German aristocracy about 1890. Nietzsche and the modern German "Kultur" could have taught nothing to Frederick the Great except some semi-scientific jargon of words for his ideas.[1]

Meanwhile side by side with the hard materialism of Frederick, there were being molded amid the masses of Germans other character elements of a different kind. For centuries Germany had been divided into hundreds of little semi-independent states, seldom united in actions either of peace or war. In consequence, the land had been repeatedly ravaged by victorious foreign armies; the people had learned their helplessness, and had learned, alas, to cringe and bend before the storm. Then under Prussian leadership, quite suddenly after 1866, they became strong in a military sense, the strongest nation in the world. Had such strength come to them slowly, with the training in pity and in kindly tolerance that should go with strength, the German people might

[1] See § II, "The Kultur of Germany," by Elkin, Nietzsche, etc.

have grown worthy of their high position. But alas, power had come too swiftly to allow of that gradual development of racial character which requires many generations. The Germans had not forgotten how to cringe.

Now, the man who will not stand up for his own human rights in defiance of superior force, cannot understand and will not anticipate such an attitude in others. The coward knows no law save that of brute force. Give him the upper hand and he will surely use it like a brute. There was no more illuminating incident through the whole war than the reproachful meeting between the Belgian and German socialists in 1915. Why, demanded the Belgians, did you not prevent your government from attacking us? But, protested the Germans, if we had interfered we would have been shot! And then they asked in rebuttal, But why did you resist our soldiers? "We had to," said the Belgians, "in defense of our independence and honor." "That," said the Germans, "is simply not sense." The whole essence of the Great War lies in that brief dialogue. Germany really believed that every man of sense, every human being not actually insane, would and should cling to the bare husk of living, at any sacrifice of principle. Hence the Germans, having acquired the power to take away life from the other nations, expected the nations to worship their strength, as Germans had once worshiped it in others. When mankind refused to bow before them, they felt that mankind was not "playing the game," *their* game; and they went to war to make us do it.

The Teutons of the past had been truly a great race, great in brute strength even in the far off Roman days, great also in their patience, their earnestness and their cleanliness. But when, because of centuries of misery, they extended their patience into passivity and their endurance into submissiveness, they lost their birthright. A person who merely follows orders, who obeys passively, submissively, loses his power to think. He ceases to be a reasoning creature. His life is guided not by intelligence but by blind emotion. That is what happened to the mass of the Germans. Their new government had given them union and the world power in which they so delighted. Hence they were ready to follow that government anywhere, believe anything it told them. And it deceived them to the height of their folly.

The world has never before seen such astounding examples of mass-hypnosis, the instant uprising on command of a fervid and genuine emotion in an entire people. The German government had only to give its order, "Hate the Belgians, they have wickedly tortured our holy and pure-hearted soldiers!" "Hate the Russians, they have wantonly attacked our gentle peace-loving people!" "Hate the Britons, they have suddenly snared our straightforward government in a trap long prepared!" and the German people swung to the new emotion with the smoothness of a pendulum and the regularity of a military platoon.[1] Intellectually of course they knew that their soldiers were not holy and pure hearted, that they themselves were not gentle and peace-loving, that their government was not straightforward. But the intellect of the mass of Germans had long ceased to function. Its last remnants had been submerged in the passion of self-worship, ecstatic worship of their power as world-rulers. The German of 1914, in the few moments when he sank to cold thought, was still a cringing, logically calculating, life-clutching creature; but in his hours of excitement he became again the ferocious barbarian of ancient ages, often recklessly heroic and wholly unintelligent.

Now, consider this huge, unreasoning child of the world, with his strength and vanity, his cringing and cruelty, his intellectual submissiveness and emotional hysteria, this monstrous yet splendid beast which the blunders and oppressions of Europe had created. Consider that he was ruled by an ambitious, military aristocracy of Prussian junkers and Rhineland financiers,[2] shrewd soulless materialists bred up by Frederick the Great and the mad philosopher Nietzsche. Under such leaders was not the beast's sometime rush of destruction a thing inevitable? If it had not been already so, the one other necessary element was the German lack of humor.

[1] See Lissauer's "Hymn of Hate," page 403.
[2] See § XIV, "The Kaiser's Decisive Step," by Thyssen, etc.

Perhaps the importance of this final factor in the disaster has not been fully recognized. The lack of an eye for incongruities and a pleasure in them will not, let us hope, be among the failings of future "great peoples." Tell an American that he is a fine individual specimen of the finest race of the world, and he will laugh with you good-naturedly. Tell the same to an Englishman, and he may at heart think you are right, but outwardly he knows you are "spoofing" him. Tell it even to an Arab or a Turk, and his eyes close with suspicion of so crude a snare. Tell it to a German, and he will swell with satisfaction, and begin angry question as to why you have delayed your salaam so long. The Germans for a generation before 1914 had been bowing in ecstatic admiration before themselves. Treitschke, the great Berlin lecturer, started them on this course as early as 1878, and they proved eager pupils. One marvels in reading through their pre-War literature at the universal easy assumption of Germany's *right* to world rule. The only trouble from the German viewpoint was that the other, lesser races of mankind were so stupidly slow in joining the delightful chorus.

Energy in authority, obedience in submission, these combining with patient toil in every rank, built up in Germany an effectiveness of organization such as the world had never before known. It was a new form of coöperation, dependent on the subordination, more or less willing, of the individual to the good of the community—as interpreted by the aristocracy. The German really believed that he had evolved a higher order of society, and that it was his mission to enforce his culture on the outside world of selfish individualism.[1]

When once we have recognized the Great War as being based thus upon the German character too hastily developed since 1866, we shall question less anxiously the extent of influence of any particular incident in leading toward the explosion. A volcano must erupt somewhere, and there is

[1] See § IV, "Germany's Economic Organization," by Hauser and Naumann.

small use in clapping a lid over some one of its more obvious ventholes and then sitting firmly on that special lid.

THE RESPONSIBILITY OF OTHER NATIONS

On the other hand, no one would represent as persecuted angels the nations which opposed Germany in the War. Perhaps the only European government which will ultimately be adjudged wholly guiltless of contributing to the antagonisms of 1914 will be poor martyred Belgium. In the East, Russia, while she had no insuperable quarrel with Germany, had often deliberately made trouble for Austria. The Austrian subject Slavs were encouraged in resistance by secret Russian agents; and though Russia may have acted in **this** partly because she loved the Slavs, yet many of her **military** chiefs were eager for a war in which to prove **their** power. In Turkey, the whole brutish misrule was unspeakable. In each of the Balkan states there was constant selfish scheming to extend boundaries at the expense of one another, constant intrigue, Russian, German, Austrian and Italian, and constant warfare.

As for Serbia, against which the Great War nominally began, and which was to suffer worst of all Europe from its devastation, Serbia could not possibly have wanted war in 1914, she was too wholly exhausted by her recent and repeated fighting. Presumably, therefore, she had no direct part in either of the Serajevo assaults. Yet Serbia had for years and years encouraged the spirit of revolt among the Austrian Slavs, her brothers; and in this she had not always confined herself to methods strictly polite and legal. When a huge and wholly inconsiderate neighbor persists in trampling upon you with hobnailed boots, it is not easy to restrict your resistance to legal methods or the formal punctilio of the duel. Moreover, Serbian propaganda could not have roused the Austrian Slavs to revolt had they not been already embittered by such genuine cause for discontent as made war seem better to them than peace. In the essence of her Austrian quarrel, Serbia was right and would always be so, as long as a single Serbian peasant was held in unwilling subjection by the Hapsburg autocrats.[1]

[1] See § IX, "National Spirit Among the Serbs," by Trevelyan. etc.

So also in the West. It was Frenchmen's own arrogance and recklessness which had enabled Prussia to entrap them into the disastrous war of 1870. Afterward, it was their own constant talking of "Revenge"—a revenge which most of them had long abandoned except as an emotional phrase —that made Germany eternally suspicious of them. This was at least in part what led the German people to bow their necks so meekly beneath the heavy yoke of Prussian militarism.[1]

As for Britain, her "imperialism" made Germans envious. Britain's mastery of the seas caused Germany, believing only in force, to fear that her sea-trade might any day be stripped from her. Britain's treatment of Ireland led Germany to justify her own tyranny over subject peoples. And lastly Britain's blocking of Germany's colonial expansion in Africa and commercial aggrandizement in the Orient, made Germany sullenly resolute to win by force what she had failed to accomplish by diplomacy. No one can deny that there had been something of the dog-in-the-manger attitude in Britain's outlook on "world politics."

Germany had long secured her own safety by the "Triple Alliance," in which Austria was her willing and Italy her unwilling ally. France and Russia, driven by fear of Germany, formed an opposition alliance. To this Britain, also fearful of Germany, linked herself in 1907 though only in such loose fashion that their agreement was not called an alliance, but the "Triple Entente." The strength thus banded against Central Europe startled the Germans in their turn. Their leaders talked angrily of the "encirclement" of their land by these strong enemies, as though the encirclement had been an original threat against Germany, instead of a necessary counter-defense. German statesmen constantly emphasized to their people the country's so-called "isolation," which they vehemently insisted was due to British "scheming" rather than to Europe's well-founded dread of German militarism.[2]

[1] See § VIII, "Alsace-Lorraine," by Hazen Davis, etc.
[2] See § XI, "Freedom of the Seas," by Balfour, Gaevernitz, etc.

GERMAN EXPANSION AND AMBITION UNDER WILLIAM II.

With our minds thus cleared as to the degree of responsibility of other nations in the Great War, and as to its real sources in Austrian and German autocracy and in the unbalanced development of the German character, let us trace now the more obvious and immediate steps which led to its outbreak.

When William II. ascended the imperial throne of Germany in 1888, he found his country already well-advanced upon that road of marvelous commercial prosperity which was to make her the most successful business corporation the world has ever known. He found his people already possessed of that idealizing elevation of the State above the individual which led so many of them to ignore self for "Germany." He found his own hand and brain in a position to control all the stupendous machinery of diplomatic and military absolutism which Bismarck had built up. In a word the new Kaiser was possessed of such power as might well have overthrown the humility and self-balance of a far greater soul than his. If ever man had an excuse for thinking himself God-chosen to direct the universe, William Hohenzollern was that man.

He soon proved himself unequal to his wondrous opportunity. He failed to direct the mighty German forces toward the benefit of the universe. He did not even marshal them successfully toward that narrower ambition, the benefit of Germany. He dismissed Bismarck, rather than endure a divided authority; and under William's personal rule, Germany no longer won such diplomatic triumphs as Bismarck frequently had gained for her. The new emperor next sought socialistic approval and passed socialistic laws, only to find the socialists grimly ungrateful and so increasing in numbers they seemed like to crowd him from his throne. He then encouraged his military associates to build up the army's power over civilians, only to find at last that the army had grown stronger than he. In brief, he thrust himself into every field, encouraged many a mighty growth, but kept a wise control over none.

GROWTH OF THE PLOT FOR WORLD RULE

Just when William definitely accepted the idea of world rule as necessary to reëstablish his vanishing ascendancy, it must always be impossible to say. The vision of world rule was already bright in Germany when the Kaiser began founding the new German navy in 1898, and when in that same year he visited Turkey and the Holy Land and spoke there of his will to be the great protector of all Moslems— including those under French or British rule. But it is doubtful if William then had either the callous soul or the stubborn will for deliberate world war. There has been much denial of responsibility in Germany since the war, much pointing the finger at some one else as the real world villain. But the general judgment in other lands has been that William began in 1898 a mere playing with the idea of world rule—and found it a delightful plaything—without deep serious intent.

His admiring subjects encouraged his high juggling with the sword. The German war machine was kept always ahead of every neighbor in numbers and efficiency. Any increase in military expenditure anywhere in the world was made the excuse for a still larger expenditure in Germany. Money taxes mounted toward the breaking point. So also did the "man tax," that is, the ever lengthening years of compulsory military service, the increasing severity of discipline, the increasing submission exacted from the civilian.[1] The military autocracy which William so pompously encouraged soon strode on beyond him. It began seriously to will and plan the foul thing, a world-wide murder out of which the German Army should arise in glory.

Up to 1907 the German merchant classes, the great money princes, still held out against this costly military madness. They hoped to win the world through trade. But then came the diplomatic struggle with Britain over the building of the Bagdad railway. That giant enterprise, dear to every German heart, was to insure German ascendancy through all the "Near East" from Vienna to Constantinople, and from Bag-

[1] See § VII, "Woe to the Conquered," by Barker.

dad to the very edge of India. It was the first great move
in the plans for a mighty "Middle Europe" empire. And
when British diplomacy blocked the Bagdad railway, the
German merchant classes took a long step towards entering
the conspiracy for war.[1]

By 1911 Kaiser William, who had once been the most
outspoken of the advocates of force, found himself at heart
perhaps the least eager for it among all his associates. The
more enthusiastic military leaders began sarcastically criti-
cizing his weakness, turning from him to his youthfully im-
pulsive son, the Crown Prince Frederick William. The latter pushed himself somewhat ostentatiously forward as the
champion of military arrogance. Wild rumors flew about
that William might be forced to abdicate in favor of his more
"resolute" son. There are many evidences that under this
pressure William took the final step in 1912, committing himself and his nation definitely to "war for world conquest."

After that there were only the details to be arranged—
preparations to be made, a date set, and fitting occasion
found. The Germans hoped to accomplish much against Britain with their newly constructed navy. As early as 1898 their
naval officers began drinking as a toast, "The Day" when
they should meet the Britons upon equal terms. The Kiel
Canal, which almost doubled the value of a German war-
ship by enabling it to shift at will between the North and
Baltic seas, was too shallow for the huge "dreadnoughts,"
having been built before their invention. So the enlargement of the canal was pushed forward with all possible haste.
It reached completion in the early summer of 1914. Meantime taxes were still further enlarged, until they pressed so
heavily upon the upper classes as to rouse bitter protest.
There was also possible one further extension of the demand on German youth for military service. That extension
was made in 1913, though it almost stung the poorer classes
and the socialists to revolt.

Outside observers began to say that the weight of German militarism was surely on the point of breaking the
back of the German empire. The enormously costly mili-

[1] See § X, "The Bagdad Railway," by Jastrow and Rose.

tary machine must very shortly justify its existence by successful war or must disappear. The new troops gained in 1913 were ready trained in 1914. The new sums raised by taxation had been converted into war munitions. Never had Germany been so ready for stupendous war, war upon the moment, before the threatening breakdown came, and before France and Russia could again match her latest military enlargement.[1]

Why did we not all see that the hour of German war was about to strike? Many people did rouse to apprehension when Franz Ferdinand was slain at Serajevo. But Austria deceived the world by at first treating the affair with such sad and simple dignity as a private Hapsburg sorrow.

Then came the conferences at the Kaiser's Potsdam palace on July 5th. The German leaders had resolved to use the tragic circumstances of the Serajevo murder as the occasion for assuming world mastery. Either by terrorizing other nations, or preferably by fighting them, Germany was to take the decisive step in establishing that mighty "Middle Europe Empire" which she had long planned. Her leaders did not intend, however, to appear as the aggressors. They had well learned the subtle Bismarckian teaching that to win the full support of their own people they must appear to be defending themselves against an unjust attack, but that to win battles they must really begin the attack thmeselves, and must even select the moment for launching it unexpectedly. So they welcomed this fortunate opportunity to put Austria forward as the disturber of the peace.

The Kaiser, on July 5th, gave secret assurance to the envoys of Austria that at last they might work their wicked will upon Serbia, that if they would seize the present occasion for crushing their little foe, he would support them to the uttermost, lend them all the strength of his armies, support them, no matter how impossible their demands. In fact, the more abrupt, severe and even ferocious an ulti-

[1] See § XII, "Germany at the Breaking Point," by Jordan, Bernhardi, etc.

matum the Austrians could devise, the better. On that same day the chief German officials were also called to Potsdam and were warned that this pledge to Austria made war almost certain, and that every preliminary step must be made so as to insure instant readiness. Rumor says that at this point the financial leaders demanded two weeks' delay, so that they might sell such foreign securities as they must lose in war. Another reason for delay was found in the fact that President Poincaré of France was at the moment visiting Russia, a fact that might make French and Russian co-operation uncomfortably swift. So the conspirators waited until Poincaré had left Russia; and meanwhile the Kaiser went on a yachting trip so that all the world might be assured he had not a single war-like thought.[1]

Next in importance to uniting the German people for a supposedly defensive war, the great conspirators considered it essential to keep the other nations disunited and unsuspicious of the German aim. Austria, by accepting Germany's aid, would become definitely bound to her, and in case of widespread war must soon become subordinate to her. The conspirators sought to draw Turkey also to their chariot wheels, and Italy if they could, and Rumania and Bulgaria and Greece. With all of these they started secret negotiations; since all might be considered as in some sort rivals of Serbia. As to supporters of the Serbs, Russia was well known to be pledged to their defense. Yet the Russian Czar might well hesitate to defend the accused assassins of another monarch. If on the other hand Russia abandoned Serbia to the spoilers, Russian influence in the Balkan States was gone forever; German supremacy was established without a blow, and presently German generals would be commanding every Balkan army as they already did in Turkey.

On the whole then, Russia would almost surely fight. And if she did, France, her ally, was pledged to join her. Here were two powerful foes well-nigh assured; but both

[1] See § XIV, "The Kaiser's Decisive Step," by Morgenthau, Muhlon, etc.

hesitant to fight for so poor a cause, and likely therefore to be slow of action and half-hearted. As for Great Britain, she was to some slight extent bound to these two, but would be interested in the Serbian cause even less than they; so the conspirators were very confident that Britain and all the more distant nations could be cajoled or confused and misled at least for the moment. Before any of them awoke to the real meaning of Germany's great stroke, Russia's awkward strength could be broken and France crushed forever.

For more than two weeks the dread ultimatum to Serbia was thus held back. It was only vaguely whispered of in highest German circles, or guessed at in Eastern European chancelleries. It was the great diplomatic secret of the century. Then, when all was ready, on July 23rd, the ultimatum was suddenly hurled at Serbia with the abruptness of a thunderbolt.

THE "THIRTEEN DAYS"

Not for generations had there been such a tumult among high state officials in Europe as that ultimatum created. Its demands had been purposely made so extravagant as to render Serbia's submission impossible. The German Government had purposely remained unaware of the exact terms prescribed, as the German conspirators aimed to make Austria feel herself the leading spirit in the attack. Yet even this suddenly extravagant trust from a usually cautious ally did not wake Austria's suspicions. She pressed blindly ahead, confident that her chance for crushing Serbia had come. As for Germany, had she not sold her foreign securities at a loss, and sent secret orders to her military officers! For her the Great Adventure was already begun; and if Austria could not strike the opening spark, the German government knew of those who would.

It is now an open fact that Europe's diplomatic efforts did almost check Austria's savage rush upon her victim. The British foreign secretary, Sir Edward Grey, was most earnestly determined to keep the peace. France was most unwilling to fight in what seemed so poor a cause. Of the strictly correct forbearance of Russia's diplomatic attitude, we have not sufficient evidence to make us equally sure. The Russian people as a whole were pacifically inclined; but they felt in honor bound to protect Serbia. The weak, unhappy Czar certainly did his best to preserve "peace with honor." On the other hand, the Russian bureaucracy was already so honeycombed with treachery, there were so many high officials taking Germany's pay and doing her bidding that if she desired a flow of offensive incidents to emanate from Russian government offices, she had only to command her troop of trained and hungry hyenas. Moreover, there was a Russian "war party," headed by the Czar's uncle and chief general, the Grandduke Nicholas, which openly preferred almost any war to any peace.

As a whole, however, the British, French and Russian influence for peace was so strongly exerted upon Serbia that she sent Austria an extremely submissive response, such as would have ended any real quarrel where the real grounds for quarrel had been stated. But since Serbia's submission was not, as it could not possibly have been, absolute, Austria found excuse for declaring the response treacherous, elusive and several other adjectives; and she declared war on Serbia on July 28th.[1]

Even then the Great War was not fully inaugurated; for while Russian began gathering her forces to protect Serbia, Sir Edward Grey with true British obstinacy continued to insist that a way of pacific settlement could and must be found. He assailed every foreign office with ever new suggestions for peace. The whole world owes Sir Edward a debt of gratitude for his conduct through all those trying "Thirteen Days" of negotiation—not that he could in any way have prevented war. We now know that was impossible. But his persistency made so crystal clear the fact that every Power was honestly eager to check the war, except Austria and Germany.

Briefly outlined, this is what occurred. All the Powers except Germany had already appealed to Austria not to de-

[1] See § XVII, "Austria Opens the War," by Count Apponyi, etc.

clare war on Serbia so abruptly, but to give them time to join with her, judge the case against Serbia, and make the latter's punishment, if guilty, an international affair. Russia now went further, declaring that if her brother Slavs in Serbia were attacked without further preliminaries, she must and would defend them with her arms. Every one then appealed to Germany to restrain her Austrian ally. Germany refused, on the plea that Austria's honor was at stake—a strange survival of that medieval madness which declared a man once started on a reckless deed must carry it to the end no matter how disastrous to himself and others, and that all his friends must support him in his reckless wickedness! A nation was to be destroyed, or a world plunged into war, rather than that the "honor" of an Austrian autocrat might be dimmed by holding back his hand from the massacre! Is it any wonder the world has swept away forever the old "diplomacy" which intrenched itself behind such debasing and unhuman falsities![1]

To this first betrayal of the "Imponderables," the German government added a second, by announcing that the only way to escape world war was to "localize the conflict" and that for this reason no other Power must interfere in "the war between Austria and Serbia," as Austria's sudden pounce upon her helpless victim was now blandly termed. In other words, if Russia persisted in saving the Serbs from destruction, Germany would attack her. For Russia such a surrender of her brethren to massacre was impossible; and even western Europe could scarce in righteousness abandon Serbia. Yet Germany would do no more than keep repeating, parrot-like, her speciously phrased demand. It is an all-sufficient comment upon the state of the mentality of the German people in 1914 that they listened seriously to such a shallow subterfuge, and still prated of their government as seeking peace.

Austria now began, from her side of the Danube River, to bombard the Serbian capital, Belgrade. Russia resolutely gathered her armies for Serbia's defense; and France

[1] See § XVI, "Breakdown of Diplomacy," by Sir Edward Grey, Prince Lichnowsky, etc.

announced herself as pledged to support Russia. Britain, as we have seen, continued protests equally insistent though less warlike. Austria seems suddenly to have become alarmed at this weight of opposition; and on July 30th she sent word to Russia that she would step back and submit the whole dispute to arbitration.

Was Austria in earnest? Had there flashed upon her startled vision some realization of the awful destruction into which the vaster German plot had lured her? Or was this a mere pretense by which Austrian subjects were to be convinced, like the Germans, of their government's peacefulness of purpose? In either case, the offer to arbitrate was useless; for Germany herself now took the decisive step. On July 31st, she precipitated world war by dispatching to Russia an ultimatum, as extravagantly impossible as that which had been hurled at Serbia.[1]

How far this ultimatum had, like Austria's, been intended from the start we cannot say. Affairs had not gone exactly as the Potsdam conspirators had planned. The Kaiser was distinctly less eager for war on July 31st than he had been on July 23rd. The world was not being wholly deceived as to Germany's underlying aggressiveness. Italy, which had been counted on to join her allies, Germany and Austria, in a "defensive" war, was evidencing quite clearly that she regarded Austria's savage swoop as an "offensive" and would have no part in it. Britain also was less patient and less blind than had been expected; and since the conspirators already knew of their own intent to invade neutral Belgium, they had an increasing fear that this would be the final straw to bring Britain into arms against them. Thus the unfolding situation for their war was by no means so favorable as they had counted on.

On the other hand, they were being driven to a state of nervous fear lest their other great advantage, that of being the first to strike, might also be snatched from them. Negotiations were dragging along; both Russia and France were perforce arming. Suppose these two dangerous foes

[1] See § XVIII, "Germany Declares War Against Russia," by Von Reventlow, Markoff, etc.

should suddenly snatch the initiative and attack Germany! The German "High Staff" insisted on instant action, before its military plan of campaign could be forestalled. The startled Kaiser, forced at last to face reality instead of speech-making, wavered. In his notes he jotted down frantic curses against Britain; he would destroy her and himself and the world together. Then he let the High Staff have its way.

Thus the ultimatum to Russia was dispatched. It declared that Germany regarded the Russian mobilization of troops against Austria as being directed also against herself, and hence if Russia did not completely demobilize within twelve hours, Germany would attack her. Such a sudden abandonment of Russian preparations would have been impossible. Even the attempt at it would, in face of Germany's own gathering of troops, have been suicidal.

The ultimatum was delivered in the Russian capital at midnight; twelve hours later, at noon of August 1st, it was followed by the German declaration of war against Russia. The final step had been taken. The Great War was no longer the mere dream of the Nietzschian devotees of "hardness" and the "superman." It was the grimmest and most awful fact in human history.

THE CAMPAIGN OF FALSEHOOD

The German assault was thus suddenly launched upon a civilization which had been so befogged and misled by the craft of the German leaders that men everywhere stood uncertain, not seeing what the struggle really meant. German craft could hope but one point further in its favor. If France, which was pledged to aid Russia, would start to invade German territory, the Kaiser could again cry, "Protect the Fatherland"; and every German would rush eagerly to arms. France, however, did not repeat her vainglorious blunder of 1870. She was very careful to avoid the faintest appearance of being the aggressor. So Germany took the next step in her long calculated campaign. She declared war on France, asserting, in absolutely obvious falsehood, that France had attacked her.

So far as the great majority of half-hypnotized German subjects were concerned, the effect of this accusation was the same as if it had been true. In a furor of patriotism they rushed to sacrifice themselves for the punishment of France.

Germany next announced, equally without one shadow of knowledge or of truth, that Belgium was aiding France; and on this pretext Germany assumed the right to invade Belgium, as the easiest road for assailing France. Another ultimatum was dispatched. Belgium must welcome the German soldiers as masters, or suffer the consequences of battle. Surrender without resistance or be destroyed! To the eternal honor of Belgium's king, Albert, he chose the latter alternative! And to the eternal honor of all Belgians, his people upheld his choice.[1]

Therein lay Germany's first colossal blunder. She thought that all people, like her own in colder moods, would bow to fear. Had she been willing to accept International Law and common obvious justice as her guide, had she spared Belgium and attacked France along the more difficult Rhine border, the war might indeed have been what Germany had so craftily intended, a contest in which she and Austria were allied against France and Russia, and almost sure of victory. Germany overreached herself. She revealed too soon the Nietzschian beast of prey behind the mask of the disinterested ally of an injured Austria.

May the world never again behold a sight so terrifying and so shameless as when the German beast sprang, ravening and rending, upon helpless Belgium! Falsehood was now the German government's weapon and defense upon every side. The German Chancellor made his notorious statement, that he admitted his country's guilt towards Belgium but was driven to it by necessity—the necessity of punishing the single murder at Serajevo by perpetrating thousands of far more hideous murders upon the wholly guiltless Belgians! Surely here was a world of unreason gone hopelessly absurd.

[1] See § XX, "Belgium Resists for Honor," by De Gerlache, King Albert, etc.

In the very moment of pledging himself to protect the Belgians, the Chancellor abandoned them to plunder and massacre. Germany vowed to restore Belgium after the war, and at the same time made obvious preparations for the land's permanent annexation. The Kaiser himself sent to the United States government an official statement asserting the impossible and oft disproven charges that France and Belgium had begun the war. And when in later years the United States government referred to this "imperial" statement, German officials flatly denied its existence. When it was then officially made public, German writers for America insisted that it must have been forged, ignoring the fact that it was but an echo of Germany's own solemnly proclaimed grievances upon which she based her Declaration of War.

THE GERMAN EXPLANATION OF THE WAR'S BEGINNING

While many intellectual Germans today agree frankly with almost every point of this exposition of the origin of the War, there are still many official or unofficial "explainers" who noisily deny the guilt of the German government. Their lines of argument are twofold. Either they quote extracts from Teuton officials, written in 1914, to show that these individuals were not expecting war, or they point to the warlike words and deeds of officials of other nations to show that others were equally at fault. No one of the arguments thus patiently woven together has ever for one moment shaken the essential facts. Dozens of letters from individual Germans declaring they knew nothing of any mobilization have no weight as against one from the German government commanding *secret* preparation. Even the Kaiser's weeping over a flower on the battlefield and poetically vowing that he "had not willed this," have no weight as against the same Kaiser's official orders to have Serbia forced into fighting.[1]

Of German charges against other nations, the vehemently advanced have been three. The first was that made officially by the German government against poor little

[1] See § XVI, "Breakdown of Diplomacy," by the Kaiser, etc.

Belgium, of having secretly formed with Britain an offensive alliance against Germany. The charge was based on
two worthless documents found by the Germans during
their occupation of Belgium. It was obviously untrue, con-
cocted carelessly in a hurried moment to divert pity from
Belgium (see Volume II, page 52). The second charge
was made against Russia, by German apologists in general, when the Russian Republic in 1917 brought the former Russian general, Sukhomlinoff, to trial for treason.
All that the evidence at this trial really established was
what has been already stated above, that some Russians in
high places acted as German agents and that not the Russian government but some Russian military officials desired
war. The third charge was that made by French Socialists
after the War, that the French president, Poincaré, had
desired and encouraged its outbreak. President Poincaré
overthrew this attack by showing that his attitude had been
that shared by all Frenchmen; he feared that war would
come, and he made every preparation to meet it, *but he did
not start it.*

There, of course, lies the logical weakness of all the
German efforts to shift responsibility. Everybody feared
and to some extent prepared against the coming of a world-
wide war; but Germany deliberately incited it. She used
the threat of it to establish her empire over Middle Europe
and the Near East, and was fully resolved to enforce the
threat if her domination was not submissively accepted.
The difference is obvious, even when partisan spirit attempts to gloss it over. So long as armies exist there will
always exist in any large country some men of military
type who seek war—or the spoils of war—rather than
peace. But only in Germany and Austria were such war-
seekers in control of the government.

HOW DEMOCRACY AWOKE TO ITS DEATH-MENACE

Pause now to see in its full terror the awful menace
which suddenly confronted the world in those midsummer
days of 1914. By such ways of craft and open menace,
a greedy monster of autocracy had been enabled to pounce

suddenly upon its unready victim, the slowly built up civilization which had been developing through all the ages, advancing confusedly, doubtfully, but ever groping onward towards universal knowledge, peace and brotherhood. This civilization of light, such light as man has managed to attain, was to be devoured by this monster wolf of old Teutonic legend, Fenris, the world-destroying wolf of evil, born of the darkness of the Teuton gods. And this monster was now no hollow painted demon of a stage spectacle. It was the mightiest autocracy the world had ever seen, splendidly armed, elaborately organized, scientifically prepared, and relieved from every scruple of conscience by the long taught doctrine that any crime was right and noble if it served that glorious idol of a glorified selfishness, "Deutschland over all."

To this stupendous outburst of armed materialism, the only sufficient source of resistance in all the human universe lay in that other and yet mightier force, "Democracy." But Democracy, for all its strength, is blind, and easily confused, and must move openly. It is many-headed and therefore many-counseled. Autocracy is single-headed, and can move in secret. Hence, the outcome of the struggle between them is, even at Democracy's best, most dangerously insecure, more so than Democracy's leaders have been quite willing to admit. Moreover, when the great Demos wins a victory, he sleeps again. His soldiers scatter joyously, each to resume his own home work and play. Then the foes of Demos recommence their crafty brewing of confusion. Only in some God-given hour of human clarity of vision does the whole world realize, as it did in 1917, that Demos must awake and strike.

France, indeed, recognized at once the nature of the opposing forces in the Great War.[1] She had ever been a leader in Democracy, and she knew well that by Democracy she must stand or fall. From her the main and most immediate resistance to the great war-plot came. But for safety's sake France had previously bound herself to the

[1] See § XIX, "France Accepts the Struggle to the Death," by Poincaré and Viviani.

autocratic Russian government; and she had taken on
with Russia an autocratic tinge. Thus even she at first
was no clear champion of human brotherhood, a leader
around whom all earnest men might rally.

Britain also knew herself to be Democratic at heart.
But her outward appearance of world empire made her
seem even more the autocrat. Her navy gave her at least
the garb and voice of despotism. Germany honestly believed that in Britain she had a rival more hypocritical,
though less strong and crafty, than herself. In truth, however, Britain's essential Democracy was clearly visible
through those last days of diplomatic effort to avoid the
struggle. Sir Edward Grey had repeatedly to say to friend
and foe, "I am not sure Britain will fight for that." He
could not shake an armed fist and announce his ultimatum
as could the autocrats of Russia, Austria and Germany.
He knew that he must first have the support of the British
populace. The first moment when he could speak positively, sure that all the weight of Britain's Democracy
stood behind him, was when Belgium was invaded. For
the first time, then, his voice rang sure and stern as ever
Germany's had been. "If you touch Belgium, it means
war with Britain." Autocracy had roused Democracy to
the full; yet the haughty, blinded Prussian lordlings did
not even recognize the meaning of the new and mightier
contest that confronted them.

Had Germany been more dangerously wise, she would
have made any and every concession to Britain and to Belgium, and to world-sentiment generally, so as to have kept
her war of conquest on its first deceptive basis of moral indignation against Serbia. But again, as always, autocracy
failed to measure truly the weight of the "Imponderables."
Germany had aimed her plans of invasion and conquest first
at Belgium; the machine had started and must not be
stopped. What matter if it overrode mere righteousness,
a useful diplomatic word indeed, kindly of sound, but without one cannon at command, without a single new device
of war concealed in secret armories.

Perhaps even after that first Belgian blunder, Germany

might have accomplished her purpose, might in her terrible strength have triumphed over Britain also, if she could have sufficiently changed her fierce wolf nature, and so avoided rousing the United States. In the great western Democracy, many thinkers long remained in doubt as to the real causes of the War. Had not the new Germany finally convinced Americans of her essential paganism, had she not by her own brute ravages shown beyond question that this War was indeed "Armageddon," the decisive clash between tyranny and brotherhood, America might still have held her strength apart. In that event the Great War would have reached a different and perhaps cataclysmic end.

Germany's disaster lay in that her government could not believe that other States were not as she in at least secret rejection of the Imponderables, that other people were not like her own in the practice and acceptance of deception. Hence we have the amazement of the German authorities over Britain's sudden defiance, the frenzied and now historic appeal of their Chancellor, "Would you go to war over a scrap of paper," a mere British promise to protect Belgium![1] No wonder that Chancellor was in despair! He had thought himself dealing with another autocracy; and he had cajoled and deceived and offered it bribes such as should have rendered it wholly subservient. He was flatly incapable of understanding that Britain, being a Democracy, simply must in the long, long run be truthful —must stand by her plighted word.

For Democracy is not a word but a reality. It is the voice of those Imponderables, which are the Inevitables. It is the expression of man's faith in man.

[1] See § XXI, "Britain Enters the War," by Asquith, Bethmann-Hollweg, etc.

CHRISTENDOM AFTER TWENTY CENTURIES

By far the most famous artist and cartoonist created by the War was Louis Raemaekers. Being a citizen of Holland, he was nominally a neutral, though his mother was of German birth. His earlier war-cartoons contained criticism of England as well as of Germany; but intense sympathy for Belgium gradually made him an impassioned supporter of the Allies' cause. Germany made every possible effort to suppress the Raemaekers cartoons, realizing with what mighty force they were blazoning her shame before the world.

THE STARS

"Those are the Orders of Honor that have been awarded to the dear God for his services to the House of Hohenzollern."

This cartoon depicts a baby Hohenzollern prince explaining the heavens to his brothers and sisters. It is by Theodore Heine, and appeared in the great German comic paper, *Simplicissimus,* as far back as 1903. Many Germans of that day recognized the enormous arrogance of their Emperor and his sons. But, apparently not realizing to what disaster this vanity tended, they made it the subject of light jest rather than serious reprobation. *Simplicissimus,* being not a Prussian but a Bavarian paper, ventured further than any other in cartooning royalty.

THE OPPOSING FORCES

AUTOCRACY AND DEMOCRACY

HENRI BERGSON   OTFRIED NIPPOLD

KARL LAMPRECHT

Our review of the causes of the Great War may best begin with its ultimate or philosophic cause. In the deceptively quiet days before the War, Henri Bergson had been widely hailed as the world's greatest philosopher. His native France had conferred upon him her highest literary and scientific honors. He was President of her Academy of Moral and Political Sciences. In Britain, Germany and America he had been equally welcomed, equally admired as the teacher of a new spiritual faith, at once poetic and scientific, a new and universal tolerance.

Tolerance is of course the traditional attitude of the philosopher. Watching all things, searching back to their origins, he comes to regard them all as natural growths, steady of approach and perhaps inevitable, horrible sometimes and sternly to be suppressed, but never beyond the pity and the helpfulness of the Highest God. From the philosopher Bergson, therefore—and especially as he speaks for France, which among the larger nations has suffered most—let us gather our first broad view of the meaning of the War. Was it inevitable? What were the vast and eternal forces which clashed? I believe the whole world will ultimately accept, perhaps it has already accepted, M. Bergson's interpretation as to the elemental antagonisms which precipitated the struggle. It was a giant phase of the war forever being waged between Life and Death.

To balance this French thinker's view of the world movement of 1914 with an equally honest, comprehensive and philosophic study from the German standpoint, has not been easy. The broadest view yet taken by a German is perhaps the one here given by Professor Otfried Nippold. It also explains why his countrymen have not been able to view the conflict broadly. Of course, Professor Nippold's view is not the official one of Germany. Indeed, his frankness and independence of officialdom in the days before the War resulted ultimately in his leaving Prussia, of which he was a native, and settling in Switzerland. There he became Professor of International Law at the University of Berne, a world-recognized authority on his subject, and a leader in the peace movements before the War. In 1913 he wrote a book of warning against the rising war spirit in Germany, a caution directed to his own beloved German people. That book stirred the lazy world to its first faint tremors of anxiety as to the approaching crisis. In 1918 Professor Nippold, in continuation of his earlier work, wrote "The Awakening of the German People," the essence of which is given here.

In contrast to this independent German attitude we give also the official viewpoint of the German Government as repeatedly expressed throughout the War. It is voiced here by Dr. Karl Lamprecht, who before the War was the most widely known and justly celebrated among German historians, Professor of History at the University of Leipzig. Dr. Lamprecht wrote this appeal especially for the American public in the first heat of the War. Whether we regard the German attitude of those days as one of blindness or as one of deliberate misrepresentation, the article certainly distorts plain facts. To an ignorant and trustful person, it would be dangerous reading. Hence, while Dr. Lamprecht's words are here given exactly as written, footnotes have been added to supply the reader with the established facts when these seem most perverted or not widely known. The glaring inconsistencies and inaccuracies of the article may do more than could either Bergson or Nippold to convince the reader that Dr. Lamprecht's scholarship belongs to a different "culture" from our own.

C. F. H.

BY HENRI BERGSON

"TO understand and not to be enraged"; this has been said to be the last word in philosophy. I believe none of it; and, had I to choose, I should much prefer, when in presence of crime, to give my indignation rein and not to understand. Happily, the choice has not to be made. On the contrary, there are forms of anger which, from a thorough comprehension of their objects, derive the force to sustain and renew their vigor. Our anger is of that kind. We have only to detach the inner meaning of this war, and our horror for those who made it will be increased. Moreover, nothing is easier. A little history, and a little philosophy, will suffice.

For a long period Germany devoted herself to poetry, to art, to metaphysic. She was made, so she said, for thought and imagination; "she had no feeling for the reality of things." It is true that her administration had defects, that she was divided into rival states, that anarchy at certain times seemed beyond remedy. Nevertheless, an attentive study would have revealed, beneath this disorder, the normal process of life, which is always too rank at the first and later on prunes away its excess, makes its choice and adopts a lasting form. From her municipal activity there would have issued at length a good administration, which would have assured order without suppressing liberty. From the closer union of the confederated states would have arisen

that unity in diversity which is the distinguishing mark of
organized beings. But time was needed for that, as it always is needed by life, in order that its possibilities may be
realized.

Now, while Germany was thus working out the task of
her organic self-development, there was within her, or
rather by her side, a people with whom every process tended
to take a mechanical form. Artificiality marked the creation
of Prussia; for she was formed by clumsily sewing together,
edge to edge, provinces either acquired or conquered. Her
administration was mechanical, it did its work with the regularity of a well-appointed machine. Not less mechanical
—extreme both in precision and in power—was the army,
on which the attention of the Hohenzollerns was concentrated. Whether it was that the people had been drilled
for centuries to mechanical obedience; or that an elemental
instinct for conquest and plunder, absorbing to itself the
life of the nation, had simplified its aims and reduced them
to materialism; or that the Prussian character was originally
so made—it is certain that the idea of Prussia always invoked
a vision of rudeness, of rigidity, of automatism, as if everything within her went by clockwork, from the gesture of her
kings to the step of her soldiers.

A day came when Germany had to choose between a
rigid and ready-made system of unification, mechanically
superposed from without, and the unity which comes from
within by a natural effort of life. At the same time the
choice was offered her between an administrative mechanism,
into which she would merely have to fit herself—a complete order, doubtless, but poverty-stricken, like everything
else that is artificial—and that richer and more flexible order
which the wills of men, when freely associated, evolve of
themselves. How would she choose?

There was a man on the spot in whom the methods of
Prussia were incarnate—a genius, I admit, but an evil genius,
for he was devoid of scruple, devoid of faith, devoid of pity,
and devoid of soul. He had just removed the only obstacle
which could spoil his plan; he had got rid of Austria. He
said to himself: "We are going to make Germany take

over, along with Prussian centralization and discipline, all our ambitions and all our appetites. If she hesitates, if the confederate peoples do not arrive of their own accord at this common resolution, I know how to compel them; I will cause a breath of hatred to pass over them, all alike. I will launch them against a common enemy, an enemy we have hoodwinked and waylaid, and whom we shall try to catch unarmed. Then when the hour of triumph shall sound, I will rise up; from Germany, in her intoxication, I will snatch a covenant, which, like that of Faust with Mephistopheles, she has signed with her blood, and by which she also, like Faust, has traded her soul away for the good things of earth."

He did as he had said. The covenant was made. But, to insure that it would never be broken, Germany must be made to feel, for ever and ever, the necessity of the armor in which she was imprisoned. Bismarck took his measures accordingly. Among the confidences which fell from his lips and were gathered up by his intimates is this revealing word: "We took nothing from Austria after Sadowa because we wanted to be able one day to be reconciled with her." So, then, in taking Alsace and a part of Lorraine, his idea was that no reconciliation with the French would be possible. He intended that the German people should believe itself in permanent danger of war, that the new Empire should remain armed to the teeth, and that Germany, instead of dissolving Prussian militarism into her own life, should reënforce it by militarizing herself.

She reënforced it; and day by day the machine grew in complexity and power. But in the process it yielded automatically a result very different from that which its constructors had foreseen. It is the story of the witch who, by a magic incantation, had won the consent of her broomstick to go to the river and fill her buckets; having no formula ready to check the work, she watched her cave fill with water until she was drowned.

The Prussian army had been organized, brought to perfection, tended with love by the Kings of Prussia, in order that it might serve their lust of conquest. To take possession of neighbors' territory was then the sole aim, territory was almost the whole of the national wealth. But with the nineteenth century there was a new departure. The idea peculiar to that century of diverting science to the satisfaction of men's material wants evoked a development of industry, and consequently of commerce, so extraordinary that the old conception of wealth was completely overthrown. Not more than fifty years were needed to bring about this transformation. On the morrow of the war of 1870 a nation expressly made for appropriating the good things of this world had no alternative but to become industrial and commercial. Not on that account, however, would she change the essential principle of her action. On the contrary, she had but to utilize her habits of discipline, method, tenacity, minute care, precise information—and, we may add, of impertinence and spying—to which she owed the growth of her military power. She would thus equip herself with industry and commerce not less formidable than her army, and able to march, on their part also, in military order.

From that time onwards these two were seen going forward together, advancing at an even pace and reciprocally supporting each other—industry, which had answered the appeal of the spirit of conquest, on one side; on the other, the army, in which that spirit was incarnate, with the navy, which had just been added to the forces of the army. Industry was free to develop in all directions; but, from the first, war was the end in view. In enormous factories, such as the world had never seen, tens of thousands of workmen toiled in casting great guns, while by their side, in workshops and laboratories, every invention which the disinterested genius of neighboring peoples had been able to achieve was immediately captured, bent from its intended use, and converted into an engine of war. Reciprocally, the army and navy, which owed their growth to the increasing wealth of the nation, repaid the debt by placing their services at the disposal of this wealth: they undertook to open roads for commerce and outlets for industry. But through this very combination the movement imposed on Prussia by her kings, and on Germany by Prussia, was bound to swerve from its

course, whilst gathering speed and flinging itself forward.
Sooner or later it was bound to escape from all control and
become a plunge into the abyss.

For, even though the spirit of conquest knows no limit in
itself, it must limit its ambitions as long as the question is
simply that of seizing a neighbor's territory. To constitute
their kingdom, kings of Prussia had been obliged to undertake a long series of wars. Whether the name of the spoiler
be Frederick or William, not more than one or two provinces
can be annexed at a time: to take more is to weaken oneself.
But suppose that the same insatiable thirst for conquest enters into the new form of wealth—what follows? Boundless ambition, which till then had spread out the coming of
its gains over indefinite time, since each one of them would
be worthy only a definite portion of space, will now leap all
at once to an object boundless as itself. Rights will be set
up on every portion of the globe where raw material for industry, refitting stations for ships, concessions for capitalists, or outlets for production are seen to exist. In fact, the
policy which had served Prussia so well passed at a bound
from the most calculating prudence to the wildest temerity.
Bismarck, whose common sense put some restraint on the
logic of his principles, was still averse to colonial enterprises;
he said that all the affairs of the East were not worth the
bones of one Pomeranian grenadier. But Germany, retaining Bismarck's former impulse, went straight on and rushed
forward along the lines of least resistance to east and west;
on the one side lay the route to the Orient, on the other the
empire of the sea. But in so doing she virtually declared
war on the nations which Bismarck had managed to keep
allied or friendly. Her ambition looked forward to the
domination of the world.

Moreover, there was no moral restraint which could keep
this ambition under control. Intoxicated by victory, by the
prestige which victory had given her, and of which her commerce, her industry, her science even, had reaped the benefit,
Germany plunged into a material prosperity such as she had
never known, such as she would never have dared to dream
of. She told herself that if force had wrought this miracle,

if force had given her riches and honor, it was because force had within it a hidden virtue, mysterious—nay, divine. Yes, brute force with its train of trickery and lies, when it comes with powers of attack sufficient for the conquest of the world, must needs be in direct line from heaven and a revelation of the will of God on earth. The people to whom this power of attack had come were the elect, a chosen race by whose side the others are races of bondmen. To such a race nothing is forbidden that may help in establishing its dominion. Let none speak to it of inviolable right! Right is what is written in a treaty; a treaty is what registers the will of a conqueror—that is, the direction of his force for the time being. Force, then, and right are the same thing; and if force is pleased to take a new direction, the old right becomes ancient history, and the treaty which backed it with a solemn undertaking, no more than a scrap of paper. Thus Germany, struck with wonder in presence of her victories, of the brute force which had been their means, of the material prosperity which was the outcome, translated her amazement into an idea. And see how, at the call of this idea, a thousand thoughts, as if awaked from slumber, and shaking off the dust of libraries, came rushing in from every side—thoughts which Germany had suffered to sleep among her poets and philosophers, every one which could lend a seductive or striking form to a conviction already made! Henceforth German imperialism had a theory of its own. Taught in schools and universities, it easily molded to itself a nation already broken in to passive obedience and having no loftier ideal wherewith to oppose the official doctrine. Many persons have explained the aberrations of German policy as due to that theory. For my part, I see in it nothing more than a philosophy doomed to translate into ideas what was, in its essence, insatiable ambition and will perverted by pride. The doctrine is an effect rather than a cause; and should the day come when Germany, conscious of her moral humiliation, shall say, to excuse herself, that she had trusted herself too much to certain theories, that an error of judgment is not a crime, it will be necessary to remind her that her philosophy was simply a translation into intellectual terms of her brutality, her appetites and her vices. So, too, in most cases, doctrines are the means by which nations and individuals seek to explain what they are and what they do. Germany, having finally become a predatory nation, invokes Hegel as witness; just as a Germany enamored of moral beauty would have declared herself faithful to Kant, just as a sentimental Germany would have found her tutelary genius in Jacobi or Schopenhauer. Had she leaned in any other direction and been unable to find at home the philosophy she needed, she would have procured it from abroad. Thus when she wished to convince herself that predestined nations exist, she took from France, that she might hoist him into celebrity, a writer whom we have not read—Gobineau.

None the less it is true that perverse ambition, once erected into theory, feels more at ease in working itself out to the end; a part of the responsibility will then be thrown upon logic. If the German race is the elect, it will be the only race which has an unconditional right to live; the others will be tolerated races, and this toleration will be precisely what is termed the "state of peace." Let war come; the annihilation of the enemy will be the end Germany has to pursue. She will not strike at combatants only; she will massacre women and children and old men; she will pillage and burn; the ideal will be to destroy towns, villages, the whole population. Such is the conclusion of the theory. Now we come to its aim and true principle.

As long as war was no more than a means to the settlement of a dispute between two nations, the conflict was localized to the two armies involved. More and more of useless violence was eliminated; innocent populations were kept outside the quarrel. Thus little by little a code of war was drawn up. From the first, however, the Prussian army, organized as it was for conquest, did not take kindly to this law. But from the time when Prussian militarism, now turned into German militarism, had become one with industrialism, it was the enemy's industry, his commerce, the sources of his wealth itself, as well as his military power, which war must now make the end in view. His factories must be destroyed that his competition may be suppressed.

Moreover, that he may be impoverished once and for all and the aggressor enriched, his towns must be put to ransom, pillaged and burned. Above all must the war be short, not only in order that the economic life of Germany might not suffer too much, but further, and chiefly, because her military power lacked that consciousness of a right superior to force by which she could sustain and recuperate her energies. Her moral force, being only the pride which comes from the material force, would be exposed to the same vicissitudes as this latter: in proportion as the one was being expended the other would be used up. Time for moral force to be used up must not be given. The machine must deliver its blow all at once. And this it could do by terrorizing the population, and so paralyzing the nation. To achieve that end, no scruple must be suffered to embarrass the play of its wheels. Hence a system of atrocities prepared in advance— a system as sagaciously put together as the machine itself.

Such is the explanation of the spectacle before us. "Scientific barbarism," "systematic barbarism," are phrases we have heard. Yes, barbarism reënforced by the capture of civilization. Throughout the course of the history we have been following there is, as it were, the continuous clang of militarism and industrialism, of machinery and mechanism, of debased moral materialism.

Many years hence when the reaction of the past shall have left only the grand outline in view, this perhaps is how a philosopher will speak of it. He will say that the idea, peculiar to the nineteenth century, of employing science in the satisfaction of our material wants had given a wholly unforeseen extension to the mechanical arts and had equipped man in less than fifty years with more tools than he had made during the thousands of years he had lived on the earth. Each new machine being for man a new organ—an artificial organ which merely prolongs the natural organs—his body became suddenly and prodigiously increased in size, without his soul being able at the same time to dilate to the dimensions of his new body. From this disproportion there issued the problems, moral, social, international, which most of the nations endeavored to solve by filling up the soulless void in the body politic by creating more liberty, more fraternity, more justice than the world had ever seen.

Now, while mankind labored at this task of spiritualization, inferior powers—I was going to say infernal powers—plotted an inverse experience for mankind. What would happen if the mechanical forces, which science had brought to a state of readiness for the service of man, should themselves take possession of man in order to make his nature as material as their own? What kind of a world would it be if this mechanism should seize the human race entire, and if the peoples, instead of raising themselves to a richer and more harmonious diversity, as *persons* may do, were to fall into the uniformity of *things?* What kind of a society would that be which should mechanically obey a word of command mechanically transmitted; which should rule its science and its conscience in accordance therewith; and which should lose, along with the sense of justice, the power to discern between truth and falsehood? What would mankind be when brute force should hold the place of moral force? What new barbarism, this time final, would arise from these conditions to stifle feeling, ideas, and the whole civilization of which the old barbarism contained the germ? What would happen, in short, if the moral effort of humanity should turn in its tracks at the moment of attaining its goal, and if some diabolical contrivance should cause it to produce the mechanization of spirit instead of the spiritualization of matter?

There was a people predestined to try the experiment. Prussia had been militarized by her kings; Germany had been militarized by Prussia; a powerful nation was on the spot marching forward in mechanical order. Administration and military mechanism were only waiting to make alliance with industrial mechanism. The combination once made, a formidable machine would come into existence. A touch upon the starting gear and the other nations would be dragged into the wake of Germany, subjects to the same movement, prisoners of the same mechanism. Such would be the meaning of the war on the day when Germany should decide upon its declaration.

She decided, he will continue, but the result was very different from what had been predicted. For the moral forces, which were to submit to the forces of matter by their side, suddenly revealed themselves as creators of material force. A simple idea, the heroic conception which a small people had formed of its honor, enabled it to make head against a powerful empire. At the cry of outraged justice we saw, moreover, in a nation which till then had trusted to its fleet, one million, two millions of soldiers suddenly rise from the earth. A yet greater miracle: in a nation thought to be mortally divided against itself all became brothers in the space of a day. From that moment the issue of the conflict was not open to doubt. On the one side, there was force spread out on the surface; on the other there was force in the depths. On one side, mechanism, the manufactured article which cannot repair its own injuries; on the other, life, the power of creation, which makes and remakes itself at every instant. On one side, that which uses itself up; on the other, that which does not use itself up.

Indeed, our philosopher will conclude, the machine did use itself up. For a long time it resisted; then it bent; then it broke. Alas! it had crushed under it a multitude of our children; and over the fate of this young life, which was so naturally and purely heroic, our tears will continue to fall. An implacable law decrees that spirit must encounter the resistance of matter, that life cannot advance without bruising that which lives, and that great moral results are purchased by much blood and many tears. But this time the sacrifice was to be rich in fruit as it had been rich in beauty. That the powers of death might be matched against life in one supreme combat, destiny had gathered them all at a single point. And behold how death was conquered; how humanity was saved by material suffering from the moral downfall which would have been its end; while the peoples, joyful in their desolation, raised on high the song of deliverance from the depths of ruin and of grief!

BY OTFRIED NIPPOLD

Before the outbreak of the Great War it can scarcely be said that any real attempt had been made to give an account

of the powerful force which suggestions are capable of
exercising even in the life of nations, and particularly in
our German nation. At that time only a few writers had
devoted their attention to "Mass-suggestions." Thus it happened that people had not become aware, or at any rate wide
circles of them were still ignorant, of the way in which the
war-makers in Germany had systematically been at work in
recent years to influence the soul of the German people by
the instrumentality of certain catchwords. In my book on
"German Chauvinism," which appeared in 1913, I undertook
the task of producing documentary evidence of this systematic activity on the part of those forces which in Germany
were exerting themselves in the direction of a war. I used
the term "Chauvinists" comprehensively to include all these
classes, not merely the military party who longed for war in
itself, but also the Pan-German politicians and imperialists
who for political or other reasons chose to represent it as
desirable and inevitable. I further showed the catch-words
of which use was made in these circles to make the German
people, in itself peace-loving, "mellow" for war. In this undertaking the "encirclement" inevitably played a part from
the outset, as did also the "French thirst for revenge," the
"envy of the English" and the alleged danger of "Panslavism." All these had to do their part in the task of representing to the German people that war was in the first place inevitable. The war-intriguers, however, did not stop at this
stage. In recent years they advanced to the theory of the
preventive war and advocated quite openly a war of aggression. In justification of such a war they in no way restricted
themselves, however, to pointing out the necessity of choos-
ing the right moment for a war, but they represented even an
aggressive war as being simply in the interests of an "active"
German policy and of an extension of German power. Thus
these war-intriguers had in the end really arrived at the point
of recommending to the German people a predatory war,
without the public opinion of Germany revolting against the
suggestion; indeed, they were able to put forward these views
amid the general approval of the multitude and more particularly of the Press.

The German people, unfortunately, was not aware of the growing danger that menaced its soul. The number of those who fell within the spell of these suggestions was constantly increasing. In 1913, in my "German Chauvinism," I was obliged to confirm the fact that even then very extensive classes of the German people believed in these catch-words. Even if before the war the number of the real and conscious Imperialists in Germany was limited, scarcely extending to the circle of those imbued with Pan-German sentiments, it still remains a fact that the great majority of the German people had nevertheless fallen under the spell of the catch-words that were scattered abroad, in this sense that they began to desire that "the bomb might at last explode if, as they say, war is inevitable." As a result of the year-long incitement to war, the German people had in fact been made "mellow," so mellow that in the end even men who were in themselves peace-loving directly longed for the dreaded war. Before the war it was only a relatively small section of the population, drawn from eminent men of intellect, from democrats belonging to the civil parties and social democrats, who had remained deaf to the suggestions of the war-intriguers.

It was under these circumstances that the year 1914 approached. Here I pass over all the portents which some months beforehand could not have failed to intimate to the careful observer the approach of the catastrophe. These indications would in themselves form an interesting chapter. In consequence of the machinations of the war-intriguers the German people's nervousness, sensitiveness and responsiveness to suggestion had gradually reached an abnormal development. As a result the circle of these intriguers felt that they were near their goal. Writing in *März* of July 18th, 1914, I believed that I might still warn the German Government against these intrigues:—"How is it possible in authoritative circles to hope, when the decisive hour arrives, to be able to master the evil, when it is continually being allowed to grow greater, and nothing is done at the right time to seize the appropriate counter-measures? What may not be an immediate danger to-day may become so overnight." A few days later the decisive hour had arrived. The German Government not only failed to master the evil, but capitulated to it.

Nevertheless the Government did not venture to tell the truth to the German people, no matter how "mellow" it had gradually been made. The truth would not have seized the people in the way considered necessary in a war. Thus a new catch-word was added to those used in pursuing mass-suggestions before the war, that, namely, of the "ruthless attack" and of the "war of defense forced upon us." For the unprejudiced, objective onlooker it cannot be said to be very ingeniously devised; for, indeed, this catch-word, when the whole situation is considered, was in reality only devised for political babes. Only the poor German people had already in fact been brought so far that it blindly believed everything, and thus it even believed in a "ruthless attack." The German people, down to the last man, believed it as gospel truth. If before the outbreak of war a section of the population had not yet fallen within the spell of these catch-words, the position in this respect was now at once altered. And thus Militarism and Pan-Germanism had gained the upper hand in Germany, not merely over the people but over the Government as well.

Militarism now held unrestricted sway, and beside it a Nationalism in which imperialistic tendencies now manifested themselves in a more unveiled form than heretofore. In its issue of September 19, 1916, the Berlin Conservative paper, *Die Post,* could quite correctly write with reference to my controversy with Von Sybel in the *Neue Züricher Zeitung* that imperialistic efforts in Germany were before the war restricted to a narrow circle, and were indeed from time to time officially repudiated. An Imperialism could, however, only operate in a really expansive manner when it penetrated into the great mass of the people and had permanently established itself there; every individual must have accepted imperialistic ideas in such a strong measure in his own circle of thoughts, that the imperialistic direction of his actions was in fact no longer present to his consciousness. It was only during the war, *Die Post* continued, that the German people had found the soil on which the imperialistic idea could take root and bring forth fruit. This was indeed the case. On the outbreak of war the whole German people did in fact fall under the spell of the suggestions of the war-makers.

And since then the German people has slumbered and dreamed a fair dream. It dreams of victories and of glory and of the respect which it has instilled into the whole world by its deeds of heroism and by its spirit of sacrifice; it dreams of the position of power which the future Germany will enjoy in the circle of the nations, and it dreams of peace. It continues to dream and it does not see and cannot see the crude reality. For the war-makers carefully seek to guard it against an awakening from its fair dream. Every day the newspapers tell the German people of new victories. The peace that is to come will thus be based on a German victory; not in vain will the sacrifices have been made. The truth is jealously kept from them, lest they awake. Nothing is allowed to pass the German frontier that could disturb the fair dream. And within Germany nothing is written or spoken that could rob the population of this illusion. Thus to-day the German people has no longer any knowledge of how it was incited into this war. Everything that took place before the war is forgotten. The German people is innocent of this war. It did not want it; it did not provoke it; it is merely defending itself and safeguarding its national existence. And as it is innocent of the outbreak of war, so also it is innocent of the continuation of the war. It has conquered and is ready for peace. What more can one ask? It cannot realize that there can be people who attribute to Germany itself the guilt of the war, and who also despite everything hold it responsible for the continuance of the war. That can only be done by the enemies of the German people, that is to say, the wicked Englishmen and Frenchmen, Russians and Japanese, and, unfortunately, many neutrals as well. Yes, indeed, the whole world seems to-day to have risen against Germany. They are surrounded by enemies. The enemies are everywhere—but not in their own land, not there where the dreaming German people continues to be carefully guarded against awakening.

What will this awakening reveal to the German people? What will the crude reality look like, when the dream is at an end? The thought is a bitter one. Every dream must come to an end some day; from every sleep there must be an awakening. And then the reality is seen. Then the German people will see that the rest of the world passes a different judgment on the question of the responsibility for the war from that current in Germany on the basis of the German official accounts. It will then recognize that while, no doubt, the German armies have often been victorious, they have not always been so, that the other side also has gained many a victory, that there was a battle on the Marne which completely frustrated the German plan of campaign, and that while it is certainly possible to dream of a German victory, such a victory cannot be experienced. It will recognize that even if Germany may perhaps be unconquerable it nevertheless cannot conquer, a fact which for an aggressor is necessarily a sorry business and cannot but destroy all dreams of victory. And further, what on awakening will be the outlook as regards their other dreams of glory and respect and honor? Has the German conduct of the war in fact been such as to increase the glory of the German name? Has it not rather been placed in the service of terror, branding the German name for centuries to come, for the sake of momentary petty advantages? Have not the German army leaders, in agreement with the German Government, violated Belgian neutrality and often enough ridden roughshod over international law on many other occasions as well? And is it not the fact that German scholarship has declared its solidarity with all these actions, and has thus robbed itself of the glory which it enjoyed throughout the whole world? And has not the German Press done its utmost to feed the flame of universal hatred enkindled by these things—hatred, of course, against other nations who are innocent of all these matters, not hatred against the enemy who sits in their own land, working on the soul of their own people?

Thus, on awakening, the German people will really see itself confronted by a world of enemies, and it will be constrained to recognize that for many years to come it has

UNCONQUERABLE

The Kaiser. "SO, YOU SEE—YOU'VE LOST EVERYTHING."
The King of the Belgians. "NOT MY SOUL."

October 21, 1914.

Most widely known and noted among British War-cartoons is the above. It appeared originally in *Punch* from the hand of the renowned cartoonist, Bernard Partridge. It echoes most emphatically the conflict of German materialism with the spiritual forces of the universe.

THE FIELDS OF FLANDERS

"Where are the Dead?
"There are no Dead."

MAETERLINCK ("The Blue Bird").

This is a Canadian sketch by J. A. Shepperson, emphasizing that high hope on which the true Culture of the world has been building for twenty centuries. Mankind, outside of Germany, believed that all the doctrines of materialism break down just because they reckon the dead as dead, and take no heed as to what a man's labors here shall make him fitted for when he passes beyond earth's Death. Hence when the Britons and Canadians sacrificed their lives by thousands on the "Flanders Fields" through all the years of the War, their faith was symbolized by Maeterlinck's allegory in "The Blue Bird." He makes the trembling searchers for the terrible field of death find it beautiful instead; for it blossoms into a field of lilies.

gained, not glory and honor, but hatred and contempt. Yes, the thought of this awakening of the German people is bitter in the extreme! It cannot but wring one's very heart to think of this brave people and of the millions it has sacrificed in life and wealth, and then to picture the awakening of this people from its dream!

BY KARL LAMPRECHT
Written in February, 1915

The gravest and perhaps most widely spread misconception about us Germans is that we are the serfs of our Princes, servile and dependent in political thought.[1] That false notion has probably been dispelled during the initial weeks of the present war.

With absolute certainty the German Nation, with one voice [2] and correctly, diagnosed the political situation without respect to party or creed and unanimously and of its own free will acted.

But this misconception is so deep rooted that more extended discussion is needed. I pass on to other matters.

The essential point is that public opinion have free scope of development. Every American will admit that. Now, public opinion finds its expression in the principles that govern the use of the suffrage. The German voting system is the freest in the world, much freer than the French, English, or American system, because not only does it operate in accordance with the principle that every one shall have a direct

[1] All university professors in Prussia were appointed by the Government, and a similar situation existed in Saxony, the home of Prof. Lamprecht. He himself was commonly accused of seeking court favor by flattery. He wrote of William II, "Listening to his ministers, we are again and again amazed at the extent to which they merely repeat the Emperor's ideas. Even opponents when coming from an interview are dominated by the charm of his personality." Any teacher or professor who expressed views not approved by the Imperial Government ruined his career. Tragic cases of this kind have been frequent. A similar system of official interference with opinion extended to almost every rank in society, operating through permits, pensions, rewards, or public condemnation.

[2] The German Socialists repeatedly objected to the threatened war. Even after it had begun and protests were treated as treason, the Socialists in the parliament only voted the money for war most unwillingly.

and secret vote, but the powers of the State are exercised faithfully and conscientiously to carry out that principle in practice. The constitutional life of the German Nation is of a thoroughly democratic character.[3]

Those who know that were not surprised that our Social Democrats marched to war with such enthusiasm. Already among their ranks many have fallen as heroes, never to be forgotten by any German when his thoughts turn to the noble blood which has saturated foreign soil—thank God, foreign soil! Many of the Socialist leaders and adherents are wearing the Iron Cross, that simple token that seems to tell you when you speak of its bearer, "Now, this is a fearless and faithful soul."

Let it be said once and for all: He who wants to understand us must accept our conception that constitutionally we enjoy so great a political freedom that we would not change with any country in the world.[4] Everybody in America knows that our manners and customs have been democratic

[3] Except for the fact that the German "voting system" was in some but not all elections free and secret, there is not one true statement in this paragraph. The German parliament was wholly undemocratic; because its upper and more powerful house was not elected at all but filled by the German princes. The lower or elected house was so powerless as to be ridiculed everywhere. Germans themselves nicknamed it the "debating society" and the "hall of echoes." The chief elective body having any real power was the lower house of the legislature of Prussia. Elections to this were notoriously arranged so as to favor overwhelmingly the upper classes, and to expose to their resentment any one who ventured to vote against them.

[4] This view was honestly held by many Germans. Commenting on it in an article in the N. Y. *Sun,* the present editor said:

"What makes the German so ready to assert 'I am freer than you, for all your boasted democracy?' In the first place, he is an orderly soul who loves to have his paths marked out for him. When a German sees a road labeled Verboten he never dreams of using it. He welcomes laws, even in their most restrictive form.

"In the second place, the German Government has really made excellent laws for the advantage of its working classes, old age pensions and the like. And it has very carefully refrained from restricting its voters on the subjects where they find their real enjoyment. A German can act toward his wife and children or in a dozen other every day affairs as an American could not—and would not wish to. So the German naturally says, 'I am freer than you.' Of the larger freedom by which a people controls its own destiny, he has so little knowledge that he does not even know he lacks it."

for centuries, while in France and England they have been ever aristocratic. Americans, we know, always feel at home on German soil.

But the Kaiser, you will say, speaks of "his monarchy," therefore must the Germans be *Fuerstenknechte* (servants of Princes).

First of all, as to the phrase "Fuerstenknechte." Does not the King of England speak of his "subjects"? That word irritates a German, because he is conscious that he is not a subject, but a citizen of the empire. Yet he will not infer from the English King's use of the term in formal utterances that an Englishman is a churl, a "servant of his King." That would be a superficial political conception.

As to our Princes, most of us, including the Social Democrats, are glad in our heart of hearts that we have them. As far back as our history runs, and that is more than 2,000 years, we have had Princes. They have never been more than their name, "Fuerst," implies, the first and foremost of German freemen, *"primi inter pares."* Therefore they have never acted independently, never without taking the people into counsel. That would have been contrary to the most important fundamental principles of German law; hence our people have never been "de jure" without their representatives. Even in the times of absolute monarchy the old "estates of the realm" had their being as a representative body,[5] and wherever and whenever these privileges were suppressed it was regarded as a violation of our fundamental rights and is so still regarded.

We glory in our Princes. They link our existence with the earliest centuries of our history. They preserve for us the priceless independence of our small home States.

We are accused of militarism. What is this new and terrible crime? Since the years of the wars of liberation against France and Napoleon we have had what amounts practically to universal conscription. Only two generations later universal suffrage was introduced. The nation has been sternly trained by its history in the ways of discipline and

[5] These "estates" represented only the higher classes—at first only the warriors—never the masses of the poor.

self-restraint.   Germans are very far from mistaking freedom for license and independence for licentiousness.

Germany has a long past.   She enjoys the inheritance of
an original and priceless civilization.   She holds clearly formulated ideals.   To the future she has all this to bequeath
and, in addition, the intellectual wealth of her present stage
of development.   Consider Germany's contributions to the
arts, the poetical achievements of the period of Schiller and
Goethe, the music of Handel, Bach, Haydn, Mozart, and Beethoven; the thought systems of Kant, Fichte, Schelling, and
Hegel!

The last decade has reawakened these great men in the
consciousness of the German Nation.   Enriched by the consciousness and message of an intellectual past, our people
were moving forward to new horizons.

At that moment the war hit us.   If you could only have
lived these weeks in Germany I do not doubt that what you
would have seen would have led your ripe experience to a
fervent faith in a Divinely guided future of mankind.   The
great spiritual movement of 1870, when I was a boy growing up, was but a phantom compared to July and August of
1914.   Germany was a nation stirred by the most sacred emotions, humble and strong, filled with just wrath and a firm
determination to conquer—a nation disciplined, faithful,
and loving.

In that disposition we have gone to war and still fight.
As for the slanders of which we have been the victims, ask
the thousands of Frenchmen who housed German soldiers
in 1870 and 1871, or ask the Belgians of Ghent and Bruges! [6]
They will give you a different picture of the "Furor Teutoni-
cus."   They will tell you that the "raging German" generally
is a good-natured fellow, ever ready for service and sympathy, who, like Parsifal, gazes forth eagerly into a strange
world which the war has opened to his loyal and patriotic
vision.

[6] When this phrase of astounding insolence or obtuseness was written, the Belgians of Ghent and Bruges could not speak; they were mur-
derously strangled.   Since then they have managed to find voice with
which to repudiate Germany in utmost loathing.

THE KULTUR OF GERMANY

THE WORSHIP OF THE "SUPERMAN" AS TAUGHT BY NIETZSCHE

WILLIAM ELKIN *introducing* FRIEDRICH NIETZSCHE HENRIQUE DE MENDONÇA

The "Kultur" on which Germany prided herself was certainly a large factor in bringing on the Great War. This new Kultur was itself war-like in essence; and, moreover, the Germans believed themselves divinely commissioned to extend it over other lands. In a way, theirs was a missionary spirit such as had started the wild followers of Mahomet to ravaging and conquering the world some thirteen hundred years before —though we must admit that the German soldier as a missionary was the strangest proselyter yet conceived in all the mad vagaries of the human mind.

William Baird Elkin, Professor of Philosophy in Indiana University, is an excellent American authority to give us an unprejudiced view of the German "Kultur" as expounded by Nietzsche and other leaders. Friedrich Nietzsche, upon whom is usually laid the main responsibility for the whole modern German system of thought, was as much Polish as German; and he gathered the roots of his doctrine from an earlier French writer, Gobineau. In education, however, as in outlook, Nietzsche was wholly German; and from about 1878 onward his vigorous books, especially his "Thus Spake Zarathustra," an imaginary exposition of the religion of Zoroaster, profoundly swayed German philosophy. Briefly summarized, Nietzsche's teaching was that Christianity is a weakness; might is the only right; the man of Aryan race (or rhetorically "the blond beast") is the mightiest among men, and should develop himself into the "superman," despise all lesser forms of human beings, and wipe out all other races except as he needs slaves. Nietzsche died in an insane asylum in 1900.

That the German "Kultur" shall not be seen only from Nietzsche's own view or from that of an American, committed to the antagonistic worship of Democracy, we include a résumé of Kultur's influence by a scholar from one of the "smaller nations." Senhor Henrique Lopes de Mendonça is a Portuguese statesman, Associate of the Lisbon Academy of Sciences, and author of many scientific works.

C. F. H.

BY WILLIAM BAIRD ELKIN

GERMAN philosophy of war, one might almost say German civilization, is based essentially on four ideas. These are in four books, two ancient, and two comparatively modern. The first is Plato's "Republic." In Plato's philosophy of the state, the state begins small, and the people are poor. It increases in wealth and in population. Then it expands. Expansion leads to war. For war an army is needed. If the army is to be successful, it must be well trained. Hence, the state is organized for the sake of the army; and the army is organized for the sake of the ruling class. This is an aristocracy. It is government by the few. But the few are the intelligent, the wealthy, and the efficient. Consequently, they are the best. And government by the best is thought to be the best government.

The great representatives, in Germany, of this idea were Bismarck and Treitschke. Treitschke held that England was a decadent nation. She began to decline about 1832, with the enactment of the first reform bill, when Great Britain began to become truly democratic. She became more democratic, and therefore more degenerate. Hence it was only a question of time when the British Empire would break up, and most of the fragments would pass to the country in best condition to acquire them. That country would be Germany, with her superior form of government. The process of British disintegration and German expansion might be facilitated by war. "We have already made our reckoning with Austria," said Treitschke, "with France, and with Russia; our last reckoning, that with England, will probably be the most tedious and the most difficult."

The second idea is in the Old Testament, the Hebrew conception of a chosen people, whose national mission was to take possession of the Promised Land, and then to increase and multiply until they should become like the stars of heaven, or the sand on the seashore in multitude.

The great representative of this idea is the Kaiser, as when he said, "Remember that the German people are the chosen of God." "It is, as it is written in the Bible, my duty to increase this heritage, for which one day I shall be called upon to give an account." On January 18, 1896, the writer joined in the celebration of the twenty-fifth anniversary of the founding of the German Empire. That evening the Emperor in his famous palace speech declared: "The German

Empire has become a world-empire. Thousands of our countrymen live abroad in the most distant parts of the world. . . . It is your duty, gentlemen, to see that you help me to incorporate this Greater Germany permanently into the old Fatherland. . . . You will loyally and devotedly assist me to discharge my duty, not only to our countrymen at home but to those thousands of our countrymen who dwell afar, so that when they need my protection, I may have the power to extend it to them." And, in a confidential memorandum, issued March, 1913, he said that their aim was "to fortify and to extend German power throughout the whole world."

If one inquires how this extension of power is to be effected, one comes to the third idea. It is in Machiavelli's "Prince," as expounded by Frederick the Great. "No treaty," said Treitschke, "and no alliance could ever make him [Frederick] renounce the right of free self-determination," consequently, "all his life through he was exposed to the accusation of faithless cunning." German power is to be extended partly by alliances, when Germany would have the better of the alliance, and would observe the alliance only so long as it was thought to be advantageous; and partly by war, brought on at the opportune moment.

The chief representatives of this idea are Bernhardi and the General Staff. "Let it be the task of our diplomacy," wrote Bernhardi, "so to shuffle the cards that we may be attacked by France, for then there would be reasonable prospect that Russia for a time would remain neutral. . . . But we must not hope to bring about this attack by waiting passively.

"We must initiate an active policy which, without attacking France, will so prejudice her interests or those of England, that both these states would feel themselves compelled to attack us. Opportunities for such procedure are offered both in Africa and in Europe, and any one who has attentively studied prominent political utterances can easily satisfy himself on that point."

The fourth idea is in Comte's positive philosophy, "the law of the three stages." According to Comte, civilization passes through three stages: the theological, the metaphysical, and the positive. The first stage is called the theological, because then people explained natural phenomena by means of personal agents, as when they thought that the sun was carried around the earth in the chariot of Apollo, and eclipses of the sun and moon were caused by gods or demons eating them up. After a time civilization advanced to the second stage. Then theology was relegated to a subordinate position, and people explained things by means of metaphysical principles, such as substances, essences, energies, etc. Finally, civilization advanced to the third stage. Then there is no more use for either theology, or metaphysics, since people explain phenomena in terms of antecedent and consequent, in accordance with natural law. In the third stage, science usurps the place formerly held by theology and metaphysics, and rules alone supreme.

In the latter half of the last century the Germans almost universally adopted Comte's idea. They said that theology and metaphysics were outgrown and outworn. Science alone was sufficient for the needs of modern civilization. And they applied science to agriculture, to industry, to commerce, to education, to war, to government, and to everything mechanical. This application of utilitarian scientific principles to modern life, without due regard to other equally important factors of civilization—religious, ethical, esthetic—is the peculiar and striking characteristic of German "Kultur." The Germans claim to be much farther advanced in this respect than any other people in the world. Hence they have a divine mission to civilize, to lead, and to rule all other peoples. Of course, they profess to act for the good of mankind. Thus Ostwald, the noted chemist, says: "Germany, thanks to her genius for organization or social efficiency, has attained a stage of civilization far higher than that of all other peoples. . . . Among our enemies the Russians, in brief, are still in the period of the undisciplined tribe [theological stage, perhaps], while the French and the English have only attained the degree of cultural development which we ourselves left behind fifty years ago [metaphysical stage, probably]. Do you ask me what it is that Germany wants? Well, Germany wants to organize Europe, for up to now

Europe has never been organized. The moment has come, I believe, for remodeling the map of Europe."

Summarizing what has been said: The Germans, according to their own view, have the best form of government; they are an elect people with a divine mission, which they seek to carry out in a strictly scientific way, in accordance with natural law, and, consequently, the will of God.

We come now to a discussion of the German ethics of war. Ethics may be defined as the science of right and wrong. Here two questions arise: (1) What is right? and (2) How do we know it? These constitute the two fundamental problems in ethical theory: the highest good, and conscience.

The next question is, What is the highest good? Two general answers are given. Some people say the highest good is happiness. Others say, not happiness, but perfection, or some form of development. If we say the highest good is happiness, then another question arises: Whose happiness? mine, or others? the happiness of the individual, or the happiness of all people? If we say that the happiness of the individual is the highest good, the ethical theory is called Egoistic Hedonism. If we say the happiness of mankind, the theory is called Altruistic Hedonism, or Utilitarianism. If we say the highest good is perfection, a similar question arises as before, Whose perfection? the perfection of the individual, or the perfection of all people? If we say the perfection of the individual is the highest good, the theory is that of self-realization. If we say the perfection of mankind, the theory is that of social welfare, closely akin to social service.

Our next inquiry is, What is the German highest good? For the common people the highest good is the Fatherland, a modification of the fourth ideal. But the common people are not Germany. The common people exist for the sake of the Fatherland. "In the German view," said Münsterberg, "the state is not for the individuals, but the individuals for the state." And the Fatherland exists for the sake of the ruling class. The ruling class of Germany molds and makes both the Fatherland and the common people. The ruling class is the real Germany. And the highest good of the ruling class is self-realization.

If space permitted, it might be interesting to trace the development of the German highest good from the time of Luther, through the sixteenth and seventeenth centuries, then through the Romantic movement in the eighteenth century, and the Prussian school system in the nineteenth century, until the rise of Nietzscheism in recent times. Nietzsche did not make the theory, he found it. And it is his distinctive merit, or demerit, that he took up this theory of the highest good and developed it to its ultimate logical conclusion, in his doctrine of the superman.

Nietzsche's greatest book is his "Zarathustra." Of it he said: "I have given to mankind the profoundest book it possesses, my 'Zarathustra.' This profoundest book in the world, according to the author, proclaims that God is dead! But if God is dead, what are men to do? How get along without God? All that is necessary is for men to become gods themselves, and thus take God's place; or if they cannot do that, then they ought to do the next best thing, viz., become supermen. To become a superman means to be, to do, to get, and to hold, all raised to the nth power. But every one cannot become a superman. Hence there are two classes of people: supermen, and back-worldsmen; or, briefly, masters and slaves.

Accordingly, there are two systems of morality: the morality of the masters and the morality of the slaves. But as it is better to be a master than a slave, the master morality is the good morality, the slave morality is the bad morality. The slave morality is essentially the same as Christian morality. It is fit only for "shopkeepers, Christians, cows, women, Englishmen, and other democrats." Nietzsche thinks it is impossible to say anything too severe against Christianity. It is the greatest evil that ever appeared in the world, because it tends to prevent the realization of the highest good, and the development of the superman. In the "Antichrist" he says: "The Christian concept of God—God as God of the sick, God as cobweb-spinner, God as spirit—

is one of the most corrupt concepts of God ever arrived at on earth."

"Every expression in the mouth of a 'first Christian' is a lie, every action he does is an instinctive falsehood—all his values, all his aims are injurious, but *he whom* he hates, *that* which he hates, has value. . . . Have I yet to say that in the whole New Testament, only a *single* figure appears which one is obliged to honor—Pilate, the Roman governor? To take a Jewish affair seriously,—he will not be persuaded to do so. A Jew more or less—what does that matter?"

Finally: "With this I am at the conclusion and pronounce my sentence. I *condemn* Christianity. I bring against the Christian church the most terrible of all accusations that ever an accuser has taken into his mouth. It is to me the greatest of all imaginable corruptions. . . . The Christian church has left nothing untouched with its depravity, it has made a worthlessness out of every value, a lie out of every truth, a baseness of soul out of every straightforwardness. Let a man still dare to speak to me of its 'humanitarian' blessings! . . . The 'equality of souls before God,' this falsehood, . . . this explosive material of a concept which has finally become revolution,—is Christian dynamite. . . . This eternal accusation of Christianity I shall write on all walls, wherever there are walls, . . .—I call Christianity the one great curse, the one great intrinsic depravity, the one great instinct of revenge for which no expedient is sufficiently poisonous, secret, subterranean, mean, —I call it the one immortal blemish of mankind. . . ."

Contrasted with Christian or slave morality is the morality of the superman, the morality of the masters. Thus Zarathustra spake unto the people: "I teach you the higher man. Man is something that must be overcome. What have ye done to surmount him?

"All beings hitherto created something greater than themselves; and would ye be the ebb of this great flood, and rather go back to the beast than surmount the human?

"What is the ape for men? A laughing-stock or a painful disgrace. The same shall man be for the higher man—a laughing-stock or a painful disgrace. . . . See, I teach you the higher man."

"Ye have heard it said of old, blessed are the meek, for they shall inherit the earth; but I say unto you, blessed are the valiant, for they shall make the earth their throne; and ye have heard men say, blessed are the poor in spirit; but I say to you, blessed are the mighty and free in spirit, for they shall enter Valhalla. And ye have heard men say, blessed are the peacemakers, but I say unto you, blessed are they who make war, for they shall be called not the children of Jahve, but the children of Odin, which is greater than Jahve."

From the German theory of the highest good a few practical conclusions follow:

First, justification of war. Nietzsche did not invent this doctrine. He found it already prominent in German thought, and emphasized it. Frederick the Great said, "War opens the most fruitful field of all virtues."

Hegel: "Just as the movement of the ocean prevents the corruption which would result from perpetual calm, so by war people escape the corruption which would be occasioned by a continuous peace."

Moltke: "Perpetual peace is a dream, and not even a beautiful dream. But war is a link in the divine system of the universe."

Treitschke: "War is a biological necessity of the first importance," and "efforts directed toward the abolition of war are not only foolish, but absolutely immoral, and must be stigmatized as unworthy of the human race."

Nietzsche: "Ye shall love peace as a means to new wars, and the short peace better than the long." And "I do not advise you to work, but to fight. I do not advise you to conclude peace, but to conquer. Let your work be a fight, your peace a victory! . . . Ye say, a good cause will hallow even war? I say unto you: a good war halloweth every cause." And again, "Oh, blessed remote time, when a people said unto itself: 'I will be—*master* over peoples!' . . . For, my brethren, what is best, shall rule; what is best, *will* rule! And where the teaching soundeth different, the best is—lacking."

A second conclusion is the justification of Germany's claim to a place in the sun, the acquisition of more colonies and the extension of commerce. In 1912 Delbrück, Treitschke's successor in the chair of history in Berlin University, dealt with this subject in his own periodical, the *Preussische Jahrbücher*. He thought the time had come to remodel the map of Africa, so that Germany might have a colonial empire in that continent. Not that Germany had colonists to send there. Germany was not an emigrant country, but an immigrant country. She employed annually upwards of one million foreign workmen. But the situation was this: Suitable positions were not available at home for the many young men of birth and wealth highly educated by the German school system. In other words, there were so many high officers in the army and navy, so many high officials in the government, and so many nobles and wealthy men throughout the country, that suitable positions for their sons could not be obtained in the Fatherland. Hence Germany needed a colonial empire which these young men could organize and develop. Germany, in short, needed colonies where her ambitious youths might have an opportunity to exploit the native inhabitants, and thus to become supermen.

How officials in the German colonies succeeded in carrying out this policy of exploitation a writer in the *Nineteenth Century* for July, 1915, informs us. In German Southwest Africa the native population decreased from nearly 1,000,-000 to less than 100,000 during the thirty years in which the Germans administered the affairs of the colony, and in 1913 the Colonial Secretary admitted that 105,000 natives in Togoland had been killed, during the preceding ten years, by German expeditions sent against them. The Germans could not make their colonies pay. And in order to make them pay, they wanted the natives to work almost without pay, hence insurrection and war. This policy of annihilation had the approval, not only of Germans at home, but of some Germans abroad. A writer in a German-American paper expressed himself as follows: "When we have humbled our enemies and confiscated their lands, let but any one of the former natives of the soil, be he English, French, Italian,

American, or a man of any other lower race, lift up his voice louder than a sigh, and we will dash him to pieces against the earth.

"And after we have demolished their worm-eaten cathedrals and the rest of their hideous structures, together with the temples of India and the other countries of heathendom, we will build much bigger cathedrals and more splendid temples in which to honor our noble Kaiser and the great deeds of his people, who are the destroyers of the decadent races of the world.

"Oh! how we thank God for having chosen our great and incomparable Kaiser and his people to accomplish this mighty mission, for has Darwin not said (and no doubt he borrowed this idea from some of our great German professors) that only the fittest shall survive? And are the Germans not the fittest in all things? Therefore let all us Germans say: Perish the carrion! Only the Germans are noble men."

Another conclusion from the German theory of the highest good is Pan-Germanism, that is, the world for Germany. For if the native races of the colonies were exterminated what would the administrators do? As supermen they could not live on one another. Then they would need other countries to govern, and other peoples to consume. The following are a few of the many statements that might be cited from German Molochs in support of their cherished Juggernaut:

Major General von Roehl: "Only one people has the right to play a leading rôle in the political world, and that people is the German people."

The Kaiser: "The ocean reminds us . . . that on it and beyond it no great decision may henceforth be made without Germany and the German Emperor."

Vossische Zeitung: "As we are the supreme people, our duty, henceforth, is to lead the march of humanity itself. . . . It would be a sin against our mission to spare the people who are inferior to us."

Rommel: "The time is at hand when the five poor sons of the German family, allured by the resources and the fertility of France, will easily make an end of the solitary son of the French family. The land between the Vosges and the Pyrenees was not made by the Almighty just in order that 38,000,000 Frenchmen should vegetate there without growing, when 100,000,000 Germans could live and flourish there as well, according to the divine law."

Treitschke: "Then when the German flag flies over and protects this vast empire, to whom will belong the scepter of the universe? What nation will impose its wishes on the other enfeebled and decadent peoples? Will it not be Germany that will have the mission to ensure the peace of the world?"

Evangelical League: "The King at the head of Prussia, Prussia at the head of Germany, Germany at the head of the world."

Still another conclusion which follows from the German theory of the highest good may be mentioned, viz., the German language ought to become the language of the world. The argument on this subject is clear and brief: All other European languages are based on the roots of dead languages. The roots of dead languages are dead. Therefore, all languages based on these roots are decadent. Q.E.D.

The position of English is peculiarly unfortunate, for English is based on the roots of two dead languages, Greek and Latin; therefore it is doubly decadent. On the other hand, the German language came straight from God, and is thus, in every respect, preëminently fitted to be divinely instrumental in spreading the culture of mankind. Says a prominent writer in the *Deutsche Tageszeitung:* "It is a crying necessity that German should replace English as the world language. Should the English language be victorious and become the world language the culture of mankind will stand before a closed door, and the death knell will sound for civilization. Here we have the reason why it is necessary for the German, and with him the German language, to conquer. And the victory once won, be it now or be it one hundred years hence, there remains a task for the German, than which none is more important, that of forcing the German tongue on the world. On all men, on men of all colors and nationalities, the German language acts as a blessing which, coming direct from the hand of God [or from his mouth?], sinks into the heart like a precious balm and ennobles it. English, the bastard tongue of the canting island pirates, must be swept from the place it has usurped, and forced back into the remotest corners of Britain, until it has returned to its original elements of an insignificant pirate dialect."

We come next to the treatment of conscience or the moral faculty. Conscience was formerly defined as the voice of God in the soul of man. That definition may have done very well in the theological stage of civilization, but it is not satisfactory in the scientific. Conscience must now be explained in terms of antecedent and consequent like any other natural phenomenon. The usual account of the moral faculty, in the first three stages of its development, is somewhat as follows:

At first the child has no conscience, just as it has no language. But it has the capacity of acquiring both. As it grows it gradually acquires a conscience and a language, and it acquires the one in much the same manner as the other. Brought up in one country, it acquires one language; brought up in another country, it acquires another language. Similarly, the child brought up in one country develops one kind of conscience; brought up in a different country, it develops a different kind of conscience. The first form of conscience which the child acquires may be called the conscience of the home, and is derived largely from its mother. This is conscience on the first level, to speak in the language of psychology.

But the child goes to school, to church and Sunday School, meets and plays and works with other children and with other people. Thus its conscience grows, as its language grows. And after a time the youth acquires the conscience of the community. This is conscience on the second level. It is the conscience of custom. Whatever is in accordance with custom is right, and whatever is contrary to custom is wrong. This conscience can scarcely be regarded as an individual faculty; rather it is social faculty, a collective faculty; the common conscience of the people. And this is as far as the development of conscience often goes.

For some persons, however, there is a third stage in the development of conscience. This is the result of a process called individualization. People who are accustomed to do their own thinking, or who read some of the masterpieces of literature, or who study science, philosophy, ethics, or religion gradually advance from the second level to the third level, from the collective conscience to the individual conscience. Then they may criticize the customs of the community, which they formerly accepted without question. Some customs they approve, others they disapprove. Some modes of conduct they commend, others they would change or abolish. They have acquired a higher conscience than that of custom. This is properly an individual conscience, in contrast with the collective. It has been acquired through contact with the thought of other minds, and exists in the higher ideals of one's community, of one's country, or of the race.

It should be observed further, that in this process of individualization there are two paths or directions, either of which conscience may take: the upward path, and the downward path. A person may acquire a higher conscience than that of custom, or a lower one. Not only may a person acquire a perverted conscience, or a seared conscience, but may lose the conscience one formerly had, and proclaim complete emancipation from all moral restraints whatever. This experience may be illustrated in the sphere of knowledge. A thinker examines many different theories,—scientific, philosophical, or religious,—and as a result of his examination he may arrive at the correct view. He has then a higher idea of truth than before. He is in a position to criticize other theories, and say this one is true, or that one is false, as the case may be. But he may also arrive at a degree of bewilderment, or dissatisfaction, such that he may say this theory is false, and that theory is false—they all are false; truth is not to be discovered anywhere; there is no such thing as truth. The case is precisely similar in the sphere of ethics, during the process of individualization. Some

persons rise to a higher level of conscience, others sink to
a lower. Of the two paths in the moral life, one leads up
the front stairs to the treasure-house of virtue; the other
leads down the back stairs to the charnel house of vice.

There is a fourth stage in the development of conscience,
that which implies the existence of a transcendental factor;
but it does not call for treatment here, as very few Germans now advance to this stage.

Naturally the next question is, To what stage of development does the German conscience attain? The conscience of
the common people is on the second level. The common people have a collective conscience, that of custom. The ruling
classes, on the other hand, have advanced to the third level.
But in the process of individualization most members of the
ruling classes seem to have gone on the downward path, instead of on the upward, and have acquired a perverted conscience, or a seared conscience, or have lost their conscience
altogether. This seems to be particularly true of the officers
of the army and navy, of the members of the diplomatic
corps, and of government officials generally.

Thus much as to the theoretical treatment of the German
conscience. It only remains now to show how the peculiar
brand of conscience, universally known as "Teutonic," has
been developed in the German people through the influence of
their chief institutions as directed and controlled by the
Kaiser and his government.

Many years ago when the writer was in Germany, he was
interested in education, and visited Jena University, then
the Mecca of American educators. In conversation with an
American fellow-student one day, I asked him what he
thought of the German schools. He replied: "Not very
much. They scarcely teach anything but God and the
Kaiser." He ought to have said "the Kaiser and God," for
that is the way in which instruction in a German elementary
school impresses an American. One fine morning a normal
school man from West Virginia proposed to me that we take
a day off and visit a village school. And we did. We went
out some twenty miles on the train, reached our destined
village, and obtained admittance to the school. German vil-

lage schools are much alike. I had already visited several, but my friend saw this world-renowned phenomenon then for the first time.

In this school there were some seventy or eighty pupils. There were two teachers, an old man and a young man, but only one schoolroom. In the afternoon the old man took charge, with all the children in one class. He taught a great lesson in history, on the German Kaisers. Long, lank, and earnest he stood before the class, and delivered his message with animation and with power. In all seriousness and with glowing fervor, he told the pupils what grand and glorious deeds the wonderful and incomparable Kaisers had done for the German people and their beloved Fatherland. God did not have even second place; the Kaisers were the whole thing. The schoolroom was decorated with many pictures of the Emperor and other Hohenzollerns, as indeed are the walls of all German schools. The teacher may have taught many other subjects that afternoon. I remember only the history lesson. It is as vivid now, after a lapse of twenty years, as is any experience of yesterday. And I believe the impression made on the children was no less strong than that on me. In this manner the German school develops what may well be called a "Kaiser" conscience.

Dr. Busch, in his secret "Life of Bismarck," has told us how the German government controls and directs the press. Busch was Bismarck's right-hand man in this field for three years. And Bismarck kept him busy, Sunday and Monday, sometimes day and night, sending at any hour a messenger to call him, if a press communication demanded dispatch. "I sometimes saw him," says Busch, "as often as five or even eight times in one day." At their first interview Bismarck said: "I intend to get you to write notes and articles for the papers from such particulars and instructions as I may give you. You will also arrange for others doing so."

"At these interviews," wrote Busch, "I had to take good care to keep my ears well open, and to note everything with the closest attention. Through practice, I gradually succeeded in retaining long sentences and even whole speeches, practically without omissions, until I had an opportunity of committing them to paper." Busch gives a list of newspapers to which "articles thus prepared were supplied," and mentioned several writers to whom he himself gave "instructions and material for publication," among them "Herr Heide, who had previously been a missionary in Australia and was at that time working for the 'North German Correspondence,' which had been founded with a view to influencing the English press."

As an illustration of the character of Bismarck's instructions we may take a brief item of March 11, 1870: "Attention is to be directed, at first in a paper which has no connection with the Government, to the prolonged sojourn of Archduke Albrecht in Paris as a suspicious symptom. In connection with it rumors have been circulated in London of an understanding between France and Austria. Our papers will afterwards reproduce these hints."

In this way Bismarck and Busch helped to develop in the German people a "Kaiser" conscience. And their policy still continues. On July 27, 1914, Austria was "wild with joy at the prospect of war with Serbia." A few days later Germany was wild with joy at the prospect of war with Russia. The German press had made thorough and effective preparation for the Great War, as later it made thorough and effective preparation for the destruction of merchant ships by submarines. The result for the government in both cases was similar. To the editor of the New York *Nation* Darmstaedter of Göttingen University wrote: "I find the sinking of the *Lusitania* was *just, necessary,* and *useful,* and I may add that the whole German nation has the same opinion."

The Church also helped to develop a "Kaiser" conscience. Every clergyman when taking his oath of office swore: "I will be submissive, faithful, and obedient to his Royal Majesty. . . . In particular, I vow that I will not support any society or association, . . . which might endanger the public security. I will inform his Majesty of any proposals made, either in my diocese, or elsewhere, which might prove injurious to the state. I will preach the word as his Gracious Majesty dictates."

It is not surprising that an observant publicist like Rohrbach bewailed the slight influence of religion on the German
conscience. Writing a few years before the war he acknowledged that the problem of religion was one of the most difficult that the German people had to face. "Are the churches,"
he asked, "capable of dealing with the demoralization of our
national conscience owing to the idolatry of class distinctions, by awakening a strong Christian religious consciousness?" He admitted that the outlook was not encouraging,
because the Lutheran church, as he asserted, "appears from
the first to be the church of princes and classes, and has
remained so faithful to itself that the principle of worldly
authority and class superiority has been better developed
within its walls than anywhere else."

The theater, similarly, is an important factor in molding
the German conscience. "When I succeeded to the throne,"
said the Kaiser, "I was convinced and had firmly determined
that the Royal Theater, like the schools and the universities,
must be an instrument of the monarch. . . . The theater
is also one of my weapons."

The university is one of the most effective weapons of
the Kaiser in the development of the German conscience.
The University is a state institution. The government controls and may prescribe the subjects of instruction. The
present Emperor, soon after his accession, ordered the Minister of Education "to discourage as far as possible the study
of the French Revolution in German schools and universities." Later he changed his mind and recommended it,
with the direction that "we should learn from it to know the
powers of darkness and of destruction and attach ourselves
by so much the more closely to monarchy and authority."

The government appoints the professors, promotes those
who please it, and dismisses or disciplines those who do not.
Dr. Arons, a teacher of physics in the University of Berlin,
was dismissed, not because of his teaching, but because he
was a Social Democrat. Hueffer relates "the case of the
brothers X,"—a burgomaster, a professor, and an assistant
professor. The burgomaster wrote for a Liberal paper an
article which displeased the government. He was tried *in*

camera for this offense and deprived of his office. Then the
Minister of Education presented to the other two brothers
for signature a paper disavowing the liberal opinions of the
burgomaster. They refused to sign. The assistant professor was not only dismissed, but the Prussian government endeavored to prevent his appointment at any other university
in Germany. And the professor was boycotted in the following manner: He was deprived of his seat in the university senate; he was prohibited from examining students; the
students were warned that if they attended his lectures their
subsequent careers would be prejudiced; and another professor was appointed to offer his courses. And yet, so peculiar
is the German mental constitution, that soon after the outbreak of the present war one of these professors wrote
Hueffer making a spirited defense of Germany, "as the true
land of culture and of democratic progress."

Of course it will be asserted that all the factors named
thus far are not sufficient to explain the real character of the
German conscience, as it has been revealed in this world war.
They explain it in part. But they do not explain the fiendish
cruelty of German soldiers as manifested in the most horrible atrocities committed on a stupendous scale. And they do
not explain the general acquiescence of the German people
in the wholesale massacres of noncombatants, and in the in-
credibly inhuman methods of warfare carried on in Belgium,
in Poland, in Armenia, and on the high seas. Two additional
considerations, however, will serve to indicate how the German conscience has been molded along these lines.

First, as to the soldiers. Most Americans have no idea of
the methods of training and discipline which prevail in the
German army.[1] If American officers treated their men as
German officers treat theirs, the American army would soon
be without officers. German soldiers are brutalized in a manner wholly unknown to soldiers serving under a democratic
régime. They tend to lose all the little element of conscience
that they ever had, except obedience to their officers. And
their officers, as already stated, usually have little or no conscience or else a perverted one. When passing from the sec-

[1] See the later article on German Militarism.

ond level of conscience to the third, they go down the back
stairs instead of up the front.

Enough, perhaps, has now been said to indicate how the
German army became an immense breeding-place for un-
natural, as well as natural, vices. Hence the abominable and
diabolical acts of barbarity and bestiality, countless and in-
excusable, committed in France and Belgium, by privates and
officers alike, against innocent and defenseless women and
children, acts that are now heralded throughout the world,
and the record of which will ever remain to the everlasting
shame of the German aristocracy and of the German army.
As Morgan says, to the end of time they will be remembered,
"and from one generation to another, on the plains of Flanders, in the valleys of the Vosges, and on the rolling fields
of the Marne, oral tradition will perpetuate this story of
infamy and wrong."

Secondly, the people. It is necessary to bear in mind that
at the beginning of the war, and during the first few weeks
of the conflict, the German people passed through an experience such as no people ever passed through before, on such
an extensive scale. Their press, their preachers, teachers, and
leaders made them believe that they were attacked by their
enemies, who wished to destroy them. The common people
were made to believe that they would easily and quickly
vanquish all their enemies, and, further, they were led to believe that the war would result in great material and spiritual
advantages to themselves. The events of the first month
seemed to confirm all their expectations. They read of nothing but victories, day after day, on all the battle fronts. In
a few weeks they would be in Paris, in a few months in
London, and then the whole world would lie at their feet.
For the first time in their history the entire population became supermen. Nietzsche's doctrine reached its culmina-
tion. The following quotation from the press campaign of
that time may serve to portray the national feeling:

"There are two kinds of races, master races and inferior
races. Political rights belong to the master race alone, and
can only be won by war. This is a scientific law, a law of
biology. It is *unjust* that a rapidly-increasing master race

should be struggling for room behind its own frontier, while a declining, inferior race can stretch its limbs at ease on the other side of that frontier. The inferior race will not be educated in the schools of the master race, nor will any school be established for it, nor will its language be employed in public. Should it rebel, it is necessary to use the most violent means to crush such insurrection, and not to encumber the prisons afterwards. Thus the conquerors can best work for the annihilation of the conquered, and break forever with the prejudice which would claim for a beaten race any right to maintain its nationality or its native tongue."

We come now to an examination of the few fundamental principles of German philosophy of war.

Plato's principle of aristocracy, government by the best is the best government, is a sophism. The practical justification of democracy, in a few propositions,—as there is not space for discussion,—is as follows:

In general, people attend to their own business better than other people would attend to it for them.

In general, people govern themselves better than another people would govern them.

All the people are more likely to govern themselves better than any one party, class, or sect would govern them, for this reason: Government is an exceedingly difficult and complicated matter, and mistakes are continually occurring. But when all the people have a voice in the government, if a mistake is made, those on whom the evil of the mistake falls are in a position to help correct the mistake, and thus remove the evil; and they have a tendency so to do. That is, in a democracy the corrective force lies within the government. Hence the natural tendency of democracy is progress and improvement.

In an aristocracy, on the other hand, when a mistake is made the resulting evil usually falls on those without the government. And these persons have little or no power to remove the evil by correcting the mistake. Hence the natural tendency of an aristocracy, no matter how good the government was originally, is to grow gradually worse. After education becomes universal, aristocracy is an anachronism.

The Hebrew idea of a single chosen people is one-sided. Later writers in the Old Testament arrived at a truer and juster conception. Thus Isaiah and Jeremiah regarded God as the God of all peoples, of the Egyptians and Babylonians as well as of the Hebrews. Of course it is eminently becoming for every one to think that one's own country is the best, just as it is meet and right for every man who is married to think that his wife is the best woman in the world. But such thought seems to be a process of the idealizing imagination, rather than a judgment of the understanding.

Machiavelli was a keen observer, and a versatile writer; but he was not a profound thinker. He failed to perceive that the moral order lies at the basis, as the very essence of human affairs. As Morley said, in his Romanes lecture: "The modern conception of a state has long made it a moral person, capable of right and wrong, just as are the individuals composing it."

Comte's law of the three stages is a superficial generalization, and is consequently inaccurate. He did not distinguish between the terms "theology" and "mythology." If he had said that civilization passes through two stages, the mythological and the scientific, he would have been correct; or he might have said that it passes through three stages, the mythological, the transitional, and the scientific. For this is the order in which civilization always has advanced. As theology and metaphysics arose out of mythology, likewise did ancient science. Mythology was the great mother science. And as the special sciences gradually freed themselves from mythology and became more strictly scientific, so did theology and metaphysics also. Hence, instead of Comte's statement being true, that theology and metaphysics have become outgrown and useless, precisely the contrary is the case. With the methodical and logical advance of the special sciences, theology and metaphysics have advanced in like manner. Theology, metaphysics, and science have all advanced in concert, or in close relation to one another, sometimes one, sometimes another being in the lead. And there is not any rational ground for inferring that the course of civilization, in this respect, will be different in the future from that in the past. As long as human nature endures, theology, meta-physics, and science will stand or fall together.

Regarding lonely and unhappy Nietzsche two brief re-marks must here suffice: (1) Nietzsche was a specialist. He may have been a great scholar in philology,—though even in this field his unfortunate prejudices sometimes lured him aside from the straight and narrow path of scientific pro-cedure. But he wrote on anthropology, psychology, sociol-ogy, philosophy, ethics, and religion, subjects about which he knew comparatively little. Hence his religious and philo-sophical opinions are largely of the nature of personal guesses, not logical or valid conclusions. Frau Wagner's criticism on "Human, All-too Human" applies to many of his books; superficial in matter and pretentious in manner. And although the pretentiousness increased until he boasted that he had attained to "an elevation" where he spoke "no longer with words, but with flashes of lightning," the superficiality alas! remained. (2) The last eleven years of his life Nietzsche was hopelessly insane; and for the ten years pre-ceding this period he was a confirmed invalid, suffering part of the time, if not all, from a lesion of the brain. Conse-quently his writings, particularly the later ones, are not to be taken as the expression of a normal or rational mind. They are of practically no value, except from the subjective point of view. They are of interest to the psychologist, or to the pathologist as they serve to throw light on the gradual prog-ress of nervous disease in this remarkable, but erratic and unbalanced man.

For nearly a generation Germany has been intoxicated with Kaiserism and Nietzscheism. Recently the *Deutsche Zeitung* proclaimed: "Down with the world-conscience! Away with the spirit of world-brotherhood! Let the Ger-man spirit of power alone be our commander and leader! Its cry is more power! More German power! That is the legacy bequeathed to us by our dead heroes, and written in the flame-red letters of their blood. May those who trifle with this legacy be struck by the curse which will rise from their graves to God's heaven! He whose 'world-conscience' or sense of 'responsibility toward humanity' causes him to say or write anything less than that which the power of the German sword commands is, and always will be, a feeble political dreamer, a gloomy wanderer in the clouds." The social tissue of the German nation has become diseased. The public mind is delirious. National responsibility is paralyzed. A surgical operation is required. After the diseased portions of the body politic shall have been removed, the nation will doubtless return to its right mind, and recognize that world-empire, at the present stage of political evolution, is but an atavistic phantom of a deranged imagination.

BY HENRIQUE LOPES DE MENDONÇA

The great majority of crushed, impoverished, bereaved mortals, cast into grief and misery by the most tremendous war that history has ever witnessed, these are the men who interest me, who interest us all. It is their voice which speaks through the lips of the great statesmen of the belligerents, proclaiming their desire for peace, but an honorable peace, a lasting peace, a peace which shall free future generations from the anguish and tortures assigned by destiny to ours.

This brings me to the point of my thought; but let us turn back a little. For sacred discourses I find myself lacking in the one essential thing, and perhaps the greater portion of my audience may be in like case—we have not the gift of faith! For want of it, the heart of many of us has for long been desolate and shrouded in gloom. This I deplore for my hearers as I do for myself. To live in a dream is still the most blissful, perhaps the only really happy form of existence on earth. And the dream of the supernatural is the supreme hope, for without hope the soul of man sinks into darkness. This it was which inspired Dante to record, over the gateway to his Inferno, the fateful legend: *Lasciate ogni speranza, ó voi che entrate.*[2]

And indeed, with an eternity of despair, no other torment was required to make a hell of Hell.

But let us desist from vain regrets. It is possible that the philosophic mission of Christianity may be on the point of vanishing from the world. Sincerely I hope not. But its

[2] All hope abandon, ye who enter here.

social mission still survives, despite revolutions and cataclysms, as the source of all morality among the civilized nations of Europe and America. Be we devout, skeptical, or atheistic, we still remain saturated with its doctrine, and thus fail to conceive, outside the domain of savagery, any society which does not revere its precepts. The ideals of justice on which all democratic legislation is based spring from the blood so unjustly shed on Calvary. The ideals of love, which kindle our hearts, take their rise from the sacred lips which proclaimed: "Love one another." The ideals of equality and fraternity, never yet attained, were from the same sublime source. Yet it is remarkable that those very revolutionaries who are the fiercest in their zeal for stripping Christ of His divine attributes should inscribe on their banner of social regeneration, in the name of Humanity, the identical words which epitomize the doctrine preached in the name of God.

Hence my conclusion is this: be our sentiments as regards religion what they may; be we believers or skeptics, mystics or atheists, in the depths of our souls we are all Christians—Christians from the moral standpoint, Christians in our mutual relations with the Godhead. Twenty centuries of Christianity have accumulated in our consciences a store of ethical sentiments which no storm will ever sweep out, unless we are prepared to revert to primitive savagery. Conceptions of honor, of duty, of respect for the rights of others, of charity towards the unfortunate, of pity for the oppressed, of horror for unjust violence, of hatred for tyranny, of execration for perfidy and crime: all these have become engrafted into our very being as essential principles, incontestable and indispensable to our social life. Without them we should lapse into the cavern-life of troglodytes, seizing with tooth and claw, with the knife and other weapons of death, the bread we require to keep us from starvation.

True, the good seed of the Gospel has not yet expelled evil from the world. But in the human animal it has at least softened those instincts of rapine, the proximate or remoter source of all social conflagrations. War itself, the organic fatality of societies, from the time when Christ's word poured balm upon the soul of the warrior, has become less atrocious in its methods. In that long period of ten centuries known as the Middle Ages, when a northern barbarian came on the scene, flooding the lands of the sun in the hope of restraining the advance of the Græco-Roman civilization, a gleam of hope filtered into the dungeons of the captives, a ray of pity flashed against the swords of the invaders. Faith, honor, adherence to the plighted word, respect for innocent and defenseless life, protection for the unjustly persecuted: all these notions of justice and dignity, which Roman law had formulated and Christ's apostles had acclaimed, found their way into a code tacitly accepted by all civilized peoples, even by those who, like the Mussulman, were themselves outside the pale of the Church. Such was the code of chivalry, which for centuries stood as the safeguard of millions of oppressed, the refuge of the weak, a shield against the tyranny of the strong, and a mitigation of the violence of armed savagery in war.

By this I do not mean, and it would be senseless to affirm, that, times without number, brute force did not gain the mastery over law and reason; that might was not the supreme arbiter of unbridled ambition. But it is certain that brute force itself paid homage to justice by cloaking its misdeeds under moral pretexts more or less specious. It was in the name of Catholic faith that the Spanish conqueror slew the Indian, that his kings bathed Flanders in blood. It was under color of a resistance to despotism that Napoleon I. undertook by force of arms to forge his own despotism upon Europe. And in the various wars of succession, the ambitions which crossed swords always invoked the protection of divine right, universally acknowledged as the source of monarchical power.

What I mean to say is that greed or wickedness invariably clothed itself in the guise of some sacred ideal, and at least in modern times—never till now—has it dared to affront the conscience of mankind by a cynical parade of its true intentions.

Never till now, I have said; never till yesterday, I ought to have said. For it was but yesterday, in the full daylight of civilization, that a European nation struck the cultured world full in the face, proclaiming over all the globe the supremacy of might as the dogma of her moral culture. It was but yesterday, to the shame of civilization, that the most admirable conquests of modern science, carefully turned to account during forty years of painstaking preparation, were brought into play to crush the weak, to surprise the unsuspecting, to trample under the brutal weight of her armies the most generous aspirations of the human soul—all this, according to the impenitent confession of her warriors and philosophers, with the sole object of riveting upon the world at large the iron bondage of German rule.

History repeats itself. Some fifteen centuries before, Attila, king of the Huns, devastated all Europe, proclaiming that never again would grass grow where the hoofs of his steed had trod. Just in the same spirit German arrogance boasted itself that never again, in the regions swept by German cannon, would popular liberty be reborn. Over the whole world of old, with Attila, dark night came on. But mark the fateful coincidence: it was on the banks of the Marne, in the Catalaunian plains, that the defeat of the Hunnish hosts dispelled the fearsome gloom; and it was in the battle of the Marne that the first dawn of victory gleamed in our eyes. Let us be of good cheer: the same fate is in store for the modern Hun.

The modern Hun has to go under, if we so will it. Let us strengthen our will, not only against the transitory vicissitudes of war, but—note this well—against the persistent insinuations of peace. Yes! For almost half a century these influences, slowly infiltrating, have threatened to pervert our thought and deprave our conscience, just as they have succeeded in doing within the borders of Germany herself. For the present war is the explosion of deleterious forces which, sapping Germany, have brought her back to the first stage of normal civilization. In attempting to establish the Teutonic hegemony of the world, those forces have shaken the foundations upon which human society rests; they have con-

verted social life into a fierce struggle of individual egoisms
in perpetual revolt against the preponderant egoism.

The Germany of which I speak, please remember, is not
the Germany which captured the admiration of thinkers,
philosophers and artists. It is not the Germany which under
the hand of Luther broke the fetters of religious intolerance,
which illuminated human thought by the brilliant beacon of
Kant, which through the sublime genius of Goethe shed its
renovating rays over universal literature, which with Beethoven and Wagner brought fresh charm into the Divine Art.
No! From the day when the most unprogressive of Germany's races, that race which to-day stands for the truculent
energies of barbarism, hurled over her the chariots of its steel
colossus, *that* Germany, great and mighty, sank into oblivion. The German nation (though blindly and unconsciously so) is to-day the victim of Prussian militarism.
Aided by a tenaciously malevolent intelligence, the germs of
that poison, spread ever since the eighteenth century at the
instance of Frederick the Great, have been filtering into the
organism of Germany, there to develop with intensity, above
all since the war of 1871 placed the Imperial crown on the
head of the King of Prussia. From that time onward the
pest overflowed the frontiers and began to contaminate the
whole world. To-day, and only to-day, has the consciousness of this infernal perversion of men's minds begun to be
perceived, up to now accepted as it has been by the *snobbism*
of the world at large as if it were a salutary transformation.

Yes! Many of our contemporaries, and among them
some of the best informed, have been reading eagerly and
assimilating with delight the Nietzschian doctrine that for
those organisms endowed with an excess of energy, the so-
called supermen, all mankind should make way. And this
abominable doctrine, based on a sophistication of scientific
principles, the negation of all morals and all justice, the con-
secration of violence and rapine, has been received without
protest, nay even with sympathy, by minds rooted in Christianity, by social workers whose activities had for their motive force the deepest respect for the dignity of man.

But if the tares spread beyond the German borders, what

wonder that they should have flourished within them, where an environment had been so assiduously prepared for their reception! The State, with singular astuteness, turned to its own ends, if it did not actively promote, the vagaries of genius so as to mold the German mentality. Nietzsche's monstrous theory was practically given a collective interpretation. The superman was expanded into the super-nationality. The professor and the soldier effectively collaborated with the philosopher in the work of moral perversion. Into the Germanic conscience was infused the mystic conviction that the German people was that chosen by the Deity to shepherd the human flock. The pride of moral and intellectual supremacy became ingrained in the soul of the people, inspiring her claim to an indisputable dominion over all the races of the earth. She presented an amazing crisis of general megalomania, which the imminence of defeat has not yet cured.

Of this fact there are abundant proofs, but want of time and the character of this discourse forbid my enlarging upon them. Suffice it to mention, as the latest instance of this form of arrogance, the expression used in 1916 by Professor von Stengel, of the University of Munich. "The whole war up to now," his iron pen wrote, "has shown that Germany has been selected by Providence to guide all other nations. Let us march at the head of them, and we shall lead them to a permanent peace. For this mission we have the strength, and likewise the spiritual gifts, as we are the crown of all civilization. The whole world, and especially the neutral nations, have only one means of profitable existence, and that is to submit themselves to our direction, which is superior to all others from every point of view. No nation surpasses us in the widest and highest ideals and sentiments, and under our dominion none need concern himself as to the defense of his rights."

Be it specially noted: the words I have just recited were penned in cold blood, inside the walls of a German University, by a man whose brain was saturated with science, at the very period when two years of war-pressure at the hands of the Allies had begun to make itself cruelly felt within the

borders of Germany. Yet this document unmistakably manifests the ambition of universal dominion, its threats not
even sparing the neutral Powers. It portrays in gloomy per-
spective a future for humanity under the iron-shod jack-boot
of the Teuton.

Should not the universal conscience, that of the whole
civilized world, be it inspired by Christ or Muhammad, by
Buddha or by the goddess of Reason, combine in revolt
against this formidable hypertrophy of national egoism?
With all sincerity I confess it: in the midst of this tremendous conflagration, what most alarms one, the epidemic
of war-madness in Germany synchronizing with a world-
wide blindness elsewhere, is that Germany should have allies
at all, and that a single neutral should continue to exist in
the world. When, with an effrontery such as this, a whole
people forsakes its rudimentary moral sense, boasting its own
brute force as the sole sanction of its boundless pride, we
feel we are confronted with a pack of ravening wolves.
These it behooves us to hunt down with all our available energies, unless we all, every man among us, mankind in the
mass, are willing to be torn to pieces by their death-dealing
fangs.

To hunt them down, yes! To destroy them utterly, no!
This would neither be practicable, nor humane, nor yet bene-
ficial. Our vision is one of a reconstituted Germany, relieved
of Prussian militarism, dedicated to her own prolific task
of peace and science, unoppressed by the horrid nightmare of
which her only record is a universal hatred. Freed from
the illusive fumes of vainglory, her eyes fixed on the supreme
ideal of liberty, her robust hands wielding the instruments
of honest toil, her powerful brain applied to invention, a Germany such as we portray would be a potent lever of incalculable value towards human progress. During long years
of apparent prosperity, though the latent virus was mining
her organism, she showed the world the greatness of her
genius, the pertinacity of her toil, the excellence of her manufactures. She contributed largely to the material comfort
of mankind, rendering life easier and more joyous, and giving the poor a share in that luxury which used to be the

monopoly of the rich. It may have been that to this end this unfortunate people was ignorantly sacrificing its old ideals of dignity, burning on the altars of despotism the last remnants of its democratic pride. But however great her services to us may have been, the price she demanded from us in return was out of all proportion. It was an ignoble serfdom, this transformation of free men into a gang of convicts, toiling on the endless task of filling their coffers. The first onslaughts of hunger should have led them to see the senselessness of such an aspiration.

What a pity that to this distracted people, the progenitor of heroes and geniuses, so cruel a disillusionment as this should alone have remained! But, should it open her eyes to her true position, she may be able later on to say, having regained full possession of her senses, that it was not she who was defeated, but the ancestral forces which overwhelmed her from within, the atavic eruption of barbarism bursting through the noble sentiments acquired by her as the work of many centuries of civilization. That formidable outburst over, she will have been released by the hands which, when fighting her, were purifying her from the malign ferment which has poisoned her culture—a culture of which she was so proud, yet one which only attains its true fecundity when the rays of the Latin sun are allowed free play upon it.

For half a century the Germanic genius, shrouded in a mantle of pride, has sought to withdraw itself from those vivifying rays. The result is what we are now witnessing. Given up entirely to herself, Germany has by insensible transitions been sliding down the declivity into barbarism. Kept going by her undeniable internal energy, her products have been colossal, but monstrous; flourishing, but aberrant. A depraved philosophy: a brutalized art. In applied science alone, served by an admirably methodical mind, and on the utilitarian side of civilization alone, thanks to an astounding tenacity, has German genius during that period earned an indisputable title to the gratitude of mankind.

But it is equally certain that this very savagery of greatness in her conceptions has blinded her. I have already referred in passing to the fatal influence of German philosophy.

That influence has not restricted itself to the limited orbit of those thinkers who alone possess the brains capable of the laborious assimilation of such metaphysical dainties. Lamentable though it may be, it would not be altogether an evil had they, sequestered in their own lazarettos, refrained from contaminating society at large. But around the thinkers there hover the restless, petulant multitude, the chattering, pervading army of snobs, and it is they who are the transmitters and the propagators of the virus. Filtered through this layer, those philosophical principles change their form, either crystallizing into dogmatic aphorisms or diffusing themselves in subtle emanations which spread throughout the whole body social. Often even the most beneficent of them, by excessive concentration, assume deleterious properties: what, then, of those which, as in the present instance, are by their nature dissolvent?

In this way the pernicious principle of the supremacy of force over right, elevated into a body of moral doctrine, the inspiring idea of the Nietzschian philosophy, has been worked to its full extent so as to arouse into mischievous activity the savage instincts slumbering in the minds of the many. Recourse to violence, intolerance of control, the rebellion of the ruled, exacerbations of the egoistic passions, refusal to yield where interests conflict, all emerge as the fatal and ultimate consequences towards which we have long been ignorantly drifting. And indeed many minds at present hostile to Germanism have nevertheless become tainted by it. Everywhere idealistic tendencies are carped at, humane precepts ridiculed, disinterestedness scorned, the struggle for life accentuated. Our old romantic ideals are tied up into bundles and slightingly labeled "sentimentalism."

A curious thing! The Germanic spirit, prone to expansiveness like all its earlier contemporaries, used to indulge from the first in the most exaggerated flights of romantic idealism. We have a familiar instance of the kind in the youthful creation of Goethe—Werther. Remember how he could find no other means of ridding his brain of a criminal passion than by shattering it with a pistol-shot. The vogue created by this romance became so extraordinary throughout

Germany that imitators arose on all sides. An epidemic of passional suicide ran through the nation. Goethe had to hasten to check it, and succeeded in doing so by cauterizing the evil he himself had created, in his later work, "The Basis of Sentimentalism."

And now, a century and a half later, the torrent of German materialism and overweening self-adulation has not merely subverted the exaggerated sentimentalism of the ultra-romantic school, but has stripped off the foliage and withered the flower of romance which gave the human soul its only perfume. It has thus destroyed the only check upon the corrosive influence of egoistic passion, the only restraint upon savagery and crime. And this time there is not the slightest hope that the disseminators of the pestilence will repent and provide the remedy for the evil they have wrought.

How dark a future would be reserved for mankind had chance not opposed a barrier to this devastating torrent, and, after it had been dammed back, had some germs of good, deposited by the flood, not been left in the world.

But, as the apothegm of the old Roman poet hath it: *"Quem Jupiter vult perdere dementat prius."* [3] It was thus that Germany, materially prosperous, aggrandized from the worldly standpoint, allowed herself to be deceived so far as to attempt a gigantic and decisive blow towards making good her own monstrous megalomania. The blow was prematurely delivered. The world had not yet been sufficiently sapped by the corruption previously spread abroad. It was still but a minority of thoughtless persons who, impelled by a craving for the new and the extravagant, by the deplorable obsession of political passion or of despicable interests, received and welcomed the advent of the movement. The others, the well-meaning, not entirely contaminated by the virus, had their eyes opened in time to the menace as revealed in the crushing of innocent populations, in the vandalistic destruction of revered monuments, in terror glorified as the true system of warfare, in unscrupulous rapine, in slaughter without pity, in ferocity without limits. Taken thus by surprise, the nations armed themselves to resist the barbarians.

[3] Whom Jupiter would destroy, he first makes mad.

THE CULTURE OF DEMOCRACY

HUMANITY'S LONG STRUGGLE TOWARD EQUAL RIGHTS AND JUSTICE

ROBERT N. McELROY   THEODORE RUYSSEN

In sharpest opposition to the German Kultur stands that other Culture which had at the same time been growing up in the world outside of Germany, the culture which is founded on Democracy, on the faith that every other man has rights equal to our own, that we want to give him whatever is justly his, and to live in harmony with him, not in authority over him. This spirit has been developed chiefly, but by no means wholly, in America.

Robert Nutt McElroy, whose words on Democracy's ideal are here presented, was Professor of History and Politics at Princeton University, and was chosen by the American Government during the War to direct, in all schools and colleges, through the National Security League, the educational work of teaching why the nation entered the war. Theodore Ruyssen is a noted French scholar and author, Professor of Philosophy at Bordeaux University, and long president of the leading patriotic Peace Society of France.

From Ruyssen as the standard authority, we may learn the European view upon Democracy and the equal rights of the smaller nations. The American review of the two hundred year long struggle toward Democracy is here presented by her own writers. To America the Great War was but a single phase in the centuries of effort; but to Europeans many of these ideas of equality, especially as applied to the "little peoples," uprose for the first time during the War. Americans have called this the War for Democracy; but many Europeans, even among the Allies, had at the beginning of hostilities still to learn much of what Democracy believes and represents. They have learned its lessons swiftly, and sometimes adopted them more valiantly than the earlier Democracies.   C. F. H.

BY ROBERT N. McELROY

WHEN you say "an American," what do you mean? Do you mean a person of English blood? The Americans without English blood are vastly more numerous than those whose ancestors were English. "American" is a term which has no relation to blood. You may be of pure German blood and yet be a real American. You may be of pure Irish blood and yet be a real American. You may be of Russian, Hebrew, Italian, Polish, French, Belgian or Austrian blood and yet be as real an American as if your ancestors had come to this country on board the *Mayflower,* or had fought with Washington to create the Republic, or later, with Lincoln, to save it. There are more than twenty-six million people in the United States to-day who were born in other countries, or whose parents were foreign born. Each and every one of these is or may easily become a real American, if he has but the spirit of loyalty to the ideals which have made this nation out of many races.

In most nations the race tie is the idea at the basis of political unity. In each of them, one race so far outnumbers all other races that the national name implies a blood kinship of its citizens. But in our nation, in the United States, the tie is not of blood, but of belief in an ideal of liberty; therefore race does not count in determining whether or not one is an American. In that respect America is unique among great, independent nations.

Our Republic was founded by people of many races, all intent upon one idea—political liberty. From many lands there came to these shores men and women who cherished the idea of political liberty above race or creed or financial interest. By their devotion they made here a nation with liberty and equality for all. That ideal furnishes the real test of Americanism. No man, woman or child who wishes special privileges is a real American. No man, woman or child who knowingly denies to another equal rights is a real American: for all Americans must "hold these truths to be self-evident, that all men are created equal; that they are endowed by their Creator with certain unalienable rights; that among these are life, liberty, and the pursuit of happiness."

Governments are created among men to make these rights secure. The best and noblest men and women of every race have always been ready to sacrifice private interests, and even life itself, to preserve them to the world. Resistance to these ideas is treason to the best that is in every race; the defense of them is the supreme duty of every

American, and our history is glorious just in so far as we have defended them.

The American Revolution was not a fight between England and America. It was a war which resulted from an attempt of the arbitrary rulers of England, led by a king of German origin, to deny these rights and thus to destroy political liberty in America, as they had already destroyed it in England, and as other arbitrary rulers had destroyed it upon the continent of Europe. America did not stand alone in her fight to preserve political liberty. To her aid came Englishmen and Frenchmen, Poles and Germans, Irish and Scotch, as well as natives of the Colonies. The Fathers of the American Revolution did not all live in America. Some of them never saw our shores. William Pitt, a Father of America, in his speeches in Parliament, used the bold words, "our armies in America," when referring to the troops which were fighting against the king. Edmund Burke, a Father of America, eloquently pleaded in England the cause of America as the cause of human freedom. The gallant Frenchman, the Marquis de Lafayette, a Father of America, was fighting for the interests of France and America when he carried out the orders of General Washington. Kosciusko, a Father of America, struck for Polish and American freedom when he fought in the American army; while the brave German, Baron von Steuben, a Father of America, unsheathed his sword in the cause of Germany and America when he taught our ragged troops at Valley Forge how to plan a campaign.

The victory at Yorktown was not merely an American victory. It was a world victory. It meant that free government, the hope of all nations, and kindred, and tongues, was to survive, not for America only, but for the good of all men, in all future ages, and in all countries.

As soon as the American Revolution had saved free government in America, other countries began to feel the effect. People with souls for freedom, in many lands, began to struggle with new courage for political liberty. France was the first to catch the infection. As the French soldiers, who had fought side by side with the Americans during "the days that tried men's souls," sailed back to sunny France and their Bourbon despots, they carried in their hearts the ringing phrase, "All men are created equal," and soon the throne of the Bourbons was rocking under the blows for "Liberty, Equality and Fraternity." A few years later the Marquis de Lafayette sent to Washington the key to the royal prison-house, the Bastille, which had been taken by the revolutionists; and he labeled it "the spoil of despotism."

England, too, soon felt the effects of a forward movement which the success of the American Revolution revivified. Parliament, under the leadership of William Pitt, the Younger, was soon made once more a really representative assembly, a character which it had lost many years before the American Revolution began. The Reform Bill of 1832 restored free government to England, and this Reform Bill had been made possible by the failure of George III. to crush free government in America.

Thus representative government returned to England, and to-day Americans and English acknowledge the same sovereign. That sovereign is not the descendant of King George III., however, but the "Sovereign People." And it is a glory to America and to Great Britain alike that wherever our flags have been unfurled, the love of that sovereign has since been the theme of political teaching.

From free America, and free France, and free England the ideals of a government "of the people, by the people and for the people" spread slowly into many lands. It was this march of free government for the peaceful and beneficent conquest of the world for the good of the world, that the gallant French people had in mind when they erected in New York Harbor that wonderful statue of "Liberty Enlightening the World."

Until August, 1914, the spread of American ideals of freedom was steady and almost uninterrupted. The world saw one country after another adopt the ideas for which the heroes of many races had fought at Yorktown; and the friends of freedom began to hope and plan for a lasting world-peace, resting upon the idea of the right of self-government.

But the peaceful conquest of the world for free government was watched with jealous foreboding by the Prussian
military autocracy, whose power had been built upon the
theory that "might makes right." From the beginning of
her history Prussia has cherished the belief that government
is something with which the masses of the people, the merchant, the farmer and the laborer, have no concern. Her
ideals have always been ideals of government from above.

"We Hohenzollerns," said the Kaiser, in frank contempt
for the idea of government "of the people, by the people
and for the people"—"We Hohenzollerns take our crown
from God alone. On me the spirit of God has descended.
I regard my whole task as appointed by Heaven. Who
opposes me I shall crush. Nothing must be settled in the
world without the intervention of the German Emperor. He
who listens to public opinion runs a danger of inflicting immense harm on the state."

In this statement William II. is merely summarizing the
philosophy which Prussia has always followed. In the history of Prussia we miss the stirring conflicts for the people's rights, which lend a charm to American, English and
French history. There are no Runnymede Barons in the
history of Prussia, no Simon de Montforts, no Oliver Crom-
wells, Pitts, Washingtons, Lafayettes or Lincolns. From
the first, Prussia has been what she remained to 1918, a
nation whose profession is war. Slowly, but with a terrible certainty, she imposed her ideals upon the rest of Germany, until Germany became merely an expanded Prussia,
a military autocracy, thinking in terms of force, and dreaming dreams of world-conquest.

The philosophy of Prussianized Germany taught that
the world must some day be brought, by force of arms, into
subjection to the will of the iron masters of Germany. The
philosophy of America and England and France, on the
other hand, teaches that the rights of small nations are
sacred and must not be disregarded. Contrast the words in
which the Kaiser told why Germany was at war with the
words in which President Wilson states the aims of
America.

The Kaiser said, "The triumph of the greater Germany which some day must dominate all Europe is the single end for which we are fighting." And, in a still more striking statement, he presents the dream of empire which has deluged the world with blood: "From childhood I have been under the influence of five men,—Alexander, Julius Cæsar, Theodoric II., Frederick II., and Napoleon. Each of these men dreamed a dream of world-empire (and) they failed. I am dreaming a dream of the German World Empire, and my mailed fist shall succeed."

President Wilson thus declared our aims: "These are the things we shall stand for:

(1) "That all nations are equally interested in the peace of the world, and in the political stability of free peoples, and equally responsible for their maintenance.

(2) "That the essential principle of peace is the actual equality of nations, in all matters of right and privilege.

(3) "That peace cannot securely or justly rest upon an armed balance of power.

(4) "That governments derive all their just powers from the consent of the governed, and that no other powers should be supported by the common thought, purpose, or power of the family of nations.

(5) "That the seas should be equally free and safe for the use of all peoples . . . accessible to all upon equal terms.

(6) "That national armaments should be limited to the necessities of national order and domestic safety."

What does this contrast mean to your mind? It should mean something very definite, if you are a real American. It should cause you again to say with pride, "America means freedom for the world."

BY THEODORE RUYSSEN

In his speech delivered before the House of Commons on August 6, 1914, in justification of the participation of the British Empire in the European War, Mr. Asquith, the English prime minister, expressed himself to this effect: "We are fighting to vindicate the principle that the small nationalities are not to be crushed, in defiance of international good faith, by the arbitrary will of a strong and overmastering power." On several occasions, members of the British and the French cabinets have emphasized the same idea, that the small nations, even the weakest among them, have an equal right to existence with the greatest, and that it is in defense of this right, violated to the injury of Serbia and of Belgium, that the allies are risking the lives of hundreds of thousands of men. "The people are resolved to dispose of themselves in freedom," proclaims M. Viviani. In terms yet more precise, Mr. Lloyd George thus defines the object of the war: "This," he declares, "is a war of nationalities." No utterance, I think, could better characterize the gigantic struggle deployed before our eyes throughout the entire European continent.

It is not, or rather it is no longer, only Serbia and Belgium which are at stake in the fighting at Artois, in the Vosges, and along the Dvina, the Dniester and the Isonzo. By far the most striking feature of this war is the way in which it has raised, one after another, most of the "national" questions of Europe and even of the Orient, not only those which yesterday menaced the equilibrium of Europe, such as the Balkan problems, but even the most ancient of them, slumbering in the obscurity of the past, and in regard to which public opinion has retained only an academic and, so to speak, a conventional interest. As a matter of fact, who save a few special students concerned himself in June, 1914, about the Polish question or that of Syria? Even among those who maintain the honorable tradition of according their sympathy to unjustly treated peoples, how many were aware of a Ukrainian, a Ruthenian, a Lithuanian question?

Thus, through a long train of successive events which should be recognized as something more than a mere series of accidents, manifold national questions, which statesmen and diplomats had attempted to disregard because they interfered with their political schemes, have entered the war. Already on July 26, 1914, the uncompromising ultimatum addressed to Serbia by Austria-Hungary gave notice that the Hapsburg Empire had determined to begin, beyond Bosnia and Herzegovina, the first step of the "advance to the East"

(*Drang nach Osten*), and gain a decisive start on the road to Salonika; thereby bringing into question the independence of Serbia and with it that of Bulgaria and Greece, disturbing again the intricate tangle of Balkan problems of which the treaty of Bucharest and the Convention of London had just relieved the wearied hands of the diplomats. On August 15th, the Grand Duke Constantine made a solemn promise to restore to Poland her territorial unity as well as her political autonomy. A little later, an imperial rescript informed the Russian Jews that henceforth they would enjoy an equal position in the Empire with that of Orthodox subjects. By the pretensions of certain German publicists the Finnish question was discovered as involving a branch of the Germanic stock which extends from the Baltic coast to the Adriatic.

With the entrance of Turkey into the war, all the national questions of the Orient were again thrown open; Russia no longer conceals her intention to conquer Armenia, of which she already holds the Caucasian region; Syria and Arabia are growing restless, and, finally, with the fate of Constantinople and the Dardanelles, the very existence of the Ottoman Empire, its final expulsion from Europe, and, perhaps, its dismemberment in Asia have come into question; this would mean the parceling out of Asia Minor into colonies or spheres of influence. More generally, the whole problem of the relation of the Moslem to the Christian world has risen anew in all its magnitude. The Germans have clearly recognized this, and from the first days of the war they tried to stir up difficulties for Russia in Persia, for England in India and Egypt, for Italy in Tripoli, for France in the whole of northern Africa, up to the day when the Ottoman Empire itself was dragged into their quarrel.

This military alliance of the Protestant Kaiser, the Catholic Emperor at Vienna, and the Moslem Commander of the Faithful is a fact of great symbolic significance. Its importance can hardly be exaggerated. It demonstrates conclusively—despite what certain writers may have said who saw nothing in the ruins of Belgium but an act of Lutheran vandalism—that the age of the great religious wars is past

and that even where religious passion plays a part, as no
one will deny it does, it is only an auxiliary to national sentiment. The alliance of Berlin, Vienna and Constantinople
is no artificial arrangement, but the expression of the natural
and necessary solidarity of the three European Empires
which are drawn together by the one common characteristic
that they have never granted nor desired to grant justice
to conquered peoples.

No doubt one may detect certain differences in the rule
established by these empires. That of Austria-Hungary has
been the least harsh; she has granted parliamentary institutions to many nationalities within the Dual Monarchy and,
of the three divisions of Poland, Galicia has undoubtedly
been the best treated. Even Germany has never, like Turkey, made wholesale massacre an instrument of government. The fact remains, however, that Austria-Hungary,
Germany and Turkey are conglomerations of imperfectly
absorbed and unequally treated nationalities. None of these
states has been able to assimilate its conquests. In Alsace,
in Lorraine, in Schleswig, and in Poland, Germany, in spite
of the most indefatigable efforts, has been able to "Germanize" only by importing Germans, by expropriating the land
owners or by forcing them through persecution to expatriate
themselves. In the Hapsburg monarchy, at least a dozen
heterogeneous, jealous and hostile nationalities are crowded
together, none of which has a decisive preponderance over
the others.

As for the Turks, it has been justly said that they have
been contented to camp, saber in hand, among the subjected
population. We must, however, do them the justice to admit that they have not attempted to impose Islamism upon
the conquered, and that they have shown themselves very
tolerant in one respect, that they have never made an attempt to win over to their type of civilization the Greeks,
the Balkan Slavs, the Armenians, the Christian communities
of the Orient. The lack of mutual understanding between
victors and vanquished has remained as profound after six
centuries of occupation as at the time when the first horse-
men, coming down from Turkestan, directed their daring

raids against the Byzantine Empire; and whenever the taxes were not paid promptly, or whenever the civil population threatened to become rebellious, great hecatombs soon restored order among the discontented and gold to the public coffers.

In the absence of any real fusion of the ethnical elements in the three empires into a homogeneous unity or any voluntary coöperation of the nationalities remaining distinct, it has been necessary to obtain unity through force: military force to begin with, thereafter administrative. Artificial combinations of alien or mutually hostile peoples, some of which knew themselves to be deprived of the political and even of the civil rights accorded to others, Germany, Austria-Hungary and Turkey were doomed to remain military empires, to place the army above the civil law, to perpetuate and to renew noble castes, one of whose privileges it is to monopolize the higher grades of the army, to put this caste and this army at the disposal not of the nation but of the ruler, and, finally, to make him, notwithstanding certain concessions to modern parliamentary polity, the arbiter of national destiny, the master of war and peace.

In opposition to this triptych, a view of the "allied" forces presents a remarkable unity, despite some incontestable divergencies. It is doubtless necessary to avoid oversimplified generalizations and merely verbal distinctions. It would be false as well as arbitrary to divide the contending nations which dispute with each other the empire of the world into the oppressors and the defenders of nationality. Germany herself achieved her unity in the name of the nationalist principle, and it may even be said that, in a certain sense, Pan-Germanism is nothing but a monstrous perversion of that principle. On the other hand, nobody will be apt to forget that in the tragic history of nationality, the record of the allies is far from immaculate. Nations without faults exist only in legend. The most liberal of western nations, England, has borne in her side for centuries the sore wound of the Irish question, and the admirable solidarity shown by the British Empire to-day cannot make us forget that on the very eve of war it was an open question whether the introduction of Home Rule in Ireland might not inflict upon the United Kingdom the horrors of a civil war. France is far from having made such efforts to elevate the dignity of her Mohammedan subjects in northern Africa as might have been expected from the country of the "Rights of Man." As for Russia, not even her best friends could forget that during the past twenty years she has continuously infringed the liberties of Finland by restrictions as unconstitutional and unjust as they were tactless, and that her attempts to Russify eastern Poland have equaled the German attempts to Germanize Prussian Poland.

All these facts are only too true and should be frankly admitted. But these admissions only add force to the statement that, as a whole, the group of allied powers represent in their struggle against the empires of armed force the continuity of that liberal tradition to which the nationalities which were enfranchised in the course of the nineteenth century owe their liberation. There is hardly a national movement to which France, England and Russia, separately or together, have not given the support of their political influence or even of their arms. Russia, whatever may have been her faults in respect to the Finns, Poles and Jews, has been an indefatigable helper in the liberation of the Balkan Slavs. England has aided in the freeing of Greece and Bulgaria, and has always shown herself the protectress of small states. As for France, it is needless to recall what Greece, Belgium, Rumania and Italy have owed to her in the conquest of their national independence.

And where have all the patriots who have been persecuted for dreaming of the emancipation of their respective nationalities found an asylum? Where were the committees for the protection of all the martyred nationalities organized, the "Leagues of the Rights of Peoples," the "Nationalist Headquarters"? Where are the pamphlets printed, where are the periodicals published, which are intended to defend before the tribunal of public opinion the interests, so easily forgotten, of the peoples held in bondage? Is it at Berlin? Is it at Vienna? No; but in the two capitals which have been equally hospitable to oppressed peoples and to "Kings in Exile," London and Paris.

For whom, after all, did men fight in 1914 from the Yser to the Niemen, from the Adige to the Caucasus? In the first instance, Russia arose to defend Serbia, already sacrificed by Europe at the end of the second Balkan War, from the menaces of Austria. England and France responded in their turn to the pathetic appeal of Belgium, crushed under the heel of one of the powers which had guaranteed by their signature her neutrality. Thus from the very outset, the European war disclosed its original character, which has continually become more apparent. It was a war of nationalities. Without question, it was also something more; it has so profoundly shaken the old structure of the European balance of power that one may well wonder what great social, political, economic, or even religious interest there is that it has not imperiled.

GERMANY'S ECONOMIC ORGANIZATION

THE PROSPERITY THAT URGED CENTRAL EUROPE TOWARD EXPANSION AND WAR

HENRI HAUSER   JOSEPH FRIEDRICH NAUMANN

The marvelous economic organization of Germany before the war, and the colossal commercial prosperity which sprang from it, were in part the product of the new Kultur. More largely, however, they sprang from the natural German energy and perseverance in toil. The unhappy result of this prosperity was to enlarge the German self-confidence. The whole nation became desirous of expansion, demanding it as a right and duty, with very little consideration of the rights of other nations against whose commerce or across whose lands they might expand. Chiefly their ideas looked towards the possession of a Middle-Europe Empire (*Mittel-Europa*), with Turkish, African and South American dependencies.

The most able and successful book that appeared in Germany during the War was the "Central Europe" of J. Friedrich Naumann, one of the most influential of Germany's radical statesmen, an economist, clergyman, newspaper editor, and member of the Imperial Reichstag. Until his death in August, 1919, Naumann was a leader in the reorganization of the less far-spreading Germany which survived the War. Instead of being blindly boastful, like most German war utterances, Naumann's "Central Europe" is keenly analytical, patriotic but philosophic. He is thus enabled to present in its strongest form the usual plea of his countrymen that they must have space for expansion, both in trade and in territory. Naumann also saw the really new impulse which German organization had introduced into civilization, and so drew the striking picture, which follows, of Germany's economic progress.

Of course it scarcely occurred to Naumann, or to the other German leaders of his hour, to consider the pressure their expansion must exert on other peoples. The superman wastes no remorseful pity on those he tramples down in his glorious progress. Naumann's picture of prosperity driving Germany toward war is almost wholly unconscious—and perhaps for that very reason the more impressive.

The conscious view of what this lordly expansion involved for the rest of Europe is therefore presented here by the standard French authority on economics, Professor Henri Hauser of the University of Dijon, a member of the Institute of France.

C. F. H.

BY HENRI HAUSER

ONE of the favorite arguments used by pacificists in recent years was that the development of industrial civilization made all war henceforward impossible, and so to say
unthinkable. The ties formed between modern peoples by
industry and commerce are so manifold and so subtle that
interest, even in the absence of sentiment, makes it impossible to break them.

Nevertheless war has broken out. More than that, war
has been declared by a people whom we were pleased to consider the most remarkable creation of industrial civilization.
And we are bound to recognize that, in the unanimous enthusiasm with which this people has welcomed the dawn of
bloodshed, among the most eager voices have been those of
the commercial and manufacturing classes. Financiers, man-
agers of works, workingmen themselves, have all figured in
the front ranks of the defenders of Imperialism.

How are we to explain this paradox? And first let us
get rid of a possible misunderstanding. Certain thinkers tell
us, "It is not true that economic causes played a preponderant
part in the explosion of July, 1914. Germany was not threatened by over-population, she had no urgent need of colonies." But the truth is that what counts in the history of
humanity is not the actual facts, but the form in which men
picture them to their minds. Political economy and history
are in their essence psychological sciences. What we are
concerned to know is not whether Germany was actually suffocating. Germany thought she was suffocating, she yielded
—to use the very words of one of those who contradict us
—to the haunting fear of aggressive "encirclement," which
she felt bound to shatter at all costs. It is this "pathological
phenomenon of collective psychology" which we must attempt to explain.

What strikes us at the very outset in the evolution of
German industry is the actual greatness of the phenomenon.
There is something impressive in the spectacle of this people, which forty years ago scarcely counted at all in economic
geography, and yet had become on the eve of the war one of

the great forces of the world. With her 5,000 millions [1] of
foreign commerce Germany reckoned in the second rank of
mercantile nations, after England. Outstripping England
herself, she had achieved the second place in the smelting
and production of iron and the second also in the manufacture of steel. Her mercantile marine, inferior to that of
France in 1870, was in 1913 surpassed only by those of England and the United States.

All this won our admiration. Are we to disavow the
admiration we have expressed, because Germany has dishon-
ored herself by crimes? No! For Frenchmen the truth is
always the truth. History will certainly record the prodigious effort of will by which Germany, victorious on the battlefield in 1870, has won her place by main force in the
economic world. I do not know whether it is true that Friedrich Karl said, on the night of the surrender of Metz, "We
have just conquered in the military sphere: our task is now
to fight and conquer in the industrial sphere." It matters little whether the words are apocryphal: they express a profound and symbolic truth, and admirably render the thought
of an entire nation.

We do not hesitate then to recognize that the German
people, since the foundation of the Empire, have given proof
of remarkable qualities. First and foremost they have
worked with intense energy, not with the feverish excitement which raises mountains in a few days, but with persistent and patient everyday labor, regular and methodical.
Ostwald is right when he attributes to the Germans the
faculty and genius for organization. They have carried to
perfection the art of making use of men, of putting every
man in his place and of getting the maximum of output from
each individual. If the genius for great discoveries seems in
recent times to have deserted Germany, the Germans are
past masters in the application of the discoveries of science to
industry. The statement has often enough been made: It
is the union of the laboratory and the workshop which is the
foundation of German wealth. This truth was emphasized

[1] The figures given by M. Hauser in *milliards* (= 1,000 millions of
francs) are here given in dollars.

in 1897 by M. Raphael-Georges Lévy. In an article in the
Revue des Deux Mondes, which was a revelation to many
Frenchmen, he wrote: "The sphere in which science wins
its triumphs is that of industry. It is difficult to find a more
striking demonstration of this truth than that furnished by
the chemical industry of Germany. That industry came
from the laboratories of great men of science such as Liebig
and Hoffmann, and its continued prosperity is due to the
incessant coöperation of hundreds of chemists who come
every year from the Universities. Germany is covered with
laboratories, several of which have cost over $100,000, and
the yearly upkeep of which requires hundreds of thousands."

Again, in one point this analysis was incomplete. Side
by side with the union between laboratory and workshop, it
is necessary to call attention to the union between the office
of the business-director and the library of the economist, the
geographer and the historian. For the method which the
Germans applied to the production of a new aniline color
they also carried into their search for commercial outlets,
and their organization of channels of commerce. The German chemist and the German commercial traveler marched
in step to the conquest of the globe.

This rise of Germany was a great and, we are prepared
to say, in a certain sense, a fine spectacle; but its very rapidity contained an element which gave some ground for anxiety.

The evolution of Germany has borne a startling and almost catastrophic character. From the complex of agricultural states, dotted with industrial patches, which constituted the *Zollverein* in 1870, the industrial Empire has
sprung up in a few years by a sort of historical "right-about-
face," without any of that slow and secular preparation
which marked the rise, for instance, of the English power.
Time has had no share in producing industrial Germany:
like nearly everything else in modern Germany it is an upstart. A few dates and figures will bring this out clearly.
Karl Lamprecht has noted the fact that towards 1880 the
infant industry of Germany still needed protection against its
older rivals, and this protectionist movement started, by re-

action, the French movement of 1892. In the midst of the internal struggle over the question of canals in 1894-1901 it is still a matter of debate "whether the majority of occupations and interests in the Empire is still agricultural or has become industrial and commercial." But facts give the answer: In 1893 the consumption of raw iron *per caput* of the population did not rise to 220 pounds a year; in 1899 it amounted to 340 pounds. The consumption of coal rises from 4,200 to 6,000 pounds a head. In the same period the production of iron and pig-iron rises from five million to more than eight million tons, that of coal from 95 million to 136 million. In these six years the fate of Germany was decided by an increase in production so intensive that it seemed "unwholesome," and was destined to lead to the crisis of 1901. The country which was poor had suddenly become very rich. In 1895 the income from the fortunes of the Empire was estimated at four billion dollars; in 1913 the estimate varied from eight to ten billions, while the wealth of Germany was estimated at 64 billions. Such are the figures proudly produced by Dr. Helfferich, Director of the Deutsche Bank, the Minister of Finance of the King of Prussia, at the twenty-fifth anniversary of the accession of William II.

This sudden increase in German wealth had very serious consequences for the character and distribution of the population of Germany. The two most notable results were the progressive disappearance of the rural population and the abrupt cessation of emigration. It is repeatedly stated that the Germans were forced into a policy of expansion and conquest by the increase in their population. This was indeed the excuse they put forward to justify their attempts to create colonies of settlement in Morocco and Asia Minor. A pitiless Malthusian law had forced them, it was said, to find for themselves a "place in the sun." Now there could be no idea more false than this of Germany as an over-populated country. It is quite true that since 1871 the population of the Empire has increased from 40 to nearly 70 millions. It is quite true that in spite of a decline in the birth rate, the increase in the population of Germany was 800,000 a year: that is, 800,000 more births than deaths, 800,000 more

mouths to feed. But this increase was far from being excessive, for every year 700,000 Slav laborers came in to work on
the great estates of the East, not to mention the Italian,
Croatian, Polish, etc., labor employed in towns, mines and
works.

As for German emigration, it was no longer more than
a memory. Between 1880 and 1883 it exceeded 200,000 a
year, in 1914 it did not reach 20,000, very much the same
figure as our own, and the French are regarded as a people
who emigrate very little. The number of arrivals far exceeds that of departures. Germany has ceased to be a country of emigration and is becoming a country of immigration.

There is indeed an emigration in Germany, but it is an
internal emigration, from the country to the town, from the
agricultural regions to the industrial districts. Since 1895
the population living on the land has ceased to be half of the
total population: at the present time it is not 44 per cent.

Out of 67 million Germans scarcely 17 millions are agricultural or live on agriculture. Every year an enormous
number of peasants quit the land and rush into colossal factories. It is thus that the number of towns with a population
over 100,000 exceeds 45, it is thus that armies of labor are
formed which put 15,000 workmen at the disposal of a firm
like Mannesermann, more than 30,000 under Thyssen,
73,000, nearly two army corps, under Krupp. In these figures I include all the works belonging to one firm.

Germany has definitely passed from the type of the agricultural state to that of the industrial state. The equilibrium
between the land and the workshop has been upset.

The Industrial State has very imperious needs and requirements, which are not shared by the Agricultural State;
the Agricultural State lives on itself and for itself, and can
live within its own limits. The Industrial State, to use the
phrase of Lamprecht, is a "tentacular" State.

To begin with, it has need of supplies of food. It is calculated that 20 millions of the 67 millions of Germany depend for their maintenance on foreign harvests and foreign
cattle. A dangerous position, since it compels Germany to
secure for herself at all times not only free passage over her

land frontiers, but, above all, freedom of communication by sea. We know what it costs Germany to-day to be cut off from receiving the wheat of Russia, America and Argentina.

The Industrial State is in pressing need not only of capital but of raw material. Germany, when she entered the lists, was regarded as a country rich in coal and iron. She has remained rich in coal; but by working her iron mines intensively I do not say she has exhausted them, but she can no longer extract from them the total amount of ore required by her metallurgical works. Krupp is more and more dependent on Sweden, Spain, North Africa and France. In the same way the spinning and weaving factories of Saxony and Silesia are dependent on Texas and Louisiana. If Sweden, which has nationalized her mines, puts barriers on the export of her ores, or the price of corn undergoes an abnormal rise in the market of New Orleans, it means famine for the crowds which throng into the Westphalia district or to the north of the Bohemian mountains.

Raw cotton bulks larger than any other article imported into Germany, to the amount of considerably more than $125,000,000. The cotton industry employs more than 1½ millions of work-people and manufactures goods to the value of more than $250,000,000. Now, two-thirds of the raw cotton consumed in the world is supplied by a single country, the United States. In 1894, a syndicate, the "Sully cotton corner," took advantage of this situation to produce an enormous rise of prices and to reserve the cotton for the American factories. On the Bremen Exchange, in February, the price paid for cotton was 85 pfennige a pound, while in December, when the corner had been broken up, it fell to 35. Germany lost in the operation $30,000,000 paid to the foreigner. A reduction in the production of cotton textiles and widespread dismissal of workmen were the results of this veritable cotton famine, which at the same time disastrously affected our own industries in the Vosges and in Normandy as well as those of Lancashire.

The Industrial State has need of capital. In spite of the prodigious increase in German wealth, German industry has an enormous appetite for capital. No sooner is capital created than it is used up in constructing new works or in remodeling machinery. In the formidable industrial struggle in which Germany entered, she was condemned to make new conquests every day, for any defeat, nay more, any check, would be fatal. It would be true to say that capital is swallowed up before it comes into being, for it is anticipated by credit. Companies with imposing capital dependent on industrial banks, these again dependent on central banks and especially on the Deutsche Bank, these great banks in their turn absorbing all available wealth, including a proportion of foreign capital—all this forms a marvelous but fragile structure. The very denials of the German financiers prove that they cannot afford to disregard the assistance of foreign capital. Let but one of the streams which feed the mighty river happen to dry up, and the crisis comes with violent and widespread consequences.

Customers are necessary to Germany even more than capital. In spite of their power of increase, in spite of their rapid advance in wealth, in spite of their appetite for enjoyment, the German people cannot by themselves alone absorb the enormous output of the German factories. They are bound to turn more and more to the outside world and to become an exporting industry.

All causes then combine to make Germany a "tentacular State," spreading out in every direction over the world. The general staff of the industrial world needs a "world-policy" to find interest for its capital and to pay the wages of its workmen. The proletariat have need of it to give them a full day's work and save them from starvation. That is why German Socialism is Imperialist. You know what a hue-and-cry was raised against the French Socialist who dared to make this discovery. We are compelled to-day to recognize that M. Andler was too painfully right. Even as early as 1900 the defenders of the German Naval Law wrote: "The freedom of the seas and vigorous competition in the markets of the world are therefore questions of life and death for the nation, questions in which the working classes are most deeply interested." We know by recent examples what Germany means by "questions of life and death," and what methods she is in the habit of using to answer such questions and to deal with any obstacles that bar the way to their solution. Only yesterday the Social Democrat, Konrad Hoenisch, ex-member of the Reichstag, exclaimed: "The social interests of the German proletariat even more than political considerations make victory for Germany necessary."

Thus we see the Industrial State condemned to "World-policy." Its first business is to find means to develop its policy of export. The first means adopted is the system of bounties. As German industry is working less for the home market than for foreign markets it is logical to sell cheap, sometimes even to sell at a loss beyond the frontier in order to win new markets and to discourage all competition. Thanks to the system by which the chief economic forces are grouped in *cartels,* the process is easy enough. In 1902 the coke-syndicate compelled the German consumer to pay four dollars a ton, while at the same time it agreed to sell large quantities abroad at less than three dollars. In the second half of 1900 the iron-wire syndicate had sold abroad at $1.60 per 100 lbs., while the home price was $2.85. It thus made a minus profit on the foreign market, and on the home market a plus profit of larger size. This gave a balance on the right side. But this time the trick was overdone, for the result was that German iron was bought up abroad to be reëxported to Germany at a profit. Next to the system of bounties comes that of treaties of commerce, which favor the importation of provisions and of laborers (Slavs, for example), and which secure a moderate tariff for German goods abroad. Such is the basis of the Russo-German Treaty of 1904, the tendency of which was to make Russia an economic colony of Germany.

In order to meet the want of iron, Germany had to conquer new supplies of iron ore. Peaceful conquest to begin with. The expert adviser attached to the commissioners of delimitation in 1871 allowed the iron-ore strata of the Woévre to escape, from ignorance of their real importance and also because he thought them inaccessible by reason of their depth, unworkable because of their high percentage of phosphorus. But the application of the Thomas process in 1878 converted the Briey basin into the most important iron-field at present being worked in the world. That is why Thyssen made his way into this region at Batilly, Jouaville and Bouligny under fictitious names. At the same time he sent his divers to Diélette to search for ore under the sea: he planted his agents in the mining and metallurgical company of Calvados, started under some one else's name the company of mines and quarries at Flamanville, and then the powerful company of smelting and steel-works at Caen. By these operations he gained the double advantage of buying ore from us and selling coke to us. With the iron of Lorraine and Normandy and the coal of Westphalia, Germany would be the mistress of the world.

To make sure of this supremacy it was of importance to remove all competition and establish German industry in the very heart of the country of her rivals. A description was given before the war of the extraordinary control acquired by German manufacturers over French works producing chemical materials, electricity, etc. At Neuville-sur-Saône it was the *Badische Sodafabrik* which, under a French name, provided the madder-dye for the red trousers of the French army, and possibly it even inspired the Press campaign, conducted with the support of sentimental arguments, in favor of a color which was dangerous from a military point of view. The Parisian Aniline Dye Company (*Compagnie parisienne des couleurs d'aniline*) was nothing but a branch of Meister, Lucius and Bruning, of Hoechst. We have been told how a Darmstadt company for producing pharmaceutical goods came and established a branch at Montereau in order to destroy a French factory which was there before, and how the *Allgemeine Elektrizitätsgesellschaft* got hold of Rouen, Nantes, Algiers, Oran and Châteauroux.

The same conquests were won at Seville, Granada, Buenos Aires, Montevideo, Mendoza, Santiago and Valparaiso. Turkey, Russia, Italy and Switzerland shared the fate of France.

A remarkable study of the same subject in Italy has been made by M. Giovanni Preziosi in some articles which appeared in 1914 in the *Vita italiana all' estero,* and were collected in pamphlet form in 1915 under the significant title, "Germany's Plan for the Conquest of Italy." It was indeed a war of conquest, conducted with admirable organizing faculty. At its center was a financial staff, constituted by the *"Banca commerciale . . . italiana,"* which naturally is called "Italian," just as the companies in France are called "French" or "Parisian." This product of German finance is described as a "Germanic octopus," the very image of the "tentacular State" before described. Establishing itself within the directing boards, and, by means of a system of secret cards, employing a regular system of commercial espionage to ruin all who resist it, it succeeded in gradually absorbing the economic energies of an entire people—establishments of credit, shipping companies, manufacturing firms; it was even able to corrupt political life, overthrow ministries and control elections. Here, as in Switzerland, the pseudo-Italian German banks "act as a pump which pumps out of Italy and pumps into Germany." Italy, which is considered a poor country, provides capital for rich Germany.

To back up this policy of economic conquest the prestige and the strength of the Empire must be put at the service of the manufacturers. To make the State as the Germans understand it, the instrument of German expansion—this is the meaning of what the Germans have well named the policy of "business and power," *Handels und Machtpolitik.* Nowhere is the confusion of the two ideas more clearly exhibited than in the report forwarded to London in February, 1914, by Sir Edward Goschen, on "An Official German Organization for Influencing the Press of Other Countries." This important document is too little known in France, perhaps because, outside the Blue Book, it has not appeared in England except as an ordinary "White Paper." But how instructive it is!

The object of this company was to promote the manufacturing prestige of Germany abroad. It supplied full information gratuitously or at a low price to foreign journals in their own language concerning Germany and favorable to Germany. It withheld the service from those who showed themselves deaf to instruction. "To reply to news meant to influence opinion on Germany and to meet attacks upon her, and to make the true situation of German industry widely known"—such was the program. In an article so naïvely transparent that its publication was thought inopportune and orders came from above not to reproduce it or make any allusion to it, the *Deutsche Export Revue* crudely remarked: "It is better to choose men already connected with the various journals, who will serve German interests without attracting so much attention."

This fusion of *Weltpolitik* and business policy was peculiarly dangerous for the peace of the world. If Imperialism, if "the tentacular State" puts its strength at the disposal of manufacturing interests, the temptation is strong and constant to use this strength to break down any resistance which stands in the way of the triumph of these interests. If a crisis comes which causes a stoppage of work (there are sometimes 100,000 unemployed in Berlin) the neighboring nation which may be held responsible for the crisis has reason to be on its guard. "Be my customer or I kill you," seems to be the motto of this industrial system, continually revolving in its diabolical circle, always producing more in order to sell more, always selling more in order to meet the necessities of a production always growing more intensive.

Russia was for Germany both a reservoir of labor and a market. France was a bank and a purveyor of minerals. What a temptation to dip deep into the jealously guarded stocking and fill both hands! What a temptation, too, to repair the blunder made in the delimitation of 1871! Even in 1911 the *Gazette du Rhin et de Westphalie* put forward the view that the iron ores of Lorraine and Luxembourg ought to be under the same control as those of Westphalia and the Saar. And I am told that the great journals of Paris, when informed of this campaign, refused to take this "provincial journal" seriously, being blind to the fact that it was the organ of the great manufacturers of the Rhineland and of the Prussian staff. What a temptation again to take the port of Cherbourg in the rear from Diélette!

As for England, the direct competitor of Germany in all the markets of the world, and manufacturing the same goods, she was the enemy to be crushed. Had she not acquired the habit, and had she not taught it to France, of refusing to lend money to poor States except in return for good orders? The time was beginning to go by when it was possible to do German business in Turkey with French or English gold. Germany's rivals have learnt from her the lesson of *Handels und Machtpolitik*. But what is to become of Essen, Gelsenkirchen, and all that immense industrial city of which Westphalia consists, if Rumanians, Greeks, Serbians order their guns and their ironclads, their rails or their locomotives at Glasgow or at Le Creusot? Germany thought war preferable to this economic encirclement, and the velvet glove gave place to the mailed gauntlet.

Little by little the idea of war as necessary, of war as almost a thing to wish for, laid hold on the industrial classes. The proof is to be found as early as 1908 in a popular book by Professor Paul Arndt, one of those small shilling books which served to instruct the German mind. All of us, even the best informed, must reproach ourselves for not having studied or studied closely enough these small books, which would have made the danger clear to us. In this volume the author, after a pæan to German greatness, begins a chapter "On the dangers of Germany's participation in worldwide trade." He shows that this participation increases Germany's dependence on the foreigner and makes her vulnerable by sea as well as by land. If international relations are disturbed there will be "many workmen without food, and much depreciation of capital," and that from causes "in great measure beyond the control of Germany" in countries which may seize the opportunity to weaken Germany. And in a hypothesis which is prophetic he describes the effects of the blockade.

But he accepts without hesitation these risks of the World-Policy. "No doubt, if we wish to be and to remain a great people, a world power, we expose ourselves to serious struggles. But this must not alarm us. There is profound truth in the dictum that man degenerates in peace time. The call to arms is often needed to rouse a world benumbed with apathy and indolence. Those who can look far and deeply into things see that warfare is often a blessing to humanity."

I have shown how the over-rapid industrialization of Germany led by a mechanical and fatal process to the German war. If any doubt were felt on the part played by economic causes in this war it would be enough to look at the picture of German victory as imagined by the Germans in their dreams during the early months of war. It is an industrial victory, a forced marriage between German coal and foreign iron, the reduction of nations into vassals who are to play the part of perpetual customers of the German workshops.

"The metalliferous strata of French Lorraine and Russian Poland," wrote Baron Zedlitz-Neukirch in 1915, "supplement in some degree our own mining works." If we ask the impetuous Max. Harden what is to become of martyred Belgium, he replies, in October, 1914, "Antwerp not against Hamburg and Bremen, but with them; Liège, working side by side with the arms factories of Hesse, Berlin and Swabia; Cockerill in alliance with Krupp; Belgian and German iron, coal and textiles under one control. From Calais to Antwerp, Flanders, Limbourg and Brabant, up to and beyond the line of fortresses on the Meuse, all Prussian." The German dream is the dream of a conquering man of business, a counting-house romance founded on Freytag's novel of *"Soll und Haben"* ("Debit and Credit"). The victory of Germany meant for them security of iron-supply and enlarged markets: it meant Briey, Ouenza, Casablanca, Bagdad.

The vision has faded and the building of their dreams has crumbled away. But the dream has left its lessons for us, which demand attention not only in the future but to-day. Let us cherish no illusions. Germany, though conquered and curtailed, will not cease to exist. It is idle to suppose, as some publicists write, that we are going to suppress a whole people. Even if we had the military power to do it, policy and morality would forbid us. After our victory there will once more be a Germany which will patiently and persistently resume its labors. The great war will no sooner be ended than the other war, the economic war, will begin again. If we do not wish to be crushed we must to-day begin to prepare our mobilization for this new war.

BY FRIEDRICH NAUMANN

During the war we were all wondering why we Germans, and especially we Germans of the Empire, were so little beloved by the rest of the world. To many well-meaning and sociable people this international dislike is something quite horrible, and they rack their brains to discover what we must do in order to find favor again. But they often look for the source of the ill-will of other nations in very secondary matters, such as perhaps in the lack of social good tone in those who travel abroad, loud-voiced German tourists dressed in Tyrolese homespun, or in the theatrical sword-clanging of some discharged general, and not in the economic national type itself; because they share in the economic and mental changes of their own nation much too unconsciously. It hardly even occurs to them that we are unloved because we have found a method of work in which now and for a long time to come no other European nation can imitate us, and which consequently the others do not regard as fair. It is this to which we have just referred as the transition to the impersonal capitalism of the second stage, a process which with us has demanded about a century and a half of work and education.

In order by illustration to make clearer at the outset the distinction between the older and the newer creed of capitalism I will begin with a little story about London. I wanted to look at the London docks, and said so to a respected English friend, whom in spite of the war I greet from across the trenches. He replied, "No one here goes to look at the docks." Then I inquired at the International Tourist Offices of Cook and Son whether they arranged for visits to the docks. Answer: No, because there were no London docks like, for instance, the Hamburg docks, which one could visit and inspect as a whole; the London docks are an unsystematic succession of many very big establishments, each of which belongs to a separate private firm. Thus, as to quantity, labor, money value, goods, the London trade exceeds that of Hamburg, but as to unity, articulation, organization, they already represent a more antiquated form of life. Hamburg learned from London, but added to its learning quite of itself something peculiarly German, which at the outset appeared like some chance additional characteristic, merely as stricter police supervision and regulation, but which developed in course of time into an essential feature. Why, we ask, does the smaller German sea trade possess the greatest companies?

Or another example: in 1900 I was in Paris during the Exhibition and was talking to a German wood carver who had worked for a long time in France, about the difference between Germans and French. The man, so far as I can remember now after fifteen years, spoke somewhat thus: If a French joiner has thirty workmen and can get a larger order employing more than this number he accepts it indeed, but puts it out on commission, because he has not sufficient confidence in himself or will not take the trouble to deal with more than thirty workmen. Meanwhile the corresponding German employer would accept the order for himself, would enlarge his workshop, and by reason of this enlargement would seek further new orders. If one of the Frenchmen acts differently, then he is certain to be from Alsace or Switzerland. Thus the Germans have the greater organizing ability both in medium-sized businesses and in skilled handwork.

The peculiarity of the Germans does not consist in an essentially new attribute which has not appeared elsewhere in the world, but in the methodical, trained progress in an ability which has existed and does still exist among the hitherto leading nations, but has not been so systematically and intentionally developed. From our own point of view we are still a long way from having arrived at perfection of organization, but in the eyes of others we have already deviated far from their style of living. They regard us as an unfree people, because we have learnt better than they have how to carry out our work on a common plan and to a common rhythm. And this applies to all types of work. It is not as if industrialism were a special German characteristic, for the English are an industrial, machine-using, manufacturing nation, and were so before us. Moreover, the peculiar German spirit of which we are speaking shows itself at least as much in our agricultural occupations as in our manufactures.

Of course there are all sorts of attempts at organization and coöperation in English and French agriculture, as, for example, among the wine growers in Southern France. But when examined closely these attempts are nearly all quite feeble, whereas German agriculture, although the independence of the peasantry is definitely safeguarded, is already almost entirely managed by systematic coöperation, or at least is making daily progress towards this goal. By the joint action of agricultural boards, agricultural schools, loan banks, granaries, and dairies, a strong net is woven round the individual. He has become a peasant coöperator, member of a definite profession. He can, no doubt, evade all these regulations, but it is to his own injury if he does so. For the sake of personal interest he becomes a member of an impersonal institution and works for it as for himself. This insertation of the individual ego into the joint ego is our special ability, by which we attain a more intensive cultivation, a better assorted production, and better marketing qualities for international trade. Individualism is fully developed, but it is then carried up into the next higher form of economic coöperative existence.

Owing to a like intrinsic impulse, our industrial life is similarly full of ideas of organization and regulations for combining. We have extensive economic syndicates or cartels; moreover, during the last twenty years our German industries have taken on an entirely new appearance. In growing they have become interlaced. By means of employers' federations, payment cartels, zone compacts, and price agreements, a complicated machinery of spheres of business and subordinations has come into being, in which the outsider can hardly find his way, but which has been created step by step as needed, and by means of which the private employer of the old style has quite gently slipped over into the disciplined, industrial community, and that in the course of one

generation and even when at the outset he was quite unwilling. He has become a federated employer. The employers of the first and second generations perhaps only
adapted themselves reluctantly to these developments and
would rather have remained individualist capitalists in the
West European sense; but the employer of the third generation is for the most part born into a combination from the
outset. Thus in a certain sense he becomes the free, directing employee of a society which produces steel or yarn or
sugar or spirits. The industrial basis of the age is thus discovered, and its spirit is now steadily penetrating deeper. In
another twenty years we shall see before us the whole scheme
of a powerful industry with its domestic regulations and its
divisions of labor. The regulation of production is on the
way. Things that forty years ago would have seemed like
the unreal idealism of socialist and state-socialist dreamers,
now appear with incredible certainty as realities which have
come into being in the interval. Germany is on the way to
become not merely an industrial State, but above all, an organized State.

In complete correspondence with this is our experience
with the wage-earners, and following their example, with all
the employees in the higher groups. The old ideal of the individual who sells his working strength when, where, and
how he likes, has almost disappeared in the social ideal of
the common unions of wage-earners and workers. The non-
unionist is still numerous, it is true, but he is in no way the
leader. And what distinguishes the German trade unionist,
so far as we can see, from the older English type, is his
greater coherence and discipline, which he has painfully but
successfully won by fighting, in spite of socialistic law and
police intrigue, against the policy of the Government and of
the employers. The German masses mean to make their
advance as organized groups; that is their guiding principle.
It is inadequate to say that they combine in order to secure
increased wages. Any one who knows the unionists knows
that calculated self-interest is only one side of their existence, and that, especially in the case of the leaders, it is
the least decisive influence. They have formed their trade

unionist ideal of conduct, narrow and inflexible, as could hardly be otherwise with people of moderate means who have but little scope for action in their lives, but yet firmly decided upon and definite in itself. The idea of a super-personal economic leadership of the masses in work, and in sale and consumption of its products, is prevalent and becomes a mere matter of course. In this the German working classes differ from all the Latin nations, for what in France and Italy is called socialism is indeed related in word and theory to the German workmen's unions, but has none of the sternness of inward determination which has been attained by our social democrats, or even by other unionist groups.

All travel along the same path: engineers, teachers, headteachers, scholars, doctors, even artists. The guilds of handworkers are coming to life again and adapting themselves to the altered conditions of the time. We are a uniform nation in spite of the quarrels among the numerous associations of opposing interests, magnificently uniform in this method of organizing our daily work and life. Primary schools, universal conscription, police, science and socialistic propaganda, have all worked together to this end. We were hardly aware that we desired all this in reality: this disciplined work of the second period of capitalism, which may be described as the transition from private capitalism to socialism, if the word socialism be not applied solely to a proletarian vision of great businesses, but is understood, broadly, as an ordering of the nation for the increase of the joint product of each for all.

This new German type is incomprehensible to the individualist nations, to whom he appears partly as a relapse into past times of constraint, and partly as an artificial product of coercion that belies and overcomes humanity. In educated circles in Paris and London they feel a mixture of pity, fear, respect and aversion towards this German type. Even if they could produce the same thing there, they would not wish to do so, for they have no desire for this disciplined soul. They do not desire it because it would be the death and surrender of the individual soul. No one can quite understand this unless he has occasionally tried to look at Germany with the eyes of a foreigner. To the German who

knows only Germany, the intrinsic strength of this opposition
must necessarily remain hidden; he does not realize how
strange he has already become to even the best men of the
Western nations, not owing to any particular thing which he
does, but merely owing to what he is.

This new German character has by no means been produced among us in the German Empire without opposition,
for it is something distinct from the old German condition of
life and heart. The old German was much more natural,
slower, wilder or weaker, just as it happened. All our Ro-
manticism lacks the organizing spirit; it is loyal, self-sacri-
ficing and companionable, but it is wanting in any guiding
idea of aim. The good, ridiculous Germans of former days
were thus no objects of general enmity. People thought of
them at times as coarse, and wished they had a larger share
of French politeness, but foreign peoples had at bottom nothing against the worthy bears, who let themselves be pushed
hither and thither and yet laughed at it themselves. No one
ever supposed that this old, comfortably coarse, downright
fellow would one day shake off his dream and stand up as
the thinker of labor.

Even when philosophers of the highest rank appeared
amongst us, foreigners never thought that this signified a
practical and economic change in the German character. Indeed, we ourselves hardly noticed how much our philosophers were practical prophets. They were regarded as artists in ideas and as reformers of the world, without its being
realized that, emanating from them, a spirit of labor inspired
by reason would transform the entire world in the course of
a century. Indeed, the thinkers themselves did not perceive
to what purpose they were there. They thought about pure
and practical reason in the sense of intellect and morality.
But after them came their followers, and tried to introduce
into Government, Law, and Administration the reason which
they had conceived. They were, it is true, only partially successful, but again, in the next generation, keen, highly trained
thinkers about actual possibilities were found in all departments of work. Neither Bismarck nor Savigny nor Helm-
holz nor either of the two Siemens is conceivable without

this philosopher's oil poured out for the second and third time. Our technical and agricultural schools are German institutions for thought which aims at realization in fact, and are nowadays almost more characteristic of our national nature than the old-established universities. The "high school" with a practical object is a novelty which we first had to assimilate ourselves, and which the people of older civilizations most heartily grudged us when it appeared, because for them knowledge was more an amusement than a practical ability.

In the quite recent past, and until our character was thus transformed in this matter of technical organization, the English were always very friendly to us Germans. The great English thinker Carlyle, it is true, understood what was preparing in the German spirit; but his fellow-countrymen accepted what they saw before their eyes: the Germans have good schools and buy English machinery! It was not until by reason of these schools the Germans set up their own machines and offered them to foreign nations that they lost the English goodwill. How could the learned brother on the continent be so bold as to mix himself up in business? This learned German technical scholar appeared in all occupations like something essentially improper. The old English world was not adapted to make a systematic working alliance between thought and international trade! From the time of this memorable change onwards, the educated Englishman felt himself deceived by the German and called him a dangerous competitor, as indeed he really was, and that too in virtue of the English universal watchword, "Free play for the strong," but with a quite differently trained strength.

How closely the new German method of work is a continuation of the German trained thought can only be realized from a comparison between German management of important undertakings by leading men and the corresponding foreign non-German management. Our financial policy has a perceptible doctrinaire tendency, but on this very account is most successful. Our military education is markedly scientific, but is not injured thereby. Our great merchants are almost economists and statisticians by profession. Our woodcraft is almost as logically thought out as a textbook on grammar. Our ship building is highly mathematical; our steel plates are scientific works; our dyes are chemical inventions. Into everything there enters to-day less of the lucky spirit of invention than of patient educated industry. Or to put it otherwise: we believe in combined work.

That connection with systematic science which we find throughout in the new agriculture and in all the more extensive industrial undertakings was and still is the peculiar quality of German social democracy. Dr. Engels, the friend of Karl Marx, said of it that it was the heiress of German philosophy, and if the saying is not taken to mean the sole heiress, then there is a large kernel of truth in it. Of all working classes, only the German (and the German-Austrian) is theoretical in its group instruction in the sense of pure Marxism. This instruction may often be false in details and may be far over the pupils' heads and remote from present day problems; but the actual fact that we possess the most theoretical labor movement in the world is part of the picture of German economic life. This working class in combination with its educated employers, with our syndicate leaders, with our Civil Service and officers, does not offer the most charming and amusing society possible, but does constitute the most practical, safe and durable human machinery. This living national machine goes its way whether the individual lives or dies, it is impersonal or super-personal, has its frictions and interruptions, but is as a whole something that has never come to pass exactly in this way before. It is the historically developed German character.

We are all being much confirmed in this our German method of work by the progress of the war. From the very first days this war, which had been forced upon us, was regarded as a necessary and quite universal duty and task which must be performed. Every one looked to those in responsible positions for a planned organization reaching even to the smallest details. As soon as it was felt that this existed, the troops and the workers at home showed themselves ready for the greatest and most exceptional efforts, without crediting themselves with this as any special merit.

The war was really only a continuation of our previous life with other tools but based on the same methods. In this indeed lies the secret of success. We conquer less through individuals than through the disciplined feeling for combined difficult work; and those who take the field to amend us after their own pattern must try in battle to equal us.

If our opponents like to label this intrinsic connection between the work of war and peace as "German militarism," we can only regard this as reasonable, *for Prussian military discipline influences us all in actual fact, from the captain of industry to the maker of earthworks.* All that we object to is the secondary implication which has associated itself with the word militarism, and which in the management of barracks in the peace years it was difficult entirely to avoid. But after this war we shall certainly remain much more closely agreed in our common esteem for the voluntary discipline of a great national, military or industrial army so long as the men are still living who have kept at their posts during this struggle. Happen what will, the German spirit has received its baptism of fire: the national genius was and is a reality. Both to ourselves and to the outside world we have shown ourselves as in essence a single unit. Now it is our concern to carry through to its goal this essential German character, proved in the most sinister of wars. This will and must be set on foot directly peace is concluded.

For on this day all Imperial and State officials and all parties and societies will produce their memoranda wherein are noted the things that must be altered after the war. I wager that three-fourths of this memoranda will contain the words: better organization! Our foreign service, our Red Cross, our hospital system, our military clothing, our military purveying, our horse-breeding, our food-supply, all this and much else must be much more rigidly thought out and calculated for beforehand, so that we shall not again be so situated as now in the ill-advised debates on food. But all organization consists in statistics, grouping, analysis, synthesis, control and regulation, and thus there grows up from all sides a State or national socialism, there grows up the "systematized national economy." Fichte and Hegel nod approval from the walls: now, after the war, the German is at last becoming heart and soul a political economic citizen. His ideal is and will be the organism and not free will, reason and not the blind struggle for existence.

This constitutes our freedom, our self-development. By its means we shall enjoy our golden age as other conquering nations in other ages and with other abilities and excellences have done before us. Our epoch dawns when English capitalism has reached and overstepped its highest point, and we have been educated for this epoch by Friedrich II., Kant, Scharnhorst, Siemens, Krupp, Bismarck, Bebel, Legien, Kirdorf and Ballin. Our dead have fallen on the field for the sake of this our Fatherland. Germany, foremost in the world!

GERMANY'S DREAM OF WORLD EMPIRE

THE WORSHIP OF THE WAR GOD THOR AS TAUGHT BY TREITSCHKE

PRINCE BERNHARD VON BÜLOW
MAXIMILIAN HARDEN   RICHARD GRELLING

We turn now from the unconscious to the conscious lust for War. In Napoleon's day Frenchmen had worshiped "Glory" and dreamed their dream of world-empire. The tremendous military successes of Germany in 1870 stirred her people to a similar evil obsession. A popular poet in 1878 wrote:

> Thor stood at the midnight end of the world,
> His hammer flew from his hand:
> "So far as my thunderous weapon I've hurled
> Mine are the sea and the land!"

> And onward hurtled the mighty sledge
> O'er the wide, wide earth, to fall
> At last on the Southland's furthest edge
> In token that His was all.

> Since then 'tis the joyous German right,
> With the hammer, lands to win.
> We mean to possess the world by might,
> As Thor the Hammer-God's kin.

Chief teacher and prophet of this demon worship in its early day was Heinrich von Treitschke, who died in 1896. As Professor of History in the University of Berlin he spoke in brilliant, passionate lectures of the splendor of Germany's new power and the coming wonders of her future. All the young aristocrats of Berlin heard him and thrilled to his inspiration. William II. called him "Our national historian." Yet ironically enough Treitschke, the inspirer of Germany's war-lust, was probably of Slavonic parentage, just as Nietzsche, the inspirer of her new philosophy, was of Polish origin.

Even Chancellor Von Bülow opens his renowned book, "Imperial Germany," with a reference to the youthful inspiration which he had caught from Treitschke. Von Bülow is generally regarded as the ablest and strongest of the Imperial Chancellors after Bismarck. His book, published shortly before the Great War, spoke so frankly of Germany's hopes of world power that foreigners scarcely took it seriously. Such visions seemed impossible to those days. Yet so exactly had this shrewd prince and statesman weighed his words that when, a year after the War had begun, he republished his book, he changed scarcely the least of its ideas. The only exception was in his treatment of the German Socialists. In his first edition he could find no words too harsh for them—they threatened to block the wheels of war. In his later edition, he rewrote the entire chapter on the Socialists and praised them heartily. That was their reward for bowing at the shrine of the war-god Thor.

Prince Von Bülow's words in the following and most noted section from his book offer us therefore the highest German official viewpoint as to Germany's destiny. Of course his words are diplomatically restrained. In one of his official speeches more than a decade before the War, while urging military expansion, he said to an eager audience, "You will understand that in my official position I can not say much; I can not dot all my i's." He then hinted that America as well as Europe was included in his schemes of conquest. So for contrast with Von Bülow's "restraint" we give a fiery outburst from Max. Harden, generally regarded as the most sincere voice of Germany during the War. As editor of a leading radical paper, Harden was a constant thorn in the side of the Imperial Government—not that he lacked war enthusiasm, but that he was too straightforward about it. He said what he meant; whereas the Government constantly and obviously said what it did not mean, preparing its terrible aggressive strokes in secret, while publicly lamenting that other nations insisted on attacking poor, peaceful Germany. Thus Harden was sometimes far ahead of the Government chorus and had to be restrained. At other times he was equally far behind and was reproachfully spurred onward.

Yet a third type of German voice is here given from the remarkable book "I Accuse." No other war book roused such excitement as this and its later continuation, "The Crime." These were written by a German and one who knew the national situation thoroughly. With resolute severity he tore the mask from all the pretenses of the Imperial Government, and pointed out the truth as to how it had deceived its people and plotted to deceive the world. "I Accuse" was published anonymously in Switzerland, but its combination of intimate knowledge and bitter condemnation drew to it the swift attention of all nations. The German official press could find no words too savage for the "traitor" author, particularly when he was learned to be Dr. Richard Grelling, a professor already academically punished for too much freedom of opinion. Yet in after-war days most Germans have admitted the justice of Grelling's every word.

Thus the following expressions of Germans' judgment upon Germany were all three written in the heat of war, after their country had tasted her first victories, before she had to face her final defeat.

C. F. H.

BY PRINCE VON BÜLOW

"IN spite of the length of their history, the German people is the youngest of the great nations of Western Europe. A period of youth has twice fallen to their lot, and with it the struggle to establish their power as a State, and to gain freedom for civilization. A thousand years ago they founded the proudest kingdom of the Germans; eight hundred years later they had to build up their State anew on quite different foundations, and it is only in our times that, as a united people, they entered the ranks of the nations."

These words, with which Treitschke begins his "German History," not only show deep historical knowledge, but also have a very modern political significance. Germany is the youngest of the Great Powers of Europe, the *homo novus* who, having sprung up very recently, has forced his way by his own superior capacity into the circle of the older nations. The new Great Power was looked upon as an uninvited and unwelcome intruder, when, after three glorious and successful campaigns, it entered the company of the Great Powers of Europe a formidable figure and demanded its share of the treasures of the world. For centuries Europe had not believed in the possibility of the national unification of the individual German territories as one State. At any rate, the European Powers had done their best to prevent this. In particular, the policy of France, from the time of Richelieu to that of Napoleon III., was directed towards maintaining and intensifying the disruption of Germany, as it was rightly recognized that the ascendancy of France, *la prépondérance légitime de la France,* depended primarily on this state of affairs. Nor did the other Powers desire the unification of Germany. On this point the Emperor Nicholas and Lord Palmerston, as well as Metternich and Thiers, were at one. Nothing could show more clearly the marvelous way in which the mature wisdom of our old Emperor coöperated with the genius of Prince Bismarck than the fact that they effected the unification of Germany, not only in the face of all the difficulties with which they were confronted at home —long cherished rivalries and hatreds, all the sins of our past, and all the peculiarities of our political character, but also in spite of all opposition, avowed or secret, and of the displeasure of the whole of Europe.

Suddenly the German Empire was in existence. More quickly even than had been feared, far stronger than any one had guessed. None of the other Great Powers had desired the regeneration of Germany; each of them, when it actually took place, would have liked to prevent it. Small wonder that the new Great Power was not made welcome, but was looked upon as a nuisance. Even a very reserved and pacific policy could effect but little change in this first verdict. This union of the States of the Mid-European continent, so long prevented, so often feared, and at last accomplished by the force of German arms and incomparable statesmanship, seemed to imply something of the nature of a threat, or at any rate to be a disturbing factor.

In the middle of the nineties, in Rome, where I was Ambassador at that time, my English colleague, Sir Clare Ford, said to me: "How much pleasanter and easier it was in the world of politics when England, France and Russia constituted the areopagus of Europe, and at most Austria had to be occasionally consulted." Those good old days are past. More than forty years ago the council of Europe had to admit another member entitled to vote, one that had not only the wish to express its opinion, but also the power to act; a power which our enemies in the world war have been made to feel even more fearfully than they had feared.

A strenuous task in the history of the world had reached completion in the masterpiece of Prince Bismarck. The unflinching purpose of the Hohenzollern dynasty for centuries required the patient heroism of the Prussian army and the resolute devotion of the Prussian people, until, after many changes of fortune, the Mark of Brandenburg rose to the rank of a Great Power as the kingdom of Prussia. Twice the prize seemed to slip from the grasp of the Prussian State. The crushing defeat of 1806 hurled Prussia down from the dizzy heights, which had filled her contemporaries with admiration and fear, and which she had attained under the rule of the great Frederick. Those people seemed to be right who had always considered the proud State of the great King to be nothing more than an artificial political structure, that would stand and fall with the unique political and military genius of its monarch. Its rise, after the overwhelming disasters of Jena and Tilsit, proved to an astonished world what innate and indestructible strength this State possessed.

Such self-sacrifice and such heroism on the part of a whole people presuppose long-established national self-confidence. And as the people of Prussia did not rise in lawless rebellion like the much-admired Spaniards and the honest Tyrolese peasants, but placed themselves one and all, unquestioningly, at the orders of the King and his advisers, it appeared, to every one's surprise, that amongst the Prussians consciousness as a nation and as a State were one and the same thing; and that the people had been transformed into a nation under the strict discipline of Frederick's rule. The reorganization of the State under the guidance of men of creative power during the years 1807 to 1813 won for the Government not only the obedience of its subjects but also their affection. In the war of liberation, from 1813 to 1815, Prussia gained the respect of all, and the confidence of many of the non-Prussian Germans.

It was a rich inheritance that the great period of upheaval and liberation left behind. But owing to the reaction of a feeble and inglorious foreign policy, and to a home administration which never knew when to be open-handed and when to refuse, this inheritance was to a large extent squandered in the course of the following decades.

In Goethe's "Wilhelm Meister," when the melancholy Aurelia finds fault in many ways with the Germans, Lothario, a man of experience, replies that there is no better nation than the Germans, so long as they are rightly guided. The German, of whatever stock he be, has always accomplished his greatest works under strong, steady and firm guidance, and has seldom done well without such guidance, or in opposition to the Government and rulers. Bismarck himself has told us in his *"Gedanken und Erinnerungen"* ("Reflections and Reminiscences") that he was from the first quite clear on this point. With the intuition of genius he found the way in which the hopes of the people and the interests of the German Governments might be reconciled. Probably no other statesman ever had so deep a knowledge of the history of the nation he was called upon to guide. Behind the external sequence of events he sought and found the motive forces of national life. He, who was born in the year of Waterloo, and was confirmed by Schleiermacher in the Church of the Trinity in Berlin, never forgot the great times of the liberation and the rise of Prussia; at the beginning of his career as a molder of the destinies of the world, the remembrance of these days was always with him. He realized that in Germany the will-power of the nation would not be strengthened, nor national passions roused by friction between the Government and the people, but by the clash of German pride, honor and ambitions against the resistance and the demands of foreign nations. So long as the question of German unification was a problem of home politics, a problem over which the political parties, and the Government and the people wrangled, it could not give birth to a mighty, compelling national movement that would sweep nations and princes alike along on a tide of enthusiasm. When he made it clear that the German question was essentially a question of European politics, when on this the non-German opponents of German unification began to move, Bismarck gave the princes the opportunity of putting themselves at the head of the national movement.

By this means national policy was interwoven with international policy; with incomparable audacity and constructive statesmanship, in consummating the work of uniting Germany, he left out of play the political capabilities of the Germans, in which they have never excelled, while he called into action their fighting powers, which have always been their strongest point.

By a happy dispensation, Bismarck found a general such as Moltke and a military organizer such as Roon to support him. The military achievements which had enabled us to regain our position as a Great Power in Europe also assured that position. They long discouraged any attempt of the Great Powers to deprive us of our right to a voice in the councils of Europe, a right which we had won in three victorious campaigns, and which has since then, for nearly half a century, never been seriously disputed, although it was unwillingly granted. With the single exception of France, every one, in all probability, would have gradually become reconciled to Germany's political power if her development had ceased with the founding of the Empire. But the political unification was not the end of our history but the beginning of a new era. In the front rank of the Powers, Germany once more participated in full in the life of Europe. For a long time, however, the life of Europe had formed only a part of the life of all the nations of the world.

Foreign politics had become more and more concerned with the world at large. The path of world politics lay open to Germany too, when she had won a powerful position on a level with the older Great Powers. The question was whether we should tread that new path, risk the "grand game," as Disraeli used to call world politics, or whether we should hesitate to undertake further hazardous enterprises for fear of compromising our newly acquired power.

In the Emperor William II. the nation found a clear-sighted, strong-willed guide, who led them along the new road. With him we trod the path of world politics; but not as conquerors, not amid adventures and quarrels. We advanced slowly, and our rate of progress was regulated, not by the impatience of ambition, but by the interests we had to promote and the rights we had to assert. We did not plunge into world politics, we grew, so to speak, into our task in that sphere, and we did not exchange the old European policy of Prussia and Germany for the new world policy; as is clearly shown by the course of the Great War both on the economic and the military side, our strength to-day is rooted, as it has been since time immemorial, in the ancient soil of Europe.

"It is the task of our generation to maintain our position on the Continent, which is the basis of our position in the world, and at the same time to foster our interests overseas and pursue a prudent, sensible and wisely restricted world policy, in such a way that the safety of the German people may not be endangered, and that the future of the nation may not be imperiled." With these words I attempted on November 14, 1906, towards the close of a detailed exposition of the international situation, to formulate the task which Germany must perform at the present time, and, as far as man can judge, will have to perform in the future: a world policy based on the solidly laid foundation of our position as one of the Great Powers of Europe.

At first voices were raised in protest when we trod the new paths of world politics, for it was considered a mistake to depart from the approved ways of Bismarck's Continental policy. The fact was overlooked that it was Bismarck himself who pointed out the new way to us by bringing our old policy to a close. His work, in fact, gave us access to world politics. Only when Germany had attained political strength was the development of German commerce and industry to a world position possible. It was not till the Empire had secured its old position in Europe that it could think of defending the interests which German enterprise, German industry and commercial foresight had created in all quarters of the globe. It is certain that Bismarck did not foresee the course of this new development of Germany, nor the details of the problems of this new epoch; and it was not possible for him to do so.

The course of events has long driven German policy out from the narrow confines of Europe into the wider world. It was not ambitious restlessness which urged us to imitate the Great Powers that had long ago embarked on world politics. The strength of the nation, rejuvenated by the political reorganization, as it grew, burst the bounds of its old home, and its policy was dictated by the new interests and needs. In proportion as our national life has become world wide, the policy of the German Empire has become a world policy.

In the year 1871 the number of inhabitants dwelling within the new German Empire was 41,058,792. They found work and a living in their own country, and, moreover, both were better and easier to get than before; this was due to the protection afforded by increased national power, the great improvement in the means of communication effected at the founding of the Empire, and the blessings of the new common German legislation. In the year 1900 the number of inhabitants had risen to 56,367,178, and to-day it has reached 68,000,000. The Empire could no longer support in the old way this immense mass of humanity within its boundaries. Owing to this enormous increase of population, German commerce and industry, and in consequence German policy, was confronted with a tremendous problem. This had to be solved, if foreign countries were not to profit by the superfluity of German life which the mother country was not able to support. In the year 1883 about 173,000 Germans emigrated; in 1892 the number was 116,339; in 1898 only 22,921; and since then the average has remained at this last low figure.

The German Empire, such as it emerged from the baptism of fire of Königgrätz and Sedan, the belated fruit of the slow evolution of our nation, could not come into existence until German intellect and the Prussian monarchy joined forces. They were bound to join forces if a united German State of lasting power was to be achieved.

German history, eventful as it is, discloses an abundance of great and mighty deeds: the struggle of the German Emperors for the heritage of the Cæsars, German arms victorious on the shores of the Great Belt and the Mediterranean, in Asia Minor, and in the heart of what is now France; and after the intellectual refining process of the Reformation, the greatest development of artistic and scientific life that the world has known since the days of Hellas and the Cinquecento.

The result, however, of these glorious activities, as far as the State and politics are concerned, was the dissolution of all forms of government in the nineteenth century, and the fact that German power was outstripped by the younger States of Eastern and Western Europe. In a thousand years of work, from the point of view of culture, the highest had been accomplished, but politically, nothing had been achieved. The Western and Southern domains of Germany, greatly favored by Nature, accomplished indestructible work in the sphere of German intellectual life, but could not raise sufficient strength for the sterner business of creating a State.

We modern Germans do not share Treitschke's harsh opinion that the small German States were worthless. During the decades in which we have enjoyed union as an Empire, we have recovered a clear perception of the manifold blessings we owe to the small States. Side by side with the sins of German separatism we must place the encouragement and protection afforded to the intellectual life of Germany by the Princes and the cities. The Court of the Muses at Weimar achieved the highest in this respect, but it by no means stood alone.

The history of most of the non-Prussian States is connected with the name of some one or other of the men of Science and of Art who have helped to raise the magnificent edifice of our intellectual life. When Prussia woke to a consciousness of her duties with regard to the spiritual achievements of Germany, in those terrible but yet splendid years when, as Frederick William III. so well expressed it, the Prussian State must make good by its intellectual powers what it had lost physically. German intellect had already reached its zenith without the help of Prussia. German intellectual life, which the whole world has learned to admire, and which even the first Napoleon respected, is predominantly the work of the South and West, achieved under the protection of her Princes, small States, and free cities.

But the people who lived on the sandy soil of the Mark, in the plains east of the Elbe and the Oder, so scantly favored by Nature, during the centuries which witnessed the growth of German culture in other parts of the country, prepared the future of Germany as a State in battles and privations under the rule of heroic and politic kings.

German intellect was developed in the West and the South, the German State in Prussia. The Princes of the West were the patrons of German culture; the Hohenzollern were the political teachers and task-masters.

It took a long time before the importance of Prussia, in which even Goethe only loved her great King, was recognized in Germany; before it was realized that this rude and thoroughly prosaic State of soldiers and officials, without many words but with deeds that were all the greater, was performing a task of enormous importance in the work of German civilization: preparing the political culture of the German nation. Prussia became for Germany what Rome was for the ancient world. Leopold von Ranke, intellectually the most universal and at the same time the most Prussian of German historians, says, in his "History of the World," that it was the task of antiquity to permeate the Greek spirit with the Roman. Classical culture, in which the intellectual life of Western Europe is rooted, was preserved by the Roman State, which, with its legal and military foundation, gave to the ancient world its political shape. The Prussian State became the guardian of German intellectual life, by giving to the German people a united State and a position on a level with the great Empires of the world.

Through the foundation of the Empire we acquired national life as a State. In so doing our political development embarked on a new and a safe course. But it has not yet reached its goal. Our task has been begun but is by no means yet completed.

We must secure and cement the unity of our intellectual and political life by the fusion of the Prussian and the German spirit. That is what I meant when, not long before my retirement, I said in the Reichstag, with reference to the fact that in the death chamber of Prince Bismarck the only ornament I noticed on the wall was the portrait of Ludwig Uhland, that this juxtaposition summed up all German history, for only the union between the energy and discipline of old Prussian Conservatism and the magnanimous spirit of German Liberalism could insure a happy future for the nation. A century ago Fichte challenged the nation to overcome the difference between thought and being within itself, and thus consciously to create itself; this challenge is also addressed to us. Prussian State life and German intellectual life must become reconciled in such a way that both their growths become intertwined without weakening each other.

Such a reconciliation had not quite been achieved before the Great War. The representative of German intellectual life was still sometimes inclined to regard the Prussian State as a hostile power, and the old Prussian at times to regard the free and untrammeled development of German intellect as a destructive force. And again and again in Parliament and in the Press accusations were leveled in the name of freedom against Prussia, and in the name of order against the undauntable German intellect, which in its breadth, its philosophic depth and its poetic charm has never been equaled since the days of the Greeks.

My late friend, Adolph Wilbrandt, in a pleasing play, has a scene between an official belonging to the North German nobility and the daughter of a savant of the middle classes. At first they repel each other and quarrel. "I represent the Germany of Schiller, Goethe and Lessing," says the woman, and the man replies: "And I represent the Germany of Bismarck, Blücher and Moltke." We often hear similar things from the lips of clever and serious men. Our intellectual and political future depends on whether, and to what extent, we succeed in amalgamating German intellect with the Prussian monarchy.

Bismarck, the Prussian, realized better than any one else that in Germany strong government could only be based and maintained on the monarchic principle. The work of union could only be permanent if the monarchy was not a purely ornamental part of the fabric of the Empire, but was made to be the actual support of the union.

And if the creative power of Prussian monarchy, well tested in the course of centuries, was to be enlisted in the interests of the new Empire, then the King of Prussia must, as German Emperor, be more than the bearer of shadowy dignities; he must rule and guide—and for this purpose must actually possess monarchic rights such as have been laid down and transcribed in the Constitution of the Empire.

Germany would never, or at best very slowly and imperfectly, have achieved union as a State by following the paths of democracy along which other nations have reached the goal of national development. As a monarchy, with the Federal Princes represented in the Federal Council, and the King of Prussia at the head, we became a united German Empire. Had we been entrusted entirely to the care of quarreling parties in Parliament, the idea of the Empire would never have gained so much ground, would never have been able to win the heart of Germans to such an extent as is actually the case since the unity of the Empire was placed under the protection of the monarchy.

At the beginning of the sixties in the nineteenth century, Crispi, later President of the Ministry in Italy, wrote to Mazzini that he had been converted from the Republic to the Monarchy, because the latter would unite Italy, whereas the former would disintegrate her : the same applies to us. And it is particularly true in our case because the German Empire, situated in the middle of Europe, insufficiently protected by Nature on its frontiers, and surrounded by great military powers, is and must remain a military State. And in history strong military States have always required monarchic guidance.

We have seen that at the moment when Germany's existence was seriously threatened on the outbreak of war, all hearts turned spontaneously to our Imperial leader, all faith and confidence were placed in him. The whole German people expressed its devoted patriotism and loyalty to the State by an unpremeditated and instinctive manifestation of monarchic feeling. And during the whole course of these terrible struggles on all fronts and in all climes Germany has realized with satisfaction that, thanks to monarchic leadership, in the war she is superior to her opponents in her readiness to strike promptly and in the uniformity of her military action.

The higher the tide of hatred and rage, of injustice and envy, rises during this war and because of this war, the less will we allow ourselves to be deterred from pursuing our aims, or to be diverted from them. In future let us not forget what a very small part gratitude plays in politics. In the life of nations a debt of gratitude, in that it hurts national pride, is more apt to lead to silent wrath than to true friendship. The wise founder of the Constitution of the United States, George Washington, told his fellow-countrymen that there was no more grievous error than to think that nations can act magnanimously and unselfishly toward each other.

We must also be clear on the point that in politics it is not right alone that decides. Pitt, the greatest English statesman, said that the might of no realm would endure for

longer than from sunrise to sunset if absolute justice were
to prevail. It was a Frenchman, Pascal, who said that right
without might is powerless, and might is mistress of the
world. If right decided things, the world would have looked
very different for the past three thousand years, and the
German people would not have had to undergo such suffering as they were exposed to in the seventeenth and eighteenth
centuries and up to the middle of the nineteenth century.

Stress must be laid, however, upon the fact that it would
be a gross mistake to confound a clear and robust practical
policy with a misapprehension of the imponderables. Nothing is less in accordance with practical policy in the true
sense of the word, or with a Bismarckian policy, than to over-
look the importance of imponderables. We can learn from
French, English and Russian history how largely our neighbors have been guided in their policy by their interests, their
wish for power and their keen desire for mastery, both political and economic. But we can also learn from the history
of our neighbors how clever they were on the banks of the
Seine, of the Thames, and even of the Neva, at cloaking
practical motives and instincts in high sounding words which
make them seem beautiful. As the wise Greek said, men
are moved not so much by things as by their views on things,
and it is often not truth but the semblance of truth which
rules the world.

The man who pursues a practical policy knows better
than any one else what an important factor feeling is in the
life of the nation, what weight imponderable things have,
which, as Prince Bismarck said on February 6, 1888, weigh
far, far more heavily than material objects. A clumsy word,
a thoughtless phrase, can do more harm at times than defeat
in battle. It is a question whether ill-chosen words cannot
do more damage than imprudent writings or even deeds,
whether the Latin dictum, *"Verba volant, scripta manent,"*
might not more properly be reversed. The expression *"cœur
léger,"* which Emile Ollivier allowed to escape his lips in
1870 at the beginning of the war, straightway labeled the
war for millions of people in the world, and the impression
created by them persisted for many years.

In practical politics and in the administration of affairs dogmatic adherence to principles and unpractical theories is mischievous. Ernest Renan, himself a philosopher, rightly said that philosophy had as little connection with politics as with mechanics or chemistry. The principles of practical politics must be applied in a practical manner, they must not be proclaimed from the housetops in the form of an extreme theory. Otherwise we shall cover Germany with odium, with an evil repute which our noble people assuredly do not deserve, for we have for centuries actually pursued a policy which is essentially more humane, and in the best sense of the word more idealistic, than France from the times of Philip the Fair, Henry IV. and Richelieu to those of Napoleon; than Russia from the days of Peter the Great and Catherine to the present time; than England in all her history.

Owing to our seriousness and our logic, owing also to our thoroughness, which at times becomes clumsiness, many a thing sounds cruder on German lips, and is more offensive when expressed in German fashion, than if it had been uttered by others. Pascal, probably the deepest French thinker, discriminated between the *esprit géometrique* and the *esprit de finesse*. The former causes much mischief in politics, the latter prevents many things and achieves some.

The outbreak of war was calculated to force the German nation with sudden violence to realize how greatly the course of foreign politics affects the fate of every German, and that questions of greater politics are like dynamite cartridges which, if they are clumsily handled anywhere in the world, may produce terrible explosions; it was calculated to show us how urgent is the necessity for cool judgment and sensible determination where the web of international relations is concerned in which our national life, in its entirety and in its details, is entangled; how indispensable, in dealing with these relations, are experience, knowledge of men and things, psychological insight and the right estimation of others which it enables us to form; how desirable is that quality which the Frenchman describes by the untranslatable expression *"le doigté,"* which Prince Bismarck demanded of every one who had anything to do with foreign and diplomatic affairs. It depends upon the lever of the pointsman whether two railway trains pass one another or collide with fearful violence.

Politics, as Prince Bismarck often said, is an art. Hence goodwill, which in matters of morality is everything, is of little or no account, and ability is the only thing that tells. A short time ago in the Reichstag a deputy opined very truly that all the misfortunes in the world arose from goodwill, coupled with incapacity. We need a skillfully conducted foreign policy all the more because we are situated in the middle of Europe, wedged in between races hostile to us, and must always reckon with the possibility of attack. We have been encircled for a thousand years, ever since by the Treaty of Verdun the German tribes of Charles the Great were separated from the others and started life as an independent State under the Carolingian king named Ludwig the German. Hemmed in by Latins and Slavs, we must suit our foreign policy to our geographical position.

The present, which is full of great and serious political problems, and still more so the future after the war, require a political generation. It is Germany's great hope that men of political insight will some day return home from the fiery ordeal by which their souls are tried in this gigantic struggle among the nations. Great-hearted men who will not let their considered judgment on practical questions of home politics be crippled by the pressure of the doctrines of party politics, strong-willed men who will demand of the Government as well a determined policy with great aims, which shall be energetically carried out.

When from the bloody seed of this world war we shall reap the increased glory of the German Empire, the important point will be to concentrate the wealth of German intellect, the indestructible German capacity for work, the unwearied German energy upon the interrupted task of German progress. Fighting so tenaciously for many months of warfare, the mighty powers and means at Germany's disposal have with invincible might and unshakable confidence in victory, mastered, and with God's help will continue to master the monstrous fate which overtook us so unexpectedly. These powers were fostered and grew during forty-five years of work in times of peace—work which was restless, sometimes somber and sullen, much debated, but always unwearied, steadfast and fruitful. This war was the tremendous test of the strength of the edifice erected in peace. Germany has stood the test. In April, 1813, Gneisenau, a great man at that time, wrote: "Prussia will never again be subjugated, for the whole nation participates in the struggle; it has developed a greatness of character which makes it invincible." What was true of Prussia at that time is true of Germany to-day.

Less than half a century of peaceful progress along the new path of history, into which Bismarck's strong hand had guided them, was vouchsafed to the German people. The German Empire, whose forces were welded together on battlefields, must now fight innumerable battles against a world of foes; and the German nation has met the threat of ruin with the determination to wrest from the struggle a glorious peace which shall clear and prepare the way to a brilliant future in international politics. It was Germany's hope and Germany's desire to strengthen and develop her position among the nations of the world by peaceful work and competition. But it has ever been the fate of the German people, as it is at the present time, to fulfill its own destiny, and hence its destiny in the history of the world, by treading a thorny path.

Our nation has never quarreled with its fate, nor does it do so now. With wonderful unanimity and determination it shows the world that its will, its might, its courage rise superior to history and to destiny. It hopes and believes that these qualities, which no nation has ever displayed with such deep and unswerving faith in God, such pure hearts, such simple acquiescence, with never-failing devotion and with such unanimity, will surely get its due reward: a peace worthy of such deeds and sacrifices, worthy of our past, a serious, real and secure guarantee for our future.

It betokens an unscientific and unpractical mode of thought to assume that after this world war an era will dawn which in its broad outlines as in its details is diametrically opposed to the past decades before the war, an era that will break with traditions and earlier development, instead of carrying them on. We are well aware of this. We cannot even desire it, for it is steady organic evolution, and not sudden change, which insures sound growth. Taine, as the result of his lifelong study of the French Revolution, came to the conclusion that, *En fait d'histoire il vaut mieux continuer que recommencer*.[1] We do, however, hope that the purifying, clarifying and civilizing influence of the war, which we have seen at work in the course of the war, will continue to act on the intellectual and public life of Germany after it is over, on the nation in general, and in detail on the Government and the parties. But experience teaches us that, however great the events, however heavy the blows of fate, neither men nor circumstances change suddenly or become the contrary of what they were before—especially not in Germany. Even the tremendous change betokened by the transition from Germany of the period of the Federated Diet, of the worthy small folk, to Germany, the new Empire and Great Power, left untouched the nature of the German, the roots of our character and the fundamental conditions of our existence.

The number of problems a nation has solved is always small compared with the number that await solution. That was Germany's experience after the wars of liberation and the wars of union. The German nation knows it to-day too. It knows that Goethe depicted the German nation in human guise, not in Wagner, who is filled with satisfaction by the contemplation of all the fine things we have at last achieved, but in Faust who, with high self-confidence, ever strives to achieve more, and who gives utterance to this truth as the ultimate conclusion of wisdom: *Nur der verdient sich Freiheit wie das Leben, Der taglich sie erobern muss*.[2]

May the consideration of the welfare of the country in Germany always prove stronger than party interests and the claims of special groups. May every German be ever

---

[1] Where history is concerned, it is better to continue than to begin afresh.

[2] He alone deserves liberty and life who must conquer them daily anew.

conscious of the duties which two thousand years of history have imposed on us, a history which led us through the stormy times of the *Völkerwanderung* (migration of nations), by way of Charles the Great and Frederick Barbarossa, by way of Fehrbellin and Leuthen, Leipzig and Waterloo, Königgratz and Sedan. May every German at all times be ready to defend the Fatherland, may every German heart for all time subscribe to the sacred vow: *Deutschland über alles!*

BY MAXIMILIAN HARDEN
Written in 1915

THEY write and talk much about the great scourge of war. That is all quite true. But we should also bear in mind how much greater is the scourge which is fended off by war. The sum and substance of the matter is this: In looking upon the office of war one must not consider how it strangles, burns, destroys. For that is what the simple eyes of children do which do not further watch the surgeon when he chops off a hand or saws off a leg; which do not see or perceive that it is a matter of saving the entire body. So we must look upon the office of war and of the sword with the eyes of men, and understand why it strangles and why it wreaks cruel deeds. Then it will justify itself and prove of its own accord that it is an office divine in itself, and as necessary and useful to the world as is eating, drinking, or any other work. But that some there are who abuse the office of war, who strangle and destroy without need, out of sheer wantonness—that is not the fault of the office, but of the person. Is there any office, work, or thing so good that wicked and wanton persons will not abuse it?

The organ tone of such words as these at last rolls forth once more in their native land.

Therefore cease the pitiful attempts to excuse Germany's action. No longer wail to strangers, who do not care to hear you, telling them how dear to us were the smiles of peace we had smeared like rouge upon our lips, and how deeply we regret in our hearts that the treachery of conspirators dragged us, unwilling, into a forced war.

Cease, also, you popular writers, the degraded scolding of enemies that does not emanate from passion but out of greedy hankering for the applause of the masses, and which continually nauseates us amid the piety of this hour! Because our statesmen failed to discover and foil shrewd plans of deception is no reason why we may hoist the flag of most pious morality.

Not as weak-willed blunderers have we undertaken the fearful risk of this war. *We wanted it.* Because we had to wish it, and could wish it. *May the Teuton devil throttle those whiners whose pleas for excuses make us ludicrous* in these hours of lofty experience. We do not stand, and shall not place ourselves, before the court of Europe. *Our power shall create new law in Europe. Germany strikes.* If it conquers new realms for its genius, the priesthood of all the gods will sing songs of praise to the good war. . . .

We are waging this war not in order to punish those who have sinned, nor in order to free enslaved peoples and thereafter to comfort ourselves with the unselfish and useless consciousness of our own righteousness. We wage it from the lofty point of view and with the conviction that Germany, as a result of her achievements and in proportion to them, is justified in asking, and must obtain, wider room on earth for development and for working out the possibilities that are in her. The powers from whom she forced her ascendancy, in spite of themselves, still live, and some of them have recovered from the weakening she gave them. Spain and the Netherlands, Rome and Hapsburg, France and England, possessed and settled and ruled great stretches of the most fruitful soil. *Now strikes the hour for Germany's rising power.* The terms of a peace treaty that does not insure this would leave the great effort unrewarded. Even if it brought dozens of shining billions into the National Treasury, the fate of Europe would be dependent upon the United States of America.

We are waging war for ourselves alone; and still we are convinced that all who desire the good would soon be able to rejoice in the result. For with this war there must also end the politics that have frightened away all the upright from entering into intimate relations with the most powerful Continental empire. . . .

Not only for the territories that are to feed their children and grandchildren is this warrior host battling, but also for the conquering triumph of the German genius, for the forces of sentiment that rise from Goethe and Beethoven and Bismarck and Schiller and Kant and Kleist, working on throughout time and eternity.

Never was there a war more just; never one the result of which could bring such happiness as must this, even for the conquered. In order that that spirit might conquer we were obliged to forge the mightiest weapons for it. Over the meadows of the Scheldt is wafted the word of the King:

> How proud I feel my heart flame
> When in every German land
> I find such a warrior band!
> For German land, the German sword!
> Thus be the empire's strength preserved!

This strength was begotten by that spirit. The fashioning of such weapons was possible only because millions of industrious persons, with untiring and unremitting labors, transformed the poor Germany into the rich Germany, *which was then able to prepare and conduct the war as a great industry.* And what the spirit created once again serves the spirit. It shall not lay waste, nor banish us free men into slavery, but rather it shall call forth to the light of heaven a new, richer soul of life out of the ruins of a storm-tossed civilization. It shall, it must, it will conquer new provinces for the majesty of *the noble German spirit (Deutschheit) that never will grow chill and numb, as that of the Roman did.* Otherwise—and even though unnumbered billions flowed into the Rhine—the expense of this war would be shamefully wasted.

BY DR. RICHARD GRELLING

The official version states that the Triple Entente has attacked us. "We have to protect our holiest possessions, the Fatherland and our own hearths against a sudden ruthless attack." So said the Emperor in his speech of August

6th. "The sword must then decide. In the midst of peace the enemy falls upon us, therefore to arms! Every hesitation, every delay, would be treachery to the Fatherland. The existence of our empire is at stake—the existence of German power and German character."

Such is the official version which crops up in a thousand various forms from the Chancellor down to the last street-sweeper.

Semi-officially, however, and in the confidence of secrecy many Germans can be heard asserting that we *were* not, it is true, attacked, but that we *would have been* attacked later, if we had not now begun the war at a moment favorable for us. Should we then ask for evidence in support of this hypothesis, most of those who maintain this view have nothing to say, or else they declare that the intention of the enemy to attack us was so obvious that any proof would be superfluous. "What did they mean by their enormous preparations" is what they most frequently say. And what about our preparations? I reply, which were certainly greater and more comprehensive than in any other country in the world. Did ever any country in time of peace act as we did in 1913 when we suddenly raised the strength of our army on a peace footing by 140,000 men, that is to say, from 720,000 to 860,000, and when we rose to an extraordinary war tax of £50,000,000? "What was the meaning of the Entente, the celebrated policy of 'encirclement' (*Einkreisung*), if they did not mean to attack us?" is what they next say. And what, I reply, was the meaning of the Triple Alliance which involved even stricter obligations than the Entente, and in spite of this, according to our assertions, was defensive in its nature? "Yes, but think of the Pan-Slavs!" is urged as an objection against me. And what about the Pan-Germans? I venture to answer. Are our "All-deutschen," our national party, our Pan-Germans of the school of Treitschke and Bernhardi, in any way better or less aggressive than the Pan-Slavs? Such "Pan-tendencies" are to be found in all countries. They are harmless, so long as they do not advance to action. The decisive act was, however, taken by our Pan-Germans, when they drove us into this horrible war—a war desired and openly proclaimed by them.

And they had and still have friends and patrons in high places. They have gradually acquired more influence in our authoritative circles than ever the Pan-Slavs exercised at the Russian court. I need not mention by name the person who for years has been the influential head and the battering-ram of this movement against the originally peace-loving mind of the Emperor. Every one knows to whom I refer.[3] The Zabern telegram, the message of farewell to the Danzig Hussars, the open demonstration from the tribune of the Reichstag against our Morocco policy, which was at the time still peaceful in intention—these and countless other occurrences and suggestions leave not the slightest room for doubt as to the quarter and the camp from which the inciters to war have discharged their destructive missiles over Germany. One has but to wander along the streets of Berlin to see in all bookshops the work of Frobenius, entitled "The German Empire's Hour of Destiny," with the commendatory telegram of the exalted gentleman on the outside. In his recommendation he expresses the desire that this "distinguished book" which he has "read with the greatest interest" will find the widest circulation among the German people. And this Frobenius is a comrade in thought of Bernhardi, and the whole purport of his book is that we should strike before it is too late; since the others mean to attack us, we must anticipate them and attack them. Of course no proof, not the shadow of a proof, is advanced in support of this premise, which in reality is but a pretext, and which is denied by Bernhardi himself.

But that does not inconvenience these great minds; they do not recognize the defects of their logic. They do not see that of the two assertions only one can be true. Either we have been attacked, in which case we are conducting a defensive war, or else we were going to be attacked, and in that case we are conducting a preventive war. If the second statement is true the first must be untrue; and in that case all official utterances from the Imperial speech from the

[3] The Crown Prince Frederick William.

Palace on the 31st of July down to the speech of the Chancellor on the 2nd of December are branded as lies.

If the assertion that it is a defensive war is true, the idea of a preventive war is at once put completely aside, and it is superfluous to discuss further whether the presuppositions of a preventive war in fact existed, or whether such a preventive war politically and morally can be defended. Bismarck, who after all knew something about politics, emphatically answered this latter question in the negative, in stating that "even victorious wars cannot be justified unless they are forced upon one, and that one cannot see the cards of Providence far enough ahead to anticipate historical development according to one's own calculation." [4]

This dictum of the great man of the past appears to have fallen into oblivion. While monument after monument has been erected to his memory, this sentence might have been inscribed in brass and in marble in the walls of the palaces of kings and of governments in places where it would at all times have been visible; then perhaps the German people and the world might have been spared this most terrible of evils. Bismarck also after 1870 was repeatedly urged by generals and by the instigators of war to undertake a new campaign against France in order to crush once for all and to make harmless for all time the country that was again raising its head. All such efforts he constantly rejected with unyielding energy, and the idea of initiating a war because it must come sooner or later, he declared to be "criminal" and "insane."

The saying is apposite, and those whom it fits will not be able to escape its application.

The Imperial War—The Place in the Sun

It will be obvious from all that I have so far said that I regard the present war neither as a defensive nor as a preventive war. *This war is purely a war of conquest, born of imperialist ideas and serving imperialist ends.* It is nothing else.

It is a war for the celebrated *"Place in the sun,"* which

[4] Bismarck, *"Gedanken und Erinnerungen."*

it is supposed is being refused us, and which we must take forcibly with the sword in our hand.

What is the meaning of the "Place in the sun"? No one says clearly what it is, and every one understands the phrase in a different sense.

The idea is so alien to the people that it may be presumed that they would not have allowed themselves to have been sacrificed, if it had been said to them: "You must gain for us a place in the sun."

For the initiated, however, it is the magic spell which unites their imperialistic desires. "Only thus relying on the sword, can we gain the place in the sun, which is our due, but which is not voluntarily accorded to us." With this inscription, and with the motto *pro patria et gloria,* the photograph of the German Crown Prince is sold in German bookshops.

The Chosen People

The place in the sun is the world-power which is due to us, as to the *chosen people of God.* From the point of view of the psychology of the nation it is remarkable how the old Jewish idea has mastered the good, Christian, Protestant, anti-semitic Empire, and how it has ousted the true teaching of Christ, that all men are brothers.

We change our religious ideas, like our uniforms, according to our needs and our circumstances.

The God whom in war we invoke every day, whom we entreat to grant that we may destroy as many of the enemy as possible, and to whom we give thanks when he fulfills our prayers, is the old Jewish God, Jehovah, the God of battles and of vengeance, to whom no sacrifice appears too great, if it is to serve the power and the dominion of his chosen people. The Christian God, however, and his "only-begotten Son," who wandered about on earth preaching love and sacrifice, whose kingdom is not of this world—they have nothing to do with this shedding of blood, which is entirely contradictory to the doctrine they taught.

If it were known in certain places in Germany how educated men and religious people throughout the whole world judge these continual blasphemous appeals to God!

Luigi Luzzatti, one of the most distinguished politicians and most important thinkers in Italy, who, as is well known, has more than once been Prime Minister (be it observed a strict Jew—this I mention as an example to Germany, whose mission is to "bring freedom," although in time of peace it does not go so far as to promote a Jew to be a Second Lieutenant), Luigi Luzzatti has recently published in the *Corriere della Sera* a remarkable article bearing the title "The abuse of the name of God," from which I quote some sentences:

"From the day on which this fearful war broke out Princes (not the people, it must be said) have bored every one by the use and abuse of the name of God. In the telegrams which were recently exchanged between the Austrian Emperor and the Sultan the Almighty makes his appearance. The matter would take on an ironical tinge if up in Heaven the conquerors and the defeated of Lepanto and the soul of John Sobieski were to hear of it. One could have wished that at least on this occasion they might have felt enough shame to induce them to leave heaven in peace out of the question! . . . Fortunately God has not yet appeared in the telegrams exchanged between the monarchs of England and Japan. And indeed it would have been a difficult matter to reconcile in the same fearful uproar of war Jesus and Buddha, a religion without God and a religion which rests on a personal God and Saviour. We are reminded of a bitterly ironical saying of Voltaire, who observed 'Since God created man in his own image, how often has man endeavored to render a similar service to God.' . . . Let us save God from such profanation! Let us leave in peace the Father of all mankind who punishes guilt and rewards virtue, and who gives no one the right to represent Him on earth, and to claim for himself His omnipotence in this tragedy of war."

Such is the judgment of serious men abroad on certain German peculiarities and on the presumption of Germany to be the chosen people of God.

The place in the sun which is due to us as the chosen

people, thus represents the true object of this war, even if it is not admitted to the nation that this is the object.

Germany's Brilliant Development

If any one seeks a place in the sun, and seeks it sword in hand, it must be assumed that hitherto he has stood in the shadow. Is this so in the case of Germany? I maintain that the opposite is the case, and in support of this assertion I rely on those very people who have pressed the sword into our hand to enable us to seek a place in the sun. In the chapter entitled "Financial and Political Preparation for War" Bernhardi gives a comprehensive view of the brilliant and unprecedented economic development of Germany since the Franco-Prussian war. He points out, and supports his assertion freely with statistics, that the increase of wealth continues on an ascending scale, and that the advance in trade and industry since the foundation of the Empire has been extraordinary. He quotes a lecture delivered by Professor Dade before a general meeting of the Finance and Tax Reformers held on the 22nd February, 1910, from which we gather that the value of German imports and exports in the last years before 1910 had increased from 300 million pounds sterling to between 725 million pounds and 800 million pounds. In 1912 German imports and exports reached a value of approximately 1,200 million pounds sterling.

This brilliant picture of our industrial development, which could be supported by a series of other figures, is naturally of use to General Bernhardi, only in so far as it enables him to represent as tolerable a further increase of military burdens. He forgets, however, that in thus demonstrating our continuous increase of national wealth, and in particular in emphasizing our increasing advantage over England, he cuts from under his own feet the ground on which there should be erected the edifice of his Imperialism. If we already have such a sunny corner in the sun, *what is still lacking? What more do we want?*

If in many respects we, the most recent industrial State in the world, the growth of scarcely more than two generations, are already placing England, the oldest industrial State, in the shadow, we certainly cannot complain of any deficiency of sunshine.

What about extension of territory? What about Colonies? Does the happiness of nations depend on the number of square miles which they possess, or does it depend on their Colonies? If that were the case, small countries like Belgium, Holland, Switzerland, Denmark, Sweden, and Norway would necessarily be poor in comparison with Great States, whereas as a matter of fact the opposite is the case. The highest figures for imports and exports per head of the population are shown by Holland, followed by Belgium, Switzerland, and Denmark, and then only *after* these the great Powers. The Belgian 3 per cents. stood at 96 when the German stood at 83 per cent. The Norwegian 3½ per cents. stood at 102 when the Russian could be had at 81. Similar figures may be adduced in every sphere of economic life. *The greatness of a country, and in particular the extent of its Colonial possessions, has no relation to the prosperity of a country.*

The best proof for this fact is found in Germany itself. No one, not even the most fanatical nationalist, will or can dispute the fact that the increase in prosperity of Germany in the last forty years, and in particular in the twenty-six years which have elapsed since the present Emperor ascended the throne, has been without precedent in the history of the world. On the occasion of the celebration of the twenty-fifth anniversary of the accession of William II. a compilation appeared under the title, "Social Culture and the Well-being of the People during the first 25 Years of the Reign of William II." This work describes, and supports with statistics, the prosperity of Germany in all branches of human culture during this period. It is superfluous to reproduce here these well-known figures.

The increase of the national income and the national wealth correspond to the commercial and industrial development of Germany. Dr. Karl Helfferich, Director of the German Bank,[5] in his contribution to the compilation men-

---

[5] Afterward Secretary of the Treasury.

tioned above, summarizes his conclusions in the following words:

"The wealth of the German people amounts to-day to more than 15,000 million pounds, as against about 10,000 million pounds about the middle of the nineties of last century.

"These solid figures summarize, expressed in money, the result of the enormous economic labor which Germany has achieved under the government of our Emperor."

That is the place in the sun which we occupy, which no one has disputed, can dispute, or means to dispute, a place in the sun for which we are indebted to the spirit of enterprise, the pertinacity and the skillful methods of our merchants and our manufacturers, but not to the braggart company of our nationalists, and just as little to the sword of our generals or the plans of campaign of our General Staff.

It is exclusively the work of the German merchant and his motto "My field is the world," exclusively the result of the long-enduring condition of peace, which, to judge from the experience of the past, the longer it lasted would have more and more promoted the prosperity of the German people.

The Place in the Sun for Us—The Place in the Shadow for the Others

In reality our imperialists are seeking to achieve something quite different. They also know, even if they do not say it to the stupid people (and Bernhardi's book proves that this is so) that we have indeed the place in the sun, that no one seeks to dispute it, and that if any one were to seek to do so, he would necessarily fail. But it is something else that they want. They want *the exclusive place in the sun; they are striving for the world-dominion of Germany,* and *that,* at any rate, is what the others are not prepared to yield to them.

The German Wehr-Verein, in a meeting held in the House of Representatives, has quite recently expressed this

with all the lucidity that can be desired. In this manifesto
we find the following words:

"We need room and air for the further development of
our German nationality. The time for moderation is past.
Relentlessly thinking only of our interests, we must and
we will dictate peace. Only one peace can be thought of, a
peace which assures the permanent leading world-position
of Germany. . . . The criminal breakers of the peace . . .
England, France and Russia, must be so weakened that in
future they will cease to be a danger to the peace of the
world."

Thus we find, on the one side, breakers of the peace,
and on the other a permanent leading world-position! Explain this to me, Count Oerindur! Here we find truth and
falsehood mingled in a most dexterous manner. On the
one side the true aims of the war-party are openly proclaimed, and yet on the other the pretense that the peace
was broken by the other party is boldly maintained. Nevertheless, these gentlemen do not succeed in their somer-
sault over logic. If to extend our nationality we must obtain for Germany the permanent *leading* position in the
world, that is equivalent to saying in other words that we
must compel the others to subject themselves to our leadership, since to-day we already enjoy equal privileges with
others, but not a leadership. If, however, we do this, it is
we who are the breakers of the peace, and not the others.

In reality that is the position of affairs, as I will point
out.

It is leadership that we seek, not merely equal privileges
with others. It would be nonsense to say that we seek the
latter, since we already possess in the fullest measure such
equal privileges. If we are not, as a German professor has
expressed it, "morally and intellectually beyond all comparison superior to all other nations," there is at least *one* superiority which has willingly been granted to our Prussian
Germany by the rest of the world for a century and a half.
I refer to our military superiority. While *we* need only
fear God, but nothing else in the world, Germany has been
feared by all—almost more than God Himself. Even Taci-

tus long ago pointed out that the defectiveness of the German frontiers was made good by fear of the Teutons. The fear of Germany produces the effect that our word weighs heavily in the council of the nations despite all "encirclement," and despite the wretchedness of our diplomacy.

On a certain occasion recently the most important conditions of peace were being discussed in a lively conversation. Frenchmen, Germans, and Englishmen living abroad were taking part in the discussion seated round the common table, and in the end they almost arrived at an agreement as to the terms of peace. Then, however, the German observed in jest, "One more condition; you French must take over *en bloc* our German diplomatists." The Frenchman sprang up in indignation and broke off the peace negotiations, exclaiming, "*Ah ça, non! Ca c'est trop. Nous continuerons à combattre.*" [6] And with these words he left the restaurant.

The lack of dexterity shown by our diplomacy—where could all the high-born Borussen and Saxo-Borussen be expected to learn skill in business!—the defects of our diplomacy are constantly made good by the weight of the army, standing in the background. For long the Triple Alliance was indeed only a sham, but it looked quite well from the outside, and it worked almost like a being of flesh and blood.

Thus in all the conflicts of recent years Germany, in union with Austria and Italy, has come out quite well in the end, and her allies, relying on the power of Germany, have been able to bear home spoil, with which it would scarcely be proper to compare the acquisitions of the Triple Alliance. Was Austria not able in 1908 to bag Bosnia and Herzegovina, a fat morsel of more importance than twenty Moroccos? Was Italy not able to appropriate without a European conflict Tripoli and the Ægean islands—acquisitions which it can scarcely be expected to disgorge again? In addition to the open door in Morocco, which is of more value than any costly rights of possession demanding the expenditure of blood, have we not got into the bargain a considerable piece of the French Congo—an exchange which

⁶ "That, no! That is too much. We will continue to fight."

cost Caillaux, the Minister responsible for it, his prestige and his position, and which almost cost his wife her life? Did we not, acting with our ally Austria, achieve in her interests the great feat of gracefully turning the Montenegrins out of Scutari, which they had purchased with streams of blood, and of introducing there an international garrison? Was not the creation of that mannikin-kingdom of Albania, that "vile abortion of filth and fire," [7] accomplished exclusively in the interests of our allies, Austria and Italy? Were we not able to complete with England and Turkey an agreement that was favorable to us in connection with Asia Minor and the Bagdad line?

This list of successes could be considerably lengthened. I need not emphasize the fact that, from my point of view, many—indeed nearly all—of these diplomatic bickerings, these alterations and annexations of territory have not the slightest connection with the real interests of the nations. When we reflect that a European war almost broke out in 1912 on the question whether Serbia should receive her celebrated "window on the Adriatic"—when we reflect that nearly every one of the questions mentioned above brought Europe for the time being to the verge of an armed conflict, while these so-called "vital questions" frequently had not in any way decisive importance for the well-being, in the true sense of the word, of the States immediately concerned, we are constantly constrained to admire anew the lamb-like patience of the nations and the craziness of the diplomatists.

[7] *Spottegeburt aus Dreck und Feuer—Faust.*

THE POISONS BREWED BY MILITARISM

WHAT MILITARY METHODS DID IN GERMANY

FRIEDRICH VON BERNHARDI
EUGENE ETIENNE   CHARLES ALTSCHUL
FREDERICK WILLIAM HOHENZOLLERN

That military training has wide values and might even, under proper methods, breed high virtues, no thoughtful man denies. But the picture of what actual militarism, carried enthusiastically to its fullest power, produced in Germany, warns us that it may easily become a weapon more suited to devils than to men. To make this picture clear, to show the progress of German militarism through enthusiasm to falsehood and treachery, and through strictness to brutality and vilest foulness, the German writers are here called on to speak for themselves.

First comes the high-priest of militarism before the War, General Bernhardi. He wrote several books which were much honored in Germany, and which preached a sort of Darwinian scientific theory that war is the chief means of advancing civilization, because it results always in the "survival of the fittest," that is, of the Germans. At the opening of the War, Bernhardi was given a command on the Russian front; later he commanded one of the western armies. We give here his teaching as expressed in his last book just before the War, "Our Future—A Word of Warning to Germany." In this book, while urging all the splendors of war, its uplifting character, its delights, its profits, Bernhardi closes his introduction with the grim warning to his people that the crisis is close at hand and that they "can pass through this crisis and reach victory only if they are determined to the utmost to win and to endure the heaviest burdens and sacrifices."

This ominous forecast of suffering is very different from the author's usual cheerful war-praise. The glory of militarism, as Bernhardi usually presents it, was obviously the side the German leaders intended their people to see. In startling contrast is its other face of treachery and cunning, as revealed in our second article.

This is an official bulletin from the French Minister of War, M. Etienne, who declared that it was a secret German official document secretly secured by him. France guaranteed this document publicly to the world; and Germany has, at least by silence, admitted its authenticity. Comment is unnecessary as to its methods and its criminality.

A still blacker side of militarism is discussed by Mr. Altschul, a well-known American citizen. He draws his evidence wholly from German sources, to prove the barbarity of Germany's process of military training, and the resulting barbarity and submissive obedience of her troops. This evidence is largely quoted from the notorious trial of

Rosa Luxemburg, the socialist leader since killed in the German tumults of 1919. The examples of evil practices are here limited to a few; they might have been expanded indefinitely to establish that each foulness was not an exceptional case but a common custom, often unprintable in its gross details.

Lastly, in contrast to these terrible cumulative German voices, we let the noisy younger "War Lord" speak for himself. The Crown Prince of the German Empire shouldered his share in the intellectual preparation of his countrymen for the War, by writing in 1913 a book of his own, called "Germany in Arms." Perhaps it is not a very great book; but it will at least enable readers to understand the writer, who, when the War was over, altered his voice and spoke in less self-assertive tones.   C. F. H.

BY GENERAL BERNHARDI

IT is quite clear that the decisive factor in all diplomatic negotiations is always the factor of actually existing and therefore effective force. Consequently, it is most important for every State which desires to maintain its position among the Powers, to enlarge its sphere of influence, *and it is particularly important that it should increase all its instruments of power,* its army, its navy and its finances. At the same time, it is at least as important to increase the moral and mental strength of the population in every way. Superior moral and mental force alone can form an equivalent for superiority in the material factors which one's opponents may possess. An advancing civilization and increasing armaments must go hand in hand. Only then can the greatest efficiency be obtained. It follows that absolutely the most important task of a modern State consists in making its armed force as powerful as possible, not only in order to be able to be victorious in war, but also with a view to being successful in diplomatic negotiations. The expansion of the armed forces of the nation is particularly valuable, because military service is perhaps the most important means for increasing the mental and moral forces of the nation.

A statesman who does not appreciate the close interdependence between armed strength and policy, and who tries to negotiate with his opponents without constantly relying on the living forces of the State—he need, of course, not continually and demonstratively show his reliance upon force—can never reckon upon success. A leading German

statesman has expressed the opinion that continual reliance
upon Germany's army, while negotiating, would before long
involve Germany in differences with all the world.[1] If that
opinion is founded on his conviction and is not merely a
phrase, it would show that he does not understand the very
elements of foreign policy. Reliance on our military power
is the *only* means whereby we can obtain what we require
without war. Respect of our armed forces will cause our
opponents to be cautious in dealing with Germany. Besides,
our readiness to throw the army into the diplomatic balance
will encourage our friends, and will powerfully encourage
them.

If in diplomatic negotiations, in the course of which we
show our reliance upon our armed strength, we do not succeed by peaceful means either in carrying our point or in
adjourning the decision: if, for instance, in case of serious
differences concerning a question of territory, we cannot
obtain its neutralization or the preservation of the status
quo, then we must go to war and defend our justified claims
The stronger our armed forces are, the greater is the probability that we shall be successful. Besides, the better our
army and navy are organized, the more highly developed is
the military, moral and mental strength of the nation and
the greater is the confidence in the political determination
of Germany among her allies, the more likely will be Germany's victory.

War is the continuation of foreign policy with non-
diplomatic means. It is the most powerful, but at the same
time the most dangerous instrument of policy. It may be
asserted that *the possibility of war is a necessary instrument of foreign policy.* One cannot imagine foreign policy without the possibility of an appeal to arms. If two
States are in disagreement, and their disagreement cannot
be settled by peaceful means, then no settlement is possible between them except by war. Only the knowledge of
the disadvantages to which war may give rise is able to
induce a State to sacrifice part of its valuable interests to its
opponent.

[1] Von Bethmann-Hollweg.

It is not generally recognized that this is the case. Even in leading circles the erroneous view is often expressed that one can obtain real political advantages by means of negotiations. There are people who believe that one can induce one's opponent to sacrifice his own interests solely by diplomatic means. Many people even endeavor to eliminate war from international life, and to replace it by international laws and law courts, by arbitration. These say that war is a relic of barbarism which brings untold misery upon mankind, that it is a violation of right, that it appeals to the brutal instincts of humanity, that it stands in contradiction to the law of Christian love, and is therefore unworthy of a modern and progressive civilized State.

The progress of civilization and the closer economic relations among nations, many assert, create constantly increasing common interests among nations, and should tend to make wars impossible. The abolition of war should further become probable through the progress of morality. These ideas which, in Treitschke's words, come to the front only in times when nations become soft and decadent, have obtained such importance during the last few years that even governments have allowed themselves to be influenced by them. It is noteworthy that, owing to the pressure of public opinion, ex-President Taft has gone so far as actually to propose the conclusion of general arbitration treaties.

In Germany the desire to preserve the peace has, since 1871, exerted an unfavorable influence upon foreign policy. The desire for peace has created a political situation in Germany which I cannot consider favorable to the country. The desire to preserve the peace which everywhere and always is placed in the foreground in Germany, seems to justify our faint-hearted peace policy. To support such views can only do harm and is likely to lame public opinion.

We must strenuously combat the peace propaganda. War must regain its moral justification and its political significance in the eyes of the public. It is necessary that its high significance as a powerful promoter of civilization should become generally recognized. We must learn to understand that economic and individual interests alone must never be the decisive factor in a truly civilized State. We must recognize that the most valuable treasures of a nation are not material, but moral, that it is necessary to make sacrifices and to suffer in the interests of a great cause, that sacrifice and suffering are more precious than enjoyment. In short, we must become convinced that a war fought for an ideal or fought with the intention of maintaining one's position in the world, is not a barbaric act, but the highest expression of true civilization, that *war is a political necessity, and that it is fought in the interest of biological, social and moral progress.*

In the life of individuals and of States there is no standing still. They must rise or decline. I believe it is absolutely wrong to contemplate only the barbaric and pernicious side of war, and to omit its practical and ideal benefits. Those who look only upon the harm done by war have never clearly contemplated a great and serious war. Those who have taken part in war will judge differently. How great and holy was the patriotic wave of 1870! All egotistical interests disappeared before the glorious feeling which united all Germans and moved them to offer themselves unselfishly to the Fatherland!

On the other hand, one must not judge of wars by those wars of the past which have arisen from dynastic or personal reasons, or from sheer lust of robbery.

A war always leads to brutalities and to suffering. But at the same time it gives rise to the noblest actions, especially when the freedom, honor and future of a nation are at stake. Then the brutalities and wrongs of war disappear before the idealism which animates the whole. The common danger unites all in a common effort, and this unifying factor is a force which frees the mind of the people and elevates them for a long time. Wars destroy the shams of peace, reveal great personalities and place them in power. They give scope to strength, greatness and truth to all the virtues, to unselfishness and to the joy of sacrifice.

One ought not to overestimate the economic damage done by war. Although wars bring about economic crises, and do harm to the business of many individuals, *the victor usually derives the greatest economic advantage from his victory.* Germany's great economic development was made possible only by the victories of 1866 and 1870-71. Throughout history we find that increasing prosperity and increasing political power go hand in hand, because capital and labor require the security of armed power to develop freely. If peace has to be bought with a diminution of political power, the economic damage done by it may prove greater than that inflicted by a sanguinary war. Lastly, it should be remembered that a war which has been chivalrously fought with honest arms is a more moral form of competition than one fought with gold and intrigue under the appearance of peace. Victories of intrigue and gold are won by those who possess gold and lack conscience and morality. They are not triumphs of civilization.

Wars are ennobling because small-minded men are swamped in the greatness of the movement. The nations and States are at their greatest when fighting with their whole strength for liberty, independence, and honor. Only in States which calculate with the possibility of war will the character of the nation possess that energy which enables them to develop their moral and mental forces to the highest degree.

War has its ideal side and peace has its blessings. At the same time, peace is no blessing if it lasts too long, especially if its maintenance has to be paid for with the abandonment of the national ideals. Such a peace dishonors a nation, and in such a peace small-mindedness and selfishness flourish, while idealism is destroyed by materialism and the simplicity of manners by luxury. In such times money becomes all powerful, and character is of little value. The more deeply we penetrate into history, the more clearly we recognize that peace is the normal and the desirable state, but that wars are required from time to time in order to cleanse the moral atmosphere. Political tension can become so great and the irreconcilable interests so acute and so involved that the Gordian knot can only be cut with the sword. When a nation sees its power jeopardized, when its ability to solve its problems in its own way is threatened, and when the highest possessions of a nation can no longer be preserved by compromise, then *war becomes a moral duty.* Such situations will arise as long as the nations look at the development of the world from different points of view. *When the pursuit of their ideals leads to differences, war becomes the highest expression of the will to civilization* and idealism makes it a necessity.

In view of the compelling logic of those considerations it seems surprising that the peace movement has obtained so great an influence. Its success is due to the fact that it is supported by powerful private, and especially by large capitalistic, interests. There is a great contrast between the views of the United States and Germany on the question of peace and war. The United States have conquered their independence and unity on the field of battle, and they have acquired a great heritage of glory, self-consciousness, and liberty. At present the United States have many competitors, but no enemies. Their relations with England are secured by the community of language, not of race. Their differences with Japan cannot endanger their vital interests, should it come to war. America need not fear overpopulation, in view of her vast and thinly peopled districts in the South and West. The natural wealth of the country makes the Americans independent of foreign States, and their struggle with nature steels their muscles and enables them to undertake the greatest and most difficult tasks. Under these circumstances it is only natural that the Americans look upon the peace movement with sympathy, for peace can only bring them advantage, while war can only harm them by impeding the development of the country and upsetting the money market.

Germany is in a totally different position. Since the collapse of the ancient German Empire the German nation has had to fight against its enemies. It has wrested from the Slavs the territories in the East, and to-day the Slavonic flood beats against its frontier with renewed hostility. Towards the West and South the Germans had to defend themselves against the Latin nations, and to preserve their political independence during centuries of war, without being able to disarm the hostility of the fanatical French. The most recent political and economic development of Germany has at last made England also our most bitter enemy. England fears that she may lose the mastery of the sea and her trade supremacy. She opposes us throughout the world with hostility, and prevents us acquiring colonies, the possession of which is for Germany a question of life or death.

If we consider our national circumstances, it is evident why the peace idea has many adherents in Germany, but that idea is not much appreciated by the patriotically inclined and by the educated. History has taught us that a State which is in Germany's position can preserve that position only sword in hand.

BY EUGENE ETIENNE

French Minister of War

Paris, April 2, 1913.

I have just received from a reliable source the following official secret report concerning the strengthening of the German army:

[Memorandum of the German Headquarters Staff on the strengthening of the German army, March 19, 1913.]

The increase has taken place in three stages:—

(1) The Conference of Algeciras has removed the last doubt with regard to the existence of an *Entente* between France, England, and Russia. Moreover, we have seen that Austria-Hungary was obliged to keep some of her forces mobilized against Serbia and Italy; finally our fleet was not at that time sufficiently strong. At the end of the dispute the first matter taken in hand was the strengthening of our coast defenses and the increase of our naval forces. To meet the English plan of sending an Expeditionary Force of 100,000 men to the Continent, it would be necessary to make a better formation of reserves, to be used according to circumstances in the protection of the Coast, in fortresses and in siege operations. It was already clear at that time

that it would be absolutely necessary to make a great effort.

(2) The French having violated the Morocco Conventions, brought on the incident of Agadir. At that time the progress made by the French army, the moral recovery of the nation, the technical advance in the realm of aviation and of machine guns rendered an attack on France less easy than in the previous period. Further, an attack by the English fleet had to be considered. This difficult situation opened our eyes to the necessity for an increase in the army. This increase was from this moment considered as a minimum.

(3) The war in the Balkans might have involved us in a war in support of our ally. The new situation in the south of Austria-Hungary lessened the value of the help which this ally could give us. On the other hand, France was strengthened by a new *loi des cadres;* it was accordingly necessary to anticipate the date of execution contemplated by the new military law.

Public opinion is being prepared for a new increase in the active army, which would insure Germany an honorable peace and the possibility of properly insuring her influence in the affairs of the world. The new army law and the supplementary law which should follow will enable her almost completely to attain this end.

Neither ridiculous shriekings for revenge by French chauvinists, nor the Englishmen's gnashing of teeth, nor the wild gestures of the Slavs will turn us from our aim of protecting and extending *Deutschtum* (German influence) all the world over.

The French may arm as much as they wish, they cannot in one day increase their population. The employment of an army of negroes in the theater of European operations will remain for a long time a dream, and in any case be devoid of beauty.

Aim and Obligations of Our National Policy, of Our Army, and of the Special Organizations for Army Purposes

Our new army law is only an extension of the military education of the German nation. Our ancestors of 1813

made greater sacrifices. It is our sacred duty to sharpen
the sword that has been put into our hands and to hold it
ready for defense as well as for offense. *We must allow
the idea to sink into the minds of our people that our armaments are an answer to the armaments and policy of the
French.* We must accustom them to think that an offensive
war on our part is a necessity, in order to combat the provocations of our adversaries. We must act with prudence so
as not to arouse suspicion, and to avoid the crises which
might injure our economic existence. *We must so manage
matters that* under the heavy weight of powerful armaments, considerable sacrifices, and strained political relations, *an outbreak (Losschlagen) should be considered as
a relief,* because after it would come decades of peace and
prosperity, as after 1870. We must prepare for war from
the financial point of view; there is much to be done in this
direction. We must not arouse the distrust of our financiers, but there are many things which cannot be concealed.

We must not be anxious about the fate of our colonies.
The final result in Europe will settle their position. On
the other hand, we must stir up trouble in the north of Africa
and in Russia. It is a means of keeping the forces of the
enemy engaged. It is, therefore, absolutely necessary that
we should open up relations, by means of well-chosen organizations, with influential people in Egypt, Tunis, Al-
geria, and Morocco, in order to prepare the measures which
would be necessary in the case of a European war. Of
course in case of war we should openly recognize these secret allies; and on the conclusion of peace we should secure
to them the advantages which they had gained. These aims
are capable of realization. The first attempt which was
made some years ago opened up for us the desired relations.
Unfortunately these relations were not sufficiently consolidated. Whether we like it or not it will be necessary to
resort to preparations of this kind, in order to bring a campaign rapidly to a conclusion.

Risings provoked in time of war by political agents need
to be carefully prepared and by material means. They must
break out simultaneously with the destruction of the means

of communication; they must have a controlling head to be found among the influential leaders, religious or political. The Egyptian School is particularly suited to this purpose; more and more it serves as a bond between the intellectuals of the Mohammedan World.

However this may be, we must be strong in order to annihilate at one powerful swoop our enemies in the east and west. But in the next European war it will also be necessary that *the small states should be forced to follow us* or be subdued. In certain conditions their armies and their strong positions can be rapidly conquered or neutralized; this would probably be the case with Belgium and Holland, so as to prevent our enemy in the west from gaining territory which they could use as a base of operations against our flank. In the north we have nothing to fear from Denmark or Scandinavia, especially as in any event we shall provide for the concentration of a strong northern army, capable of replying to any menace from this direction. In the most unfavorable case, Denmark might be forced by England to abandon her neutrality; but by this time the decision would already have been reached both on land and on sea. Our northern army, the strength of which could be largely increased by Dutch formations, would oppose a very active defense to any offensive measures from this quarter.

In the south, Switzerland forms an extremely solid bulwark, and we can rely on her energetically defending her neutrality against France, and thus protecting our flank.

As was stated above, the situation with regard to the small states on our northwestern frontier cannot be viewed in quite the same light. This will be a vital question for us, and our aim must be to take the offensive with a large superiority from the first days. For this purpose it will be necessary to concentrate a large army, followed up by strong Landwehr formations, which will induce the small states to follow us *or at least to remain inactive in the theater of operations, and which would crush them in the event of armed resistance.* If we could induce these states to organize their system of fortification in such a manner as to constitute an effective protection for our flank we could abandon the proposed invasion. But for this, army reorganization, particularly in Belgium, would be necessary in order that it might really guarantee an effective resistance. If, on the contrary, their defensive organization was established against us, thus giving definite advantages to our adversary in the west, we could in no circumstances offer Belgium a guarantee for the security of her neutrality. Accordingly, a vast field is open to our diplomacy to work in this country on the lines of our interests.

The arrangements made with this end in view allow us to hope that it will be possible to take the offensive immediately after the complete concentration of the army of the Lower Rhine. *An ultimatum with a short time-limit, to be followed immediately by invasion, would allow a sufficient justification for our action in international law.*

Such are the duties which devolve on our army and which demand a striking force of considerable numbers. If the enemy attacks us, or if we wish to overcome him, we will act as our brothers did a hundred years ago; the eagle thus provoked will soar in his flight, will seize the enemy in his steel claws and render him harmless. We will then remember that the provinces of the ancient German Empire, the County of Burgundy and a large part of Lorraine, are still in the hands of the French; that thousands of brother Germans in the Baltic provinces are groaning under the Slav yoke. It is a national question of restoring to Germany her former possessions.

BY CHARLES ALTSCHUL

The Great War has focussed the attention of all Americans upon political and social conditions in foreign countries, and has familiarized them with many matters which had not occupied their minds before. The feature which probably attracts more attention than any other is the difference in the respective points of view of the Teutonic and of the English-speaking nations, as revealed in all matters relating to war and warfare. Character and habits of other peoples have been more closely studied than ever before, and the aggressive leaders of the group of enemy nations, the Germans, have quite naturally come in for the closest scrutiny.

Accustomed as these leaders have been for many years to universal military service, to a large standing army, to officers drawn principally from the ranks of the nobility, and to marked class distinctions, they have absorbed certain notions which to us, who have grown up under very different conditions, seem like worship of constituted authority and the unwarranted surrender of individual responsibility.

The gradual development of these very notions has brought about an inordinate influence of the military group in public affairs, which at the present moment is frequently referred to and much discussed. It may therefore not be amiss to try to throw some side-lights on the subject.

At the outbreak of the war, the German army was acknowledged to be the most stupendous military machine imaginable. It was in all its branches efficient, scientifically developed, thoroughly up to date, and very ably officered. It consisted of a small contingent of professional soldiery and of a mass of men made available by universal military service, and seemed truly representative of the entire nation. To belong to any branch of the service carried, as a matter of fact, a certain prestige at home, and the ambition of almost all educated men was to be appointed officers of reserve after concluding the regular term of service with the colors.

The disappointment in this country at the receipt of the horrifying news about the conduct of this representative body of men when the German army broke into Belgium, was as great as it was sincere. The stories seemed beyond belief; it was incredible that fathers, sons, brothers, could have been so unmindful of their education, of their heritage of whole-souled and humane instincts! But the sickening and revolting details were confirmed, and repeated from different districts, until one could no longer resist the conviction that frightfulness was to be a feature of German campaigning, to be carried out as ruthlessly as the commanding officers saw fit.

Although fully aware that war conditions usually result in the commission of atrocities by every army—because all restraint of normal life is removed, and the lack of normal surroundings brings about a deplorable abandonment of self-control—yet the world stood aghast at this display of license and brutality.

The question very naturally presented itself, whether our earlier very favorable impression of the German army had been warranted or whether insufficient knowledge had driven us to wrong conclusions? What had contemporary opinion in Germany been on this very important matter? What did the daily press reveal—the best mirror of passing impressions everywhere?

In a country in which the influence of Governmental agencies on the press is as great as we now all know it to be in Germany, one cannot expect a frank expression about an institution as closely interwoven with the Government as the army is, except in the opposition newspapers. The press of Germany, as that of most countries, caters nowadays assiduously to the taste of its readers, and devotes much space to matters in which its particular public is especially interested. On this account, the fullest discussion of conditions in the army is likely to be found in those newspapers which circulate most widely among the masses, from which the bulk of the army, the common soldier, is drawn. The best source of information for our purposes would therefore seem to be the daily newspaper *Vorwärts,* the official organ at that time of the Social Democratic party, the party which secured about one-third of all the votes cast for the Reichstag at the last election before the war—not only socialistic votes, but those of liberals of every description as well, who could in no other manner give expression to their anti-Governmental views.

The trial, in 1914, of the socialist, Rosa Luxemburg, one of the active workers in the field of socialistic propaganda, brought to light much information of value in connection with what one of the representatives in the Reichstag, Schulz, called "the gloomy, barbarous bestiality of maltreating soldiers (*Scheusäligkeiten der Soldatenmisshandlungen*) which recalls the Middle Ages." Rosa Luxemburg was tried because, at a public meeting, she had used the expression, "It is surely one of those tragedies (*Dramen*) which are enacted in the German barracks day after day, but the groans of the participants rarely reach our ears."

She explained at her trial that she meant by tragedies, "Any abuse of a soldier, of course particularly such as leads to suicide, desertion, or such as have similar consequences. Whatever instances of maltreatment are to be proved here, are tragedies. . . . It can also be proved that these incidents of daily occurrence are considered tragedies by the witnesses. . . . Was it not a tragedy when a soldier in Bautzen threw himself from a fourth story window, and was unfortunate enough to miss his goal and was court-martialed and sentenced to six months' imprisonment for desertion?"

In answering the statement of the public prosecutor to the effect that, according to the complaint of the Minister of War, defendant had by her remark insulted all the officers, non-commissioned officers, and besides, all persons attached to the Prussian army, her attorneys expressed their readiness to prove the correctness of the defendant's statement. They said: "We do not intend to prove single blows and knocks, but innumerable ones. The examination of this evidence is startling. We may assert that not one per cent. of it has ever reached the public or the courts-martial. There is an endless chain of complaints which no one has, so far, heard of. Scarcely a witness will speak of two or three blows only, but it is always the question of a chain of incredible cases of maltreatment stretching over a period varying from a month to several years. . . . We have submitted hundreds of decisions of courts-martial from the year 1907 to 1913, in which alone tens of thousands of cases of maltreatment of soldiers have been judicially established."

When the prosecution of the defendant was first announced, an appeal was issued through the *Vorwärts*, calling upon all to come forward and testify whose own experiences in the army were apt to substantiate the statement of the defendant. It is no slight matter in Germany to

espouse openly the cause of one who is being prosecuted by
the Government in a matter as zealously guarded as the
reputation of the army; nevertheless, when the trial started,
922 men from all parts of Germany had responded, and
were ready to testify to something like 30,000 separate instances of brutal treatment of soldiers.

Before the trial came to an abrupt end, the attorneys for
the defendant had stated in court what testimony they were
prepared to produce in support of the defense, and had mentioned the names of witnesses and the evidence which was
to be proved by each. These witnesses were not called to
the stand and did not have the opportunity to testify to
these facts; the trial was adjourned before that. But the
statement that they were ready to do so was made in open
court by the attorneys of Rosa Luxemburg, and their standing as *Rechtsanwalt*—a title conferred on lawyers in Germany when they have borne themselves faultlessly in following their profession a certain length of time—is a war-
ranty of the integrity of their statement.

It will suffice to select from the mass of material presented some particularly striking examples. One witness
would testify that:

"He was struck in the face with the fist by Lieutenant
Erler so that a tooth bled and got loose. He was beaten till
he was bleeding, but report of the case was not sent higher
up. Musketeer Hempel shot and killed himself after drill,
because he had been grossly insulted by a corporal in front
of the company. A reservist threw himself in front of a
railroad train, another drowned himself, because they could
no longer stand the abuse of N.C.O.[2] Huebner."

"Another witnessed maltreatment so severe as to cause
blood to flow; spitting at soldiers by superiors; cursing
by officers, one of whom made two soldiers poke the head
of another, who was bodily and mentally weak, into the
snow up to his neck. This lieutenant stuck his sword between a soldier's hands which were tied behind his back, so
that when he walked, the point struck the hollow of his
knee."

[2] The letters N. C. O. mean "non-commissioned officer."

"A Polish recruit was maltreated so fearfully by a N.C.O. that he finally hanged himself. The N.C.O. got the soldiers to certify that they had seen nothing."

"An officer struck him when he did not succeed in an exercise which had not been practiced and which was not according to regulations. Disgusting invective was used and maltreatment practiced by officers. When the adjutant took his deposition and he wanted to testify to instances of brutality, the adjutant did not want to hear about it and said that the soldier had not got enough."

"Captain von Rock used terribly offensive language. His body servant (*Bursche*) attempted suicide owing to bad treatment. A N.C.O. broke two ribs of a soldier who while bayoneting dodged a little because he was timid. Neither had the courage to file a complaint."

"Soldiers were struck in the face during instruction. Were made to bend their knees while stretching out the rifle, until they dropped. Holes in the clothes were intentionally torn open, and the soldiers told jeeringly that they would now be worth while mending. Witness saw hundreds of times helmets pressed down and the bands which held them under the chin pulled so that the soldiers got red in the face. Alsatians and Lorrainers particularly were maltreated and frequently called 'damned French-heads,' 'French skulls,' etc. The N.C.O.'s warned men against complaining, promising worse treatment for such cases."

"Witness knew of a case of suicide in consequence of maltreatment. Witness himself, after complaining about a sergeant, was abused by the captain and got five days' light arrest for improper conduct towards a superior."

"A recruit was so badly abused by a N.C.O., in the room, that he cried and said, if that had happened to him in civil life he would have smashed the fellow's head; he was too much ashamed to tell what had really occurred."

"A merchant by the name of Schuchardt shot himself in 1907 on account of abuse. This case was not brought into court."

"Witness received his training from two N.C.O.'s who had already been punished for maltreating soldiers. Several N.C.O.'s maltreated regularly and grossly. Recruits were compelled to sweep the rooms of the N.C.O.'s from nine till eleven at night with tooth-brushes. One recruit was tortured until he went insane and was then dismissed as unfit for the service."

"Lieutenant Schmidt boxed a soldier's ears, then ordered all the men to leave the room, and one heard only groaning and cursing. The recruit was injured in such a manner that he had to be discharged, and received a pension for injury in the service."

They would have continued to present to the court the details of their evidence, but before the trial had proceeded very far the Minister of War gave notice that he would submit to courts-martial all cases that had been mentioned, which had not been passed upon by such courts before, and were not yet outlawed. This attempt to force before courts-martial the witnesses who had volunteered to testify in favor of Rosa Luxemburg before a civil court, was looked upon as a veiled threat, because these witnesses were more likely to be treated as if they themselves were the accused, if the military authorities desired to frighten off others from testifying.

At the request of the Government, but against the vehement protest of the defendant, this interesting trial was then adjourned to give the Minister of War an opportunity to carry out his plan. The outbreak of the present war, soon after the last court proceedings, resulted in the case being dropped.

There is other material available from which to gather information concerning the conditions in the German army in times of peace. On April 8, 1914, the *Vorwärts* published an article on "German *Kultur* in the Barracks," which commences: "When we hear different Prussian Ministers of War talking in the Reichstag about the maltreatment of soldiers, we might be led to believe that a great improvement had taken place with respect to this deep-seated evil in the army. However, he who attentively follows the incessant flow of instances of cruelty, shudders at the abyss of brutality which is still yawning. We wish to submit but a small

selection from the record of cases of maltreatment which
have come into court during the last fifteen months; they
will suffice to put all attempts at whitewashing in their right
place."

The details then fully presented cover the cases of eight
officers and of about fifteen non-commissioned officers. The
instances of brutality are about the same as mentioned in
our former list; but these non-commissioned officers seem
to have outdone those whose records we listened to before.
We hear that—

"In the fourth squadron of the Regiment Garde-du-
Corps, two acting corporals and three 'professional regulars'
maltreated recruits in the most brutal manner with ropes,
snaffles, horse brushes, the sword, etc. One of the victims
became temporarily insane.

"In the Queen Augusta Guard Regiment No. 4, Sergeant
Waske ordered a grenadier to lie down before a cuspidor and
then called out 'Drink.' The grenadier drank from it quite
obediently, which proves that 'servile obedience' (*Kadaver-
gehorsam*) is no idle phrase."

Glancing further through this illuminating file of papers,
we come across an article by Richard Gädke on "Maltreatment in the Army," from which a few extracts follow:
"It is likely that but a tenth part of all the reprehensible
acts comes to the notice of the superiors, and only at a public
trial, exposed as by a stroke of lightning, does one see what
is really going on. It is the system that must be attacked,
bitterly and relentlessly. The system which has sprung from
old, bad, and moldering custom, from antiquated views of
the time of the armies of mercenaries. The nature of our
entire military organization still resembles that of a troup
of *lansquenets,* gathered from the roughest elements of the
people, rather than an army of the people which draws into
its fold the flower of our youth for the sole purpose of teaching them the use of arms and preparing them for a defense
of the Fatherland. Thus, we reach the idea of purely passive, purely suffering obedience; and many a commander
is still subconsciously controlled by the opinion of Frederick

the Great, that a soldier should fear his superior more than the enemy."

Further on, we find extracts from a book by a retired Prussian captain, Hans Pommer, "Twenty Years as Officer of Infantry in the Imperial Provinces" (*Reichslanden*), who says, among other things: "The disciplining of German soldiers is still done by coercive measures, which may have been warranted under feudal serfdom, but which must be considered a mockery of human rights when employed in a modern army of the people.

"I knew a captain who insulted his men in the commonest manner and made a habit of striking the man who held his horse when he dismounted, who maltreated his body-servant (*Bursche*), and yet no one had the courage to proceed against this torturer of soldiers. This captain, who should really have been retired from the army, was even honored with a command in China. Another captain, who closed his career only after having been appointed brigade commander, was so blinded when in rage that he did not mind riding down three rows of men in order to punish a man in the fourth."

From time to time other news-items and articles have appeared in the German press, all reciting similar instances of outrage upon the person or dignity of the soldier. The cumulative proof of brutality is shown in the relentless and unexpected light which Germans themselves have thrown upon the conditions in their army in times of peace. If Americans had been familiar with these details, they would have expected the worst during the stress of a campaign, and would have been less unprepared for the unheard of barbarities practiced in so many places where the Germans set foot. If officers, non-commissioned officers, and professional regulars treat their own recruits in the fashion described, in times of peace, what could be expected of troops commanded by such ruffians in enemy country, under the terrific excitement of combat, and particularly when "frightfulness" is the slogan? It is not contended that all German officers are addicted to these practices. There are, no doubt, a great many, perhaps a majority among them,

who are themselves opposed to such conditions. But the
system has evidently continued in spite of the more humane,
and has become so thoroughly ingrained that it showed its
true colors as soon as the first opportunity presented itself.

BY CROWN PRINCE FREDERICK WILLIAM

To-day, indeed, we live in a time which points with special satisfaction to the proud height of its culture, which is
only too willing to boast of its international cosmopolitan-
ism, and flatters itself with visionary dreams of the *possi-*
bility of an everlasting peace throughout the world. This
view of life is un-German and does not suit us. The German who loves his people, who believes in the greatness and
the future of our homeland, and who is unwilling to see its
position diminished, dare not close his eyes in the indul-
gence of dreams such as these, he dare not allow himself
to be lulled into indolent sleep by the lullabies of peace sung
by the Utopians.

Germany has behind her since the last great war a period
of economic prosperity, which has in it something almost
disconcerting. Comfort has so increased in all circles of
our people that luxury and claims to a certain style of life
have undergone a rank development. Now certainly we
must not thanklessly deny that a wave of economic prosperity brings with it much that is good. But the shady side
of this too rapid development often manifests itself in a
painful and threatening manner. Already the appreciation
of wealth has gained in our country an importance which
we can only observe with anxiety.

The old ideals, even the position and the honor of the
nation, may be sympathetically affected; *for peace, peace*
at any price, is necessary for the undisturbed acquisition of
money. But the study of history teaches us that all those
States which in the decisive hour have been guided by purely
commercial considerations have miserably come to grief.
The sympathies of civilized nations are to-day, as in the
battles of antiquity, still with the *sturdy and the bold fight-*
ing armies; they are with the brave combatants who, in the
words which Lessing puts in the mouth of Tellheim, are

soldiers for their country, and fight out of the love which they bear to the cause. Certainly diplomatic dexterity can, and should, postpone the conflict for a time, and at times disentangle the difficulties. Certainly all those in authority must and will be fully conscious of their enormous responsibility in the grave hour of decision. They must make it clear to their own minds that the gigantic conflagration, once enkindled, cannot be so easily or so quickly extinguished. As, however, lightning is an adjustment of the tension between two differently charged strata of the atmosphere, so the sword will always be and remain until the end of the world the decisive factor.

Therefore every one, to whom his country is dear, and who believes in a great future for our nation, must joyfully do his part in the task of seeing that the old military spirit of our fathers is not lost, and that it is not sicklied o'er with the pale cast of thought. For the sword alone is not decisive, but the arm steeled in exercise which bears the sword. Each of us must keep himself fit for arms and also prepared in his mind for the great solemn hour when the Emperor calls us to the standard—the hour when we no longer belong to ourselves, but to the Fatherland with all the forces of our mind and our body; for all these faculties must be brought to the highest exertion, to that "will to victory" which has never been without success in history.

[Later comes this passage:] Our country is obliged more than any other country to place all its confidence in its good weapons. Set in the center of Europe, it is badly protected by its unfavorable geographic frontiers, and is regarded by many nations without affection. Upon the German Empire, therefore, is imposed more emphatically than upon any other peoples of the earth the sacred duty of watching carefully that its army and its navy be always prepared to meet any attack from the outside. *It is only by reliance upon our brave sword that we shall be able to maintain that place in the sun which belongs to us, and which the world does not seem very willing to accord us.*

[The royal author then describes a regimental maneuver of the guards on the field at Döberitz:] The steel helmets

glitter in the sunshine; in the galloping exercises every individual horseman endeavors to keep on to the man in front,
and to keep the right direction—no easy matter when there
is dust, and the ground is rough. Many a one stumbles, and
away past him gallops the company of riders. What does
it matter! When you plane wood, shavings must fall.
And there the call resounds over the field, clear and quiver-
ing amid the uproar of the galloping mass, "Front!" The
reins whirl round, and as if by a stroke of magic, the line
is formed again, with a front of five impetuous squadrons
of the guards,—and then comes the signal, "Charge!" Then
the last ounce is taken out of the horses, and with bodies
strained forward and with lances in rest with a "hurrah"
we ride to the attack. For any one who has taken part in
such attacks, there is nothing fairer in the world!

And yet to the true horseman there is one thing which
appears more beautiful: if all that were the same, but if
only at the end of the rapid charge the enemy were to ride
out against us, and the struggle for which we have been
drilled and trained, *the struggle for life and death,* were to
begin. How often during such attacks have I heard the
yearning call of a comrade riding behind: *"Donnewetter!
if that were only the real thing!"* O horseman's spirit! All
who are true soldiers must know and feel: *"Dulce et de-
corum est pro patria mori."* [3]

[3] Glad and glorious [or sweet and fitting] it is to die for one's
country.

WOE TO THE CONQUERED!

THE SUBJECT FOREIGN NATIONS WITHIN THE GERMAN EMPIRE

ERNEST BARKER

We face here another side of our review, not the sources of the German outburst, but the results which would have followed upon her success, as these results are revealed in lesser shape by her treatment of foreign races previously her subjects. Along the whole eastern border of Germany and Austria there extended, for a century, a thousand mile wide strip of country sometimes called the "Dead Lands of Europe," a desert of misery in what Nature meant to be a glorious fertility.

As Germany has never attempted to maintain that she ruled her submerged foreign peoples for their own good—except as it was supposedly good for all peoples to become German or die—the theme need scarcely be presented from more than a single viewpoint. Mr. Ernest Barker is a recognized British authority upon this theme, a Fellow of Oxford University, who has written several works upon the life of various conquered peoples.

Perhaps the War itself has taught the only necessary lesson as to Germany's treatment of subject races. The Poles when appealed to for aid by both Germany and Russia, and offered equally flattering promises by each, preferred positively and even desperately to cast in their lot with the old, autocratic, stupid, selfish misgovernment of Russia rather than trust themselves to "enlightened Germany."

BY ERNEST BARKER

FOR the last hundred years a dominant conception among the Germans has been that of "the folk" (*das Volk*). The folk—they have thought and said—is a being and almost a person; and as such it has its corresponding attributes —its sense of right; its way of speech; its songs, its poetry and its music. Law, according to a great German jurist, is the organ of folk-right; folk-music, folk-songs, folk-poetry—all these are the natural outpourings of the *Volksgeist;* while as for the folk-speech, that is not only the medium for the expression, but also the condition of the existence, of these other things. The philosophy of Hegel represents in many ways the apotheosis of this German idea of the folk. To Hegel the folk, politically organized as a state, is the home of a system of social ethics that inspires and controls the life of the individual, who finds his peace in its will and his duty in filling duly a station in its system. "The spirit of a nation controls and entirely dominates from within each person," so that "he feels it to be his own very being . . . he looks upon it as his absolute final aim," and "his life is hid with that of his fellows in the common life of his people." The "culture" of the folk—the nation or people—thus becomes a sacred tradition; and the language in which it is enshrined becomes, as it were, the vehicle which carries the holy ark of the covenant.

Imbued with ideas of this order, the Germans have shown themselves sedulously careful to maintain the purity of their language, seeking to exclude all foreign or "Welsh" words, and to express every idea and every concept by means of native Germanic words. "This movement," it is said, "has grown with the growth of national unity, and a powerful society, the *Sprachverein*, has been recently founded, and has published handbooks of native words for almost every department of modern life." Thus the language of commerce, of chemistry and of every range of thought, is made purely German; and thus the German language, unlike the English, which has borrowed freely, and continues to borrow freely, from almost every language that has been or now is spoken, remains what we may call "self-sufficient," and indebted to no other.

Much may be said, both for and against this cult of linguistic purity. A language which refuses to borrow from other languages loses that flexibility, subtlety of expression and variety of shades of meaning, which an abundance of "loan-words" enables a language that borrows such words freely to attain; but, on the other hand, linguistic purity conduces to a political result, as indeed it is largely based on a political motive—a conscious and vivid sense of national unity and national uniqueness.

But whatever may be said of the two ideals—"nationalism in language, as against borrowing; a pure, as opposed to a mixed, language"—a new and difficult problem arises, when we find the people who use the pure German tongue seeking to suppress other tongues that are used within the boundaries of German territory—the Polish, the Danish and the French. This is a policy which the Germans have more and more pursued since they finally attained their own national unity in 1870; and it is a policy which cannot but seem to most of us illogical and inconsistent. If folk-speech is a consecrated thing, because it is the vehicle of folk-culture, surely the folk-speech of Poles and Danes and Frenchmen can plead a title to existence, and a right to be used no less than that of the Germans. To inflict dumbness on a people and to mutilate its tongue, at the same time that you proclaim the pure sanctity of your own speech, is to sin against the spirit of nationality with the same breath with which you proclaim it holy.

Why, then, do the Germans seek to coerce into the use of an alien speech—a speech which is the vehicle of a culture that is not their own culture—those peoples who dwell in German territory, but do not belong by blood or tradition to the German people itself? At bottom, perhaps, the reason is an instinctive feeling that the area of German government should be also the area of German nationality, and that, if there are alien elements in the area of German government, they must be, as it were, chemically changed and transmuted until they are unified with and incorporated into the area of German nationality. Just as foreign words must be purged from the German language, so foreign languages must be purged from the German soil; and just as it is resolved that foreign words must not be used in German speech, so it is enacted that foreign speech must not be used on German soil.

The analogy here implied and used is not, of course, a true or valid analogy. It is one thing for a German who speaks German to say that he himself will use no word but German, nor does he lose his freedom if he thus abnegates the use of foreign words: it is another thing for a German to say that other peoples within the German borders, who do not speak German, shall use no language but German in schools and courts of law and public meetings, and these other peoples *do* lose their freedom when they are thus compulsorily deprived of the use of their native language. But the analogy, however untrue, is pressed, as we shall see, to its uttermost consequences.

The instinctive feeling which leads to its application is corroborated by other instincts. There is the German passion for drill and uniformity and *Polizei*. Accustomed to putting men into actual and physical uniform, the German Government has drifted, as it were, by a curious extension of policy, into the habit of seeking to put men into metaphorical and mental uniform. After all, it can be argued, the army needs a uniform language of command; and if the army demands linguistic unity, will not linguistic unity best suit the needs of the schools, the law-courts, and all public intercourse? The administration of education will be easier if schools are not bilingual; the administration of justice will be simpler if there is only one language for pleading; the whole of public administration will run on a single gear, instead of running on several, if the State addresses its subjects, and can always expect to be addressed by its subjects, in a single language.

Last, but by no means least, we have to remember that spirit of exclusive nationalism which has entered so strongly and so pervasively into German life. There is the feeling that German culture is so large, so embracing, so universal, that it is good for all to use the language which is the key to all its treasures. If men are forced to use it, they are, after all, being "forced to be free"; and at the cost of a little compulsion in their schooldays they are initiated into the large freedom of the mind, which will come from a full and liberal education in German speech, and, through German speech, in German culture.

These, then, are some of the reasons why the period between the end of the Franco-Prussian war and the beginning of the present war is filled with examples of linguistic oppression in the German Empire. That oppression takes four main forms. First and foremost, it affects the school; and since religious instruction is part of the work of the school, it affects religious instruction, and tends to result in something perilously akin to religious persecution. Secondly, it affects the law-court, the post-office and all the organs of public administration. Thirdly, it affects public meetings: and finally—and most striking of all—under decrees like that of April, 1899, which required teachers in Posen to disuse Polish in the family circle, and under police action such as that which entails domiciliary visits for the seizure of Polish literature, it affects the home itself.

Much of the oppression is based on administrative orders, such as the orders of the Minister of Education, which make the use of German compulsory in schools; some of it is based on administrative action by the police; but part of it is based on direct legislation by the German Reichstag itself, and oppression of this kind cannot be ascribed to "bureaucratic" methods, but must necessarily be referred to the deliberate will of the German people itself, as expressed by its representatives. It is a law of the Reichstag of 1908 which regulates the use of languages other than German in public meetings. Under Article 12 of that law—the law of associations—the use of German is made compulsory in public meetings, except at election times. An exception is made for those districts in which more than 60 per cent. of the population do not speak German; but even this exception is to disappear at the end of twenty years from the passing of the Act. A Polish deputy, therefore, must speak to his constituents in German, except at election times—or unless the district in which he is speaking is one which contains more than 60 per cent. of inhabitants who do not speak German.

It is necessary, in order to comprehend the methods and the results of linguistic oppression in the German Empire, to study separately the three main areas of such oppression —Prussian Poland, Danish Schleswig and Alsace-Lorraine. The methods used, and the results attained, were indeed much the same in all the three areas; and the law of 1908 applied to them all equally. But the three areas differ in some respects; and the methods and results of linguistic oppression, so far as it is based on administrative action, which in its nature varies from one area to another, have also shown a number of differences.

In this connection it must be remembered that the Poles and the Danes in the German Empire are subjects of Prussia, and as such were governed by the Prussian Ministry; while the people of Alsace-Lorraine were not included in Prussia, their country being a federal territory (*Reichsland*) governed by the federal authority. Another difference, which is also important, is that the Poles are distinct from the Germans of Prussia both in religion and language; the Danes differ in language, but not in religion; while the majority of the people of Alsace-Lorraine differ in religion (being Roman Catholics), but not in language—speaking, as they do, a German dialect.

In 1815 Frederic William III., in a rescript to his Polish subjects, promised to respect their nationality and to give their language an equal position with German in public meetings. Down to 1870 the promise was on the whole observed. Between 1830 and 1841, it is true, a governor of the province of Posen, Flottwell by name, pursued a policy of Germanization, founding schools to encourage German culture, and buying land from Polish owners to sell it again to Germans. But his policy was not extreme: the Poles remained loyal subjects of Prussia; and they fought for Prussia in the war against Austria in 1866 and the war against France in 1870. Almost immediately after 1870, however, Bismarck began a campaign against the Poles. In 1872 he embarked on a struggle with the Roman Catholic Church, which is the Church of the Poles. "The beginning of the struggle," he says in his "Reflections and Reminiscences," "was decided for me preponderantly by its Polish side"; and he refers to statistics which "proved the rapid progress of the Polish nationality at the expense of the Germans," and to official reports which showed that "there were whole villages in Posen and West Prussia containing thousands of Germans who through the influence of the Catholic section had been educated according to Polish ideas, and were officially described as Poles, though in the previous generation they were officially Germans." To meet this situation, a law of 1872 deprived the clergy of the right of inspecting schools which they had hitherto enjoyed, and gave the work to Government officials. Next year, 1873, an administrative order required that the German language alone should be employed in schools, except for religious instruction—though even for this purpose German might be used, if the pupils were sufficiently advanced to understand the language.

The war thus begun in the schools was continued and extended in succeeding years. A further step was attempted in 1883, when the provincial Government of Posen ordered that religious instruction should be given in German, if half the students in a school were of German birth. The Prussian Minister of Education at the time disapproved of the order, and it was rescinded; but a later Minister, Dr. Studt, reversed the action of his predecessor, and since the beginning of this century the principle of the order of 1883 has been enforced, the alleged grounds being "the awkwardness of a bilingual system of education, and still more the persistent efforts of the Poles to make their privileged position a means of racial isolation." By thus enforcing on Polish children religious instruction given in a language other than their own, the Prussian Government practically turned linguistic oppression into religious persecution; and, indeed, as the confession of Bismarck, quoted above, sufficiently illustrates, the anti-Polish policy of the Government was from the first also anti-Catholic in its motives.

Besides interfering with religious instruction, the Prussian Government also interfered with the life of the family. A decree of 1899, already mentioned above, required teachers—German teachers who had married Polish wives—to cease to use the Polish language in their homes. Children who are deaf-mutes are instructed in German—with the result that they cannot converse with their father and mother, their sisters and brothers. The possession of Polish books dealing with Polish history and literature renders a pupil liable to exclusion from secondary schools. Domiciliary visits by the police are the inevitable result of this rule; and such visits, in their turn, inevitably result in "incidents" and misery. At Thorn, for instance, a town in West Prussia, the police suspected a secret society of schoolboys. They visited the homes of a number of boys attending one of the schools, which they thought to be the center of the "conspiracy," and in six of the homes they found historical and religious books printed in Polish, which were immediately confiscated. Sixty of the boys were charged with belonging to an illegal society, and brought to trial. That there was a society among the boys, and that the object of the society was to study Polish history and literature (subjects excluded from the curriculum of the schools), was not denied; that there was any "conspiracy," or any "illegal" intention, was not and could not be proved. None the less, a number of the boys were expelled from the town and the district— only to be aided, by a sum of £1,000 raised by Polish students in Switzerland, to pursue their studies at Lemberg and Cracow, in Austrian Poland, where the Government was not so impossibly rigorous.

Under conditions such as these, school life becomes a burden and a torment. The German schoolmaster becomes a rigorous martinet: the Polish schoolboy becomes a sullen rebel: the school becomes a battleground. Children are punished by the police for misdemeanors committed in school: one pupil may be confined in a house of correction for not giving his answers in German during a lesson on the catechism; another may be condemned to four months' imprisonment for *lèse-majesté*, because he has spoken "treasonably" about current politics. While children are punished, parents are fined. A French author, writing in 1910, estimates the total of the fines up to that date at a sum of $50,000. The result of the whole system is truancy *en masse* and a system of school-strikes. A series of such strikes began in 1906, and lasted into the spring of 1907. They began in Posen, but they extended as far as Breslau in Silesia. In October, 1906, there were 40,000 children on strike, and in the course of 1907 as many as 60,000. The Government replied with a heavy hand, by wholesale dismissals, imprisonments and fines. For "incitement" to school-strikes 35 priests were sentenced to periods of imprisonment amounting in the aggregate to 20 months, and to fines amounting to $1,500; 1,450 parents were fined $4,500 for the non-attendance of their children at school; other persons were sentenced to terms of imprisonment amounting in the aggregate to 6½ years for offenses connected with the school-strikes.

So far of the schools. Linguistic oppression, however, has also invaded other areas than that of the school. In 1870 Polish was still used in the law courts and Government offices: a Pole might still address the Government in Polish, and still be answered in Polish. That has all been changed. German is now the only language of justice and administration; and just before the war, in 1913, Prussian postmen were refusing to transmit or deliver letters addressed in Polish. Persons with Polish names are pressed or forced to change them to a German form; a Pole called Szulc or Szuman may be fined if he fails to write himself Schultz or Schumann. Villages and streets have been rebaptized in German; over 2,000 streets, it is said, have been thus renamed in the dominant language. Shop signs must be in German; the very inscriptions on tomb-stones must be in German; railway book-stalls must not sell Polish papers. A Polish deputy, speaking in the Prussian Parliament not long ago, could say: "No Pole can plead his own cause before the courts in his mother tongue, and should he wish to employ it before the administrative authorities, he is not heard. Immemorial names are summarily abolished. Family names are distorted by the authorities. Every class meeting is held under police surveillance, and open-air meetings are prohibited altogether, Polish theatrical performances are for the most part forbidden or stopped."

The interference of the Government with public meetings and with the drama—it should also be added, with the Press—is an interference with freedom of thought and its expression only second, if indeed it is second, to interference with freedom of education. The law of 1908 on public meetings has already been mentioned. Polish drama was everywhere prohibited, except, it is said, in the town of Posen during the winter; and Polish amateurs could not produce a Polish play,

because a translation had to be presented to the police in order
that their consent be obtained—a consent which always arrived too late. Polish papers were subject to rigorous supervision, and their editors often found their way to prison,
though this, it should be added, is a fate not unknown to
editors of German papers. The result of this repression was
intellectual stagnation. It is hard for the things of the mind
to flourish under a censorship of this order; and the intellectual life of the Poles migrated steadily from Prussian Poland to the milder air of Austrian Poland.

Yet, in spite of all oppression, the unconquerable spirit of
the Poles has striven to maintain its life and vigor. Voluntary effort and voluntary associations—which have played a
great part in Poland, particularly in the economic sphere, but
also, and with almost equal vigor, in the intellectual—have
been directed to the preservation of the national life. The
"Sokol" associations of the Poles, for social and educational
purposes, are numerous; in 1914 there were said to be as
many as 1,000, each with a membership of about 100. The
congress of Sokols at Posen in 1905 decided to organize
courses of lectures and conferences on literary and historical
subjects. If Polish culture was excluded from the official
schools, it was thus fostered by the voluntary agency of educational associations, which correspond, in their way, to our
own "Workers' Educational Association"; and as long as
these associations were active, Polish speech and Polish culture could not die. The Polish Press, whatever the surveillance to which it was subject, continued to exist; its chief
organ was said to have a circulation of 70,000. Popular
libraries are also flourishing; they disseminate the national
literature, and serve, along with the Press, as an instrument
of national education.

On the whole, the German policy of linguistic oppression
failed to attain its object in Prussian Poland. Indirectly it
even benefited the Poles. Taught to be bilingual, they have
found their gift of tongues to be economically valuable, and
they have been successful competitors for business with
German rivals, who only knew and could only use a single
language. This is an undesigned mercy, which can hardly

excuse those who have been its involuntary donors. It won the Prussian Government no gratitude; while the design and the execution of its linguistic policy turned the Poles, loyal subjects of Prussia fifty years ago, into the ways of passive resistance and resolute, if quiet, defiance. A race which was, and might have continued to be, loyal, if it had been left free to speak and to use its own language, lost its loyalty when it was commanded to speak and to use an alien language as a sign of loyalty.

The perverse policy of the German Government naturally had perverse results. Intended to Germanize the Poles, it made them more Polish. Intended to incorporate them in German culture, it has driven them back on the ardent cultivation of their own. Intended to create loyalty, it destroyed loyalty. Intended to strengthen Germanism, it strengthened the Poles at the expense of the Germans.

"The Polish language," wrote a German professor in 1914, "gains not only in the country districts, but also in the towns, and even in the town of Posen. The Polish middle class grows, while the German decreases." But it is always so. He who sows dragons' teeth can only reap a crop of armed and defiant warriors.

Such is the treatment of their language that has been meted out to the 3,500,000 Poles in Prussia. That treatment was the model which the Germans followed in dealing with the Danes of Northern Schleswig. At first sight it is curious that they should have done so. There are only some 150,000 Danes in Northern Schleswig; and it could hardly have threatened German culture if they had continued to use their own language freely. The Danes, again, are Protestant, like the majority of the Germans of Prussia; and one might have expected to find a natural bond of religious sympathy between Prussia and the Danes, such as could not exist between Prussia and the Catholic Poles.

But the Prussian passion for uniformity and rule triumphed over these differences; and the Danes, in spite of the differences of their position, were treated on parallel lines with the Poles. "To conquer the school is to conquer the future," said Bismarck; and on that line, as we have seen, he acted in dealing with the Poles. It is exactly on the same line that the Prussian Government acted towards the Danes.

It is one of the tragedies of the history of German education that the school, instead of being used as an end in itself, should have been used as a means to political objects. This is the real meaning of Bismarck's saying; and it has been the real motive of much of the educational policy of the Prussian Government. Dr. Studt (the Prussian Minister of Education who was responsible for the order that religious instruction should be given to the Poles in German if half of the pupils of a school were of German birth) is reported to have said in 1907, in visiting North Schleswig, "Teachers should always remember that it is their mission to educate children by inculcating the sentiments of loyalty and love to the German fatherland." To import a political motive into education is fatal to a free and liberal education; and when that political motive results in the use of compulsion, and the drilling of a non-German population in German speech and history and culture, it is fatal to any sort of education at all.

ALSACE-LORRAINE

WHY FRANCE AND GERMANY CONTINUED
IRRECONCILABLE

CHARLES HAZEN   THE OFFICIAL PROTEST OF ALSACE
HEINRICH VON TREITSCHKE   WILLIAM DAVIS

Even more complete than the German government's failure with the Danes and Poles was its failure to satisfy the people of Alsace-Lorraine. Indeed from the time of the seizure of these lands by the newly created German Empire in 1871, their people were so ill-treated that the "Crime of Alsace" remained an ever-festering sore in European statecraft.

The question as to the original State ownership of Alsace and the German-speaking portion of Lorraine is of no importance whatever. From ancient Roman days the ownership of the west bank of the Rhine has been in constant dispute between Teuton and Gaul. Moreover no region in the world possessed any permanent nationality so long as, under the feudal system of medieval times, kings and dukes disposed of their States as private inheritances, splitting them up at will and presenting them as personal gifts to one another.

The people of Alsace only acquired a real nationality of their own in that red birth-hour of Europe's Democracy, the French Revolution. Then at last the awakened Alsatians ceased to belong to some king by his "divine right"; they came into the peoples' "divine right" of Nationality. Passionately they declared themselves French. And thereafter they were French. They sealed their love and loyalty in the blood of a hundred battlefields. In face of this great rich patriotism of the people, no argument pleading that a German emperor or duke of old once held Alsace as part of his inheritance, has any meaning for the modern world.

In 1871 the German Empire seized this French land by force, in defiance of the desperate protests of the Alsatians. That was the original crime. But time heals all ancient wrongs, and a wiser Germany might have at length won the affections of the Alsatians. She did not do so. For over forty years they remained Democrats and Frenchmen, and were persecuted as such.

The conditions of the seizure of Alsace by Germany are here described by America's foremost authority on European history, Professor Hazen of Columbia University. The persecution that followed in the Prussian military effort to force Alsace to become German is given in the words of Professor Davis of the University of Minnesota, quoted from his book, "The Roots of the War." On a theme which has so long vexed Europe we can get our clearest view from unprejudiced American scholars. The extreme German view is voiced by Treitschke, the foremost advocate of progress by conquest. As Professor of History in Berlin in the 1890's and favorite historical lecturer to the Court, he established the view of official Germany.

BY CHARLES HAZEN [1]

THE Treaty of Frankfort, which closed the Franco-German War of 1870, transferred to Germany from France a territory nearly as large as the States of Connecticut and Rhode Island, 5,600 square miles, 1,700 villages, towns and cities, and 1,600,000 human beings, the consent of not one of whom was either asked or given.

What reasons did the Germans give for this momentous act, this violent mutilation of a neighbor, this subjection of a million six hundred thousand of its citizens to an alien rule? Many different arguments were urged by many different kinds of people. Poets, historians, editors gave one set of reasons, economists another, military men and Bismarck still a different one. It was the opinions and the determination of the military men and of Bismarck that really counted and were decisive. Nevertheless the latter were entirely willing that the German masses should be influenced by considerations less harsh and materialistic, provided only they were influenced in the same direction and toward the same end. Virtue in their opinion had its place in the world of thought and action, only virtue should never become a fetish. This danger has thus far been successfully avoided in Germany.

The argument that presented the fairest exterior, and that influenced the great popular classes of Germany, justifying this forcible annexation against their will of a protesting people, was that after all these people had once been Germans, and were Germans still in all essentials, and that, as soon as they found themselves once more in the German family, the false and perverted ideas that the French régime had inculcated in them would drop away, and the "long-lost brothers" would thus be liberated not only in body but in soul from an intolerable and unworthy thraldom to the foreigner. It was widely asserted that the Alsatians were real Germans at heart despite the attempts of the French to make them French, and that annexation, as soon as it was an accom-

---

[1] Reproduced from the *Unpopular Review* by kind permission of Messrs. Henry Holt & Co.

plished fact and, therefore, safe, would be greeted by them with unfeigned satisfaction and joy.

This was the argument of Germany's historical rights, an argument which can be clearly presented only if given at length, a task from which we are precluded here. Alsace and Lorraine had once been included within the boundaries of the Holy Roman Empire. Therefore, they should be included within the new German Empire. But so had Holland and so had Switzerland been parts of the Holy Roman Empire, but had long been independent, and were entirely satisfied with their independence, and were highly resolved to maintain it, as their history and their constant attitude amply demonstrated. Was this a reason for Germany's resuming them? Nowadays the Pan-Germanists believe that Germany should do this very thing, but in 1870 the reason was not considered applicable to them, though it was considered pertinent and adequate to the case of Alsace-Lorraine. The Germans said that the annexation of Alsace to France was the work of a robber-king, Louis XIV., who had torn it from Germany; and that Germany, now that she had the power, had also the duty to take back the stolen goods. We have no desire to enter upon a defense of Louis XIV. His political morality was not fundamentally superior to that of the present ex-Emperor of Germany. But he lived in the seventeenth century, while William II. lives in the twentieth.

Moreover it is altogether too summary a statement to say that Louis XIV. simply seized Alsace-Lorraine by an unjust and wanton use of force. To say, as Count von Hertling does, that they were snatched by a robber king is an undue simplification of history. The process of annexation began in 1552 with the acquisition of Metz, Toul and Verdun, in return, it should never be forgotten, for services to the Protestants of Germany in their war against Charles V., bent upon the extermination of Protestantism. A part was secured by violence and usurpation during the succeeding period. A century later, in 1766, Lorraine was incorporated in France by an entirely natural and peaceful process, the extinction of the reigning house by death, and the passage by inheritance of the country to the related House of Bourbon.

Mulhouse voluntarily and unanimously sought incorporation in France in 1798.

Thus Alsace and Lorraine became French. The process covered therefore a period of two hundred and forty-six years. One thing is certain, the robber king did not reign or live that long. German historical exegesis is sometimes too curt.

Having acquired Alsace and Lorraine, France did something which Germany did not do after 1871. She ruled them well and humanely. She gave them the maximum of liberty. She left them largely alone, trusting to time and not to compulsion to reveal to them the advantage of the French connection. Gradually and quietly, without friction or injustice or heart-burning, the Alsatians and Lorrainers found themselves more comfortable, more prosperous, more peaceful than they had ever been. And when the French Revolution came, with its attractive, captivating message of liberty and equality, with its powerful attack upon a despotic past, upon feudalism and tyranny in social and political customs and institutions, when the tonic and invigorating spirit of the new era of democracy swept over France it found no more enthusiastic adherents than in Alsace and Lorraine. By a profound intellectual and spiritual sympathy, by a complete community of interests and convictions, those provinces became French through and through in every fiber of their being. The evidence of this complete and willing and joyous absorption of Alsace-Lorraine in the life of France is overwhelming.

The Napoleonic period continued the work of consolidation and inner fusion. Alsace and Lorraine were swallowed up, like all the other provinces of Old France, in the general history of the country. They took an honorable, wholehearted and distinguished part in the long series of Napoleonic wars. By every token a people could give, they were completely and proudly French.

On the Arc de Triomphe in Paris are inscribed the names of twenty-eight Alsatian and Lorraine generals, among others, Kellermann and Kléber, Lefebvre and Rapp, Custine and Marshal Ney. The careers and characters of these men were the common talk of the Alsatian fireside and of the camp. They were the heroes of the people, adding imperishable luster to the history of Alsace and Lorraine, their native lands.

In the face of evidence like this, it was sheer and jejune nonsense to claim, as many of the Germans did, that the people of these provinces were Germans, long-lost brothers, waiting to be delivered from bondage. Some of them knew that this was nonsense, though they would not admit it or would only half concede the facts. Heinrich von Sybel, friend of Bismarck, and historian of the Founding of the German Empire, made at the time a brief for Germany's right to the provinces, basing it on ancient possession, yet he said this in 1871 :

"We know, indeed, that the Lorrainers since 1766, the Alsatians since 1801, have become good Frenchmen, and to-day, oppose, by a large majority, the reunion with their Fatherland. For such an attitude, we do not deny, we feel respect. The inhabitants were born and brought up in the great French commonwealth; they would be men destitute of common feeling and patriotism if, notwithstanding their German speech, they did not consider themselves French to-day. But we trust to the power of Nature; water can be diverted for a time into artificial channels, but with the removal of the dam will flow with the full stream. If to-day the inhabitants find the French more sympathetic than the Germans, soon they will find themselves among their own kind in Germany. In Germany they will find the best gifts of the French State, the consciousness and security of a mighty commonwealth, a sound harvest of science and art, a wide market for their industry, and a progressive parliamentary life. They will have lower taxes, greater religious freedom, numerous schools, and in the army will meet the sons of the educated class."

It may be said in passing that the Alsatians and Lorrainers have not found their own kind in Germany since they were forced to become subjects of the Empire, nor have they participated in a particularly progressive parliamentary life, nor has their service in the German army been to their taste or advantage.

Other reasons in justification of their seizure of Alsace-Lorraine were urged by the Germans, and have been reiterated ever since. Ethnology has been invoked. Skulls in Alsace are of the German type. Ethnic unity should be represented by political unity. To which it may be replied that in Alsace are also abundantly found skulls that are of the Celtic type. Moreover if Germany has the right to annex this country by reason of ethnic affinity, by what right does she hold unwilling Polish people, who are racially utterly dissimilar, Slavs not Teutons? Evidently what is sauce for the goose is not necessarily sauce for the gander. This ethnological argument is not serious, nor is the other one that, as the Alsatians largely speak German, they are Germans and belong in the German Empire. Yet this argument has seemed to a good many superficial people to have weight. Are those who speak a given language justified in forcibly annexing others who speak it? In Switzerland three languages are spoken, and the one most widely spoken is German. Would the Germans be justified in annexing the larger part of Switzerland, France in annexing the French cantons, Italy the Italian?

If the map of Europe is to be based on the linguistic theory of one language, one people, it will have to be redrawn from top to bottom and from end to end, and will when completed along the new line present a surprising and shocking appearance. For in nearly every existing state of Europe more than one language is in use; in the British Isles, Gaelic, Welsh, English; in France, Breton, Basque, Provençal, Italian, French; in Finland, Swedish, Russian, Finnish; in Austria-Hungary at least ten different languages; in Russia a considerable number.

Moreover, one is tempted to ask if the fact that the people of the United States speak English would give England title to our country which, it will be recalled, once belonged to the British Empire. If the German Empire, created in 1871, has the right to "resume" what had belonged to the Holy Roman Empire, which died in 1806, it is difficult to deny similar privileges to the British Empire, which has never died, but has had a continuous history. And those privileges should also be extended to Spain, which once ruled most of Central and South America, where Spanish is still spoken. Evidently Count von Hertling's linguistic statesmanship leaves out of account some rather important historical factors necessary to the picture of the contemporary world. It is not a panacea for the ills of the world; it is a quack medicine, liberally advertised, and the honesty of whose proprietor is not absolutely above reproach.

But the Germans had still other arguments. In annexing Alsace-Lorraine, in drawing the western boundary as they did, they said that they were but establishing the "natural" boundary. In other words the Vosges, being mountains, are a natural obstacle of importance, therefore, a fit frontier, while the Rhine, being a river, is not one. Concerning this it may be said that the Vosges mountains are not Alps, and that the Rhine was considered a boundary by Julius Cæsar, and has always been and will always be a formidable ditch to cross in the face of an enemy controlling the other side. Moreover, in 1871, the Germans were not bound by the theory when it didn't suit them. They pushed their line west of the Vosges whenever they saw a sufficient advantage in so doing.

These various reasons for the annexation of Alsace-Lorraine were not the real ones that determined the action of the Government. They were simply so much food for gudgeon, so much dust for the eyes of excessive innocence. Military reasons were the primary reasons for the famous act. The boundary was determined largely by the military men. They wished Metz, and they took it, because, as Moltke said, it was the equivalent of an army of a hundred thousand men, though it was west of the linguistic boundary, and as French as Bordeaux itself.

The Germans took Alsace because it would be, as Bismarck said, an admirable *glacis,* a military zone behind which is a fortress, in fact a powerful first line fortification. It was on the ground of military necessity, in other words of military advantage, that Germany made the annexations of

1871. Bismarck, there is abundant reason to believe, took no stock in the other arguments to which we have alluded—that of language, that of the natural frontier, that of historical right. These theories might be valuable, as they had an influence over the popular mind. Over his own mind they apparently had none. In 1867 he expressed in an interview the following opinion: "Suppose," he said, "France entirely conquered, and a Prussian garrison in Paris; what are we to do with our victory? We could not even decently take Alsace, for the Alsatians are become Frenchmen and wish to remain so." But by October, 1870, after the Prussian victories of August and September, he sang a different tune. "Germany," he then said, "wants peace and will make war until she gets it, let the consequences be ever so lamentable from a humane point of view. . . . This peace will be secured by a line of fortresses between Strassburg and Metz, as well as by those two towns, which will protect Germany against the dread of a second attack by France." At the end of the following January, after the capitulation of Paris, his words were as follows: "As you see, we are keeping Metz; but I confess I do not like that part of the arrangement. Strassburg is German in speech and will be so in heart ten years hence. Metz, however, is French, and will be a hotbed of disaffection for a long time to come."

Military reasons then were the primary reasons for the annexation of Alsace-Lorraine. Another reason, powerful with the government, was the economic advantage to be derived. Germany wished the coal and iron mines of these provinces. She had begun the process of acquiring such lands at the expense of France in 1815 after the overthrow of Napoleon. She carried it much farther in 1871. It is to the annexation of 1871 that she is indebted for much of her industrial strength to-day, the basis of her political power and of her vaulting ambition. In 1913, out of 28,000,000 tons of iron ore extracted from German soil, 21,000,000 came from the mines of annexed Lorraine. To the rapes of 1815 and 1871, Germany owes much, as she is very well aware. The French, having lost their mines, subsequently discovered others in the part of Lorraine left to them in 1871, in the valley of the Briey.

In 1913, owing to the expansion of her industries, Germany was obliged to import from abroad 14,000,000 tons of iron ore. This is almost the exact amount annually extracted from the mines of Briey, which Germany seized at the beginning of the present war.

But there is another angle from which this famous transaction must be contemplated, the point of view of those most immediately concerned. In February, 1871, before even the negotiations for peace between France and Germany began, the people of Alsace-Lorraine protested against what they saw was coming. Their representatives in the French National Assembly solemnly declared "the immutable will of Alsace and Lorraine to remain French territory," asserted that France could not agree to the cession of Alsace and Lorraine, that the French people did not have the right to accept such a mutilation, that France might "experience the blows of force, but could not sanction its decrees," that Europe could "neither permit nor ratify the abandonment of Alsace and Lorraine," that it could not allow "the seizure of a people as a common herd" nor permit a peace which would be "a legitimate and permanent provocation to war." The conclusion of this protest was as follows: "Wherefore we call our fellow-citizens of France and the governments and peoples of the entire world to witness in advance that we hold to be null and void every act and treaty, vote or plebiscite, which would consent to the abandonment, in favor of the foreigner, of all or of any part of our provinces of Alsace and Lorraine."

Two weeks later, on March 1, 1871, immediately after the ratification of the preliminaries of peace by the National Assembly, the representatives of the sacrificed provinces again solemnly protested against outraged right. This famous protest, whose passion and whose pathos have since moved all right-thinking men for two generations and ought to arrest and fix the attention of the world to-day, should be read in full.

THE PROTEST OF 1871

The representatives of Alsace and Lorraine submitted to the Assembly, before peace negotiations were begun, a declaration affirming in the most formal way, in the name of the two provinces, their will and their right to remain French.

Handed over, in contempt of all justice and by an odious abuse of force, to the domination of foreigners, we now have a final duty to perform.

We declare once more null and void a compact which disposes of us without our consent.

Henceforth and forever each and every one of us will be completely justified in demanding our rights in whatever way and manner our consciences may approve.

At the moment of leaving the chamber where our dignity no longer permits us to sit and in spite of the bitterness of our grief, the supreme thought which we find at the bottom of our hearts is a thought of gratitude to those who, for six months, have not ceased to fight in our defense, and our unalterable attachment to France from which we are torn by violence.

We shall follow you with our wishes and we shall await with entire confidence in the future, the resumption by a regenerated France of the course of her great destiny.

Your brothers of Alsace and Lorraine, now cut off from the common family, will preserve for France, absent from their hearths, a filial affection until the day when she shall resume her rightful place there once more.

BY HEINRICH VON TREITSCHKE

In view of our obligation to secure the peace of the world, who will venture to object that the people of Alsace and Lorraine do not want to belong to us? The doctrine of the right of all the branches of the German race to decide on their own destinies, the plausible solution of demogogues without a fatherland, shivers to pieces in presence of the sacred necessity of these great days. These territories are ours by the right of the sword, and we shall dispose of them in virtue of a higher right—the right of the German nation, which will not permit its lost children to remain strangers to the German Empire. We Germans who know Germany and France know better than these unfortunates themselves what is good for the people of Alsace, who have remained under the misleading influence of their French connection outside the sympathies of new Germany. Against their will we shall restore them to their true selves. . . . Before the nineteenth century closes, the world will recognize that the spirits of Erwin von Steinbach and Sebastian Brandt are still alive, and that we were only obeying the dictates of national honor when we made little account of the preferences of the people who live in Alsace today.

BY WILLIAM STEARNS DAVIS [2]

Unfortunately the conquerors of 1871 had never learned the sage proverb: "The more haste, the less speed." If loyal subjects of the Kaiser could have been made by ministerial edicts from Berlin, the Alsatians would have been instantly contented and happy: but they were not Brandenburgers. Their lands had been trampled over by invading armies: their homes had often been desolated: Strassburg had been ruthlessly bombarded: while up and down the whole land they were still mourning their dead. On the 30th of September, 1872, the new government, however, enforced its edict compelling all the people to decide whether they wished to be Germans or Frenchmen. If Germans they must submit to the new régime. If Frenchmen they must prepare speedily to quit the land of their fathers wherein they were now counted as alien interlopers. As a result, at the very least 45,000 persons (in the main among the most intelligent and promising young men in the land) deliberately took the sorrowful road to exile. In 1914 these men, gray-headed now, were to see visions, dream dreams, and say moving things to the soldiers of France. Almost simultaneously the teaching of the French language in elementary schools was forbidden.

[2] Copyright, 1918. Reprinted by the kind permission of The Century Co.

In the city of Strassburg, where the *Marseillaise* had first been flung upon the air, it was prohibited to learn its language, save as a "foreign tongue" for advanced pupils, like English, Italian and Russian. Under French occupation a certain mongrel type of German had always been spoken in the Alsatian villages. The French had never troubled about this. It had not prevented the Alsatians from being zealous patriots. Now, by a natural reaction, many a Teuton-speaking Alsatian prided himself on chattering also a little bad French.

But what drove the annexed population to peculiar wrath, was the almost instant enforcement of the German military conscription. Their slain brethren in the French uniform were hardly cold and buried before the youth of the two provinces were commanded to don the spiked helmet and follow the Prussian drill-sergeant. Vain were protests. In 1871 a deputation of citizens went up to Berlin to expostulate. Bismarck told them brusquely, "Prussia had an immense experience of the results produced by wearing the Prussian uniform. Get the King's coat on a man's back and let him wear it for three years, and you have made not only a good soldier but a good 'burgher' [for Germany] out of him." "Yes," retorted Klein, leader of the deputation, "but you must get the coat on first and *that* is what you can never do!" Twelve thousand Alsatian young men at that time fled from their homeland merely to escape the Kaiser's livery, and entered the French army. The rest submitted outwardly, but with a sullen spirit that made them of most dubious value as soldiers. The new régime might introduce an admirable legal system and build many new railroads,—all this counted for nothing beside the tyranny of the drill-master.

The conquerors had in fact adopted a relentless policy of "thorough," and held to it with native tenacity. Under the French régime, whatever the Paris government, the Alsatians had enjoyed pretty complete local autonomy. The French prefect had usually been a lax, good-natured functionary, only meddling in serious cases. The government had no doubt been haphazard, unscientific, somewhat inefficient—and popular. Now everything was changed. A swarm of officials with all the Prussian characteristics, plus even greater rigidity—thanks to feeling themselves on the defensive and to being charged with the propagation of *Kultur*—was turned loose on the land with autocratic powers. Down to 1879 the two provinces were ruled practically by a military dictator sent from Berlin. In that year an attempt was made to set up a simulacrum of constitutional rule. The provinces were henceforth to be a "Reichsland," a dominion held by all the Empire in common, not by Prussia merely, but with the Kaiser appointing the governor-general and otherwise exercising pretty complete sway. There were to be a local elective diet and other forms of political "freedom," but the powers of the governor-general and his council (appointed by the crown) were such that the voters could do little more than register public protests by their ballots at one governmental act after another. The Berlin rulers did indeed make a serious attempt to conciliate local opinion by sending down for once a really humane and enlightened governor, Baron von Manteuffel. His intentions were good, and he tried sincerely to let the Alsatians preserve their self-respect. "I do not ask for your sympathy," he declared, "but I advise you to look on the union of Alsace-Lorraine to the German Empire as definitive."

Von Manteuffel won the personal good will of the people he was sent to govern. But his very condescension raised against him enemies at home. He was accused by his fellow Germans of "negotiating with the enemy" because he adopted mild measures; and the horde of lesser officials who had swarmed into the new province, greedy adventurers ("carpet-baggers" Americans would call them), anxious only to seize on every public post, tyrannize and grow fat, denounced him as little better than a traitor. In 1887 he died. The Alsatians mourned him, but he had not convinced them their new masters were anything but despots. At many an election the deputies Alsace-Lorraine sent up to the Reichstag were violent "protesters" against the new régime, and the friction grew rather than diminished. It was under Manteuffel that the Bishop of Metz was awarded the Prussian

Order of the Crown, which he repaid by expressing his regret at this unwelcome honor in a public letter to the governor.

When Manteuffel died, the small-fry officials felt that their time was come. Kindness had failed; "proper severity" should now teach these returned but ungrateful sons of the Fatherland, the provincials, to appreciate their blessings. What happened soon after is thus summed up by Paul Hymans, a native Alsatian,—born in 1874 after the annexation, and witness to many things. "Within a few months Alsace was subjected to every kind of German brutality. Deputies were expelled and Alsatian societies were dissolved. Political prosecutions took place on every side, for offenses such as seditious cries or emblems, membership in the 'League of Patriots,' high treason, etc. To guard the Alsatians against 'intimidation' by their French relatives, intercourse with persons beyond the frontier was made impossible by a regulation prescribing the use of passports." There was even a report that Bismarck wished there would be an insurrection in the hope of crushing disaffection once for all in blood.

The natives were too wise for such folly. They offered the passive resistance which is always so exasperating to a government which demands inward submission as well as external obedience. Of course all important government offices were retained by Germans from across the Rhine. Emigrants were sent in from Prussia to take the farms of the exiles who had gone to France, just as other colonists had been sent into the Polish lands. The newcomers naturally were treated as pariahs by the natives. Their social relations were miserable. A Prussian came to Alsace as a stationmaster. Being a domestic soul, he desired a wife; no Alsatian girl would marry him. He was obliged to send to Berlin for a consort to share his home and responsibilities. In all, about 300,000 Germans thus settled in the Reichsland; but they remained a mere army of occupation among the 1,550,000 odd natives who longed to see them go. They were only so many untactful provocatives to friction and a new disloyalty.

After William II. had ousted Bismarck, there was a partial relaxation of the worst of the régime of petty officials that had followed Manteuffel. William, however, by his speeches gave small encouragement to the hopes of the Alsatians for a revocation of the deed of 1871. "We would rather," said he in an oration, "sacrifice our eighteen army corps and our 42,000,000 inhabitants on the field of battle than surrender a single stone my father and [his generals] . . . have gained."

A new generation was growing up in Alsace-Lorraine: young men and women to whom French days were a story for their elders, but the new generation was not being won for the German régime. Unfortunately for their loyalty the Alsatians as a race had a keen sense of humor. It was not always possible for them to take their Prussian preceptors with sufficient seriousness. In 1895 occurred a typical incident at Detwiller, a village near Zabern. A certain peasant had a fine white cock with a lordly red crest. The owner most treasonably dyed the bird's tail blue— making him the veritable emblem and colors of France. This overt act was promptly denounced by the emperor's loyal police. They ordered the peasant to slaughter his sedition-teaching fowl. The man refused. The police saber then avenged the outraged fatherland: and so the feathered traitor perished. The Paris papers made merry over the tale: and diplomats more gravely observed that the incident had completely effaced all the efforts of the Kaiser to cultivate "good relations" with France at the opening of the Kiel Canal and the visit there of some French warships.[3]

From the beginning of the third emperor's reign down to the eve of the great conflict matters did not better them-

[3] German self-seriousness and lack of humor produced weird results sometimes in Alsace. A German Protestant clergyman visited an Alsatian pastor's family. He tried hard to persuade his clerical friend to speak German in his household. The other replied that "his wife insisted on speaking French." The visiting cleric vainly argued that it was weak and cowardly to be thus dominated by a woman. Finding his efforts unsuccessful, he sent his friend a treatise "On the Biological Imbecility of Woman" (*"Über den biologischen-Schwachsinn des Weibes"*). The Pan-German congress, to which he formally reported this deplorable case of demi-treason, duly applauded his patriotic endeavors.

selves. Sometimes it was a case of petty persecution, sometimes of grievous invasion of ordinary human rights

Finally in 1911 the German authorities conferred on their Reichsland a moderately complete autonomy with a real local constitution, putting it somewhat on a par with the other German states, although the governor-general was still sent down from Berlin and there were other unpleasant evidences of servitude. This long-delayed benevolence produced no lucky results. The newly elected "Landtag" promptly showed its disaffection by cutting down the governor-general's salary, and refusing to vote the annual allowance for the Emperor's hunting trips to Alsace, when he had deigned to chase a few stags and flush some partridges in the game preserves of this part of his dominions. The Prussians promptly retaliated in 1912 by canceling the orders for locomotives for their state railways which had been given to an Alsatian concern. That same year the "All-Highest" visited Strassburg and flung his imperial warning at the Mayor. "Listen! Up to now you have only known the good side of me; you might be able to learn the other side of me. Things cannot continue as they are: if this situation lasts, *we will suppress your Constitution and annex you to Prussia!*"

The Social Democrats all over the empire of course danced with glee at this threat. Their spokesman in the Reichstag declared that here was a confession, on the very highest authority, "that annexation to Prussia is the heaviest punishment one can threaten to impose upon a people for resistance against Germany. It is punishment like hard labor in the penitentiary, with loss of civil rights!" The Landtag, however, was not suitably intimidated. It answered the Kaiser by two resolutions: (1) that their new constitution was not to be altered save by the will of the Alsatians themselves; (2) that the Reichsland should have a national flag. Neither of these suggestions of course was acceptable at Berlin, and so the stress continued.

In 1913 came the notorious Zabern incident. Zabern was a pleasant little city in Alsace. In its garrison was the 91st Prussian infantry, and among the officers thereof was a youthful lieutenant of the true junker school, a certain noble Baron von Forstner of some twenty years of age, who took his honors very seriously. School children and factory lads seem to have called names at him, and he, in addressing his men, seems to have retaliated by styling the Alsatian recruits *Wackes,* a local title of derogation. There was another story that he had promised his men a ten-mark piece if one of them brought down a Social Democrat, provided it came to shooting. The reports of von Forstner's crude remarks spread; the town papers grew caustic and the colonel of the garrison, von Reuter, warned the local civil magistrate, Director Mahler, to restore order (there having been small demonstrations) or he would do so himself. On November 29, 1913, Mahler having refused to object to lawful proceedings, when a civilian crowd gathered in front of the barracks, von Reuter directed a subaltern to order it to go home. The angry burghers refused, whereupon the military charged out and arrested some fifteen civilians, including three high judges and the state prosecuting attorney himself who chanced to get caught in the throng. These four dignitaries were speedily released; the other civilians were held in durance vile over night and then released.

This clash of burgher and soldier produced wrath throughout Germany; von Reuter was already hated by the liberals as an exponent of extreme junker theories. He was tried for violating the law which forbade the soldiery to interfere in civilian matters, but was promptly acquitted by his military court on a technicality. The wrath of the liberals was great, and it was shared by many level-headed conservatives. The Governor-General of Alsace himself felt constrained to resign as a protest at this usurpation of civilian functions—but an order from the Emperor commanding the military henceforth to keep within their authority caused him to withdraw his action.

Very quickly, however, Zabern and the noble lieutenant, Baron von Forstner, again gave business for the telegraph. This highborn gentleman had not been wisely withdrawn to another garrison town less acquainted with his mannerisms. He fell into an undignified altercation with a lame shoemaker of the neighborhood. Very probably the clown presumed upon his physical weakness and made unflattering remarks. Von Forstner, not feeling that his opponent's infirmity should be any protection, drew his saber and wounded the cripple. Once more there was uproar. Von Forstner was promptly tried by court martial. In a lower court he was convicted and sentenced to one year in custody; a higher tribunal, however, promptly took up the case on appeal and acquitted the lieutenant "for self-defense"! [4]

Von Forstner had thus vindicated his "honor," so dear to every Prussian officer, by repaying revilings with a blow from the noble's weapon, but in the Reichstag civilian wrath boiled over. The defense of the government advanced by Bethmann-Hollweg was feeble and evasive; and oil was poured on the flames by the arrogance of the war minister, who spoke also, and said bluntly that von Forstner might have been overanxious to protect himself, but that such a "courageous young officer" was an asset to the nation. The chancellor was of course not so much to blame as the military officials, and behind them the Kaiser, their chief, who had allowed the folly of a subaltern workman, and the "lewd fellows of the baser sort" in an Alsatian town, to make a great national issue. But it was easier to bait Bethmann-Hollweg than William of Hohenzollern and the War Office. The Reichstag, on the 6th of December, 1913, passed a vote of censure upon the government, 393 to 54, only the ever-faithful Conservatives voting in behalf of the military.

Had this vote of censure been carried in almost any other European parliament, the Prime Minister and all his subordinates would have resigned immediately. As it was, Bethmann-Hollweg, holding his office not by parliamentary majorities but by the good favor of the Kaiser and the military, smiled blandly and continued with the next items on the government program. Only the socialists were bold

[4] The crippled shoemaker was held by two soldiers while their lieutenant slashed him. *Afterwards* a pocket knife was discovered in the civilian's pocket. It was against this that the officer defended himself.

enough to insist that he should quit office. The "National Liberals" and the "Centrum," although they had voted for the censure, were unwilling to force the issue. The Reichstag had simply expressed the opinion of a pretentious, officially recognized debating club.

Nevertheless the incident had sent panic through the junkers and the princely gentlemen in the Potsdam palaces. Doubtless they cursed von Forstner and von Reuter roundly in private as "blockheads" and "asses" even while they publicly defended them. The rift between the civilians and the military had been advertised too clearly.

The Zabern incident, in other words, taught the junkers, the Pan-German propagandists, and their allies, the great manufacturers who were clutching at world trade, that despite the great material prosperity they had brought the Empire, despite the careful drilling of public opinion, their position was getting precarious. It doubtless had its effect upon their august personal head, the God-crowned Emperor and King. Its whole effect surely was to get them all to quicken their efforts, already promising fearful success, to ease the home situation by a foreign war.

In that same year (1913) the situation became so bad that Alsatian conscripts who had lately, as a special favor, been allowed to render their army service near their home towns as were the rest of their fellow citizens, were now ordered to perform their terms in the army at a distance from their native state.[5]

Nineteen hundred and fourteen saw increased friction, with the poet-artist, Jacob Waltz, one of the most distinguished literary men in Alsace, under prosecution for treason because of satires upon the German administration in the form of books for children. For this crime he was tried before the Imperial Supreme Court at Leipzig, acquitted on the more serious charge, but sentenced to one year's imprisonment "for insulting the police and inciting to disorder." He fled to France, and very soon thereafter

---

[5] During three sojourns in Germany the author was assured that the Alsatian conscripts could not be trusted in battle on the Western front. In 1914 I understand they were actually mobilized against Russia.

the Great War began, at the outbreak of which several prominent Alsatians either escaped over the border or were imprisoned for the attempt.

When the European conflict commenced it was clear enough that the German attempt to assimilate Alsace had failed utterly. "In Alsace-Lorraine we are in an enemy's country," a Prussian statesman is quoted as saying: and the Kaiser's forces were sent through the country with a healthy anxiety lest the first defeat make the whole region blaze up in revolt behind them. Many of the "needful severities" the Germans inflicted on Belgium were explained as being absolutely unavoidable, because the experience of Alsace-Lorraine had demonstrated that a policy of "leniency" was useless for a conquered population. The fact of course was, as an American writer has well put it, that "begotten as the Prussian system had been under conditions where iron discipline was a requisite for success, thoroughly convinced of its own efficiency, it knew no law but that of force, and failed in those peaceful contests where victory must be won by conciliation."

However, the issue of the lost provinces had still larger bearings, important for all the world. A calm-minded Frenchman stated the issue as seen by his nation thus: "It is produced by *an irreconcilable opposition between two conflicting conceptions of right;* sovereignty of government by right of conquest—the principle of the German monarchy; sovereignty of the people, whence arises the right of every population to determine its nationality—the principle of French democracy."

In 1884 the "International Peace League," one of those multifarious and pathetically ineffective peace societies which were covering the earth, met at Geneva and passed this resolution: "The conquest and forcible annexation of Alsace-Lorraine constitutes the chief obstacle to [lasting] peace, and the true cause of the enormous armaments." This statement was still true with only a slight exaggeration in 1914. If Germany had been sure of the loyalty of her Reichsland and on reasonably good terms with France, Armageddon could hardly have come to pass as it actually did.

AUSTRIA FINDS DANGER IN THE BALKANS

GROWTH OF A NATIONAL SPIRIT AMONG THE SERBS

CONSTANTIN DUMBA   G. M. TREVELYAN

Let us look now, in briefer fashion, to the racial problems of Austria, her treatment of her vassal peoples, her resistance to the everywhere rising tide of Nationalism and Democracy, and her consequent difficulties with Serbia and with Russia.

Some clever maker of phrases may in some far future day dismiss the Great War as "the war about pigs." From one narrow viewpoint, that is what it was. Serbia's main product for export, her main source of national wealth, was the humble pig. But since the little mountain land was persistently barred from access to the sea, her export of pigs was largely dependent on the goodwill of her neighbors. Her eastern neighbor, Bulgaria, raised pigs also and naturally sought to bar the Serbian product in that direction. Hence for many years Serbia's chief commercial outlet for her pigs was through Austria. The Austrian government, after annexing Bosnia in 1909, declared war on the Serbian pig. He was barred from entry into Austria. Thus Serbia faced economic destruction. So serious was the situation that King Peter of Serbia and his councilors solemnly considered the necessity of surrender, of placing their land under Austria's government and so reopening the market. Instead they fought the two Balkan wars against Turkey and Bulgaria, and emerged triumphant, thinking that now surely they had won a seaport, a means of exit for the pigs. But Austria, and also Italy, in the peace treaty of 1913 in the Balkans, the Treaty of Bucharest, barred Serbia from the sea. Thus Austria still held her little rival in economic slavery. What wonder that the Serbian hatred for Austria overleaped diplomatic bounds!

This of course was only one phase of the Balkan quarrels; but Austria dealt with all problems in the same spirit. She took the calmly Teutonic attitude that her rights, her wishes, must override all others. What matter if Serbia perished, so long as Austria expanded. This faith is well expressed by Dr. Dumba, the Austrian Ambassador to the United States in 1914. In offering to explain the situation to Americans, Dr. Dumba sees the Balkan troubles solely as a crafty diplomatic struggle between Austria and Russia. He assumes as an axiom that some great Power will of course devour the little Balkan States and only exerts himself to show how wickedly Russia works and how nobly Austria conducts what he calmly calls her "natural expansion toward the east." That phrase in fact has long been the catchword of Austrian policy, the *"Drang nach Oest,"* the "Summons toward the East," the "Call of the Orient."

For a more sympathetic view of the Serbians themselves, it has

seemed better to offer not a Serbian writer but a more impartial statement by a well-known British essayist who dwelt for a time in Serbia.
It should be remembered that Britain was not, at the outbreak of the
War, pro-Serbian. She would never have fought for Serbia, but was
inclined officially to approve of punishing her for "disturbing the peace
of Europe"—even though that peace was to Serbia but a form of death.

C. F. H.

BY CONSTANTIN THEODOR DUMBA

THE war between Austria-Hungary and Russia may well
be said to be the outcome of conflicting civilizations
and conflicting aims. The controversy between the Dual
Monarchy and the Serbian Kingdom is only an incident in
the greater struggle between German civilization, as represented by Austria-Hungary, and Russian aspirations on the
southern frontier of the Dual Monarchy. To a proper understanding of the conflicting trend of these two forces—
Austria-Hungary and Russia—a realization of the respective interests of the two Powers in the Near East is essential.

Our interest in the Near East is economic, and not at all
nationalistic. Russia's interest is solely sentimental or nationalistic. The Monarchy was the dominant trade factor
in the Balkan States. Russia has no trade worth mention-
ing, either in Serbia or in any other Balkan State. The
Gagarin line of steamers on the Danube, which Russia maintained at great cost, carried hardly any freight to Belgrade,
except supplies for the Russian minister in the Serbian
capital. Austria-Hungary sent merchants and commercial
travelers into the Balkan States. Russia, on the other
hand, sent priests, consuls, agitators, and apostles of the
Slavic idea.

The natural expansion of the German Empire of Austria
toward the Near East began after the permanent expulsion
of the Turkish hordes by the victories of Prince Eugene of
Savoy. Parallel with the Austrian expansion southeastward
went the Russian advance toward the Black Sea. In an
effort to avert a clash in this parallel but gradually con-
centering expansion, Emperor Joseph and Empress Catha-
rine met late in the eighteenth century—1787—in the Cri-
mea, and reached an agreement for the dismemberment of

Turkey. Under this project of monarchs, the western part of the Ottoman Empire, including Bosnia-Herzegovina, now the bone of contention between the Monarchy on the one hand and Russia and Serbia on the other, was apportioned to Austria. To Russia's share were allotted the regions now known as Rumania and Bulgaria. It was at this period that the Russian dream of the possession of Constantinople, first broached in the form of a mythical will of Peter the Great, began to assume reality as a governing principle of Russian policy in southeastern Europe.

In the nineteenth century, Metternich, in vain, tried his conservative policy for the maintenance of the territorial integrity of Turkey. The Monarchy's championship of Turkey as a permanent territorial and political entity in Europe failed because of Russia's persistent aggressions. At the Congress of Berlin, in 1878, which adjusted the boundaries of the Balkan Peninsula after the Russo-Turkish War, Count Andrassy abandoned this policy of Prince Metternich. Under the treaty negotiated in Berlin, the independence of the kingdoms of Serbia and Rumania was recognized and the tributary principality of Bulgaria was created. In these arrangements the principle of nationality was the predominant consideration. Count Andrassy's chief interest in the proceedings of the Congress on behalf of Austria-Hungary was commercial, as Russia's was sentimental or nationalistic.

Andrassy sought to secure an outlet for our industrial products. This attitude was in accord with Austria's previous dealings with Balkan peoples. He first concluded a commercial treaty with Rumania before it was an independent kingdom. Accordingly, one of the clauses which were incorporated into the Treaty of Berlin at Austria's behest placed Serbia under the obligation to reach a commercial understanding with the Dual Monarchy. But even this obligation Serbia carried out only under great pressure from Vienna.

Another outcome of the Congress of Berlin—and a fateful one, as now appears—was the mandate of the Powers for the occupation of the provinces of Bosnia-Herzegovina by Austria-Hungary for purposes of pacification and administration.

The relations between the Monarchy and Serbia in the first years of the new order of things were satisfactory and harmonious. Hand in hand with the economic dependence of Serbia upon Austria-Hungary as the main and almost exclusive outlet for Serbian commerce, went a political intimacy between King Milan's administration and the Government at Vienna. But against this friendly relation the Radical Russophile party carried on an energetic campaign. This campaign was supported at much cost by Russia, which conferred scholarships upon hundreds of Serbian students in Russian universities, and educated many Serbian officers in Russian military colleges. In addition to these cultural efforts of the Russian Government, the so-called Slavic Benevolent Society in Moscow and St. Petersburg always stood ready with ample funds to give material support to all poor Serbs who should show a desire to avail themselves of the educational facilities of the Russian Empire. Such were the mild beginnings of the Russian propaganda in Serbia, which was destined to lead to a tragic climax in Serajevo a few years later.

After the assassination of King Alexander, son of King Milan, and Queen Draga in June, 1903, the Russophile Radical party, under Nikola Pashitch, the present premier, came into complete and almost undisputed control in Belgrade. Under King Peter, the successor of King Alexander, the Russian minister at Belgrade assumed the rôle of a sort of viceroy. Russian dominance over Serbian affairs was especially conspicuous under the late Baron Hartwig, who was at the head of the Russian legation in the Serbian capital during the two Balkan wars and until his death in 1914.

Under the influences set at work by Russia, the attitude of Serbia toward Austria-Hungary underwent a complete reversal. As Austro-Hungarian minister to Serbia before 1903, I often discussed with the king or his ministers the destiny of Serbia.

They all seemed to take it for granted that the door to the west had been closed to the Serbian nation by the Austro-

Hungarian occupation of Bosnia-Herzegovina, and only
the door to the south—in Macedonia—was open. Serbia had
given up the dream of a Serbian expansion at the expense
of the Monarchy, and was considering conquests to the
south, in Old Serbia. Accordingly, the activities of the
nationalistic societies under the department of propaganda
at the Serbian Foreign Office were cultural. They took the
form of the establishment of schools and churches in Macedonia for the spread of the national ideal, very often at the
expense of the Bulgarians. This purely educational campaign lasted until the sudden end of the reign of Alexander.
Under King Peter began the propaganda of action which
was destined to have a tragic counterpart in the assassination of the Archduke Francis Ferdinand and his consort
in Serajevo.

Bands of raiders, or comitadjis, were organized, armed
with bombs and rifles, and sent into the debatable territory
of Macedonia to convince Bulgarians and other nationalities that they were really good Serbs. These methods,
until the annexation of Bosnia and Herzegovina was announced by Austria in 1908, were applied only to Macedonia. After that event, the activities of the propaganda
under the inspiration of Russia were transferred to Austrian and Hungarian territory.

The active interest of Russia in the newly annexed lands
came in the wake of two rebuffs for Russian arms and
Russian diplomacy. During Russia's struggle with Japan,
the Monarchy had maintained the friendliest relations with
Russia, in the hope that the colossus of the North would
succeed in retaining its outlet in the Far East. With the
triumph of Japan in Manchuria, Russia swung back to a
keen revival of interest in the affairs of the Near East. But
the second disappointment—this time a failure for Russian
diplomacy—was to come.

It is the custom to speak of the annexation of Bosnia and
Herzegovina as having been carried out by Austria to the
accompaniment of profound secrecy. Such is not the case.
The Monarchy, before the formal act, had exchanged several
friendly notes on the subject with Russia. It is not gen-

erally known that Russia had even given her conditional approval of the plan of annexation in advance of its execution. At a conference in the Castle of Buchlau, in Moravia, in the autumn of 1908, Baron von Aehrenthal, the Austro-Hungarian Minister of Foreign Affairs, had obtained the consent of Iswolski, his Russian colleague, to the prospective step. In return for Russia's friendly attitude in the matter, von Aehrenthal pledged to the Russian Foreign Minister Austria-Hungary's consent to the opening of the Straits of Constantinople to the Russian fleets.

When Iswolski, on continuing his trip, presented this plan to the British Foreign Office, he was quickly convinced that the agreed-upon *quid pro quo* was impracticable. Then began the opposition of Russia to the annexation by Austria-Hungary of the country which had been rescued from anarchy and placed upon the road to progress by Austrian arms and statesmanship, and in which Austria-Hungary had expended vast sums for essential improvements. This opposition was voiced by the Russian press in a series of violent utterances and by Serbia in a campaign of incendiary and indecent attack upon the Dual Monarchy. Serbia's defiant attitude lasted from October, 1908, until the following March. Austria-Hungary was then compelled to proceed at great cost to a partial mobilization as a defensive measure.

In point of fact, the annexation of Bosnia-Herzegovina was neither a stealthy nor an unforeseen event. On the eve of the opening of the Russo-Turkish War in 1877, Austria, like England, had set down conditions for its neutrality in the coming conflict. The Monarchy, among other considerations, stipulated the acquisition of control in Bosnia, and Great Britain the inviolability of the Straits of Constantinople. Both these conditions Russia sought to evade after the defeat of Turkey. England enforced the performance of Russia's promises by the dramatic appearance of its fleet in Besika Bay; the Monarchy obtained the performance of Russia's part of the bargain with the Dual Monarchy at the hands of the Congress of Berlin.

Despite the double assent which Russia had given to our

control in Bosnia-Herzegovina, Russia picked out the Bosnian issue as the key-note of a wide appeal to all Slavic nations as an example of the "Austrian peril." Russia is extremely reactionary in its domestic policies and extremely revolutionary in its foreign policies. The character of the Russian agitation carried on in the Austrian Slavic provinces may well be designated as revolutionary. The courts in Hungary only recently finished consideration of a characteristic method of Russian propaganda on Hungarian territory. Several Ruthenians, whom the Russians call Malorussi—"Little Russians"—were convicted of high treason under the cover of religion. The chief witness for the defense was the Pan-Slavist leader Bobrinski, a member of the Russian Duma, who had come from Russia to appear before the court under a pledge of immunity. It was shown in the course of the testimony that a swarm of Bobrinski's paid agents had agitated among the Austrian and Hungarian Ruthenians, ostensibly in an effort to detach them from the United Orthodox to the Russian Orthodox Church, but actually in an attempt to develop anti-Austrian sentiment among these "lost children" of Russia. Bobrinski's guilt of the charge of plotting against the peace of a friendly State was proved with sufficient conclusiveness, but it was impossible to convict him because of the promise of immunity under which he had consented to appear on Hungarian soil.

The trial and the disclosures which it brought about created a profound feeling of resentment throughout Austria and Hungary. The Hungarian Government had caught Bobrinski—and behind Bobrinski something that loomed like a menacing cloud up in the North.

Any approach to the hard methods of Kaulbars would not be endured with patience by any great Power. Kaulbars, with his Russian diplomatic entourage, terrorized Bulgaria during the period of uncertainty that followed the abduction, on the 9th of August, 1886 (old calendar), of Prince Alexander, by Russian agents, from his bed in the palace. With Alexander out of the way, Kaulbars, assuming the powers of a viceroy under suspended constitutional guarantees, attempted to browbeat and intimidate the Bulgarian regency, and actually made a deliberate and systematic attempt to promote a revolution against the Government, by informing the people, in fiery proclamation and by a series of speeches throughout the country, that the Government had incurred the displeasure of the Czar, and that, therefore, Bulgaria would suffer untold evils unless it quickly compelled its rulers to obey the mandate of Alexander III.

The extraordinary methods of Kaulbars and his masters at St. Petersburg produced such a strong wave of indignation in Vienna that the Monarchy at that early stage was brought to the brink of war against Russia in defense of the independence of Bulgaria.

The strings that led from Prague, the capital of Bohemia, to St. Petersburg and Moscow, the center of the Pan-Slavistic movement, were estimated as ominous and significant symptoms. The frequent pilgrimages of prominent Slavic leaders—like Kramar and Klofac, the Czechs, to St. Petersburg or Belgrade, and the numerous Sokol congresses and conferences, within and outside of the limits of the Monarchy, were outward signs of the intense character of a determined and dangerous agitation.

The Government of the Dual Monarchy has been taught by experience that the Serbian Kingdom is the torpedo which Russia has launched at the body of the Monarchy. That is why the Austro-Hungarian Government, in its dealings with Serbia after the crime of Serajevo, found no alternative to insistent and uncompromising action. Any quibbling, any half-measures in repressing such intolerable activities as have characterized the Russo-Serbian propaganda on Austrian territory, would have perpetuated the peril and made the situation worse than it was. It would have been tantamount to abdication by the Monarchy of its sovereignty on its own soil. And such an abdication we are not yet prepared to make. It must vindicate its sovereignty and insure order within its boundaries, even at the risk of incurring the accusation of undue aggressiveness from those who do not realize that the patience of the Dual Monarchy has been long and its desire for peace constant.

BY G. M. TREVELYAN

Prior to the outbreak of war singularly little was known in Western Europe about the Serbians and their quarrel with Austria-Hungary, and that little was chiefly derived from Austrian and Hungarian sources. Everything that there is to say against the Russian Government—and there is much to say against it—has for years past been told to England and America. But the wrongs of the nationalities of Austria-Hungary were little known to the general public over here. The fact that these suffering races were branches of the "Slav" family prevented them from getting a fair hearing before the world.

The prejudice against "Slav" peoples was a remarkable obsession which the events of the war have served to remove. Because one Slav government, namely, the Russian Government, was a bad government (though, in fact, no worse than the Hungarian or the German in its treatment of subject races), therefore all Slav *peoples* were regarded as barbarians. It seemed quite natural that seven million "barbarous" South Slavs should be subjected to the rule of "cultured" Germans from Vienna and "chivalrous" Magyars from Buda-Pest. And if the Serbians over the border showed any desire to liberate their brothers of Bosnia and Croatia, they obtained none of the sympathy which the Piedmontese had obtained sixty years before, when they made themselves equally obnoxious to Austria on behalf of their brother Italians.

The present world-war was in its origin a "punitive expedition" against the Serbians for having the impudence to sympathize with their brother Serbs and Croats in Austria-Hungary. The expedition was to have been made in August, 1913, as Signor Giolitti revealed to the world, but owing to Italy's refusal to join the German Powers in a war of aggression it was postponed for a year until the murder of the Archduke by Austrian subjects seemed a fitting opportunity to wipe Serbia off the diplomatic map.[1]

[1] The idea that the Serbian Government was connected with the murder was put forward without proof by Count Forgách, the Austrian

The "punitive expedition" began by "chivalrous" Hungarians murdering two to three thousand men, women and children of the "barbarous" Slavs near Shabatz and Losnitza. They burnt a large number of the "barbarian" women and children alive, and gouged out the eyes of others.[2] The Serbians have not taken any reprisals; and although they captured 60,000 Austrian prisoners, those prisoners when questioned made no complaints of their treatment. The Austrian wounded were treated on an absolute equality with the Serbian, in the Serbian hospitals. In this war Slav "barbarism" shows up very well against German "culture" and Magyar "chivalry." The case for keeping the South Slavs of Bosnia, Dalmatia, Croatia, and Slavonia subject to Austrians and Magyars on the ground of inferior civilization was always a fraud, and has now been thoroughly exposed.

All the nationalist movements inside Austria-Hungary had been growing with great rapidity during the last half-dozen years before the war, especially the movement drawing the Croats towards the Serbs, who speak the same language, and are only divided from them in religion. The reign of terror that existed in these provinces during the war made it utterly impossible that the Austro-Hungarian rule could continue in the Slav and Rumanian provinces, except as the rule of the sword.

Some people ask why, if the subject races of Austria-Hungary were thus alienated from the Government, they did not rise in insurrection. The answer is because *all* the young men were taken into the army by the modern system of military slavery, and *all* the leaders were in prison or exile. If that had been done in Italy and throughout Europe in March, 1848, there would have been no year of revolutions. The modern militarist organization made revolu-

Under-Secretary of State, who had been convicted in 1909 of having documents forged with a view to securing the judicial murder of South Slav leaders. The counter suggestion that the Austrian police connived at the murder of the Archduke is far more probable, if the very peculiar circumstances of the murder are closely studied.—AUTHOR'S NOTE.

[2] See the official Memorandum and Report. Also the evidence of Dr. Reiss, of the University of Lausanne, given in lectures in London and in the *Revue de Paris*.

tions impossible; for it is young men who rise in revolt, and it was the young men who were drafted into the army, where the races kept watch over each other, and military discipline rendered mutiny the most hazardous and desperate act.

Yet even so Austria's great military weakness in this war was caused by the hatred of her subject populations, and the secret disloyalty of her soldier slaves. Large portions of her army were guarding other portions, or garrisoning disaffected districts. When they take the field, the unwilling conscripts fight well for a while—they can do no less unless they are ready to be shot—but they take the first opportunity to surrender. That is why the Serbians soon had 60,000 prisoners, most of whom, so far as I could judge by their words and conduct, were only anxious not to be caught by the Austrians and made to fight again.

It is because she is not a nation that Austria-Hungary is so weak in war. From the opening of the year 1915 she was practically occupied by Kaiser William's troops. It was the North Germans and Bavarians who came and saved Hungary, after the great defeat in Serbia in 1914; otherwise Hungary and probably Austria too would have been torn to pieces by an invasion of Russians and Rumanians coming over the Carpathian passes, which would probably have led to an Italian invasion as well. Hungary became a vassal State, protected by Germany.

It is a mistake to think of Austria and Hungary, either singly or together, as a "nation" in the sense in which Russia, Germany, France and England are nations. If we think so, we fail to understand one of the root causes of the present war. And when people suggest the restoration of the state of things before the war as the basis for a permanent peace, they forget Austria-Hungary. The Empire of Vienna and Buda-Pest was an anachronism, dependent for support upon the Prussian arms. It was the domination of two races, the Austrian-Germans and the Magyars, over half a dozen other races. And in one respect at least it was worse than the Old Turk rule of Abdul Hamid. The Old Turks, villainous as their rule was, left cultural, linguistic, and scholastic liberty to the subject races whom they pillaged and oppressed. They did not care what dirt the infidel ate in his own schools and churches. They had no wish to turn the Greek or the Bulgarian into a Turk. But the Magyars tried to suppress the language, schools, and culture of the subject races. The Magyars are vassals of the Prussian Kaiser by natural affinity. German victory would mean, in East and West alike, the continued attempt to suppress the cultural development of the smaller races.

Indeed, the present war arose quite as much out of the question of Austria-Hungary and its subject nationalities as it did out of the German ambition to dominate Europe. Even German love of domination would not alone have sufficed to set the whole world on fire, had not German Culture been in alliance with a force equally regardless of the rights of others, the determination of the Magyars of Hungary to "Magyarize" the Rumanians, Slovaks, and Croats who dwelt within the borders of their State. In theory the law of 1868 gave cultural liberty to the Slavs in Hungary, but in practice this law was a dead letter. The whole Government machinery was used to oppress any man who wished to remain a Slav or Rumanian, or to bring up his children as such. The policy of the Hungarian Premier, Count Tisza, represents this "will to oppress" on the part of the Magyars. The Magyars numbered only 45 per cent. of the population of Hungary. And Count Tisza's policy was not even the policy of the Magyar nation, but of the Magyar oligarchy who deprived even their own race of all political power.

This Magyar oligarchy was for years past the dominant force in the Austro-Hungarian partnership. Buda-Pest, knowing well what it wanted, had been able to dictate to the vacillating statesmanship of Vienna, which had occasional hankerings after a more Liberal treatment of the subject peoples. When the old Emperor Francis Joseph wanted to introduce universal suffrage throughout his wide dominions he was prevented by the Magyar politicians, who saw in it the doom of their race ascendancy. Their treatment of the subject races of Hungary became worse of recent years. In 1912 they abolished the Constitution of Croatia, and seized the funds and charters of the Orthodox Serb Church in Hungary. This steadily increasing oppression of the South Slavs was unfortunately of more account in world politics than the more liberal treatment of the Poles of Galicia, to whom the Austrians allowed more liberty than was enjoyed in either Prussian or Russian Poland.

The reason why the domestic system of the Magyars in Hungary proved so fatal to all Europe is not far to seek; this internal tyranny involved an aggressive foreign policy in the Balkans and towards Russia. For the tyranny exercised over the Croatian South Slavs in Hungary involved as a corollary the repression of the Serbian South Slavs in Bosnia (the Province abutting on Serbia, which is ruled by Austria and Hungary jointly). And the repression in Bosnia in turn necessitated a hostile attitude on the part of Austria-Hungary towards Serbia. For Serbia and Bosnia were in reality one country divided in half—a free half to the east, and an enslaved half to the west of the Drina river. Since oppression was the order of the day, the oppressed peoples naturally looked across the Drina to their brothers of free Serbia, especially after Serbia had shown herself redoubtable in war against the Turks and the Bulgars in 1912-13. For the same reason it became more than ever essential to the Austrians to prevent the further development of Serbia, after her victory over the Turks, lest she should become the liberator of the South Slavs. Hence the fatal policy of Austria in making it a *casus belli* for all Europe if Serbia got a single port on the Adriatic. By Austrian decree the Serbians were condemned to remain forever a bucolic, inland people, with no seaport, though half the eastern Adriatic coast is inhabited by their co-nationals, the South Slavs. Austria had "tied Serbia up in a sack," as the Serbs say.

This artificial seclusion from the sea was the bane of Serbia. The Austrians cut her off from civilization and then called her uncivilized. She was prevented from enjoying commercial and intellectual communication with the great European world, except by way of her enemy, Austria.

She was shut in on all sides. No one visited Serbia, no one helped her to develop her resources, no one knew what manner of men inhabited her land. It was assumed that they were all "regicides," dirty, idle keepers of pigs, as their enemies, the Viennese, reported. And, as so often happens, it was only their recent success in war which at length caused the world to remark the qualities which they have always displayed in peace. As one of the few Englishmen who visited Serbia both before and during the present war, I should like to record what the Serbians are really like.

The Serbians have the virtues and the limitations of a peasant democracy. Eighty-six per cent. of the population belongs to the class of peasant proprietors, cultivating their own farms. There is no class of landlords taking rents. There is no feudalism, no squirearchy, and as yet no important mercantile or industrial classes—no "middle class" or "working men." There are yeomen, and nothing else. The contrast is strange, as compared to neighboring Hun-gary, where the Magyars, one of the most feudal of all European races, sacrifice the wealth and happiness of the cultivating peasant to the landlord patrician, who carries off everything politically, socially, and economically. Serbia, on the other hand, is democratic and equalitarian, far more so than either America or England. There are no class questions, because there is practically only one class. Patriotism is the sole political feeling of the average Serbian, because there is no "social problem" and consequently there can be no vital politics except foreign politics. It is due to the independent manliness of the free yeoman, and to the absence of all class division, that the Serbian army won redoubtable victories in the field over the larger forces that Austria-Hungary sent into Serbia on their errand of murder, pillage, and destruction. If ever there was a pure victory of freemen over slaves who had been sent by the tyrant to destroy them, it was the Serbian victory in 1914. A few talks with the poor Austrian prisoners, only too rejoiced to be out of the fighting and uninterested in the issues of the war, were enough to show why they had been beaten by the sturdy peasant-soldiers of Serbia, united in one mood of heroism and devotion.

There are, however, defects as well as merits in this very pure form of Democracy. There is no adequate class of men to lead the people. The administrators, politicians, and army officers are all peasants at one or two removes from the soil. The leading class is an improvisation. There is no inherited tradition of leadership and administration as in the class of gentlemen or merchants in the countries with which we are familiar. It has followed that, while the peasants have been living excellent and happy lives on their farms, the improvised politicians whom they elected as their political stewards have often made a terrible mess of Serbian politics. The regicide of 1903, a vile way of ending an intolerable state of things, was the culminating point of this mismanagement. Since then things have improved rapidly, especially since 1908, when the Austrian annexation of Bosnia aroused Serbians to a sense of reality, and caused a real moral and national revival. In 1914 we had in Serbia the rule of the excellent M. Pashitch, who is about as likely as Mr. Asquith to have had a hand in the murder of the Archduke Ferdinand.

Of course, not all Serbian administration is up to the standard of M. Pashitch. The standard of civil administration in Serbia is still very low, because, as I have said, there is no class with administrative traditions. This matters the less in ordinary times in Serbia, because the administrative needs of a simple peasant community are comparatively small. But when the Serbians had to administer a large part of Macedonia, won from the Turk and kept from the Bulgar in recent wars, the want of administrative experience was more serious. In Macedonia they had to govern not only fellow Serbs, but people of different races and religions, Greek, Albanian, Turk, Vlach, Bulgar, and Macedonian Slav. It is here that their deficiency in administrative experience came out.

But the administrative weakness of the Serbians is much less marked in the army than in the civil service. The best elements of the improvised upper class go into the army.

It is a very different service now from the army that supplied the regicides of 1903, and that suffered such easy defeat at the hands of the Bulgarians in 1885. The Turks in 1912, the Bulgarians in 1913, and the Austrians in 1914 each in turn failed to realize until it was too late how far army reform had recently gone in Serbia. Without good officers not even a race of stalwart yeomen can triumph in modern warfare as the Serbians triumphed.

These officers, of whom the chief have been educated in the Paris military schools, strike me as men of superior quality, good at their profession, but modest and kindly. There is nothing of the Prussian officer about them in their relations to the men they command. They are brothers-in-arms with their soldiers. Comradeship and discipline go together. For indeed the officer is in most cases only a peasant educated to command other peasants. The small civilian professional class—lawyers, doctors, clerks, etc.—is also found in the ranks of the officers in time of war.

There is a great difference between Serbia proper and the Macedonian provinces which she recently acquired down South. Serbian Macedonia contains many races, European and Asiatic, and is still rotten with all the vices of a country but just released from Turkish rule. The inhabitants dwell in gigantic villages of five or ten thousand inhabitants each, whence they ride out every morning to till the distant fields. In this their custom resembles that of many of the Sicilians and South Italians. Indeed, the bare limestone mountains and backward civilization of Macedonia are curiously like some parts of South Italy or Sicily. But the change from South Italy to North Italy is not greater than the change from Serbian Macedonia to Northern Serbia. In Northern Serbia, which has been free of the Turks for a hundred years and where the entire population is Serbian, you have a landscape of gentle, undulating, fertile hills, cut up into fields by hedges after the English pattern. It is much more like Devonshire than the typical scenery of the Balkans or Mediterranean. The white-walled, red-roofed farms are scattered widely about this pleasant countryside, for there is no need for the inhabitants to draw together for safety at nightfall. It is this country, the richest in Serbia, that the Austrian troops sacked so ruthlessly during their invasion. The Serbians are an emotional and mercurial people. The South Slav differs in many respects from the Russian Slav. He is less stolid, having been crossed with Greek and Italian blood, and modified by Italian influence in the course of the Middle Ages. Before the coming of the Turk, the Serbian Empire produced works of Italian art of high rank, like the wonderful fourteenth-century church of Detchanic.

The Serbian peasant is not, like the Russian peasant, devoutly religious. He attends church very little, and he has not much of what we call "personal religion." He is neither clerical nor anti-clerical, but indifferent to his clergy. On the other hand, he is profoundly poetical, and his national songs about Kossovo and Marco Kralyevitch are the food on which his youth is fed. The background of his mind is occupied by the history and legend of his country, as handed down in this poetical and musical form. The modern Press and modern literature have not reached him. In the battle of Prilep in 1912 the soldiers thought they saw Marco Kralyevitch on his horse Sharatz leading them on against the Turk, as the ancient Roman farmers thought that they saw the Twin Brethren at Lake Regillus.

The Serbs are less patient in retreat than the Russian, but capable of more fierce attack and of sudden recovery of *morale* after all is apparently lost. Their *retour offensif* against the Austrians in December, 1914, when they stopped their hasty retreat, turned round and attacked the pursuing enemy and broke him to pieces, is one of the most extraordinary feats in war, and is also highly illustrative of the mercurial character of Serbian heroism.

THE BAGDAD RAILWAY AND THE LORDSHIP OF THE EAST

THE FIRST CLASH BETWEEN BRITISH AND GERMAN IMPERIALISM

MORRIS JASTROW   J. HOLLAND ROSE

EVANS LEWIN

While Austria, as we have seen, was prone to regard Teutonic interests in the Near East as being mainly Austrian interests, Germany as the world now knows, regarded Austria as being merely her temporary deputy, even in the Balkans. All that region, with all the Turkish Empire beyond, was one day to be German. The first great step toward accomplishing this mighty future was the building of the Bagdad railway.

This vast engineering project might well have changed the entire course of empire in the East. The scheme was only opened slowly to the eyes of the world; but early in this twentieth century it stood revealed as an opportunity for Germany to obtain control of all western Asia. The railroad began as a small affair back in the 1880's, a little German-owned road in a single district of Asia Minor. But soon it spread and spread. Its tracks climbed huge mountains and crossed barren deserts. It became one of the great railroads of the world, and followed the oldest, richest trade route of civilization, the route of prehistoric caravans between the East and the West, between India and Europe. From Berlin traffic could go straight to Constantinople, and from Constantinople straight to Bagdad.

Even beyond Bagdad plans were begun for carrying the railroad to the Persian Gulf, that is, to the very doors of India. Merchandise by such a route would be far cheaper than by Britain's roundabout ship road through the Suez Canal. The railway would make Germany the commercial master of the East, and by its facilities for transporting armies might easily make her the military lord as well. Britain, chief ruler of the old Mahometan world-empire, might lose control of Egypt and then of India and then of the farther East. Imperial Germany would supplant Imperial England.

Germany of course insisted officially that she had no slightest thought of conquest, that the railway was purely a commercial enterprise, a giant effort of her money kings to simplify the trade of the world. She even, with characteristic boldness, invited British, French and Russian capitalists to join in the building of the road, thus seeking to use their money, but keeping the control in German hands.

No wonder Britain was alarmed! For years the tension increased between these great commercial rivals. Britain blocked the railway beyond Bagdad. All the territory it was to cross, even to the Persian Gulf, was nominally Turkish; and Turkey had become a mere pawn in Germany's hands. But Britain encouraged the local ruler along the gulf coast, the Sultan of Koweit, to claim independence; and in his name she stopped the road.

Such however was the resolute will to peace of the British government in the last years before the War that her Foreign Secretary, Sir Edward Grey, managed to arrange terms of agreement even with Germany, and even over the Bagdad railway. The year 1913 saw a convention or treaty by which Britain was to allow the railroad to reach the Gulf under restrictions planned to keep the road—at least in theory—a commercial one.

The story of this long struggle is here told in its opening by Prof. Morris Jastrow of the University of Pennsylvania, America's leading authority on the ancient Babylonian region of which Bagdad is the capital. Professor Jastrow is a loyal American of Germanic ancestry, and hence is not inclined to be prejudiced against Germany. His story is here followed by that of J. Holland Rose, a noted British historian; and the account is then brought sharply up to 1914 by another British scholar, a notedly impartial one, Mr. Evans Lewin, Librarian of the Royal Colonial Institute of Britain.

C. F. H.

BY MORRIS JASTROW [1]

THE Bagdad Railway has been a nightmare resting heavily on all Europe for eighteen years—ever since the announcement in 1899 of the concession granted to the Anatolian Railway Company. No step ever taken by any European power anywhere has caused so much trouble, given rise to so many complications, and has been such a constant menace to the peace of the world. No European statesman to whom the destinies of his country have been committed has rested easily in the presence of this specter of the twentieth century. In the last analysis the Bagdad Railway will be found to be the largest single contributing factor in bringing on the war, because through it more than through any other cause the mutual distrust among European powers has been nurtured until the entire atmosphere of international diplomacy became vitiated. The explanation of this remarkable phenomenon, transforming what appeared on the surface to be a magnificent commercial enterprise, with untold possibilities for usefulness, into a ver-

[1] Reprinted by permission. From "The War and the Bagdad Railway" by Dr. Jastrow. Copyright by J. B. Lippincott Co.

itable curse, an excrescence on the body politic of Europe, is to be sought in the history of the highway through which the railway passes. The control of this highway is the key to the East—the Near and the Farther East as well. Such has been its rôle in the past—such is its significance to-day. . . .

England's influence at Constantinople, paramount till 1880, weakened then, largely through Gladstone's opposition to the régime of Turkey, for which there was ample justification. The Armenian massacres of 1894 shocked Europe, and Gladstone was irreconcilable in his denunciation of the "unspeakable Turk," as the Sultan and all Turkey came to be called. This, naturally, was not pleasing to Constantinople, at the time under the complete domination of Abdul Hamid. Germany was quick to seize upon the situation and under the leadership of her ambitious, restless and romantically inclined young Emperor, with his mind full of far-reaching schemes, obtained by a series of cleverly designed steps the position at the Turkish capital which England had once held. The convention of 1902-03 made it evident that Germany had stolen a march on England, and that France's prestige at Constantinople had likewise suffered through the distinct advantage that Germany would have over her in the future exploitation of Asia Minor.

The terms on which a German Syndicate obtained the concessions of the Bagdad Railroad were indeed most favorable. The concession was to last for 99 years, and this included the two branches already built, Haidar-Pasha-Angora and Eskishehr-Konia. It had been assumed that the concession would not go beyond a line to Bagdad, and England felt that as long as the Persian Gulf was not to be reached, the situation would not be serious for her, either from the commercial or the political point of view. The India trade would not be diverted to the Persian Gulf in favor of the short land route, because of the double loading involved and the water trip from the Gulf to Bagdad. When, however, the precise terms of the convention became known, it was seen that the extension not only included Basra, but also contemplated a branch from Zubeir (not far from

Basra) to a terminus on the Persian Gulf "to be determined," together with the right of navigation on the Shatt-el-Arab and the Tigris—an exclusively English privilege—during the period of construction of the railway in this region. That gave an entirely new interpretation to the convention as a whole and at once created a critical situation which steadily grew worse.

The favor shown the German Syndicate was evident on the surface. Such terms had never been secured before. No wonder that there were great rejoicings in Germany when they were announced, and gnashing of teeth outside of Germany.

The German Syndicate, to be sure, offered to English and French capitalists a share in the enterprise. Dr. Siemens and Dr. von Gwinner, the two leading spirits of the project, emphasized strongly the desire to give to the undertaking an international character; but this move was generally regarded as due to an anxiety on the part of the German Syndicate to obtain foreign capital to aid them. It was estimated that the cost of the Konia-Bagdad construction would amount to 350 million francs, and this was more than Germany was supposed to be able to carry alone. The control of affairs was so arranged, it was claimed, that it would always remain in German hands. Five of the eleven directors were to be chosen practically by the Anatolian Company, and Germany would also be in a position to control the vote of three Ottoman representatives provided for as members of the board, so that the Germans would always be certain of a majority over representatives of other shareholders. A storm of protest against the entire project arose in England and France, and the two governments were severely blamed in the press and in the legislative bodies for having permitted the convention to go through, the political significance of which when the terms of the convention became known entirely overshadowed the commercial aspects. England more particularly felt that not only were her interests in the Near East threatened through the trade and freight that would pass to the route of the railway, but that her domination in India was endangered. She had good grounds for this fear, seeing the open manner in which advocates of national expansion in Germany pointed out the possibilities involved in securing for Germany a continuous route from Hamburg to the Persian Gulf in seven or eight days only, with four additional days by steamer to reach India. The Pan-Germanists, whose voice had become blatant in Germany by this time, added coals to the fire by their equally open jubilation at the prospects of a complete German control of the Turkish possessions in Asia. German colonization in Asia Minor was to be encouraged, following in the wake of the commercial advantages to be gained by the railway, and thus the diplomatic supremacy of Germany in Constantinople was to be strengthened by the spread of German settlements throughout the East.

It was felt in England that if, as Napoleon is said to have remarked, Antwerp in the hands of a great continental power was a pistol leveled at the English coast, Bagdad and the Persian Gulf in the hands of Germany (or any other strong power) would be a 42-centimeter gun pointed at India.

BY J. HOLLAND ROSE

The Bagdad Railway Question closely concerns the future of Asia Minor, Mesopotamia, and Egypt. The scheme crystallized in 1898 at the time of the Kaiser's visit to the Holy Land. Outwardly he appeared as a crusader, championing the interests of Christian pilgrims to Jerusalem, for whom he gained concessions from the Sultan.[2] But he also procured from the Sultan a verbal promise for the construction of the Bagdad Railway. This happened in the year succeeding the Armenian and Macedonian massacres. At the time of those outbreaks of calculating fanaticism strong remonstrances were made to the Sublime Porte by the Western Powers. They were fruitless. For many years past Germany had supported Turkey, in pursuance of the policy of Prussia traditional since the days of Frederick the Great;

[2] "Not splendor, not power, not glory, not honor, no earthly blessing is it that we seek here: we pine, we pray, we strive alone after the sole, the highest blessing, the salvation of our souls."—KAISER WILLIAM.

and in 1897 Kaiser William emphasized the closeness of the political tie connecting the German and Ottoman Empires. Consequently poets and idealists in Western Europe raged in vain against the atrocities perpetrated by "Abdul Hamid the Damned." The power behind his throne was the Kaiser, who found his reward for the great betrayal of 1897 in the bargain for the Bagdad Railway. In 1902 the Porte issued a firman authorizing that enterprise.

Early in 1903 General von der Goltz delivered to the Königsberg Geographical Society a lecture in which he stated that the German Bagdad Syndicate had secured a concession for extending its line to Koweit on the Persian Gulf "after diplomatic negotiations with Great Britain." He also foretold that British mails for India would soon go via Vienna, Constantinople, Bagdad, and Koweit. It was evident that British trade in the Persian Gulf, especially at Basra, would largely be diverted to this railway, especially if, as was contemplated, it was connected with European lines by a tunnel under the Bosphorus. In this case, there would be through communication from Ostend or Antwerp to the Persian Gulf, with serious results to British shipping interests.

The promoters of the German Bagdad scheme showed clearly enough that political and military issues of great moment were also at stake. This appeared in a work, *"Die Bagdadbahn,"* published in 1902 by Dr. P. Rohrbach, whose travels in Mesopotamia, originating in theological motives, had of late led him to take a decidedly militant tone. He stated frankly that it was not worth while spending a pfennig for a weak Turkey; but for a strong Turkey it might be worth while to spend many million marks. He pointed out how the Bagdad Railway would enable the Sublime Porte to bring up its Anatolian troops quickly to the Bosphorus, whereas in the Russo-Turkish War of 1876-7 seven months were wasted by the troops from Mesopotamia before arrival at the front. The new lines would double the military strength of the Ottoman Empire. Further, the prosperity of Mesopotamia and Asia Minor would revive, stimulated as it would be by the immigration of numbers of Germans.

Thus, both in a financial and military sense Turkey would soon be able to resist her redoubtable enemy, Russia. Rohrbach also affirmed that agreements had been almost secured both with France and with Great Britain (this, too, in 1902).

Nevertheless, in view of the unfriendly conduct of Germany in other quarters, the Bagdad scheme had to be scrutinized closely. Her ambassador at Constantinople, Baron Marschall von Bieberstein, was openly hostile to Great Britain. On the other hand, the British opposition to the Bagdad scheme was finally declared by a German writer in the *Nineteenth Century and After* [June, 1909] to be due to Russian instigation. Clearly, the only way with so intricate and compromising a scheme was to let it alone, and allow the Germans to make the line if they could get the money for it. They failed to carry through the original scheme so far as concerned the Persian Gulf. To this extension the British Government could not assent; for it would have enabled Turkey and Germany to send troops quickly to the confines of Persia, and a further extension of the line would threaten India. The design of Germany and Austria to control the Balkan Peninsula and Asia Minor appeared clearly in the years 1908-10. In 1908 Austria annexed Bosnia; and though for a time in that year the Young Turk Movement overthrew German influence at Constantinople, yet the intrigues of Baron Marschall brought about a complete revival of Teutonic ascendancy in April, 1909. Ever since that time the Young Turks have been the creatures of Berlin. All the more reason, then, had Britain for opposing the German scheme of "pacific penetration" to the Persian Gulf, where British merchants had long before built up an extremely valuable trade. Moreover, the terminus, Koweit, was the city of an independent Sheikh whom England had more than once supported against the coercion of Abdul Hamid. In 1911 Sir Edward Grey demanded that, if a railway were made to the Gulf, it must be a purely commercial undertaking. Herein he followed the lines laid down by Lord Lansdowne, who stated that he could never allow another Power to obtain there a strong naval position "which might be used on the flank of our communications with India."

Such an assertion was all the more needed because of a recent compact between Russia and Germany. In November, 1910, the Czar visited the Kaiser at Potsdam and they conferred together on matters of State. Their meeting caused no little surprise in view of the rebuff which the Kaiser had dealt to the Czar in the winter of 1908-9 over the Bosnian Question. It now seemed that the Czar had accepted defeat and was willing to follow the lead of Germany. The meeting of the two Emperors therefore caused great concern at London and Paris; for it might betoken the break-up of the Triple Entente, lately severely strained by the death of H.M. Edward VII. The German account of the deliberations of the two Emperors is as follows: Russia agreed not to oppose the scheme, and even to link up that railway with her Persian lines; also to recognize Germany as an equal in matters commercial in that country. The Court of Berlin, on its side, recognized that Russia had special political and strategic interests in Northern Persia, as well as rights to construct railways, roads, and telegraphs. Thus, Germany said in effect, "Help me to build the Bagdad Railway through to the Persian Gulf, and I will hand over to you North Persia and as much of that land as you want." But this was not all. The Russian and German Governments also gave mutual assurances that each would enter into no engagement inimical to the other.

The Potsdam Convention was a triumph for the diplomacy of Germany. She had set back Russia's interests at the time of the Bosnian crisis; and she pushed on the Bagdad Railway until it promised to become a menace to Russian Caucasia. Then she turned round and said, "Now that I have beaten you, will you not make a bargain? Let us virtually partition Persia between us, shutting out the British; and, while we are about it, let us have a friendly understanding all round. I will not attack you in any quarter, if you will not attack me."

BY EVANS LEWIN

So far as Great Britain was concerned, the Bagdad Railway negotiations of 1911 were carried on directly with the Porte and only at a later stage with Germany; but all the time it was apparent that German influence was directly behind the Turkish Foreign Office and that the Porte was only the intermediary between the two parties. Both Lord Morley and Lord Haldane took part in the business, the former going to Germany in 1911, the latter spending a "holiday" there a little later—when questions other than those connected with the Bagdad Railway were fully discussed.

For two more years the long and tedious negotiations with the Turkish Government continued in their secret courses; but matters began to move when, in February, 1913, Hakki Pasha arrived in London in order to expedite the discussion between Great Britain and the Porte. A number of conventions were prepared and on May 30 Sir Edward Grey made an important announcement as to the scope of draft agreements with the Turkish Government. The object of the Porte in thus hastening negotiations had been twofold —to remove British objections to the proposed increase in the Turkish customs duties, and to enable Germany to carry the railway as far as Basra. The increase of the customs dues, which directly or indirectly would be applied to the construction of the railway, had to be vetoed unless British interests were protected by some binding agreement.

In the preparation of the new conventions the spirit of compromise came to the aid of the German financiers who were sheltering behind the skirts of the Turks. Great Britain not only recognized the suzerainty of the Porte over Koweit, which was to be an autonomous district of the Ottoman Empire, but also definitely left to Germany the construction of the section as far as Basra. In return for these concessions, the Porte (a) engaged not to interfere with the internal affairs of Koweit, and explicitly recognized the validity of the concessions concluded between the Sheikh and the British Government; (b) abandoned its pretensions to the suzerainty over the peninsula of Al Katr, the Bahrein

Islands, Muscat, and the territories of the Trucial Chiefs in the Persian Gulf; (c) and recognized the right of Great Britain to undertake in the future, as in the past, the duty of policing, buoying, and lighting the Gulf. In addition there were to be two British directors on the Railway Board as a guarantee against differential rates.

The agreement outlined by Sir Edward Grey also recognized that "the navigation of the river up to and beyond Bagdad is a substantial British interest which may be developed and consolidated."

The preliminary agreement was heralded in Germany as a triumph for German diplomacy. The *Berliner Tageblatt* on December 29, 1913, stated that "for years this undertaking has threatened to become a bone of contention between Russia, England, and Germany. The German Government has now, through its cleverness and tenacity, succeeded in removing all difficulties, and of bringing the line altogether into German possession." This is nothing more than a statement of fact. Without blaming our own diplomacy in the matter unduly or emphasizing its want of continuity and excess of vacillation, a measure of respect cannot be withheld from German statecraft which during the whole proceedings connected with the railway, financial and diplomatic, displayed an adroitness in meeting and overcoming the opposition of Great Britain, France, and Russia that showed the Germans to be able, if not masterly, negotiators. The position was doubtless turned to their advantage in many ways by events in the larger sphere of world-politics, but nevertheless the difficulties in the way of the Germans were sufficiently pronounced to have turned aside any diplomatists but the most tenacious and persistent.

"In tracing the development of the German expansion in Asia," states Mr. Sarolea in his book on Anglo-German relations, "we shall find one additional proof of the absurdity of the German grievance that England has pursued a policy systematically hostile to Germany. We shall see that in the case of the Bagdad Railway not only have the powers of the Entente Cordiale done nothing to oppose Germany, but that French statesmen have again and again promoted

German claims and that England in her desire to conciliate her neighbors has betrayed some vital imperial interests, and has allowed Germany to assume a formidable position, threatening both Egypt and India, a position from which she is not likely to retreat, and yet from which she will have to retreat if an armed conflict is to be avoided." An examination of the Bagdad negotiations reveals the justice of this contention.

At the commencement of the Bagdad troubles Great Britain, Russia, and France had almost equal claims to the participation in the enterprise, but each in turn abandoned these claims in favor of Germany, whose interests in reality bore no comparison with those of the Entente Powers. Russia, who in 1900 had been able to divert the line to the southward, withdrew all opposition ten years later. France, by the agreement of February 15, 1914, in exchange for the recognition of a railway "sphere of action" in the north and northwest of Anatolia and in Syria, definitely withdrew from participation in the Bagdad Railway, and Great Britain, as has been seen, withdrew all opposition in 1911, and only safeguarded her special and unique position in the Persian Gulf.

THE FREEDOM OF THE SEAS

THE MAD RACE FOR NAVAL SUPREMACY WHICH DROVE BRITAIN AND GERMANY TOWARD RUIN

GEORGE GILBERT MURRAY   ARTHUR BALFOUR
KARL KAUTSKY   GERHARD VON GAEVERNITZ

It is not easy to speak with restrained judgment of the sharply conflicting naval policies which had so large a part in causing the Great War and in driving the United States to enter it. When questions of the sea are raised, American interests become at once and seriously involved with those of Europe. Britain, long the chief sea-power of the world, had freed the ocean from Spanish monopoly and universal piracy, and gradually developed a "freedom of the seas" which was complete and satisfactory to every one in times of peace. In time of war when Britain was neutral, she naturally wanted to use her ships for trade; and when she wanted to block neutral trading with her foes. Hence her view of the "freedom of the seas" in time of war differed decidedly from that of nations who could not withstand her. On this point the United States and Britain had frequent controversies; but even here a fairly equitable "international law" was gradually built up.

To the growth of an American navy second only to her own, Britain never offered objection. She was thoroughly convinced of America's "will to peace," and while the United States navy might conceivably at some time oppose her own, it could never be with grim resolve at her complete destruction. When, however, Germany, the great military Power, began building a great naval fleet, Britain took alarm. She declared openly that she would never place herself at Germany's mercy by allowing the German fleet to equal hers, while the German army so infinitely outranked her. Hence when the new German navy was begun in 1898, Britain accepted the challenge. For every new German ship, Britain built two similar ones, or thereabout. A race began, tremendously costly, terrible in its threat to all the world.

That race could stir the blood even of an Oxford Professor of Greek, George Gilbert Murray. He, one of Britain's most honored scholars, the recipient of endless learned degrees, tells here of the long race as he and his countrymen saw and feared it. He speaks carefully, honestly, and most anxiously, though with academic restraint. Then we give the general presentation of the entire subject which was officially prepared for America by the ruler of the British navy, the "First Lord of the Admiralty," Arthur Balfour. He had been a former Conservative Prime Minister of Britain, and when the War came he joined the coalition ministry which united his country. In this powerful war ministry Balfour took charge of the navy. Later he was the leader of the British mission to the United States when that country entered the War. The German Socialistic view of the subject is presented here by Karl Kautsky, and the German governmental view by official authority. This final article, in rather more extended form, was issued as Germany's appeal and explanation to America upon this theme, in 1915. Its author, Professor von Schulze-Gaevernitz, was the Rector of the University of Freiburg, an established authority on political economy, and a member of the Reichstag. Unfortunately, in speaking for the Imperial Government, the learned von Gaevernitz speaks also as a "propagandist"; and that, according to the established Imperialist view, authorized him to distort facts, even to the extent of absurdity. It has therefore been necessary to add footnotes to inform the reader of such facts as the professor either ignores or forces into service upside down.

C. F. H.

BY GEORGE GILBERT MURRAY

AN army supreme in Europe; a power so great that no European state could move without consulting it: that was the achievement of Bismarck. But—here there is general agreement between military theorists like Bernhardi, well-informed Pan-Germans like Reventlow, and moderate and responsible Imperial Chancellors like Prince von Bülow —the position won by Bismarck was to be only a stepping-stone. Power in Europe was a means to *Weltmacht,* Power in the world. And the Kaiser, from the beginning of his reign, is said to have had the firm resolve to give Germany a fleet corresponding to her army.

We need not look for the words of extremists. The policy is announced by von Bülow and by the Kaiser's own speeches. "Sea-power is world-power." "The future of Germany is on the sea." "The trident shall pass into our hands." Von Bülow and Reventlow repeatedly explain the practical difficulty of this policy. At present England is the strongest sea-power; and the problem for Germany was not merely to build up a fleet capable of dealing with the British fleet, but to do so under England's eyes and without England's interference. "The fleet was to be built without our coming into conflict with England, whom we could not yet oppose at sea." There were two great dangers: England's enmity and England's friendship. "England's unreserved and certain friendship could only have been bought at the price of those very international plans for the sake of which we should have sought British friendship." "The alpha and omega of British policy has always been the attainment and maintenance of English naval supremacy." (Naturally; since if Great Britain loses command of the sea, she dies of starvation in a few weeks; and owing to her "consistent egoism," she does not wish this to occur.) Therefore the problem for Germany was, by long patience and concealment, to undermine Great Britain's naval supremacy without her knowing it. Then, it might be hoped, Great Britain would be wise enough to accept the new situation. If not, the German fleet could strike. The German people would heave a long sigh and cry "At last!" The day would have come.

It would be easy to multiply statements of this policy from the writings of Imperial Chancellors, of the Kaiser himself, and from Reventlow. It would be still easier to collect the sinister vaporings of various members of the German Navy League and the Pan-German League. But my object is not to make out a case against Germany; it is only to consider the disturbing effect of German ambitions upon British policy.

This ideal of *Seemacht und Weltmacht* took shape, as is well known, in the German Navy Law of 1900. This law nearly doubled the existing Navy and provided for a steady increase year by year for some considerable time ahead without further consulting of the Reichstag. As a matter of fact, the Reichstag was consulted frequently, but only with the object of accelerating, not of questioning, the rate of increase. The officially avowed object of this naval policy was to give Germany so strong a fleet that "even the strongest naval Power should not be able to challenge her with any confidence." In less official language it was that, as Germany had the strongest army in the world, so she must have the strongest navy in the world. The eagle wanted both its wings.

Sir Edward Grey's general comment on the situation is worth quoting. It is so characteristically gentle. "Now let me say this. German strength is by itself a guarantee that no other country will desire or seek a quarrel with Germany.

That is one side of the shield, and one of which Germans may well be proud. But there is another side of the shield, and that is: If a nation has the biggest army in the world, and if it has a very big navy, and is going on building a still bigger navy, then it must do all in its power to prevent the natural apprehensions in the minds of others, who have no aggressive intentions themselves, lest that Power, with its army and navy, should have aggressive intentions towards them. I do not believe in these aggressive designs (of Germany). I do not wish to have my words interpreted in that sense. But I think it must be realized that other nations will be apprehensive and sensitive, and on the lookout for any indications of aggression. All we or the other neighbors of Germany desire is to live with her on equal terms." (Sir Edward Grey, in the House of Commons, November 17, 1911.)

However much we might refuse to believe in the existence of "aggressive intentions," there was clearly in existence a new political fact which Great Britain was bound in one way or another to meet. Three lines of policy, it seems, were possible.

1. A force-against-force policy: as Germany meant to increase her navy till it was strong enough to strike us down, our policy might be to provoke a quarrel and strike her down first. This was the policy of a "preventive war," advocated occasionally by the more excitable ultra-imperialists in England, but essentially too immoral to be tolerated by the mass of the British people. Reventlow observes that if the British Government had wished for a "preventive war" in the earlier years of the century, nothing would have been easier than to find an occasion for it.

2. A policy of mere submission. I have never seen this policy advocated by any serious person, unless perhaps Mr. Brailsford could be accused of doing so in a paradoxical passage of his brilliant book, "The War of Steel and Gold." He tries there to argue that, even at the worst, suppose Germany completely conquered all opposition, nobody would really be a penny the worse, while at the same time he expresses his personal belief that "there will be no more wars

among the six great Powers." The passage was written early in 1914, and I think we may perhaps assume that the author's opinion of the comparative harmlessness of being conquered by Germany has been as much changed as his belief that there would be no more European wars. On the whole, I do not think it necessary to argue against the view that Great Britain should have said to Germany: "You want to have the biggest fleet in the world? Well, have it, and much good may it do you! We will not compete."

3. A policy of reasonable and pacific common sense. This was the policy actually followed. We said to Germany: "If you have any grievance against us, tell us and we will try to remove it: but you must understand that the command of the sea is to us a matter of life and death, and we cannot afford to lose it. Our navy is a danger to nobody, certainly not to Germany; because we deliberately keep a very small army, so that it is utterly impossible for us to attack any first-class Power. But your navy appears to threaten us in a vital point."

This policy took two forms: an attempt to get into cordial and frank relations with Germany, so as to settle any reasonable grievance which she might feel; and an attempt to come to some agreement for a proportional reduction of armaments. The two lines overlap, but may for clearness' sake be treated separately.

Let us take first, as simplest and most definite, the question of armaments. Great Britain's line was clear. "We wish for no aggression, no increase of the empire; we are ready for any treaties of conciliation or arbitration; but our national safety depends on the command of the sea. Therefore, if your intentions are peaceful, as we quite believe they are, let us have an understanding about armaments. We will make no attempt whatever to rival your army, and we ask you not to try to outstrip our navy. Short of outstripping it, or putting our command of the sea in danger, tell us what arrangement will suit you, and we can reduce our fleets together. And meantime we will give you any security you like that we will not attack you or enter any combination which aims at attacking you. But, we warn you, if you insist on building faster and faster, we shall build too and endeavor to keep up our full superiority. That means that we must both continue ruining ourselves on naval armaments until the race is checked either by a European war or a domestic revolution."

Our record on the disarmament question is above reproach. In 1898 the Czar brought the matter forward and proposed an International Conference for the reduction of armaments. Mr. Goschen, as First Lord of the Admiralty, agreed to accept a reduction if other Powers would frame a scheme. By the time of the Second Hague Conference, in 1907, Sir Edward Grey being then Foreign Secretary, we had gone further. We risked taking the initial step, and announced beforehand, in July, 1906, a large reduction of our Navy, in the hope that other Powers might be induced to follow our example. We reduced our program twenty-five per cent. in battleships, sixty per cent. in large destroyers, and thirty-eight per cent. in submarines. This step was all the bolder since the Germans had, immediately before, amended their program by the addition of six large cruisers. Next month Lord Haldane, then Secretary for War, went to Berlin as the Kaiser's guest. He was told that Germany would not discuss the reduction of armaments, and would not attend the Hague Conference at all if that subject was to be there considered. Another attempt was made at Cronberg by King Edward himself, in conjunction with Lord Hardinge. It was rejected no less summarily. Other nations, they were told, might feel the burden of armaments too much for them. Germany did not, and meant to have both her army and navy as large as she thought fit.

The British Prime Minister, Sir H. Campbell-Bannerman, still persevered. It might be that the peace-feeling in Europe would be strong enough even to influence Germany. The Social Democrats and the remains of the Liberal parties would surely respond. He wrote himself an article in the *Nation* (March 2, 1907), urging the cause of disarmament, and expressing his willingness to make further reductions in the British fleet if the other Powers would coöperate. He made this proposal officially to the seven chief naval Powers. The Russian jurist, Professor Maartens, visited the Courts of Europe with the same object. But Germany's official answer was given by the Chancellor in April, 1907: "The German Government refused to participate in any such discussion." The whole subject had to be ruled out of the Hague Conference.

There was a further increase of the German fleet this year. In the next King Edward again visited Cronberg, and approached the subject of reduction of armaments. The Kaiser's answer was that no discussion of naval armaments with a foreign Government could be tolerated by Germany. His tone seems to have been just that of Reventlow: the proposal itself was an insult. The blood of the latter boils to recount the story how an English midshipman once said to a German cadet, "We have the fleet, and you have the army." Where the insult lies is a little difficult for an outsider to see; but an insult it is, and one which, Reventlow thanks God, can never be repeated.

It is this feeling which explains a speech of Prince von Bülow in December, 1908, where he denies that definite proposals for the limitation of armaments had ever been made to the German Government. They had not been made, because, as soon as the subject was opened, Germany refused to listen and cut the speaker short. As a matter of fact, there were great suspicions of secret shipbuilding in this year and the next, and in 1909 facts which came to the knowledge of Mr. McKenna, then First Lord of the Admiralty, made him demand an unusual increase of the British program. His fears were, as a matter of fact, not realized, though the statements of fact which he made were quite accurate. But the great strain produced both here and in Germany by these suspicions made the situation even more dangerous than before. Sir Edward Grey therefore made a very characteristic proposal. He suggested, since Germany would not agree to any limitation, that at least both countries should prove their good faith by letting one another see what they were building. He proposed that the naval attachés in London and Berlin should be allowed from

time to time to see the actual stage of construction reached
by the capital ships in dock. Arrangements could be made
for preventing the disclosure of any details which were particularly secret, and the step would obviously allay anxiety
and prevent groundless panics. The German Government
refused. They did not wish, it seems, to allay the strain.

It is important to understand German feeling on this
point. It is doubtless in origin a theory conjured up to
justify the policy which Germany's instinctive ambition
craved, the Calvary, in Reventlow's words, which she had
irrevocably set herself to climb. But from whatever cause
it arose, it has been for many years a genuine feeling. To
the German Imperialist the true ideal is to put forth the extreme of human effort in the service of the Fatherland;
peace, arbitration, honest treaties, rules of war, everything
that in any way limits the need of effort and slackens the
tensity of the struggle, is in itself contemptible, and is only
sought by nations who are decadent and slack in moral fiber.
Reventlow remarks how the German-Americans lose their
true *Deutschtum.* They even "lose their comprehension of
Germany" to such an extent that a deputation of them once
came to Berlin to plead the cause of the Taft Arbitration
Treaty! "But that bubble is long burst!"

The British overtures for the reduction of armaments
continued unabated down to Mr. Churchill's proposal in 1912
for a "naval holiday." All were refused, and the two nations were thrown back on undisguised and unmitigated
competition in shipbuilding. But after 1907 the naval question begins to merge into the larger question of friendship
with Germany. We will therefore go back to that subject.

Up to 1902 or 1903, as Reventlow repeatedly emphasizes,
Great Britain was frequently in the position of suing for
German friendship. But Germany regarded such friendship
as a trap. Her aim was "World-power by means of Sea-
power"; and friendship of a sincere or permanent kind with
Great Britain could only be obtained by the sacrifice of
this policy. After 1903 Great Britain began gradually to
realize that her difficulties with Germany were due not to
any particular points in dispute. Such points as there once

were had practically all been settled long before, especially in the period of "graceful concessions" about 1890, when Lord Salisbury carried through the peaceful partition of disputed territories in Africa and gave Germany the island of Heligoland.

The present difficulties were due to some settled resolve of Germany's. We began gradually to see what that resolve was: never quite to quarrel till the Day came, yet never to come to terms; but it was long before we realized the enormous force with which it was held. Not all Germans, it was justly argued, agreed with the Kaiser and the majority of the Reichstag; and even the Kaiser might change his mind. In 1906, when the Campbell-Bannerman Government took office, it showed the spirit of its policy by its very first acts. It made a determined move at the Hague Conference towards an agreement for disarmament and pacification, and at the same time it opened confidential conversations with Germany to see in what way the two Powers could reëstablish cordial relations. Lord Edmond Fitzmaurice, the Under-Secretary for Foreign Affairs, is described as "making entreaties to Germany." But, "fortunately, Germany succeeded in foiling any such discussion." (Reventlow).

Meantime the efforts for a good understanding continued outside the course of formal diplomacy. In 1906 and 1908 came the two visits of King Edward with Lord Hardinge to the Kaiser, in 1906 and 1912 the two special missions of Lord Haldane, while in humbler spheres exchanges of visits were organized between municipal bodies, societies of working men and the like. Much was hoped on both occasions from Lord Haldane's visits. He was a man universally respected in England and known to be *persona grata* in Germany. Though he afterwards showed himself a great War Minister, he was an earnest friend of peace. But, as a matter of fact, he was simply baffled at the outset. The great men whom he met in Berlin had other aims, and aims which were not compatible with friendship for Great Britain.

At one time indeed the proposals for something like friendship seemed much nearer to accomplishment, and in this case the first move came from Germany. In 1909, after von Bülow's fall, the present Chancellor, Bethmann-Hollweg, came into power, and one of his earliest acts was an attempt to form an understanding with Great Britain. It is not clear whether he was in part sincere, but thwarted by another influence, or whether he was merely scheming to break up the Triple Entente. He suggested in general terms that there might be some understanding about the two navies, if it could be based on a general political friendship. British hopes rose high, but of course by this time the hopes were accompanied by suspicions.

Bethmann-Hollweg's naval proposal, the one side of the agreement which could be practically tested, amounted to nothing at all. He refused even to consider any reduction or any modification of the Navy Law; at most he was willing to discuss "retardation" of shipbuilding, provided that the total number of ships already arranged for 1918 were built by that year. At a later stage in the negotiations, however, even "retardation" was ruled out. The Kaiser informed the British Ambassador that he personally would on no account agree to any arrangement by which Germany was debarred from increasing her naval program as she chose. Thus the naval proposal came to nothing.

The Chancellor's general proposal of coöperation centered in an engagement that, in the event of either Power being attacked by a third Power or group of Powers, the Power not attacked should remain neutral. This sounds moderate in itself; but one observes at once its utterly different character from that of the two Ententes at which Great Britain had arrived. The Ententes were based on a full and sincere discussion of all the points at issue between Britain and France or Britain and Russia, and on the friendly relation which arose out of the loyal settlement of those differences. There was a promise of diplomatic support in certain cases, and a general understanding that neither Power would do anything behind the back of the other. But there was no mention of war, and no obligation to any particular attitude in the event of war. Where such a question subsequently arose, as in the Morocco crisis, it arose from new events in European politics: there was no military agreement in the Ententes. But German diplomacy, characteristically, puts war in the forefront. We were to promise neutrality in case Germany was ever, under any circumstances, attacked.

Of course we had no faintest intention of joining in an attack on Germany, and we offered clear undertakings to that effect. But the danger was that, by intrigue or by the interplay of alliances, Germany might maneuver some Power into making the first formal attack. As the summer of 1914 showed, it was always easy for Germany, by declaring war on Russia, to compel France to "attack" her; and indeed she did then, though in a half-hearted manner, accuse France of making the first attack. The proposed treaty would in these circumstances have bound us to be neutral. True, we might have taken the line which Italy took, and argued that the war was really an aggressive war on the part of Germany, not an attack by France, and that our treaty did not hold. But one great end would in the meantime have been attained by Germany. The confidence between France and Great Britain would have been sapped. France knew that we would not back her in any aggression, she knew that she herself contemplated no aggression. But she would have been justly suspicious if we concluded a treaty with her one great enemy, binding us to be neutral in certain contingencies.

As Sir Edward Grey said to the German Ambassador, the way for the German Government to get into friendly relations with us was to improve its own relations with France; not to make arrangements for fighting France while we stood aside. We had indeed no obligations with any Power which interfered with the formation of new ties. Sir H. Campbell-Bannerman had expressed it: "Our stock of good feeling and international goodwill is not exhausted by France. Let us hope that this wise policy will be extended. There is the great Empire of Russia. Then again there is Germany." But it appeared that the German proposals in this case involved exactly what we could not accept. "One does not make new friendships worth having by deserting old ones. New friendships by all means let us make, but not at the expense of those we have." (Grey, Nov. 27, 1911.)

After prolonged negotiations the proposals of 1909 fell through. They achieved certain minor ends, facilitating, for instance, the ultimate coöperation of Great Britain in the amended scheme for the Bagdad Railway, but in the main they left an unsatisfactory impression. In August, 1910, however, the British Government returned to the charge. They agreed not to bother Germany any more about the reduction of her naval program, and proposed an understanding on the basis of three stipulations: (1) A "temporary retardation" of the shipbuilding; (2) meantime no increase in the program and no building in secret: free exchange of information about the actual progress of work in the dockyards; (3) assurances that we had no hostile intentions towards Germany and had made no agreement with any Power which contained in it anything directed against Germany. Germany refused both (1) and (2), the Kaiser himself explaining that under no circumstances would he consent to any arrangement which bound Germany not to increase her naval program as and when she chose. As for the third offer, Germany proposed further discussion, and the British Government at length, with much disappointment, assented to the plan of discussing a political agreement without any cessation or slackening of the naval rivalry.

The sort of agreement contemplated by the German Chancellor is described in Sir E. Grey's speech of March 13, 1911. It amounted to an arrangement "more comprehensive, far-reaching, and intimate than any arrangement, short of actual alliance, that England had with any other Power. Such an arrangement was likely to cause misunderstanding in France and Russia. The British agreements with France and Russia were not based on a general political formula. They were settlements of specific questions, and the settlements had transformed relations of friction into relations of friendship. There was nothing exclusive in these friendships; the British Government had seen with unmixed satisfaction the settlement of some disputes between France and Germany and between Russia and Germany. Why should not the same thing be attempted between Germany and England?"

Thus Grey's policy is to reject a special and close treaty with Germany, specifically contemplating war, which might prove inconsistent with Great Britain's friendly relations with France and Russia, and would certainly leave Germany able to wage war upon those Powers with a freer hand. He pressed instead for a general settlement of disputes, which would bring Germany into harmony with the other Powers. In other words, we would coöperate with Germany in the maintenance of peace and the existing order; we would not coöperate with her, nor promise her a free hand, in any attempt to overthrow the existing order and assert her supremacy over Europe.

This was not what Germany desired. As Reventlow puts it, Germany had already in 1905 stood at the parting of the ways. At that time Great Britain had first appealed to Germany for a reduction of armaments or a naval understanding, and, being refused, had replied by building the *Dreadnought* and establishing a naval base on the North Sea. British friendship, says Reventlow, could easily have been secured. The ways of Germany's foreign policy would have been made smooth, but she would have had to accept British naval supremacy. She preferred, with full consciousness, "to build for her foreign politics and diplomacy a Calvary which must, *nolens volens,* be climbed."

In 1912 Lord Haldane again visited Berlin and attempted to negotiate the terms of friendship. He pleaded the cause of naval retrenchment. What was the use of the two Powers entering into a solemn agreement of amity, if both were immediately to increase their battle-fleets as a measure of precaution against their new friends? The pleading was useless. As a matter of fact, Germany chose the moment of Lord Haldane's visit to announce very large increases in both Navy and Army.

There remained the possibility of a political agreement, apart from any reduction of the navies. But Germany's

terms by now were more explicit and sweeping. She wanted
an unconditional pledge that Great Britain would maintain
neutrality in the event of Germany being engaged in war.
She wanted to climb her Hill of Skulls more untrammeled;
to be able to make war, it may be, on France or Russia, or
to annex Belgium or Holland or Denmark, with the security
that Great Britain was bought off beforehand. One is surprised that a responsible Minister could have expected us
to accept such a proposal. He may have thought that our
naval burden was even more crushing to us than it really
was, and that we would abandon everything, including our
honor and our future safety, for the sake of a breathing
space and Germany's temporary friendship. And in any
case, one is reminded of a saying of Bismarck's, quoted by
von Bülow: "If Mr. X makes you a proposal which is obviously advantageous to him and ruinous to you, it by no
means follows that Mr. X is a fool. It only follows that you
will be one if you accept." We would do nothing to make
Germany's path towards war easier. But we continued to
the last moment to make proposals for extending our
friendly relations to the Powers not in the Entente.

BY ARTHUR JAMES BALFOUR

The phrase "freedom of the seas" is naturally attractive
to British and American ears. For the extension of freedom
into all departments of life and over the whole world has
been one of the chief aspirations of the English-speaking
peoples, and efforts toward that end have formed no small
part of their contribution to civilization. But freedom is a
word of many meanings, and we shall do well to consider
in what meaning the Germans use it when they ask for it,
not (it may be safely said) because they love freedom but
because they hate Britain.

About the "freedom of the seas," in one sense, we are all
agreed. England and Holland fought for it in times gone
by. To their success the United States may be said to owe
its very existence.

For if, three hundred years ago, the maritime claims of
Spain and Portugal had been admitted, whatever else North

America might have been, it would not have been English-speaking. It neither would have employed the language, nor obeyed the laws, nor enjoyed the institutions, which, in the last analysis, are of British origin.

But the "freedom of the seas" desired by the modern German is a very different thing from the freedom for which our forefathers fought in days of old. How, indeed, can it be otherwise? The most simple-minded must feel suspicious when they find that these missionaries of maritime freedom are the very same persons who preach and who practice upon the land the extremest doctrines of military absolutism.

Ever since the genius of Bismarck created the German Empire by Prussian rifles, welding the German people into a great unity by military means, on a military basis, German ambitions have been a cause of unrest to the entire world. Commercial and political domination, depending upon a gigantic army autocratically governed, has been and is the German ideal.

If, then, Germany wants what she calls the freedom of the seas, it is solely as a means whereby this ideal may receive worldwide extension. The power of Napoleon never extended beyond the coast line of Europe. Further progress was barred by the British fleets and by them alone. Germany is determined to endure no such limitations; and if she cannot defeat her enemies at sea, at least she will paralyze their sea power.

There is a characteristic simplicity in the methods by which she sets about attaining this object. She poses as a reformer of international law, though international law has never bound her for an hour. She objects to "economic pressure" when it is exercised by a fleet, though she sets no limit to the brutal completeness with which economic pressure may be imposed by an army. She sighs over the suffering which war imposes upon peaceful commerce, though her own methods of dealing with peaceful commerce would have wrung the conscience of Captain Kidd. She denounces the maritime methods of the Allies, though in her efforts to defeat them she is deterred neither by the rules of war, the appeal of humanity, nor the rights of neutrals.

It must be admitted, therefore, that it is not the cause of peace, of progress, or of liberty which preoccupies her when, in the name of freedom, she urges fundamental changes in maritime practice. Her manifest object is to shatter an obstacle which now stands in her way, as more than a hundred years ago it stood in the way of the masterful genius who was her oppressor and is her model.

Not along this path are peace and liberty to be obtained. To paralyze naval power and leave military power uncontrolled is surely the worst injury which international law can inflict upon mankind.

Let me confirm this truth by dwelling for a moment on an aspect of it which is, I think, too often forgotten. It should be observed that even if the German proposal were carried out in its entirety it would do nothing to relieve the world from the burden of armaments.

Fleets would still be indispensable. But their relative value would suffer change. They could no longer be used to exercise pressure upon an enemy except in conjunction with an army. The gainers by the change would therefore be the nations who possessed armies—the military monarchies. Interference with trade would be stopped, but oversea invasion would be permitted. The proposed change would therefore not merely diminish the importance of sea power, but it would diminish it most in the case of non-military States, like America and Britain.

Suppose, for example, that Germany, in her desire to appropriate some Germanized portions of South America, came into conflict with the United States over the Monroe Doctrine. The United States, bound by the doctrine of "freedom of the seas," could aim no blow at her enemy until she herself had created a large army and become for the time being a military community. Her sea power would be useless, or nearly so. Her land power would not exist.

But more than this might happen. Let us suppose the desired change had been effected. Let us suppose that the maritime nations, accepting the new situation, thought themselves relieved from all necessity of protecting their sea-borne commerce and arranged their program of naval ship-building accordingly. For some time it would probably proceed on legal lines. Commerce, even hostile commerce, would be unhampered. But a change might happen. Some unforeseen circumstance might make the German General Staff think it to be to the interest of its nation to cast to the winds the "freedom of the seas" and, in defiance of the new law, to destroy the trade of its enemies.

Could anybody suggest after our experience in this war, after reading German histories and German theories of politics, that Germany would be prevented from taking such a step by the mere fact that it was a breach of international treaties to which she was a party? She would never hesitate—and the only result of the cession by the pacific powers of their maritime rights would be that the military powers would seize the weapon for their own purpose and turn it against those who had too hastily abandoned it.

BY KARL KAUTSKY

In the eighteenth century England was a grain export-ing country. In the beginning of the nineteenth century she produced wheat in nearly sufficient abundance to sup-ply her home demand. . . . In the year 1850 she was importing nearly four million quarters of wheat, and that import had been increased tenfold in 1909, as against a home production of only seven millions. Shortly before the outbreak of the war, 84 per cent. of England's wheat supply was drawn from overseas. . . . Thus England in case of war would be delivered over to famine if she did not possess command of the sea. Her control of the sea, which in the early years of the nineteenth century was little more than a weapon for the development and pro-tection of her Colonial Empire, and so, in modern language, served imperialistic ends, became in course of time indispensable for maintaining the independence of the country. Control of the sea thus changed, for the British people, from an imperialistic to a democratic necessity, at any rate for so long as it was not possible to effect general disarmament and the supersession of war. Its objects were pacific and, by reason of the perilous position of the country in time of war, very popular with the mass of the English people, even with Liberals, except the pure Socialists. The idea of sea control being thus embraced not merely by the imperialistic but also by the democratic sections of the community received not a protectionist or monopolist but a very liberal development in accordance with the basis of the open door. Thus it happened that during the whole nineteenth century no nation made any attempt to challenge England's control of the sea. Only Germany, and at the end of the century, adopted the policy of threatening that control when England's vital interests were much more decisively bound up with it than in the time of the first Napoleon.

BY GERHARD VON SCHULZE-GAEVERNITZ

The "freedom of the seas," which has been formally incorporated in the law of the nations, is valid for England only in so far as it is based upon a tacit acceptance of British naval supremacy. Even "Manchester" men and laissez-faire politicians have helped to build up the British Navy. Mr. Stead, the pacifist, had been agitating in Germany in the cause of peace. When he returned to England from his peace propaganda in Germany he advocated the construction of two British men-of-war for each German keel.

This apostle of universal peace was, at the same time, an apostle of British naval supremacy. To the same end England blocked the development of the right of private property on the sea, and upheld the right to capture, in order to kill the trade of her enemies. In this direction she has gone still further in the present conflict by extending the scope of the meaning of contraband to an extent which has paralyzed the commerce even of neutrals.[1]

In the London Declaration of 1909 the rules of international maritime law as established by custom were formu-

[1] When this statement was written, late in 1915, all the neutral maritime nations were conducting a commerce more extensive and much more remunerative than in peace times. The main menace to their ships was the German submarine.

lated. Under that declaration ore, raw cotton, agricultural and mining machinery were included in the "free list," that is, among the articles which, under all circumstances, could be dealt in freely with neutral countries. Grain is defined as "relative contraband," which is not subject to seizure if it is discharged at neutral ports and then conveyed to the enemy's territory. At present, however, England is seizing both conditional contraband and non-contraband as she pleases. British inspectors supervise Dutch trade in Holland. England forbids neutral countries to export to Germany under the threat of cutting off all supplies.

On account of the growing interdependence of nations British naval dominion now weighs on mankind far more heavily than a hundred years ago. In 1880 only the coast lines of oversea continents were opened up. Islands like the West Indies were the basis of the then existing colonial system. Oversea trade was made up of the more valuable articles of luxury, such as tobacco, coffee, sugar, and spices, which could be dispensed with. In case of need every European country could become a self-sustained State without serious inconvenience.

Since then the oversea countries have been thoroughly settled and opened up. A division of functions has taken place among the nations, and their economic life has become thoroughly interwoven by the vast increase in the volume of international trade.

The commerce of the world now consists, not of the luxuries for the rich, but of the necessities of life for the masses. To-day the weal and woe of every nation, as of every individual, depends to a large extent on the international trade, which is mostly ocean-borne. Hence mankind has been delivered to the good-will or ill-will of Great Britain, the mistress of the seas.[2]

[2] In the year 1913 Germany was still 80 per cent. self-supporting, and could easily have been wholly so. Moreover she depended for imported food supplies far more on Russia and the East than on the West. To the closing of trade routes on land Germany never objected—possibly because she could do more of it than any other Power. In the one place where Germany could control the sea trade—at the Dardanelles—she induced Turkey, even before Turkey was openly at

By cutting off oversea communications, including the cables, Britain can bring the delicate machinery of the world's industry to a complete stop. By closing the seaways to industrial Europe England condemns the million-headed armies of workmen to unemployment and cracks her whip of hunger in the huts of the poor.

European agriculture is also dependent upon exportation of farming products and the importation of necessary supplies. By cutting cottonseed meal and fodder, England stops the supply of milk in cities and treads upon the bodies of infants.[3]

In oversea countries which export raw material the producer is on principle the credit taker, and in the end pays off his interest with goods. An epidemic of bankruptcies threatens these new countries. The storm of a commercial crisis sweeps over South America and the economic existence of thousands of debtors and creditors alike has been

war, to bar all traffic. This step was largely responsible for Russia's ruin. In other words Germany shut other "masses" from the very freedom she demands for her own. Her own masses never wholly lacked the "necessities· of life" through all the War, and when these grew scant the cause was primarily because Germany set all her own masses to fighting instead of farming. The second cause was the ruin of the East by Germany herself and her allies. Britain's sea-power was only the third and smallest factor in Germany's privations.

[3] Surely German propaganda reaches in such a phrase its most astounding heights of impudent pretense. This was written, remember, before the full British blockade of later years. German military officials were at this time deliberately and directly stopping the food of infants in Belgium and Poland and northern France; and learned German professors were upholding this real starvation in patriotic and enthusiastic manifestoes. Totally ignoring this damning fact, this German professor here works out an involved accusation against Britain to the effect that, by cutting down the importation of some farm supplies, Britain lessened the product of milk in some sections, and hence —since German adults apparently insisted on drinking their full milk ration—German infants were being "trodden" on, not by their grasping elders, but by Britain. Apparently Germany's theory is that she will put her babies in the first line of attack. Then her men, sheltered behind the babes and feeding on the babes' supplies, can massacre the rest of the human race. Meanwhile the Herr Professors are to raise a howl of horror against any opponent who, in seeking to resist her men, touches the barricade of infants. This is a fair sample of the working of the German mind, even the supposedly educated mind, during the War.

ruined. The exportation of goods, the investment of new capital stops when British political interest demands that the world's industrial machinery be stopped, and yet British political interests have nothing in common with South America.

The British sea blockade of 1914 shook the industrial structure of the United States "hardly less than if the States themselves had been participants in the war." Evidence of this is the closing of the Stock Exchange, the decrease of the exportation of goods, and the levy of "war taxes."

Last of all, all real coast countries whose cities and economic centers lie within range of the British guns are unconditional vassals of the ruling sea power. If the Briton bids them, the Portuguese must risk their lives for a matter that does not concern them at all. Even Italy is unable to take part in any political combination which is not acceptable to England.

To-day, in a much larger measure than in the age of Napoleon, the "freedom of the seas" must be the political goal of all non-Britons.

But only two States are independent enough to profess openly that they want to reach that goal of humanity. They alone possess the economic means to oppose the Briton as equals on the sea. These countries are the United States and Germany.

The United States has definitely outstripped the British mother country because of the enormous natural resources and vast geographical extent, a gigantic production of raw materials, and the population twice that of England. To-day the United States is the world's largest producer of gold and silver, mineral oil, cotton, steel, and coal. Possessed of the most efficient industrial machinery, it could, if it wished, easily match or surpass British sea power. But the sentiment of the United States is against "militarism" and "navalism." The United States is a colonial country abounding in strong individuals, but with a decentralized Government.

Flattered and deftly lulled to sleep by British influence, public opinion in the United States will not wake up until the "yellow New England" of the Orient, nurtured and deflected from Australia by England herself, knocks at the gates of the New World. Not a patient and meek China but a warlike and conquest-bound Japan will be the aggressor when that day comes.[4] Then America will be forced to fight under unfavorable conditions. In the meantime, England's suicidal policy has sacrificed the foremost advanced-post of the white race and culture, German Tsingtao.

Hereby Britain has laid the north of China open to attack, while Japan, with a cold logic, has assailed Germany, the strongest white power in the Orient, has encircled the Philippines, reaches out for island bases and sea control of the Pacific, and bids fair to emerge from the war as the only sure "winner."

Thus the work of the liberation of mankind is left to Germany, and to Germany alone. On Nov. 11, 1870, Carlyle wrote to the London *Times:* "Patient, pious, and plodding Germany has coalesced into a nation, and has taken over the hegemony of the European Continent. That seems to me the most hopeful international fact which has happened in my lifetime."

Germany, the late-comer! While the Briton was conquering the world, Germany has been pushed out since the Thirty Years' War to the outer line of the world's affairs. The customary ballast of ships that were returning from Germany was sand—the "produce of Germany" (*le produit de l'Allemagne*), as the French sarcastically put it.

The Hansa merchants were like so many roosters that picked a few grains in the stable of a noble steed and were kicked out when they became a nuisance. But in that quiescent life old Germany gathered a new youth—that mysterious strength which Carlyle foreshadows in depicting Frederick William I. and his surroundings. Then, toward the end of the eighteenth century, under the protection of Prussian neutrality in the revolutionary wars, that classical

---

[4] Consult also in a later volume the more direct efforts of the German government to involve the United States in a war with both Japan and Mexico.

age arose when Germany was crowned with the wreath of intellectual achievement. Kant is the mighty figure that marks the boundary. How much philosophical thought is pre-Kantean even to-day and even with us. Oswald in Germany and English "pragmatism" are cases in point.

As long as the Germans were content to live in the clouds the Briton ceded to them the legion of intellectual empire, "the cuckoo house" and fools' paradise of philosophic speculation. He feared neither Fichte's virile "Talks to the German Nation," nor Hegel's world-embracing system of thought. But wrongly so, because that culture which seemed so remote from the world was in reality intently practical. The German culture was a new spring of inexhaustible strength which was to inspire the German idealist to a reshaping of the visible world.

With the alliance between historic Prussia and the "ideal nation"—"the German Nation"—as Fichte had visualized it—a great power arose in Europe on a thorough national foundation. This new German Empire, in the opinion of Bismarck, its founder, appeared to be "satiated in Europe," so lacking in tendencies of expansion that Great Britain ceded to it the rock island of Heligoland in 1892 without a shadow of misgiving. But the finger of economic necessities—a yearly increase of 800,000 in population on a small area—pointed beyond Europe.

By the merger of the historic Prussian customs union, principally with the West German ideas of Fr. List, Germany raised herself to the position of an economic world power, which by the restriction imposed upon a smaller Germany prepared the way for a greater Germany. List's final goal was also a political one; wealth was but the means, the end was the liberation of humanity from the mountain of British pressure. To this end List accepted Napoleon's Continental system as well as "Fichte's national idea."

"But do you," he appealed to his countrymen, "who are struggling to prevent the restoration of Gallic supremacy, find it more endurable and honorable to yield your rivers and harbors, your shores and your seas, to the sway of the British from now on?"

Step by step Germany caught up with the British model economic state, and overtook Britain first in iron and steel production, and then in chemical and electrical industries. Germany now became the seat of modern high finance; her aggregations of capital, accompanied by an even distribution of national wealth, outgrew all British proportions and began to approach American dimensions; with this difference, that the German system is more systematic and more closely coördinated with the State than the somewhat accidental, and still half colonial, capitalism of the United States.

The new German activity impinged with painful effect upon some of the old and firmly established British industries. Witness the single example of coal-tar dyes, which completely superseded the British dyestuff industry, especially indigo, which Great Britain previously produced from vegetable sources in India for the supply of the entire world. All this became the more acutely felt when German economic life, turning like that of England toward the seas, reached out mightily for the oceans of the world.

Our Kaiser's word that Germany's future lies on the sea is more than true; for our present is on the water. In all zones German wares, ships, banks, and enterprises of all sorts came into contact with those of England. But, more important still, the challenge to British industrial dominion seemed to bring into question also the political supremacy of Britain.

From this source came the ominous clouds which darkened our political sky for so many years. The question was forced upon us, Would not the Briton attempt at the eleventh hour to destroy by political means the rival who had outstripped him in the economic race? [5]

[5] "Outstripped" is here a mere word for boastfulness. In 1913 Britain's manufacturing and commercial interests were still the largest in the world, and seemed likely long to continue so. Germany and the United States were following Britain as good seconds, but neither had equaled her. As for war as a means of restoring British ascendancy, the fact was obvious then as now that war between Germany and Britain would give the United States an easy supremacy over both.

GERMANY REACHES THE BREAKING POINT

THE BURDENS WHICH MADE WAR A NECESSITY

DAVID STARR JORDAN   GENERAL VON BERNHARDI
JULES CAMBON   COLONEL PELLÉ

Looking back over the previously depicted causes of the War, the reader will feel strongly, as not a few men had grown to feel in 1914, that war was inevitable. Germany had carefully taught her people that this was so, that only by war could they escape the constant threat of their foes' "encirclement," and escape also the staggering burdens, both financial and personal, laid upon Germany by the ever enlarging army and navy. Our general introduction has pointed out why the German government itself selected 1914 rather than an earlier or a later year for its moment of attack. Delay would have meant the strengthening of all her foes, a larger French army built up by the law increasing the service period, a far more mobile and effective Russian army developed from nearly completed railroad and transportation plans, and an ever mightier British fleet. Delay might also have meant a complete internal breakdown, from the resistance both of the poor socialists who paid most of the taxes, and of the rich aristocrats who objected to paying any. Germany had to strike at once or never.

Read the following evidences of her state of mind. The first is a brief statement by one of the most noted American scholars, Dr. Jordan, for many years the active head of the great California university of Leland Stanford. He visited Germany in 1913 and foresaw the coming storm. The next is from General Bernhardi, a high German authority already quoted. In the fall of 1913, he added to his latest book on war an extra chapter from which we translate. To him the Balkan war of 1913 meant intolerable interference with German plans; for its closing treaty gave to Serbia a new lease of life, however feeble. Did not Serbia block the *Mittel-Europa* empire by which German rule was to extend through Austria to Turkey and the East? Germany must act immediately! Bernhardi's tone changes. He had always urged war in the future. Now he urges it as a matter of the immediate present.

Next come the official reports of M. Jules Cambon, the French Ambassador in Berlin at the fateful hour. Twice in 1913 did M. Cambon send solemn warning to his government of the dark change in German temper. Of especial historic note is his account of the interview between the Belgian king, Albert, and the new-spirited Kaiser, grown reckless by the pressure behind him, and the arrogant confidence of strength.

To M. Cambon's reports are added two secret diplomatic reports made public by the French Government after the War had begun. They show how careful, how shrewd and how anxious was the watch being kept on Germany by the State which had most to fear from German ambition and malevolence.

C. F. H.

BY DAVID STARR JORDAN

IN the summer of 1913 I learned of a meeting of the *Friedensfreunde,* to be held in Nuremberg in July. I attended the meeting and became acquainted with a number of leading Democrats, and with a good many others interested in peace, though not on a democratic basis. I was invited to come back to speak in the German cities, and I found time in December to give lectures in Frankfort, Wiesbaden, Mannheim, Stuttgart, and Munich. Through my friends I learned a good deal of the plans of the Pan-Germanists and especially of the German General Staff.

In brief, they hoped to bring on war in 1914. Presumably, at that time, through disturbances to be created in Alsace-Lorraine. They were then proposing to take Belgium and Holland—Holland for the sake of making Antwerp the center for the coming attack upon England. They wished especially to take the two departments of Nord and Pas-de-Calais from France. They proposed to make of Boulogne the great seaport of Germany, surrounding its broad flat bay with breakwaters, doing all this before England would enter the war, and removing the German fleet to Boulogne. They had a new German name for Boulogne, but I do not find it in my notes and do not recollect it. They were also to take Paris and exact an indemnity that would pay the expenses of the war; 25,000,000,000 marks was the figure I heard mentioned. After this, they were to treat France with great leniency, relieving her of all necessity for maintaining an army and navy and defending her from her great arch-enemy Great Britain. It was thought that France, being wholly degenerate, would not resist, and she could then devote herself to commerce and to the continuing of loans of money to finance German industry. . . .

I suppose that the Zabern incident and the arrest of "Oncle Hansi" [Jean Jacques Waltz] were moves in the direction of inciting trouble in Alsace, getting a protest from

France to be followed by a sudden ultimatum. The death of the Archduke, whether planned in Budapest or not, served to make the way to war easier, by beginning it in the southeast.

BY GENERAL VON BERNHARDI

The European situation has chiefly changed, because Germany, which formerly was politically quite unimportant, has become by far the foremost Power on the Continent. A new factor has arisen.

It can really not reasonably be expected that Germany, with her 65,000,000 inhabitants and her world-wide trade, should allow herself to be treated on a footing of equality with France, with her 40,000,000 inhabitants. It can really not be expected that Germany should allow 45,000,000 inhabitants of Great Britain (Celtic Scotchmen, Welshmen, and Irishmen side by side with Germanic Englishmen) to act as arbiters to the States of the Old World, and to exercise an absolute supremacy on the sea. It can really not be expected that Germany, with her constantly growing population, should renounce her claims to become a great colonial Power and to acquire territories suitable for settlement, while States with a decreasing or an insufficient population, such as France and England, share the possession of the Old World with Russia, which in the main is an Asiatic Power.

Germany, though she has become a world-Power only lately, is entitled to claim an important increase of her sway, corresponding to her economic and cultural importance. Circumstances compel her to strive for such expansion. On the other hand, *it cannot be denied that Germany's desire, even if she acts with the greatest modesty, is one of the reasons of the present tension.* Germany's national competitors fully recognize the power of expansion possessed by the German nation, and its necessity. They therefore conclude that Germany will, notwithstanding her proved love of peace, be at last compelled to enter upon a policy of expansion. England, France, and Russia will never be induced to believe that Germany will for all time resign herself to her present position. Therefore these countries strive to keep down Germany, and to re-create the convenient conditions which prevailed when a weak Germany occupied Central Europe. Before all, France will not, under any circumstances, abandon her claim to a position of political equality with Germany. She feels particularly entitled to claim equality, because her colonies are greater than ours. . . .

The position in the Balkan Peninsula has completely changed. The Turks have suffered a crushing defeat, and none of the European Powers have come to their aid.

A terrible awakening has taken place. The Great Powers did not for a moment think of enforcing their peace program. The States of the Triple Alliance could not find the necessary energy actively to defend their interests, while the Triple Entente desired to see Turkey weakened, if not broken. To the Entente Powers the victory of the Balkan States could be only advantageous whilst it would most seriously damage the States of the Triple Alliance. The Entente Powers would certainly have been ready to interfere in case of a Turkish victory, but they did not feel called upon to work for the preservation of that State. The Triple Alliance Powers have received their lesson, and they will find it difficult, if not impossible, now to secure for themselves the advantages which they might easily have obtained had they interfered at the right moment.

Turkey has been in a state of decay for a long time. Still, it was absolutely in the interests of the Triple Alliance to delay the expulsion of the Turks from Europe until the great European war, which will decide the fate of the Central European States, has been fought. Owing to the course of events, the Triple Alliance will now have to fight such a war under far less favorable conditions. Before Turkey's defeat Germany could calculate upon the coöperation of Turkey and Rumania. To-day all this has changed, and a state of affairs has arisen which brings with it the greatest perils for Germany and her allies.

It is clear that Turkey cannot hope to reconquer her lost provinces, and that the partition of her European territories has commenced. However this will be effected, Austria and Rumania, and therefore the Triple Alliance, too, will lose by it. If Austria agrees to the enlargement of the Balkan States, hoping to place them under her influence, she will collide with Russia, which follows the same policy. It cannot be assumed that in a competition with Russia for the favor of the Balkan Slavs Austria will be successful. It is, of course, possible that the Balkan States, supposing they remain united, will try to shake off Russia's influence and support Austria. Still, one cannot calculate upon the lasting unity of the Balkan States, as they pursue opposing interests. Serbia will be hostile to Austria as long as several million Serbs remain under Austrian rule and desire reunion with the Serbians of the kingdom, and these will remain hostile to Austria until they have obtained an outlet on the Adriatic.

We must, therefore, reckon with the possibility that, in case of a great European war, the Balkan States will be found on the side of the Triple Entente, hoping to expand at Austria's expense. Thus the Triple Alliance will lose its secure route through Turkey, by which it could receive supplies in case of a war against the Entente Powers. The neutralization of that route would be of little value in view of the insecurity of paper guarantees.

The superiority against which we have to fight has increased, and Germany's strategical war preparations must be changed accordingly.

In consequence of the Balkan war, Germany's prestige throughout the world has suffered, though without justification. Turkey's defeat is celebrated by our enemies as a German defeat. The fact that the Turkish army had Krupp guns and German instructors induces them to depreciate the German army. All England is triumphant at Turkey's defeat, which is attributed to German military training. Besides, the English clearly recognize that the Triple Alliance has lost power by that defeat. In France similar sentiments prevail. Formerly only the French army was eager for war. Now the whole nation shares these feelings. The people are sure of victory, and armaments are secretly increased in expectation of war. In Russia the Pan-Slavists are gaining ground and are attacking Austria. Even little Belgium has found that she has a French heart, and she is jubilant at the defeat of the Turks and the lost labor of the German instructors.

The peril of a general war has come nearer. The strained relations between Austria and Serbia may lead to war. Even if the present quarrel should be settled, the Austro-Serbian differences remain. We cannot expect that the Powers of the Triple Entente will not make use of their improved position. Urged on by public opinion, they may try to enforce their will upon Germany. That would be logical and natural. Hence a wise and farseeing policy must calculate with the possibility of war. France and Russia seemed hitherto not to consider the moment favorable for striking. The unexpected events in the Balkan Peninsula have completely changed the position for them. The German Government must be on its guard.

All the pusillanimous supporters of a policy of surrender who do not wish to embark upon a real world-policy, and who desire that Germany should continue to exist in its narrow Continental confines, will, under the circumstances, certainly loudly assert that Germany has no vital interest in the Balkans, and protest against energetic action. Never dare and never strive! That is the motto of those Philistines to whom peace is the most precious good, even if the greatness and the future of the Fatherland are at stake. They will energetically point out the dangers of a war against superior forces, and demand that the Government should avoid war by its moderation, instead of preparing for it by energetic action.

These German pessimists and men of little faith must be told again and again that it is the strongest and most vital interest of Germany that the position of Austria-Hungary in the Balkan Peninsula should remain intact, and that Italy's claims in the Mediterranean should be supported; that notwithstanding the altered position of affairs, Germany's own advantage requires that Constantinople and as much territory in Europe as possible should remain Turkish, as long as Russia belongs to the Triple Entente; that Germany should defend Turkey's Asiatic possessions with all means in her power, and that a "hands off" should be addressed to the French and English if they should desire to interfere with Turkey. And again, and ever again, it must be pointed out that we have no reason to be afraid of war if we act with our whole armed strength, if we do everything to be as strong as possible on the field of battle, and *if we are determined to act before Germany's opponents are ready* if it becomes clear to us that an honorable peace cannot be maintained.

Our enemies envy us not only our position and our world-wide trade, which increases our national wealth from year to year, and which we have conquered by two victorious wars. Exactly as they envied Frederick the Great Silesia, they desire now to crush us. It would be unworthy of our past and of our German name if we should bow down before their hostility without a struggle. Our claim to a great position in the world may certainly lead to a war similar to the Seven Years' War. Still, we shall be as victorious as was Prussia's hero king. That is my absolute and joyous conviction. A great war will unify and elevate the people and destroy the diseases which threaten the national health. The latent forces within our armies require arousing. They will make it unconquerable in hard times. Besides, it is not yet too late to complete our armaments. In very little time the *cadres* and the number of horses can be increased, the machine guns procured, and the cycling battalions be raised. The Army Service Corps can be reënforced with motor vehicles. Germany's highly developed industry will satisfy the highest requirements. Besides, it is necessary, in view of the changed situation, to strengthen and modernize the fortresses on the eastern frontier. The war readiness of the German navy and the strength of the coast fortifications can very greatly be increased in a short time. A strong will can achieve all this as if by witchcraft.

Our future lies in our own hands. Small men will talk finance and whine that we cannot afford it. We can find the necessary funds easily, in case of need, by loan. Goethe has told us that the character of a nation may be seen by the quality of its armies and law courts, and that finances are comparatively unimportant. The truth of this has been proved in the War of Liberation, when impoverished Prussia raised 200,000 soldiers and crushed Napoleon, although she had only 5,000,000 inhabitants.

In view of Germany's tremendous wealth, and in view of the fact that the future of State and nation are at stake, it seems criminal to speak of financial difficulties. Germany does not lack money. What we want is a firm will to greatness. Then only shall we obtain greatness. Every one must do his best. All true Germans must gather round the Emperor, ready to give their blood and their treasure for the honor, the greatness, and the future of the German nation. *"Through war to victory!"*

BY JULES CAMBON

Berlin, March 17, 1913.

Our naval and military attachés are sending to their respective Ministers reports on the new German military law. I take this opportunity of drawing the attention of your Excellency to these important documents.

The consideration of the financial expedients by which Germany intends to provide for these military measures is the sole cause of the delay in the publication of the definite proposals of the Government. *In spite of the patriotism with which the rich classes affect to accept the sacrifices asked of them, they are none the less, particularly the business circles, dissatisfied with the financial measures which have been announced,* and they feel that a compulsory levy imposed in times of peace creates a formidable precedent for the future. On the other hand, the Federal Governments have strongly opposed an innovation which grants to the Empire resources derived from direct taxation. Hitherto, taxation of this kind has been reserved to the Federal States, and the latter see in the surrender of this principle a new declaration of the corporate unity (*personalité*) of the Empire, constituting a distinct diminution of their own sovereign power.

However this may be, in increasing the strength of the

German army the Empire desires to leave nothing to chance in the event of a possible crisis.

The German changes have produced a result unexpected by that country, viz., the proposal of the Government of France to reëstablish the three years' service, and the manly determination with which this proposal has been welcomed in France. The surprise occasioned by these proposals has been utilized by the Imperial Government for the purpose of insisting on the absolute necessity of an increase of German military strength; the German proposals are represented as a reply to our own. The reverse is the case, since the immense military effort which France is undertaking is but the consequence of German initiative.

The Imperial Government is constantly rousing patriotic sentiment. Every day the Emperor delights to revive memories of 1813. Yesterday evening a military tattoo went through the streets of Berlin, and speeches were delivered in which *the present situation was compared to that of a hundred years ago.* The trend of public opinion will find an echo in the speeches which will be delivered next month in the Reichstag, and I have reason to fear that the Chancellor himself will be forced to allude in his statements to the relations of France and Germany. It was of course to be expected that national patriotism would be worked up just when fresh sacrifices are being required, but to compare the present time to 1813 is to misuse an historical analogy. If, to-day, there is anything corresponding to the movement which a hundred years ago roused Germans to fight the man of genius who aspired to universal dominion, it is in France that such a counterpart would have to be sought, since the French nation seeks but to protect itself against the domination of force.

Nevertheless, it is true that the state of public opinion in both countries makes the situation grave.

Berlin, November 22, 1913.

I have received from an absolutely reliable source an account of a conversation which took place a fortnight ago between the Emperor and the King of the Belgians, in the presence of the Chief of the General Staff—General von Moltke. This conversation, it appears, has made a profound impression on King Albert. I am in no way surprised at the impression he gathered, which corresponds with what I have myself felt for some time. Enmity against us is increasing, and the Emperor has ceased to be the friend of peace.

The person addressed by the Emperor had thought up till then, as did all the world, that William II., whose personal influence had been exerted on many critical occasions in support of peace, was still in the same state of mind. He found him this time completely changed. The German Emperor is no longer in his eyes the champion of peace against the warlike tendencies of certain parties in Germany. *William II. has come to think that war with France is inevitable,* and that it must come sooner or later. Naturally he believes in the crushing superiority of the German army and in its certain success.

General von Moltke spoke exactly in the same strain as his sovereign. He, too, declared war to be necessary and inevitable, but he showed himself still more assured of success, "for," he said to the King, "this time the matter must be settled, and your Majesty can have no conception of the irresistible enthusiasm with which the whole German people will be carried away when that day comes."

The King of the Belgians protested that it was a travesty of the intentions of the French Government to interpret them in that sense; and to let oneself be misled as to the sentiments of the French nation by the ebullitions of a few irresponsible spirits or the intrigues of unscrupulous agitators.

The Emperor and his Chief of the General Staff nevertheless persisted in their point of view.

During the course of this conversation the Emperor moreover seemed overstrained and irritable. As William II. advances in years, family traditions, the reactionary tendencies of the court, and especially the impatience of the soldiers, obtain a greater empire over his mind. Perhaps he feels some slight jealousy of the popularity acquired by his son, who flatters the passions of the Pan-Germans, and who does not regard the position occupied by the Empire in the world as commensurate with its power. Perhaps the reply of France to the last increase of the German army, the object of which was to establish the incontestable supremacy of Germany is, to a certain extent, responsible for his bitterness, for, *whatever may be said, it is realized that Germany cannot go much further.*

One may well ponder over the significance of this conversation. The Emperor and his Chief of the General Staff may have wished to impress the King of the Belgians and induce him not to make any opposition in the event of a conflict between us. Perhaps Germany would be glad to see Belgium less hostile to certain aspirations lately manifested here with regard to the Belgian Congo, but this last hypothesis does not seem to me to fit in with the interposition of General von Moltke.

For the rest, the Emperor William is less master of his impatience than is usually supposed. I have known him more than once to allow his real thoughts escape him. Whatever may have been the object of the conversation related to me, the revelation is none the less of extreme gravity. It tallies with the precariousness of the general situation and with the state of a certain shade of public opinion in France and Germany.

If I may be allowed to draw a conclusion, I would submit that it would be well to take account of this new factor, namely, that the Emperor is becoming used to an order of ideas which were formerly repugnant to him, and that, to borrow from him a phrase which he likes to use, "We must keep our powder dry."

SECRET DIPLOMATIC REPORT OF COLONEL PELLÉ, FRENCH MILITARY ATTACHÉ AT BERLIN IN 1912

We are discovering every day how deep and lasting are the feelings of injured pride and revenge provoked against us by the events of last year.

The Treaty of November 4, 1911, has proved a complete disillusion.

The feeling is the same in all parties. All Germans,

even the Socialists, bear us a grudge for having taken away their share in Morocco.

It seemed, a year or so ago, as if the Germans had set out to conquer the world. They considered themselves so strong that no one would dare to oppose them. Limitless possibilities were opening out for German manufacturers, German trade, German expansion.

Needless to say, these ideas and ambitions have not disappeared to-day. Germany always requires outlets for commercial and colonial expansion. They consider that they are entitled to them, because their population is increasing every day, because the future belongs to them. They consider us, with our forty million inhabitants, as a second rate power.

In the crisis of 1911, however, this second rate power successfully withstood them, and the Emperor and the Government gave way. Public opinion has forgiven neither them nor us. *People are determined that such a thing shall never happen again.*

SECRET DIPLOMATIC REPORT OF FRENCH FOREIGN OFFICE IN JULY, 1913

From observations which our agents in Germany have been able to collect from persons having access to the most diverse circles, it is possible to draw the conclusion that two feelings sway and irritate men's minds:—

(1) The Treaty of November 4, 1911, is considered a disappointment for Germany.

(2) France—a new France—undreamed of prior to the summer of 1911, is considered to be a warlike country, and to want war.

Members of all the parties in the Reichstag, from the Conservatives to the Socialists, representing the most different districts of Germany, university people from Berlin, Halle, Jena, and Marburg, students, elementary school teachers, commercial clerks, bank clerks, bankers, artisans, merchants, manufacturers, doctors, lawyers, editors of Democratic and Socialistic newspapers, Jewish publicists, members of trade unions, clergymen and shopkeepers from the

Mark of Brandenburg, country squires from Pomerania and shoemakers from Stettin celebrating the 505th anniversary of their association, country gentlemen, officials, priests, and large farmers from Westphalia, are unanimous on these two points, with very slight differences corresponding to their position in society or their political party.

The events of 1911 caused a profound disillusionment in Germany. A new France, united, determined, resolved not to be intimidated any longer, has emerged from the shroud in which she had been seen burying herself for the last ten years. Public opinion in Germany, from December to May, from the columns of the press of all parties, which reproached the Imperial Government for their incapacity and cowardice, has discovered with surprise mingled with irritation that the country conquered in 1870 had never ceased since then to carry on war, to float her flag and maintain the prestige of her arms in Asia and Africa, and to conquer vast territories; that Germany, on the other hand, had lived on her reputation, that Turkey is the only country in which during the reign of William II. she had made moral conquests, and these were now compromised by the disgrace of the Morocco solution. Each time that France made a colonial conquest this consolation was offered:—"Yes, but that does not prevent the decadence, anarchy, and dismemberment of France at home."

The public were mistaken and public opinion was misled.

Given this German public opinion that considers France as longing for war, what can be augured for the future as regards the possibility and proximity of war? . . .

People sometimes speak of a military party in Germany. The expression is inaccurate, even if it is intended to convey the idea that Germany is the country where military power is supreme, as it is said of France that it is the country where the civil power is supreme. There exists a state of mind which is more worthy of attention than this historical fact, because it constitutes a danger more evident and more recent. There is a war party, with leaders and followers, a press either convinced or subsidized for the purpose of creating public opinion; it has means both

THE SPIRIT OF PAN-SLAVISM

"Russia promises to leap straight from the Carpathians to Berlin."

Leon Bakst, the celebrated Russian artist, furnishes this Russian cartoon. In it he proclaims that his country will not be content merely to hold back Austria in a defensive war. When called on to defend the Serbian Slavs, she will cross the Carpathian Mountains, will overrun Austria, and is even able if necessary to fight Germany also. The Russian cartoons contain nothing of the keen insight of Dyson nor of the high spirituality of Raemaekers; they are savage, direct threats, meeting the similar German cartoons blow for blow.

CURSED BY HIS ANCESTORS
"Stupid blunderer! Foolish pupil!"

Among neutral cartoonists of the War, the most noted after Rae-maekers has been the Spanish artist Robida. This is perhaps his most striking cartoon. His designs are like those of the Russians, straight-forward, obvious and unaided by suggestion. From a gas-filled and malodorous heaven Frederick the Great looks down in fury, and Bis-marck, now become a winged cherub, glares in disgust. Both curse the blunderer who is ruining their work by stupidly misapplying their crafty falsehoods. While William II raises the crown of world empire to his own head, his son plays frivolously with the world, balancing it on a finger, and Bulgarian, Turkish and Austrian leaders smile ingratiatingly above the flames and ruin they have caused. But the World's bayonets are coming! Bismarck and Frederick see them, though the others do not.

varied and formidable for the intimidation of the Government. It goes to work in the country with clear ideas, burning aspirations, and a determination that is at once thrilling and fixed.

Those in favor of war are divided into several categories; each of these derives from its social caste, its class, its intellectual and moral education, its interests, its hates, special arguments which create a general attitude of mind and increase the strength and rapidity of the stream of warlike desire.

Some want war because in the present circumstances they think it is *inevitable*. And, as far as Germany is concerned, the sooner the better.

Others regard war as necessary for economic reasons based on overpopulation, overproduction, the need for markets and outlets; or for social reasons, *i.e., to provide the outside interests that alone can prevent or retard the rise to power of the democratic and socialist masses.*

Others, uneasy for the safety of the Empire, and believing that time is on the side of France, think that events should be brought to an immediate head. It is not unusual to meet, in the course of conversation or in the pages of patriotic pamphlets, the vague but deeply rooted conviction that a free Germany and a regenerated France are two historical facts mutually incompatible.

Others are bellicose from "Bismarckism'" as it may be termed. They feel themselves humiliated at having to enter into discussions with France, at being obliged to talk in terms of law and right in negotiations and conferences where they have not always found it easy to get right on their side, even when they have a preponderating force. From their still recent past they derive a sense of pride ever fed by personal memories of former exploits, by oral traditions, and by books, and irritated by the events of recent years. Angry disappointment is the unifying force of the *Wehrvereine,* and other associations of Young Germany.

Others again want war from a mystic hatred of revolutionary France; others finally from a feeling of rancor. These last are the people who heap up pretexts for war.

Coming to actual facts, these feelings take concrete form as follows:—The country squires represented in the Reichstag by the Conservative party *want at all costs to escape the death duties, which are bound to come if peace continues.* In the last sitting of the session which has just closed, the Reichstag agreed to these duties in principle. It is a serious attack on the interests and privileges of the landed gentry. On the other hand, this aristocracy is military in character, and it is instructive to compare the Army List with the year book of the nobility. War alone can prolong its prestige and support its family interest. During the discussions on the Army Bill, a Conservative speaker put forward the need for promotion among officers as an argument in its favor. Finally, this social class which forms a hierarchy with the King of Prussia as its supreme head, realizes with dread the democratization of Germany and the increasing power of the Socialist party, and considers its own days numbered. Not only does a formidable movement hostile to agrarian protection threaten its material interests, but in addition, the number of its political representatives decreases with each legislative period. In the Reichstag of 1878, out of 397 members, 162 belonged to the aristocracy; in 1898, 83; in 1912, 57. Out of this number, 27 alone belong to the Right, 14 to the Center, 7 to the Left, and one sits among the Socialists.

The higher bourgeoisie, represented by the National Liberal Party, the party of the contented spirits, have not the same reasons as the squires for wanting war. With a few exceptions, however, they are bellicose. They have their reasons, social in character.

The higher bourgeoisie is no less troubled than the aristocracy at the democratization of Germany. In 1871 they had 125 members in the Reichstag; in 1874, 155; in 1887, 99; in 1912, 45. They do not forget that in the years succeeding the war they played the leading rôle in parliament, helping Bismarck in his schemes against the country squires. Uneasily balanced to-day between Conservative instincts and Liberal ideas, they look to war to settle problems which their parliamentary representatives are painfully incapable of solving. In addition, doctrinaire manufacturers declare that the difficulties between themselves and their workmen originate in France, the home of revolutionary ideas of freedom—without France industrial unrest would be unknown.

Lastly, there are the manufacturers of guns and armor plate, big merchants who demand bigger markets, bankers who are speculating on the coming of the golden age and the next war indemnity—all these regard war as good business.

Amongst the "Bismarckians" must be reckoned officials of all kinds, represented fairly closely in the Reichstag by the Free Conservatives or Imperial Party. This is the party of the "pensioned," whose impetuous sentiments are poured out in the *Post*. They find disciples and political sympathizers in the various groups of young men whose minds have been trained and formed in the public schools and universities.

The universities, if we except a few distinguished spirits, develop a warlike philosophy. Economists demonstrate by statistics Germany's need for a colonial and commercial empire commensurate with the industrial output of the Empire. There are sociological fanatics who go even further. *The armed peace, so they say, is a crushing burden on the nations,* it checks improvement in the lot of the masses, and assists the growth of socialism. France, by clinging obstinately to her desire for revenge, opposes disarmament. Once for all, she must be reduced, for a century, to a state of impotence; that is the best and speediest way of solving the social problem.

Historians, philosophers, political pamphleteers and other apologists of German *Kultur* wish to impose upon the world a way of thinking and feeling specifically German. They wish to wrest from France that intellectual supremacy which, according to the clearest thinkers, is still her possession. From this source is derived the phraseology of the Pan-Germans and the ideas and adherents of the *Kriegsvereine, Wehrvereine,* and other similar associations.

We come finally to those whose support of the war

policy is inspired by rancor and resentment. These are the most dangerous. They are recruited chiefly among diplomatists. German diplomatists are now in very bad odor in public opinion. The most bitter are those who since 1905 have been engaged in the negotiations between France and Germany; they are heaping together and reckoning up their grievances against us, and one day they will present their accounts in the war press. It seems as if they were looking for grievances chiefly in Morocco, though an incident is always possible in any part of the globe where France and Germany are in contact.

They must have their revenge, for they complain that they have been duped. During the discussion on the Army Bill one of these warlike diplomatists exclaimed, "Germany will not be able to have any serious conversation with France until she has every sound man under arms."

In what terms will this conversation be couched? The opinion is fairly widely spread, even in Pan-German circles, that Germany will not declare war in view of the system of defensive alliances and the tendencies of the Emperor. But when the moment comes, *she will have to try in every possible way to force France to attack her*. Offense will be given if necessary. That is the Prussian tradition.

Must war then be considered as inevitable?

It is hardly likely that Germany will take the risk, if France can make it clear to the world that the *Entente Cordiale* and the Russian alliance are not mere diplomatic fictions but realities which exist and will make themselves felt. *The British fleet inspires a wholesome terror.* It is well known, however, that victory on sea will leave everything in suspense. On land alone can a decisive issue be obtained.

As for Russia, even though she carries greater weight in political and military circles than was the case three or four years ago, it is not believed that her coöperation will be sufficiently rapid and energetic to be effective.

People's minds are thus getting used to consider the next war as a duel between France and Germany.

THE ASSASSINATION OF THE AUSTRIAN CROWN PRINCE

WHOSE VICTIM, AND WHOSE OPPORTUNITY?

JUNE 28, 1914

AUSTRIAN OFFICIAL REPORT

CRAWFURD PRICE   SIGMUND MÜNZ

The incidents which led up to the death of the Austrian Crown Prince Franz Ferdinand have been carefully wrapped in obscurity. Briefly outlined, what we know is that the prince paid a visit of state to Serajevo, the capital of the discontented province of Bosnia. Prince Ferdinand was a strong, hard, seemingly cold man in permanent disfavor at the Hapsburg court because he had defied the family tradition and insisted on wedding "beneath" him. Moreover his bride, perhaps the only person in the world who was deeply devoted to him, was of the despised Slavic race. The aged emperor, Franz Josef, unwillingly created the lady a duchess, but she never received full recognition in the royal court. She was that peculiar fantasy of monarchial pomp, a "morganatic" wife, wedded to the man but not to the prince. Her children could never succeed their father on the Hapsburg throne. For this and other reasons there was a breach between Franz Ferdinand and the other Hapsburgs, and he dwelt mainly at his country home of Konopischt with his wife and children. Here he was visited early in 1914 by Emperor William of Germany.

After that, all is vague. There have been persistent rumors that William and Franz Ferdinand formed an alliance, and that thereafter the other Hapsburgs were determined to destroy Franz Ferdinand before he succeeded his aged father on the throne and drove them all from power. The gist of these rumors has been concentrated into two tales, two speeches. Emperor William is reported to have said on learning of Ferdinand's death, "Now, I shall have to begin my work all over again." More probable is the other bitterly natural tale that Ferdinand himself in dying said of his assassin, "Vienna will give him a decoration for this."

Before the prince went to Serajevo, the region was known to be in a ferment of discontent; and he was repeatedly advised not to risk his life by venturing there. Rumor again enters here with a tale of his unwillingness to go and of his being driven to it by Hapsburg taunts of cowardice. If these tales are false in spirit or in fact, the Austrian court has only itself to blame; for they have been bred by its policy of secrecy. What is undeniable in fact and most impressive is that, in a country long accustomed to elaborate police control, the heir of the throne was sent into an openly rebellious district and was given a police protection utterly inefficient, glaringly inadequate. As he and his wife drove through the town in procession, a man, Cabrinovic, found it easy to step close to the royal carriage and hurl at it a bomb which barely missed the doomed couple. Here again steps in rumor to picture events at the Mayor's reception after this first assault. On one hand the prince is represented as haughtily lecturing his city hosts for their insufficient protection, and as refusing their entreaties that he would not venture on a similar ride back to his hotel. On the other, he is represented as foreseeing the result, hesitating to go out, and being urged to his fate by crafty enemies. At any rate, he rode forth again, and a young Bosnian student, Gavrilo Princip, found it easy to step close up to the royal carriage with a revolver. The poor "duchess" wife, Slavic, morganatic, but a lover of her husband, threw herself in front of the revolver. Princip fired twice. The first shot slew the wife, and the second the husband. Each died almost immediately.

The burial of the royal pair was hurried, poor and unhonored by any of the dignity of royal pomp. Some desolating fear hung over it; and all of good that can be seen in the disaster is that at least if the unbefriended couple had to go, they were happy in that they went together.

Both Princip and Cabrinovic were seized by the surrounding people immediately after their attacks. They were tried secretly and condemned to secret imprisonment, their trials being under the supervision of the Austrian Under-Secretary of State Forgach. This wretch, Forgach, had previously been convicted of forging documents to convict Slavic victims in previous political trials, a crime for which he had been pardoned and promoted.

Despite our natural repudiation of any statement issued under Forgach, there seems little doubt as to Princip's personality, his purpose and his fate. He was a Slavic youth inflamed by the wrongs of his race; and he is reported to have been consumptive and to have died in prison. Cabrinovic, however, remains vague, as does the whole affair. He is reported to have been an Austrian, the son of a former official and himself a spy in the police service. His crime could thus have had no patriotic motive, no moral dignity. What became of him we do not know. Darkness has swallowed him up again, just as darkness spewed him forth, the one utterly sordid, soulless, ineffective creature in the world's great tragedy.

We give here the official statement of the Austrian court which first classes the two attacks as one, which they probably were not, and then traces them, not by evidence but by a mere chain of argument, to the Serbian Government. In contrast to this we quote a general survey of the Serajevo affair from "The Dawn of Armageddon" by Crawfurd Price, a British authority on Serbian affairs. Then follows a frank estimate of the Crown Prince and of his fate by the prominent Austrian diplomat and liberal thinker, Sigmund Münz.

C. F. H.

THE AUSTRIAN OFFICIAL REPORT

*Record of the District Court at Serajevo, touching the pro-
ceedings there instituted against Gavrilo Princip and
confederates on account of the crime of assassination
perpetrated on June 28, 1914, on His Imperial and
Royal Highness the Archduke Franz Ferdinand of
Austria-Este and Her Highness the Duchess Sophie of
Hohenberg.*

GAVRILO PRINCIP, Nedeljko Cabrinovic, Trifko
Grabez, Vaso Cubrilovic and Cetres Popovic confess
that in common with the fugitive Mehemed Mehmedbasic
they contrived a plot for the murder of the Archduke Franz
Ferdinand and, armed with bombs and in the case of some
of them with Browning pistols, laid wait for him on June
28, 1914, on his progress through Serajevo for the purpose of carrying out the planned attack.

Nedeljko Cabrinovic confesses that he was the first of
the conspirators to hurl a bomb against the Archduke's carriage, which missed its mark and which on exploding injured
only the occupants of the carriage following the Archducal
motor car.

Gavrilo Princip confesses that he fired two shots from
a Browning pistol against the Archducal motor car, by which
the Archduke Franz Ferdinand and the Duchess Sophie of
Hohenberg received fatal wounds.

Both perpetrators confess that the act was done with
intent to murder.

These confessions have been fully verified by means of
the investigations which have taken place, and it is established that the deceased Archduke Franz Ferdinand and the
deceased Duchess Sophie of Hohenberg died as a result of
the revolver shots fired at them by Gavrilo Princip.

The accused have made the following declarations, which
are essentially consistent, before the examining magistrate:—

In April, 1914, Princip, during his stay at Belgrade,
where he associated with a number of Serbian students in
the cafés of the town, conceived the plan for the execution

of an attempt on the life of the late Archduke Franz Ferdinand. He communicated this intention to his acquaintance, Cabrinovic, who also was in Belgrade at the time. The latter had already conceived a similar idea and was ready at once to participate in the attempt. The execution of an attempt on the Archduke's life was a frequent topic of conversation in the circle in which Princip and Cabrinovic moved, because the Archduke was considered to be a dangerous enemy of the Serbian people.

Princip and Cabrinovic desired at first to procure the bombs and weapons necessary for the execution of the deed from the Serbian Major Milan Pribicevic or from the Narodna Odbrana,[1] as they themselves did not possess the means for their purchase. As, however, Major Pribicevic and the authoritative member of the said association, Zivojin Dacic, were absent from Belgrade at that time, they decided to try to obtain the weapons from their acquaintance Milan Ciganovic, who had formerly been a Komitadji and was at that time in the employment of the State railways.

Princip, through the instrumentality of an intimate friend of Ciganovic, now got into communication with the latter. Thereupon Ciganovic called on Princip and discussed the planned attempt with him. He entirely approved it, and thereupon declared that he would like to consider further whether he should provide the weapons for the attempt. Cabrinovic also talked with Ciganovic on the subject of the weapons.

At Easter Princip took Trifko Grabez, who also was in Belgrade, into his confidence. The latter is also shown by his own confession to have declared himself ready to take part in the attempt.

In the following weeks Princip had repeated conversations with Ciganovic about the execution of the attempt.

Meanwhile Ciganovic had reached an understanding on the subject of the planned attack with the Serbian Major Voja Tankosic, who was a close friend of his and who then placed at his disposal for this object the Browning pistols.

[1] The chief Serbian society devoted to the cause of freedom for the Slavs in every land.

Grabez confesses in conformity with the depositions of Princip and Cabrinovic that on the 24th of May he, accompanied by Ciganovic, visited Major Tankosic at the latter's request at his rooms. He says that after he had been introduced Tankosic said to him: "Are you the man? Are you determined?" Whereupon Grabez answered: "I am." Tankosic next asked: "Do you know how to shoot with a revolver?" and when Grabez answered in the negative Tankosic said to Ciganovic: "I will give you a revolver, go and teach them how to shoot."

Hereupon Ciganovic conducted Princip and Grabez to the military rifle range at Topcider and instructed them in a wood adjoining the range in shooting with a Browning pistol at a target. Princip proved himself the better shot of the two. Ciganovic also familiarized Princip, Grabez and Cabrinovic with the use of bombs which were given them.

On the 27th of May, 1914, Ciganovic handed over to Princip, Cabrinovic and Grabez, as their confessions agree in stating, six bombs, four Browning revolvers and a sufficient quantity of ammunition as well as a glass tube of cyanide of potassium with which to poison themselves after the accomplishment of the deed in order that the secret might be kept. Moreover, Ciganovic gave them some money.

Princip had previously informed Danilo Ilic, at Easter, of his plan of assassination. He now begged the latter on his return to Serajevo to enlist certain additional persons, in order to ensure the success of the attempt. Hereupon Ilic according to his confession enlisted Jaso Cubrilovic, Cetro Popovic and Mehemed Mehmedbasic in the plot.

Only one of the bombs was made use of in the execution of the attempt. The remaining five bombs came later into the possession of the police at Serajevo.

In the opinion of the judicial experts these bombs are Serbian hand-grenades which were factory-made and intended for military purposes. They are identical with the 21 bombs which were found in the Save at Brcko in the year 1913 and which were partly in their original packing, which proved without a doubt that they came from the Serbian arsenal of Kragujevatz.

It is thus proved that the grenades which were used in the attempt against the Archduke Franz Ferdinand also came from the stores of the Army Depot at Kragujevatz.

Grabez quite spontaneously calls the grenades which were handed over to him and his accomplices "Kragujevatz bombs."

.   .   .   .   .   .

It is clear how far the criminal agitation of the Narodna Odbrana and those who shared in its views, has of late been primarily directed against the person of the hereditary Archduke. From these facts, the conclusion may be drawn that the Narodna Odbrana, as well as the associations hostile to the Monarchy in Serbia, which were grouped round it, recently decided that the hour had struck to translate theory into practice.

It is noteworthy, however, that the Narodna limits itself in this way to inciting, and where the incitement has fallen on fertile soil to providing means of material assistance for the realization of its plans, but that it has confided the only dangerous part of this propaganda of action to the youth of the Monarchy, which it has excited and corrupted, and which alone has to bear the burden of this miserable "heroism."

All the characteristics of this procedure are found in the history and origin of the profoundly regrettable outrage of the 28th of June.

Princip and Grabez are characteristic examples of young men who have been poisoned from their school days by the doctrines of the Narodna Odbrana.

At Belgrade, where he frequented the society of students imbued with these ideas, Princip busied himself with criminal plans against the Archduke Franz Ferdinand, against whom the hatred of the Serbian element hostile to the Monarchy was particularly acute on the occasion of his tour in the annexed territories.

He was joined by Cabrinovic, who moved in the same circles, and whose shifting and radically revolutionary views, as he himself admits, as well as the influence of his surroundings in Belgrade and the reading of the Serbian papers, inspired him with the same sense of hostility to the Monarchy, and brought him into the propaganda of action.

Thanks to the state of mind in which he already was, Grabez succumbed very quickly to this milieu, which he now entered.

But however far this plot may have prospered, and however determined the conspirators may have been to carry out the attempt, it would never have been effected, if people had not been found, as in the case of Jukic, to provide the accomplices with means of committing their crime. For, as Princip and Cabrinovic have expressly admitted, they lacked the necessary arms, as well as the money to purchase them.

It is interesting to see where the accomplices tried to procure their arms. Milan Pribicevic and Zivojin Dacic, the two principal men in the Narodna Odbrana, were the first accomplices thought of as a sure source of help in their need, doubtless because it had already become a tradition amongst those ready to commit crimes that they could obtain instruments for murder from these representatives of the Narodna Odbrana. The accidental circumstance that these two men were not at Belgrade at the critical moment doubtless balked this plan. However, Princip and Cabrinovic were not at a loss in finding other help, that of Milan Ciganovic, an ex-komitadji, and now a railway official at Belgrade, and at the same time an active member of the Narodna Odbrana, who, in 1909, first appeared as a pupil at the school at Cuprija. Princip and Cabrinovic were not deceived in their expectations, as they at once received the necessary help from Ciganovic.

BY CRAWFURD PRICE

During the first six months of 1914 a remarkable series of Conferences between various European crowned heads and statesmen—notably those of the Triple Alliance—were the outward sign of a troubled diplomatic situation; and principal among them stood out the meeting between the Kaiser and the Archduke Franz Ferdinand at Konopischt, where it is probable that an aggressive program was arranged between the Central Powers. During the whole of this period the Balkan situation was in a very unsettled state. The Albanian régime under Prince William of Wied had proved a conspicuous failure, and Turkey, who was in close collaboration with Germany, evidenced a desire to regain the sovereignty of the Ægean Islands, which had been allotted to Greece, and further provoked Athens by atrociously persecuting the Hellenes in Asia Minor.

What was the nature of the program elaborated at Konopischt we shall probably never learn. That it concerned a deliberate attempt to upset the Bucharest settlement and exploit the recently arranged rapprochement between Bulgaria and Turkey (together with, perhaps, the unsatisfactory situation in Albania) to the profit of Austria as the advance guard of Pan-Germanism in the Balkans, is obvious from the trend of Teuton-Magyar diplomacy and the bleatings of the officially-inspired Press. But into the prevailing unrest was suddenly thrown the assassination of the Archduke Franz Ferdinand at Serajevo on June 28, 1914.

On the morning of that fatal day the Austrian heir-apparent was driving in the town when a man named Cabrinovic threw two bombs, which fell short. A natural indisposition to take further risks appears to have been overridden by official determination, and during the afternoon's procession the assassin Princip murdered the Archduke and his consort by means of two well-aimed shots from an automatic pistol. The Administration naturally alleged the existence of a widespread plot, directed, of course, from Belgrade; but the two principals had little in common, and it is more logical to suggest that no understanding existed between them. Cabrinovic was a known anarchist and the son of an Austrian spy, while Princip was a student, remarkable for his industry and application, who had been exiled from his home and politically persecuted by the authorities. The one alleged outside instigation; the other proclaimed his individual responsibility. Both were Austrian subjects.

In effect, the Archduke was the victim of a régime which had held Bosnia in bondage for more than thirty years, and which all but openly declared that its object was to exterminate the individuality of the Serbian race. Such methods as had been employed invariably breed their own reward. While for lack of definite proof we pass over the possibility that the crime was deliberately planned by the Pan-Germanists, there is surely little occasion for surprise that some spirit more highly strung, more emotional than its fellows, should have provoked outrage in order to call the attention of Europe to conditions of existence that were fast becoming intolerable to an enslaved people.

Disraeli once said that "Assassination never yet changed the history of the world," and in this instance it would have served only for an increase of repression in Bosnia, had not Austria-Hungary, and with her Germany, been ready to utilize any and every excuse for accomplishing their desire to annihilate Serbia as a step in the direction of world hegemony. Despite the anxiety of the Vienna and Budapest newspapers to fasten the responsibility upon Serbia, there were no immediate developments. As a matter of fact, it would seem that the crime at first upset some deeply-laid German plan, for the Kaiser, on learning the news, is alleged to have remarked significantly: "All my work must be recommenced." But the Austro-Hungarian diplomats were quick to recognize the new and unlooked-for opportunity of carrying through their nefarious schemes.

"We must settle our account with Serbia," wrote Baron von Giesl from Belgrade to his Government. "Both in order that our Monarchy may preserve its position as a Great Power, and even in order that it may continue to exist as a Great Power, a war is inevitable. If we hesitate to place our relations with our neighbor on a clear basis, we must share the responsibility for the difficulties and unfavorable conditions of the conflict which must necessarily be engaged, sooner or later, in the future. If we are resolved to present formidable demands, together with a demand for a real control—for only a control of this kind will succeed in cleaning out the Augean stables of Pan-Slav agitation—we must take into consideration all the possible consequences of our action and possess, from the very commencement, the firm will to obtain our requirements. Half-measures and protracted negotiations, resulting in a mixed compromise, would be the hardest blow that could be dealt at the credit of Austria in Serbia and the situation in Europe."

In short, the Baron saw that the long-awaited occasion to secure that real control of Serbia for which Austria had so persistently striven had at length arrived. His advice obviously accorded with the opinion prevalent in Vienna and Berlin. Moreover, the situation in Europe seemed favorable. England had her Irish crisis, France her Caillaux scandal, and Russia her labor troubles. The military position was likewise propitious for the Central Powers. The Vienna *Militaerische Rundschau* declared: "The moment is yet favorable for us. If we do not decide upon war now, we shall have to fight in two or three years at the latest in less favorable circumstances. At present the initiative lies with us; Russia is not ready, the moral factors are with us, as also is the force. As we must fight some day, let us provoke the conflict immediately."

Despite the bellicose attitude of the major part of the Austro-Hungarian press and the general effort to convey to Europe the impression that the assassination was the result of a plot prepared in Serbia, the exchange of views occasioned in diplomatic circles justified a hope that there would be no untoward development. Serbia took early steps to make her position clear. On June 30th, M. Yovanovitch [2] advised Baron Macchio that "The Serbian Government most energetically disapproves of the Serajevo murder and on its part will loyally do everything possible to demonstrate that it will not tolerate on its territory any agitation or enterprise calculated to jeopardize our relations with Austria-Hungary, already so delicate." The following day M. Pashitch notified his Ministers accredited to European Courts that the crime had met with the reprobation of all classes in Serbia, where it was recognized that it might have a most unfavorable repercussion upon relations with the Monarchy. He protested, however, against the endeavor of the Austro-Hungarian press to saddle Serbia with the responsibility for

[2] The Serbian Minister at Vienna.

an act of madness committed by an Austrian subject which it was in the vital interest of Serbia herself to avert. This spirit seems at first to have been reflected or assumed by Austro-Hungarian diplomacy. On June 30th the Austrian Ambassador at Constantinople assured the Serbian *chargé d'affaires* that he need have no fear lest the event should endanger the more satisfactory relations existing between the two States, and on July 3rd Baron Macchio told M. Yovanovitch at Vienna that Austria-Hungary accused neither the Serbian people nor their Government, but "certain agitators." Finally, the aged Emperor himself, in addressing the Austrian and Hungarian Presidents of Council, declared that he was "convinced that the murder is only the work of a small group of misguided persons."

It was scarcely necessary for M. Pashitch to assure the world through his Ministers that the incident was regarded with unmixed disapproval by King Peter's Cabinet, for, apart from the obvious fact that the State had pressing need of a prolonged peace in which to repair the wastage of the recent campaigns and consolidate her conquests, the Government had striven to guard against any aggravation of their relations with the neighboring monarchy. Any anarchistic tendency in Belgrade had been carefully watched, and, indeed, the Belgrade police had actually warned their Vienna confrères against Cabrinovic—to no purpose—and on June 21st M. Pashitch himself had advised the Ballplatz of his suspicions that a plot was being organized in Bosnia. It is evidences such as these, added to the unpopularity of the Archduke Franz Ferdinand in certain Viennese circles, the Emperor's preference for the Archduke Karl, and the fact that in the alleged presence of a widespread conspiracy (signaled by the Serajevo police the following day, and of which, if it existed, they must have been well aware previously) the victim was driven into public again after Cabrinovic's abortive attempt on his life, which lent weight to the suggestion that the crime was actually abetted by the Austro-Hungarian authorities themselves.

When this has been said, however, it must be admitted that the suspicions that some of the principal actors in the

Serajevo drama were in close relation with persons at Belgrade were too strong to be passed over in silence by the Austro-Hungarian authorities.   Under the circumstances, the Monarchy very properly might have acquainted the Serbian Government with the facts and the names of those compromised by the evidence and called upon them: (1) To hold answerable those judged who were in Serbian territory, and (2) To give guarantees for a more effective control of the Pan-Serbian movement.

Had this very logical course been adopted, it is evident from the declaration made by M. Pashitch and the reply subsequently sent by Serbia to the Austrian ultimatum that the matter could have been arranged in a manner apparently satisfactory to all parties.   That the possibility of such an equitable arrangement was not overlooked in the early days following the tragedy is obvious from the assurances given to the Entente in Vienna that the conditions imposed upon Serbia would be most acceptable and such as would permit them to count upon a pacific solution of the crisis.   Further, on July 8th, the *Pester Lloyd* (Budapest) declared that—"Nothing will be demanded from the Serbian Government that can affect their natural self-consciousness or the national dignity entrusted to their care."

BY SIGMUND MÜNZ

During the last decade of Francis Joseph's reign, there were many believers who, at the time of prayer, turned their faces in the direction of Konopischt.   The Crown Prince's ideas were interpreted, it was generally believed, by the *Reichspost*—a newspaper whose programme included clericalism, anti-Semitism, militarism, war, hatred of Serbia, and detestation of everything Italian.   The old Emperor showed a far more sympathetic understanding for Italy and the Italians than his heir.   Despite his surname, d'Este, his mother's descent from the house of Bourbon-Sicily, his Este estates in Upper Italy and the neighborhood of Rome, his knowledge of fine arts, Francis Ferdinand was no favorable critic of Italy.   When I visited Luzzatti—then President of the Council—in Rome in May,

WHAT BELGIUM FACED

This is one of the series of terrible pictures with which the Belgian artist Jean Domergue illustrated the Official Belgian Report of deeds actually perpetrated by the Germans in Belgium. Only deeds sworn to by a sufferer or some eye-witness are recorded in this awful report book. The picture here is of five farmers who were driven into Lebbeke bound arm to arm, and there had their eyes put out with sharp irons. Afterward, while bound and blinded, they were beaten.

A BETTER 'OLE

"Well, if you knows of a better 'ole, go to it."

When the grim humor of the actual warfare in the trenches superseded the cartooning of the preliminaries of the War, the work of the
Britisher, Bruce Bairnsfather, stood out at once as the climax of this
style of art. Best known of all his cartoons is this one, which has
supplied a title both to books and to plays. It is typical also, in a
larger sense, of Britain's whole position in the Great War. The fight was
not of her seeking. If she could have found any possible way to a
"better 'ole" she would most eagerly have taken it, as her Foreign Minister so repeatedly proved in his negotiations. But since there was no
other place for her than in the forefront of the battle, no "better 'ole,"
she accepted her responsibility and fought the good fight as resolutely
and as stubbornly as "Old Bill" himself.

1910, one of his first remarks was: "But why is your Crown Prince, the Archduke, so very hostile to us?" I was silent, and then answered: "Perhaps the Italians are confusing strong clerical feeling and attachment to the Pope with enmity against Italy."

It was with the murder of the heir to the Austro-Hungarian throne that this terrible world-war began. Is it not in itself a frightful thought that, even if his death was not the cause but only a pretext for a world-war, one human being, however high in rank, should claim such fearful sacrifices? And this prince of the House of Hapsburg had still to prove himself the elect of mankind. To tell the truth, he had by no means the gift of making himself beloved by his people. In popularity he was far behind his old uncle, and was even said to have been put in the shade by his nephew,[1] to whom, especially immediately after his accession, nobody denied the qualities of sincere goodwill, unprejudiced love of humanity, and an honorable striving after peace. All Charles's better qualities were, of course, wrecked by his weakness of character, his unreliability, his ignorance, and his lack of talent.

Francis Ferdinand was censured for his inclination to cruelty and his extreme avarice. He showed little magnanimity towards his subordinates, and little humanity towards the poor and the oppressed. He was more of a bigoted Roman Churchman than a Christian, and, like the mob, he was hostile to the Jews. His ambition, apparently, was to become a Catholic and Austrian edition of the Emperor William II., whom he imitated in his endeavors to build a strong fleet. He seemed destined to become a scourge, rather than a helper and father, to the nations of the Dual Monarchy. If a man's character may be surmised from his face, his features showed as little distinction as his nature. His changing moods would hurl deserving friends and fellow-workers into the abyss of disfavor, and his hatred knew no bounds. Baron Beck, his adviser, who had backed up his morganatic marriage with Countess Chotek, was ruthlessly thrust aside by his Cæsarian arrog-

[1] Charles, who became Emperor in 1916.

ance, which was capable of working up into uncontrolled hatred. He never forgave the suffragan Bishop of Vienna, Marschall, who had been his tutor and friend, for ranging himself on the side of the old Emperor and the Court, who opposed the marriage, and avenged himself by thwarting his nomination as Archbishop of Vienna. And he never forgave Baron Beck, whom he had intended in due time to appoint his own Prime Minister, for accepting a ministerial appointment without his—the Archduke's permission.

The old Emperor could not feel very happy concerning him, and he had an idea that his nephew, thirsting for power and waiting impatiently for his death, enjoyed making him angry. It was in this strain, as I heard later, that the old Emperor spoke to General von Schönaich, the former Secretary of State for War. The former Prime Minister, Körber, who has since died, told me that Francis Ferdinand, who for some time had represented the Emperor in various State duties, had never had enough heart to pardon a man who was condemned to death, however forcible the reasons urging him to mercy. He hated the Liberal newspapers and every Liberal publication like the plague. He dreamed of a powerful Austria, and, to attain this end, did not, perhaps, shrink from the prospect of war, even if we must not be so unjust as positively to assert that he joined with William II. in conspiring against peace.

The murderer of Serajevo, who ended two lives at the same moment, challenged world-wide condemnation by his infamous act. Consternation at the crime, however, prevailed for only a short time over feelings of pity at the horror of the deed. Before the corpses had been lowered into the vault, it seemed as if a feeling of emancipation emerged among the greater part of the population. People breathed again. This was the Emperor they had desired least. Only some vain courtiers, some servants of his despotic moods, believed that the Divine decree had cheated them out of their guiding star. And it was for this somewhat ignoble being that the five continents of the globe were to be drained of blood for years!

THE KAISER'S DECISIVE STEP

THE HOHENZOLLERNS PLAN TO DIVIDE THE WORLD AMONG THEIR FOLLOWERS

JULY 5, 1914

HENRY MORGENTHAU   WILLIAM MUHLON
AUGUST THYSSEN   AUSTRIAN OFFICIAL RECORD

Twice during the year 1917 members of the German Reichstag referred, in their debates, to the "Potsdam meeting of July 5, 1914." These references were promptly suppressed by the German Government; but all the world now knows that on that tragic date the Kaiser conferred with his chief advisers at his palace at Potsdam and they agreed to make the Serajevo murder the occasion for establishing Germany's leadership of the world. Serbia was to be obliterated, Austria's vassalage to be increased, and France and Russia to be terrified into submission. Austria's representatives were promised unlimited support in crushing Serbia. Every man consulted knew that this meant war, and no man knew how far the war might spread.

The Austrian rulers readily concurred in this "Potsdam Plot," though we now know that they only looked to it as involving war on helpless Serbia, and expected Germany to protect them from the danger of a general European war. The publication of the Austrian Government records in 1919 gave proof of Austria's part in the plot; and the Bavarian records added further evidence.

These confirmations were, however, unnecessary. Before the end of the Great War three different Germans of high authority had given to the world plain evidence of the long-studied preparation of this plot for looting the world. The first and most important of these witnesses was one of the high conspirators themselves. This was the Baron von Wangenheim, German Ambassador to Turkey, who confidently expected to become the Imperial Chancellor, but who died of apoplexy at Constantinople in 1915. During Germany's first sweeping tide of success, Von Wangenheim boasted of the successful scheme to the United States Ambassador to Turkey, Hon. Henry Morgenthau. Mr. Morgenthau transcribed the account in his truly remarkable book, "Ambassador Morgenthau's Story," which must always remain our chief authority for all the important and dramatic events which centered around Constantinople in the early days of the War.

Our second witness is Dr. William Muhlon, a prominent German financier and diplomat. He was not himself at the Potsdam meeting, but as a director of Krupp's, the great government munition makers, he was given immediate warning of it. He says that he received the details from two of the chief leaders, Herr Krupp von Bohlen, head of the Krupp works, and Dr. Helfferich, President of the Imperial Bank, and thus the financial head of Germany. Herr Muhlon has written a book in which he describes how he watched with ever-increasing horror the evils springing from the great plot, and how he ultimately abandoned Germany in despair and dwelt in Switzerland. He first publicly announced his attitude of revolt in an open letter to Chancellor Bethmann-Hollweg in 1917. Then in March, 1918, he published in a Berlin paper a brief, crisp résumé of his knowledge of the plot. The two historic documents are both given here.

Far more astounding is our third witness. August Thyssen was before the War the chief steel magnate of Germany, a Carnegie not yet retired from business, but over seventy years old, and rich, one would have thought, beyond the gross temptation of murder for plunder's sake. In 1917 Herr Thyssen issued the statement here reprinted. It is valuable partly for its added light upon the Hohenzollern plot in its handling of the German capitalists. Even more, however, Thyssen's statement deserves closest study for its revelation of the soul—if soul it can be called—of a German money king. He tells of the world-conquest purely as a business venture. He entered it to make money; and he agreed to pay for war and wholesale slaughter, apparently without the faintest compunction, or even any conception that he was blameworthy. Far from self-condemnation, his whole money-soul is writhing only because the Hohenzollerns have not lived up to their contract and handed him his profits. Instead they have called on him for more money. That, indeed, stirs his conscience into agony. He rages at their "blackmail." He sees it as a crime, against which all men will shriek. Is murder wrong? No, nor the plot to plunder whole nations. That had been business—good business. Obviously Herr Thyssen still thinks so. But to threaten him, a money king, and attack his properties! Will mankind submit to his enduring such an outrage! Herr Thyssen thinks not.

Never perhaps since time began has any other man so utterly damned himself out of his own mouth as has this Herr Thyssen in his whining protest against the dishonest company in which he finds himself. Indeed, though the Thyssen pamphlet has been widely circulated and stands undenied, yet perhaps we may some day learn that it was a forgery. On its face it is almost unbelievable. It is too perfect for anything but fiction—too typical to be true.

C. F. H.

BY HENRY MORGENTHAU [1]

U. S. Ambassador in Constantinople

ON June 29th we heard of the assassination of the Grand Duke of Austria and his consort. Everybody received the news calmly; there was, indeed, a stunned feeling that something momentous had happened, but there was practically no excitement. A day or two after this tragedy I had a long talk with Talaat [2] on diplomatic matters; he made no

[1] Copyright, 1918, by Doubleday & Page.
[2] Talaat Bey, the Turkish Minister of the Interior, was the chief leader of the "Young Turks" and the real ruler of the country, he and Enver Bey having seized control by a murderous revolt in 1913.

reference at all to this event. I think now that we were all affected by a kind of emotional paralysis—as we were nearer the center than most people, we certainly realized the dangers in the situation. In a day or two our tongues seemed to have been loosened, for we began to talk—and to talk war. When I saw Von Mutius, the German chargé, and Weitz, the diplomat-correspondent of the *Frankfurter Zeitung,* they also discussed the impending conflict, and again they gave their forecast a characteristically Germanic touch; when war came, they said, of course the United States would take advantage of it to get all the Mexican and South American trade!

When I called upon Pallavicini [3] to express my condolences over the Grand Duke's death, he received me with the most stately solemnity. He was conscious that he was representing the imperial family, and his grief seemed to be personal; one would think that he had lost his own son. I expressed my abhorrence and that of my nation for the deed, and our sympathy with the aged emperor.

"Ja, Ja, es ist sehr schrecklich" (yes, yes, it is very terrible), he answered, almost in a whisper.

"Serbia will be condemned for her conduct," he added. "She will be compelled to make reparation."

A few days later, when Pallavicini called upon me, he spoke of the nationalistic societies that Serbia had permitted to exist and of her determination to annex Bosnia and Herzegovina. He said that his government would insist on the abandonment of these societies and these pretensions, and that probably a punitive expedition into Serbia would be necessary to prevent such outrages as the murder of the Grand Duke. Herein I had my first intimation of the famous ultimatum of July 23rd.

The entire diplomatic corps attended the requiem mass for the Grand Duke and Duchess, celebrated at the Church of Sainte Marie on July 4th. The church is located in the Grande Rue de Pera, not far from the Austrian Embassy; to reach it we had to descend a flight of forty stone steps. At the top of these stairs representatives of the Austrian

[3] The Austrian Ambassador at Constantinople.

Embassy, dressed in full uniform, with crêpe on the left arm, met us, and escorted us to our seats. All the ambassadors sat in the front pew; I recall this with strange emotions now, for it was the last time that we ever sat together. The service was dignified and beautiful; I remember it with especial vividness because of the contrasting scene that immediately followed. When the stately, gorgeously robed priests had finished, we all shook hands with the Austrian Ambassador, returned to our automobiles, and started on our eight-mile ride along the Bosphorus to the American Embassy. For this day was not only the day when we paid our tribute to the murdered heir of this medieval autocracy; it was also the Fourth of July.

The very setting of the two scenes symbolized these two national ideals. I always think of this ambassadorial group going down those stone steps to the church, to pay their respect to the Grand Duke, and then going up to the gayly decorated American Embassy, to pay their respect to the Declaration of Independence. . . .

In glancing at the ambassadorial group at the church and, afterward, at our reception, I was surprised to note that one familiar figure was missing. Wangenheim, Austria's ally, was not present. This somewhat puzzled me at the time, but afterward I had the explanation from Wangenheim's own lips. He had left some days before for Berlin. The Kaiser had summoned him to an imperial council, which met on July 5th, and which decided to plunge Europe into war.

[The author fully describes Baron von Wangenheim, the German Ambassador, as being the most important figure in Constantinople, dictating the Turkish policies, and later almost intoxicated by the early German victories.]

The good fortune of the German armies so excited him that he was sometimes led into indiscretions, and his exuberance one day caused him to tell me certain facts which, I think, will always have great historical value. He disclosed precisely how and when Germany had precipitated this war. To-day his revelation of this secret looks like a most monstrous indiscretion, but we must remember Wangenheim's state of mind at the time. The whole world then believed that Paris was doomed and Wangenheim reflected this attitude in his frequent declarations that the war would be over in two or three months. The whole German enterprise was evidently progressing according to program.

I have already mentioned that the German Ambassador had left for Berlin soon after the assassination of the Grand Duke, and he now revealed the cause of his sudden disappearance. The Kaiser, he told me, had summoned him to Berlin for an imperial conference. This meeting took place at Potsdam on July 5th. The Kaiser presided and nearly all the important ambassadors attended. Wangenheim himself was summoned to give assurance about Turkey and enlighten his associates generally on the situation in Constantinople, which was then regarded as almost the pivotal point in the impending war. In telling me who attended this conference Wangenheim used no names, though he specifically said that among them were—the facts are so important that I quote his exact words in the German which he used—*"die Häupter des Generalstabs und der Marine"*— (The heads of the general staff and of the navy) by which I have assumed that he meant Von Moltke and Von Tirpitz. The great bankers, railroad directors, and the captains of German industry, all of whom were as necessary to German war preparations as the army itself, also attended.

Wangenheim now told me that the Kaiser solemnly put the question to each man in turn: "Are you ready for war?" All replied "yes" except the financiers. They said that they must have two weeks to sell their foreign securities and to make loans. At that time few people had looked upon the Serajevo tragedy as something that would inevitably lead to war. This conference, Wangenheim told me, took all precautions that no such suspicion should be aroused. It decided to give the bankers time to readjust their finances for the coming war, and then the several members went quietly back to their work or started on vacations. The Kaiser went to Norway on his yacht, Von Bethmann-Hollweg left for a rest, and Wangenheim returned to Constantinople.

In telling me about this conference Wangenheim, of course, admitted that Germany had precipitated the war. I think that he was rather proud of the whole performance, proud that Germany had gone about the matter in so methodical and farseeing a way, and especially proud that he himself had been invited to participate in so epoch-making a gathering. I have often wondered why he revealed to me so momentous a secret, and I think that perhaps the real reason was his excessive vanity—his desire to show me how close he stood to the inner counsels of his emperor and the part that he had played in bringing on this conflict. Whatever the motive, this indiscretion certainly had the effect of showing me who were really the guilty parties in this monstrous crime. The several blue, red, and yellow books which flooded Europe during the few months following the outbreak, and the hundreds of documents which were issued by German propagandists attempting to establish Germany's innocence, have never made the slightest impression on me. For my conclusions as to the responsibility are not based on suspicions or belief or the study of circumstantial data. I do not have to reason or argue about the matter. I know.

The conspiracy that has caused this greatest of human tragedies was hatched by the Kaiser and his imperial crew at this Potsdam conference of July 5, 1914. One of the chief participants, flushed with his triumph at the apparent success of the plot, told me the details with his own mouth. Whenever I hear people arguing about the responsibility for this war or read the clumsy and lying excuses put forth by Germany, I simply recall the burly figure of Wangenheim as he appeared that August afternoon, puffing away at a huge black cigar, and giving me his account of this historic meeting. Why waste any time discussing the matter after that?

This imperial conference took place July 5th and the Serbian ultimatum was sent on July 23d. That is just about the two weeks' interval which the financiers had demanded to complete their plans. All the great stock exchanges of the world show that the German bankers profitably used this interval. Their records disclose that stocks were being sold in large quantities and that prices declined rapidly. At that time the markets were somewhat puzzled at this movement but Wangenheim's explanation clears up any doubts that may still remain. Germany was changing her securities into cash for war purposes. If any one wishes to verify Wangenheim, I would suggest that he examine the quotations of the New York stock market for these two historic weeks. He will find that there were astonishing slumps in prices, especially on the stocks that had an international market. Between July 5th and July 22d, Union Pacific dropped from 155½ to 127½, Baltimore and Ohio from 91½ to 81, United States Steel from 61 to 50½, Canadian Pacific from 194 to 185½, and Northern Pacific from 111⅜ to 108. At that time the high protectionists were blaming the Simmons-Underwood tariff act as responsible for this fall in values, while other critics of the Administration attributed it to the Federal Reserve Act—which had not yet been put into effect. How little the Wall Street brokers and the financial experts realized that an imperial conference, which had been held in Potsdam and presided over by the Kaiser, was the real force that was then depressing the market!

Wangenheim not only gave me the details of this Potsdam conference, but he disclosed the same secret to the Marquis Garroni, the Italian Ambassador at Constantinople. Italy was at that time technically Germany's ally.

The Austrian Ambassador, the Marquis Pallavicini, also practically admitted that the Central Powers had anticipated the war. On August 18th, Francis Joseph's birthday, I made the usual ambassadorial visit of congratulation. Quite naturally the conversation turned upon the Emperor, who had that day passed his 84th year. Pallavicini spoke about him with the utmost pride and veneration. He told me how keen-minded and clear-headed the aged emperor was, how he had the most complete understanding of international affairs, and how he gave everything his personal supervision. To illustrate the Austrian Kaiser's grasp of public events, Pallavicini instanced the present war. The previous May, Pallavicini had had an audience with Francis Joseph in Vienna. At that time, Pallavicini now told me, the Em-

peror had said that a European war was unavoidable. The
Central Powers would not accept the Treaty of Bucharest
as a settlement of the Balkan question, and only a general
war, the Emperor had told Pallavicini, could ever settle
that problem.

The Treaty of Bucharest, I may recall, was the settlement that ended the second Balkan war. This divided the
European dominions of Turkey, excepting Constantinople
and a small piece of adjoining territory, among the Balkan
nations, chiefly Serbia and Greece. That treaty strengthened Serbia greatly; so much did it increase Serbia's resources, indeed, that Austria feared that it had laid the
beginning of a new European state, which might grow sufficiently strong to resist her own plans of aggrandizement.
Austria held a large Serbian population under her yoke in
Bosnia and Herzegovina, and these Serbians desired, above
everything else, annexation to their own country. Moreover, the Pan-German plans in the East necessitated the
destruction of Serbia, the state which, so long as it stood
intact, blocked the Germanic road to the Orient. It had
been the Austro-German expectation that the Balkan War
would destroy Serbia as a nation—that Turkey would
simply annihilate King Peter's forces. This was precisely
what the Germanic plans demanded, and for this reason
Austria and Germany did nothing to prevent the Balkan
wars. But the result was exactly the reverse, for out of
the conflict arose a stronger Serbia than ever, standing firm
like a breakwater against the Germanic flood.

Most historians agree that the Treaty of Bucharest
made inevitable this war. I have the Marquis Pallavicini's
evidence that this was likewise the opinion of Francis Joseph
himself. The audience at which the Emperor made this
statement was held in May, more than a month before the
assassination of the Grand Duke. Clearly, therefore, we
have the Austrian Emperor's assurances that the war would
have come irrespective of the assassination at Serajevo.

BY WILLIAM MUHLON

Letter of Dr. Muhlon to Chancellor Bethmann-Hollweg on May 7, 1917

Your Excellency,

However numerous and crass the errors and faults committed by Germany since the war began, I have none the less long persisted in the belief that our leaders would eventually show themselves possessed of a belated foresight. It was in this hope that I put myself to a certain extent at your service to collaborate with you in Rumania, and that I informed you I was ready to help you in the country in which I am living at present (Switzerland), if our aim was to be the bringing together of the parties at war. That I was and still am opposed to any work other than that of reconciliation and restoration I proved, shortly after hostilities opened, by resigning once and for all from the directorate of Krupp's works.

But since the first days of 1917 I have abandoned all hope as regards the present leaders of Germany. Our offer of peace with no indication of our war aims, the unrestricted submarine war, the deportations from Belgium, the systematic destruction in France, the torpedoing of English hospital ships have so discredited the governors of the [German] Empire, that I am profoundly convinced that they are for ever disqualified for the task of elaborating and concluding a just and sincere international agreement. They may change their personal views, but they cannot remain the representatives of the German cause.

The German people will only be able to atone for the grievous sins committed against its own present and future, against that of Europe and all mankind, when it is represented by other men with a different type of mind. To tell the truth, it is only just that its reputation throughout the entire world should be as bad as it is. The triumph of its methods—the military and political methods by which it has conducted the war up till now—would mean the defeat of the highest ideas and hopes of humanity. We have only to picture to ourselves a nation exhausted, demoralized, or sick of violence consenting to make peace with a Government which has waged such a war in order to realize how gloomy and uncertain in that case would remain the path and prospects of mankind.

As a man and as a German, who desires nothing but the welfare of the sorely tried and deceived German people, I turn my back for good and all on the present representatives of the German Government. And my one desire is that all independent men should do the same and that many Germans may understand and act. Since any appeal to German public opinion is impossible for me at present, I have considered it to be my strict duty to inform your Excellency of my point of view.

Statement of Dr. Muhlon published in the "Berliner Tageblatt," March 21, 1918

In the middle of July, 1914, as on many other occasions, I had a conversation with Dr. Helfferich, who was at that time the Director of the Deutsche Bank in Berlin and is now the official representative of the Imperial Chancellor. There were certain big transactions (in Bulgaria and Turkey) in which the firm of Krupp took an active interest for business reasons (supplying war materials), and the Deutsche Bank had adopted a negative attitude in the matter. In justification of the bank's attitude, Dr. Helfferich gave me several reasons, and concluded with the following:

"The political situation has become very threatening. In any case the Deutsche Bank must wait before committing itself further in foreign countries. The Austrians have been with the Kaiser during the last few days. In eight days' time Vienna will deliver a very sharply-worded Ultimatum to Serbia. The Ultimatum, which will have a quite short time-limit, will contain demands of the following nature: Punishment of a number of officers, dissolution of political associations, criminal investigations in Serbia with the co-operation of officials of the Dual Monarchy. In fact, immediate satisfaction will be demanded on a number of definite issues, failing which Austria-Hungary will declare war on Serbia."

Dr. Helfferich added that the Kaiser had expressed his

decided approval of this Austro-Hungarian move. The Kaiser had said that he regarded a conflict with Serbia as a domestic affair concerning Austria-Hungary and Serbia alone, and that he would not allow any other state to interfere; that if Russia mobilized, he would mobilize, too; that mobilization in his case meant immediate war; and that this time there should be no wavering. The Austrians, according to Dr. Helfferich, were delighted at the Kaiser's determined attitude.

Thereupon I remarked to Dr. Helfferich that, even before his disquieting communication, I had been very much afraid that a world-war was coming, and that my fears were now converted into absolute certainty. He replied that "things certainly looked like war, but that perhaps France and Russia would after all reconsider their attitude in the matter. The Serbs decidedly deserved a lasting lesson."

This was the first communication I received with regard to the Kaiser's conversations with our allies. I knew that Dr. Helfferich stood in particularly confidential relations to those highly-placed persons who were bound to be initiated in the matter, and that his communication was therefore reliable. On returning from Berlin, I informed Herr Krupp von Bohlen und Halbach, of whose Board of Directors at Essen I was then a member. Dr. Helfferich, I may remark, had expressly authorized me to do so. [It was intended at that time to make him a member of the Council of Supervision of Krupp's firm.]

Von Bohlen seemed greatly surprised that Dr. Helfferich should possess such information, complained that "after all, these Government people can never keep their mouths quite shut," and then made a statement to the following effect:

"He had himself been with the Kaiser during the last few days. The Kaiser had spoken to him, too, about his conversation with the Austrians and its result, but had so emphasized the secrecy of the matter, that he [*von Bohlen*] would not have ventured to tell even his own Board of Directors. But, as I already knew about it, he could tell me that Helfferich's statements were correct. Indeed, Helfferich appeared to know more details than he (Bohlen) himself. The position was, in fact, very critical. The Kaiser had told him he would declare war at once if Russia mobilized. This time people would see that he would not change his mind. The Kaiser's emphatic and repeated asseveration that this time nobody would be able to reproach him with irresolution had produced an almost comic effect."

Vienna's Ultimatum to Serbia made its appearance on the very day which Helfferich had predicted to me. I was again in Berlin at the time, and said frankly to Helfferich that I found the Ultimatum, in form and in content, simply monstrous. Dr. Helfferich, however, expressed the opinion that this was only the effect produced by the German translation. He said he had seen the Ultimatum in French, and one could not regard it as at all overdone in its French version. On the same occasion Helfferich also told me that the Kaiser's Scandinavian cruise was only a blind; that he had not arranged it on the customary scale, but was keeping in constant communication [with Germany] and near enough to be reached at any moment. All one could do now was to wait and see what happened. One must hope that the Austrians—who of course did not expect the Ultimatum to be accepted—would act quickly, before the other Powers had time to interfere. The Deutsche Bank had already made its preparations, so that it was ready for all eventualities. Thus, e.g., it was keeping all gold as it was paid in, and not returning it to circulation. That could be done without exciting any attention whatever, and considerable sums were thus accumulating day by day.

Very soon after the Viennese Ultimatum to Serbia the German Government issued an announcement to the effect that Austria-Hungary had acted on its own account without Germany's foreknowledge. If one endeavored to reconcile this announcement with the events which I have described above, the only possible solution was that the Kaiser had already committed himself, without allowing his Government any hand in the matter; and that the German representatives had not attempted, in their conversations with the Austrians, to draft an agreed text of the Ultimatum.

For the contents of the Ultimatum, as I have shown

above, were known with considerable accuracy in Germany. Herr Krupp von Bohlen, with whom I discussed this German official announcement—which, in effect at any rate, was a lie—disapproved of it as much as I did, because Germany ought never to have given *carte blanche* on such a momentous issue to a state like Austria; and because it was the duty of the leading statesmen to demand, both of the Kaiser and of our allies, that the Austrian claims and their Ultimatum to Serbia should be discussed and settled in the minutest details, and that the exact program of the subsequent procedure should be fixed at the same time.

"Our leading statesmen," he argued, "had no right, whatever view they might take of the matter, to surrender themselves to the Austrians without reserve, or to expose themselves to eventualities which they had not already taken into account. In pledging ourselves to the Austrians we ought to have attached appropriate conditions." In short, Herr von Bohlen considered that the German denial of foreknowledge, if there was any trace of truth in it, sinned against the elementary rules of the art of political diplomacy; and he led me to expect that he would speak in this sense to Herr von Jagow (at that time Secretary of State for Foreign Affairs), who was one of his particular friends.

After he had spoken to Herr von Jagow he gave me the following account of the interview: Herr von Jagow persisted in assuring him that he had taken no part in composing the text of the Austro-Hungarian Ultimatum, and that Germany had never even asked to collaborate. To Herr von Bohlen's objection that this was really inconceivable, Herr von Jagow had answered that of course he himself, as a diplomat, had thought of making a demand of the kind, but that, by the time he was informed of the matter and had been called in, the Kaiser was so deeply committed that it was already too late to take any steps consistent with diplomatic usage, and that there was nothing more to be done. The situation had been such that it was impossible any longer to propose any reservations and conditions. Moreover he, Jagow, had come to the conclusion that there would be one advantage in the omission, viz., that a good effect would be produced in Petrograd and Paris by the announcement, which Germany would be able to make, that we had not collaborated in the Viennese Ultimatum.

BY AUGUST THYSSEN

I am writing this pamphlet because I want to open the eyes of Germans, especially of the business community, to facts. When the Hohenzollerns wanted to get the support of the commercial class for their war plans, they put their ideas before us as a business proposition. A large number of business and commercial men were asked to support the Hohenzollern war policy on the ground that it would pay them to do so. Let me frankly confess that I am one of those who were led to agree to support the Hohenzollern war plan when this appeal was made to the leading business men of Germany in 1912-13. I was led to do so, however, against my better judgment.

In 1912 the Hohenzollerns saw that the war had become a necessity for the preservation of the military system, upon which their power depends. In that year the Hohenzollerns might have directed, if they had desired, the foreign affairs of our country so that peace would have been assured in Europe for at least fifty years. But prolonged peace would have resulted certainly in the breakup of our military system, and with the breakup of our military system the power of the Hohenzollerns would come to an end. The Emperor and his family, as I said, clearly understood this, and they, therefore, in 1912, decided to embark on a great war of conquest.

But to do this they had to get the commercial community to support them in their aims. They did this by holding out to them hopes of great personal gain as a result of the war. In the light of events that have taken place since August, 1914, these promises now appear supremely ridiculous, but most of us at the time were led to believe that they would probably be realized.

I was personally promised a free grant of 30,000 acres in Australia and a loan from the Deutsche Bank of £150,000, at 3 per cent., to enable me to develop my business in Australia. Several other firms were promised special trading facilities in India, which was to be conquered by Germany, be it noted, by the end of 1915. A syndicate was formed for the exploitation of Canada. This syndicate consisted of the heads of twelve great firms; the working capital was fixed at £20,000,000, half of which was to be found by the German Government.

There were, I have heard, promises made of a more personal character. For example, the "conquest of England" was to be made the occasion of bestowing upon certain favored and wealthy men some of the most desirable residences in England, but of this I have no actual proof.

Every trade and interest was appealed to. Huge indemnities were, of course, to be levied on the conquered nations, and the fortunate German manufacturers were, by this means, practically to be relieved of taxation for years after the war.

These promises were not vaguely given. They were made definitely by Bethmann-Hollweg on behalf of the Emperor to gatherings of business men, and in many cases to individuals. I have mentioned the promise of a grant of 30,000 acres in Australia that was made to me. Promises of a similar kind were made to at least eighty other persons at special interviews with the Chancellor, and all particulars of these promises were entered in a book at the Trades Department.

But not only were these promises made by the Chancellor; they were confirmed by the Emperor, who, on three occasions, addressed large private gatherings of business men in Berlin, Munich, and Cassel in 1912 and 1913. I was at one of these gatherings. The Emperor's speech was one of the most flowery orations I have listened to, and so profuse were the promises he made that were even half of what he promised to be fulfilled, most of the commercial men in Germany would become rich beyond the dreams of avarice.

The Emperor was particularly enthusiastic over the coming German conquest of India. "India," he said, "is occupied by the British. It is in a way governed by the British, but it is by no means completely governed by them. We shall not merely occupy India. We shall conquer it, and the vast revenues that the British allow to be taken by Indian Princes will, after our conquest, flow in a golden stream into the Fatherland. In all the richest lands of the earth the German flag will fly over every other flag."

Finally the Emperor concluded: "I am making you no promises that cannot be redeemed, and they shall be redeemed if you are now prepared to make the sacrifices which are necessary to secure the position that our country must and shall occupy in the world. He who refuses to help is a traitor to the Fatherland; he who helps willingly and generously will have his rich reward."

All sounded, I admit, tempting and alluring, and though there were some who viewed rather dubiously the prospect of Germany being able to conquer the world in a year, the majority of business and commercial men agreed to support the Hohenzollern war plans. Most of them have since wished they had never paid any attention to them.

According to the promises of the Hohenzollern, victory was to have been achieved in December, 1915, and the promises made to myself and other commercial men in Germany when our money for the Kaiser's war chest was wanted were to have been then redeemed.

But this is what has happened in reality: In December of 1916 the Chancellor, Bethmann-Hollweg, began to have interviews once more with business men. The purpose of these interviews was to get more money from them. Guarantees were asked from seventy-five business men in Germany, including myself, that they would undertake to subscribe £200,000,000 to the next war loan. I was personally asked to guarantee a subscription of £200,000. I declined to give this guarantee; so did some others. I was then favored with a private interview with Bethmann-Hollweg's private secretary, who told me that if I declined to give the guarantee and subsequently the money I would lose a contract I had with the War Office. But not only that—I was threatened with the practical ruin of my business if I did not give the guarantee.

I described this demand as blackmail of the worst sort

and refused to guarantee a mark to the war loan. Two months later I lost my contract, and the greater part of my business has been taken over at a figure that means confiscation. Moreover, I am not to get paid until after the war, but am to receive 4 per cent. on the purchase price. Every man who declined to promise a subscription to the amount he was asked has been treated in the same manner.

The majority of men, however, preferred to pay rather than to be ruined, and so the Hohenzollerns in the main got their way. But, apart from the blackmailing of men who refused to pay any more money into the Hohenzollern war chest, let us see how the Hohenzollerns' promises are working out. A circular was sent out last March to a large number of business men by the Foreign Trade Department which contained the following suggestion:

"It will be wise for employers who have foreign trade interests to employ agents in foreign countries who can pass themselves off as being of French or English birth. German agents and travelers will probably for some time after the war have difficulty in doing business not only in enemy countries but in neutral countries. There will undoubtedly be a personal prejudice against Germans that would probably make it difficult for representatives of German firms to do business. Although this prejudice will not interfere with German trade, as it will be merely of a personal character, it will facilitate trading transactions if employers will employ agents who can pass as French or English, preferably, or as Dutch, American, or Spanish."

So this is the prospect we are faced with after the war. The meaning of this circular in plain language is this: So loathed and hated have Germans become outside their own country that no one will want to have any personal dealings with them after the war.

A large number of businesses are, moreover, being secretly bolstered up with State aid. A condition of this aid is that the owners of the businesses receiving it shall agree to accept a considerable degree of State control over their business after the war. This is part and parcel of a plan on the part of the Hohenzollerns to get the commercial classes thoroughly into their grip before the end of the war, and so minimize the chances of a revolution.

These men who have agreed to accept aid now for their businesses, and State control after the war, have received a notification from the Foreign Trade Department to the effect that, with proper organization, Germany ought to recover her pre-war trade three years after peace is declared. Here is the Hohenzollern method of redeeming promises. We are to get back our pre-war trade three years after peace is declared, and to do this we must submit to have our trading transactions controlled and supervised by the State.

Can any German to whom such prospects are held out by the Emperor fail to see that he has been bamboozled and humbugged and fooled into supporting a war from which the utmost he can hope to gain is to come out of it without national bankruptcy?

AUSTRIAN OFFICIAL RECORD

Minutes of Ministerial Council on affairs of State held at Vienna on July 7, 1914, under the presidency of the Minister of the Royal and Imperial Household and Minister for Foreign Affairs, Count Berchtold.

Also present:—
> The Austrian Premier, Count Stürkh.
> The Hungarian Premier, Count Tisza.
> The Joint Minister for Finance, Ritter von Bilinski.
> The War Minister, Ritter von Krobatin.

Keeper of the Minutes:
> Councillor of Legation, Count Hoyos.

Agenda: Bosnian Affairs.—The diplomatic action against Serbia.

The President opens the sitting by remarking that the Ministerial Council has been called in order to advise on the measures to be used in reforming the evil internal political conditions in Bosnia and Herzegovina, as shown up by the disastrous event at Serajevo. In his opinion there were various internal measures applicable within Bosnia, the use of which seemed to him very appropriate, in order to deal with the critical situation; but first of all they must make up their minds as to whether the moment had not come for reducing Serbia to permanent inoffensiveness by a demonstration of their power.

So decisive a blow could not be dealt without previous diplomatic preparation; consequently he had approached the German Government. The conversations at Berlin had led to a very satisfactory result, inasmuch *as both the Emperor William and Herr von Bethmann Hollweg had most emphatically assured us of Germany's unconditional support in the case of hostilities with Serbia.* Meanwhile, we still had to reckon with Italy and with Rumania, and here he agreed with the Berlin Cabinet that it would be better to negotiate and be prepared for any claims to compensation which might arise. He was clear in his own mind that hostilities with Serbia would entail war with Russia. Russia, however, was now playing a far-seeing game, and was calculating on a policy of being able to unite the Balkan States, including Rumania, with the eventual objective of launching them at an appropriate moment against the Monarchy. He suggested that we must reckon on the fact that in face of such a policy our situation was bound steadily to deteriorate, and all the more if an inactive policy of *laisser aller* were to be interpreted as a sign of weakness by our own South Slavs and Rumanians, and were to be a direct encouragement to the power of attraction of the two neighbor States. The logical inference to be drawn from his remarks was that we must be beforehand with our enemies and, by bringing matters to a head with Serbia, must call a halt to the gathering momentum of events; later it would no longer be possible to do so.

The Hungarian Premier agreed that during the last few days the results of our investigations and the tone of the Serbian press had put a materially new complexion on events, and emphasized the fact that he himself held the possibility of warlike action against Serbia to be more obvious than he had thought in the period immediately after the act at Serajevo. But he would never give his consent to a surprise attack on Serbia without previous diplomatic action, as seemed to be contemplated and as had unfortunately already been made the subject of discussion by

Count Hoyos at Berlin; were that done, in his opinion, our position in the eyes of Europe would be an extremely bad one, and in all probability we should have to reckon with the enmity of the whole Balkans, except Bulgaria, while Bulgaria herself being at present very much weakened would not be able to give us the necessary support.

It was absolutely necessary that we should formulate demands against Serbia and only send an ultimatum in case Serbia failed to satisfy them. These demands must undoubtedly be hard, but should not be impossible of fulfilment. Should Serbia accept them we should be able to quote a dazzling diplomatic victory, and our prestige in the Balkans would be raised. Should our demands not be accepted he himself would then be for warlike action, but even at this point he thought it essential to lay stress on the fact that the object of such action ought to be the reduction of Serbia, but not her complete annihilation; first, because this would never be allowed by Russia without a life and death struggle, and also because he, as Hungarian Premier, could never consent to the annexation of part of Serbia by the Monarchy.

It was not Germany's place to judge whether we should now deal a blow at Serbia or not. Personally, he was of opinion that it was not absolutely necessary to go to war at this moment. At the present time we must take into account that the agitation against us in Rumania was very strong, that in view of the excited state of public opinion, we should have to reckon with a Rumanian attack.

We must also remember that in the sphere of European politics the relation of French to German power would continually deteriorate because of the low birthrate, and that Germany would therefore continually have more troops at her disposal, as time went on, against Russia. These considerations ought all to be weighed on the occasion of a decision as important as the one to be taken to-day; he must, therefore, come back to this, that, in spite of the crisis of affairs in Bosnia, he would not make up his mind unconditionally for war.

The President remarked that the history of the last

years had shown that while diplomatic successes against Serbia raised the reputation of the Monarchy for the time being, the actual tension in our relations with Serbia had only increased. Neither our success during the annexation crisis, nor at the creation of Albania, nor Serbia's submission later in consequence of our ultimatum of the autumn of last year, had altered the real situation in any way. He imagined that energetic action alone would suffice to solve once for all the problem created by the systematic propaganda for a Greater Serbia encouraged from Belgrade, the disintegrating effects of which had made themselves felt as far as Agram and Zara.

As regards the danger of a hostile attitude on the part of Rumania, mentioned by the Hungarian Premier, the President remarked that this was less to be feared now than later on, when the unity of interests between Rumania and Serbia would have become more pronounced. To be sure, King Carol had let fall doubts as to whether he would be able to fulfil his duty as an ally, should occasion arise, by sending active help. On the other hand, it was scarcely likely that he would allow himself to be so far carried away as to become involved in hostilities against the Monarchy, even supposing that public opinion did not itself oppose that. Further, there was Rumanian fear of Bulgaria; even as things stood at present this was bound to a certain extent to hamper Rumania's freedom of movement.

As for the observation made by the Hungarian Premier on the relative strength of France and Germany, surely they had to remember that the decreasing birthrate of France was counter-balanced by the infinitely more rapid increase in the population of Russia, so that the argument that in future Germany would always have more troops at her disposal against France would not hold.

The Austrian Premier remarked that to-day's Ministerial Council had actually been called for the purpose of advising about the internal measures to be taken in Bosnia and Herzegovina, in order to make effective the present inquiry into the assassination, on the one hand, and, on the other, to counteract the Greater Serbia propaganda. But now these questions must give way to the principal question; should we solve the internal crisis in Bosnia by a demonstration of power against Serbia?

Two considerations now made this principal question an immediate one; first, the Governor of Bosnia and Herzegovina was proceeding on the presumption, acquired in the course of inquiries and in consequence of his knowledge of Bosnian affairs, that no internal measures would be effective, unless we made up our minds to deal a forceful blow to Serbia abroad. In view of this report from General Potiorek we must ask ourselves whether the schismatic activities originating in Serbia could be stopped at all, unless we took action against the Kingdom.

During the last few days the whole situation had received a materially fresh complexion and a psychological situation had been created, which, in his opinion, led unconditionally to an issue of arms with Serbia. He certainly agreed with the Hungarian Premier that it was for us, and not for the German Government, to decide whether a war were necessary or no; he must nevertheless observe that our decision must be materially influenced by the fact that, in the quarter which we were bound to regard as the greatest support of our policy in the Triple Alliance, unconditional loyalty was, as we were informed, promised to us and that, in addition, on our making inquiry, we were urged to act at once; Count Tisza ought to weigh this fact, and to consider that a hesitating, weak policy would run us into the danger of losing the certainty of this unconditional support of the German Empire on a future occasion. This was the second consideration which must be taken into account in forming our decision, and was additional to our interest in restoring order in Bosnia.

How to begin the conflict was a question of detail, and should the Hungarian Government be of opinion that a surprise attack *"sans crier gare,"* to use Count Tisza's expression, was not feasible, then they must needs think of some other way; but he did most earnestly hope that, whatever they might do, they would act quickly, and our trade and commerce be spared a long period of unrest. All this was detail compared with the chief question as to whether it should in any case come to armed action or not, and here the authoritative interest was the reputation and stability of the Monarchy, whose South Slav provinces he held to be lost if nothing were to happen.

They ought, therefore, to make up their minds to-day, in a general way, whether they meant to act or not. He, too, shared the President's view that the situation would not be in the least improved by a diplomatic success. If, therefore, international considerations caused them to adopt the method of an initial diplomatic action against Serbia, *this would have to be done with the firm intention of allowing such action to end only in a war.*

The Joint Finance Minister observed that Count Stürgkh had referred to the fact that the Governor wanted war. For two years General Potiorek had held the view that we must match ourselves against Serbia, in order to be able to retain Bosnia and Herzegovina. We ought not to forget that the Governor, who was on the spot, could better judge the situation. Herr von Bilinski, too, was convinced that a decisive struggle was unavoidable sooner or later.

The Hungarian Premier observed that he had the highest opinion of the present Governor as soldier, but, as regards the civil administration, it could not be denied that it had broken down completely and that reform was absolutely essential. He would not now enter more fully into this question, especially as it was no time for big alterations; he would only observe that the most incredible conditions must be reigning among the police, to make it possible that six or seven persons known to the police should have been able to place themselves along the route of the procession on the day of the assassination, armed with bombs and revolvers without a single one of them being noticed or removed by the police. He could not see why the condition of Bosnia could not be materially improved by means of a thorough reform of the administration.

The Joint War Minister is of opinion that a diplomatic success would be of no value. Such a success would only be interpreted as a weakness. From the military point of

view he must emphasize the fact that it would be better
to wage the war now, rather than later, as the balance of
power would move disproportionately against us later on.
As for the procedure for beginning war, he might be permitted to remark that the two great wars of recent years,
both the Russo-Japanese and the Balkan Wars, had been
begun without previous declarations of war. His opinion
was at first only to carry through their contemplated mobilization against Serbia, and let general mobilization wait
until they knew whether Russia was going to take action or
not.

We had already neglected two opportunities of solving
the Serbian question and had deferred decision on both
occasions. If we did this again and took no notice of this
latest provocation, this would be taken as a sign of weakness in every South Slav province and we should be inducing
an increase of the agitation directed against us.

It would be desirable from a military point of view if
the mobilization could be carried out at once, and secretly,
and a summons addressed to Serbia only after mobilization
had been completed. This would also be a good thing as
against the Russian forces, as just about this time the Russian frontier forces were not at their full strength on account of harvest-leave.

Thereupon a discussion developed about the aims of
warlike action against Serbia, and the Hungarian Premier's
point of view was accepted, to the effect that Serbia should
be reduced in size, but not, in view of Russia, entirely
annihilated. The Austrian Premier emphasized the fact
that it might also be advisable to remove the Karageorgevich dynasty and to give the Crown to a European prince,
as well as to induce a certain condition of dependency of
this reduced kingdom on the Monarchy in relation to
military affairs.

The Hungarian Premier still remained convinced that
the Monarchy could adopt a successful Balkan policy by
means of Bulgaria's adherence to the Triple Alliance, and
pointed out what a frightful calamity a European war
would be under present circumstances.

The question of war was then further argued thoroughly in the course of a long discussion. At the end of this discussion agreement was reached:

(1) That all present wish for the speediest decision which is practicable in the conflict with Serbia, whether by means of war or peace.

(2) That the Ministerial Council is prepared to adopt the point of view of the Hungarian Premier to the effect that mobilization shall only follow after concrete demands have been addressed to Serbia, and have been refused, and an ultimatum has further been sent.

(3) On the other hand, all present, excepting the Hungarian Premier, hold that a purely diplomatic success, even if ending in a startling humiliation for Serbia, *would be without value, and that, therefore, the demands to be put to Serbia must be so far-reaching as to pre-suppose a refusal, so that the way would be prepared for a radical solution by means of military intervention.*

Count Tisza observes that he is desirous of meeting the views of all present, and therefore would be prepared to concede this much, that he would agree that the demands to be put to Serbia must be very hard, yet must not be of such a nature as to cause our intention of putting unacceptable demands to become obvious. Otherwise, our legal position would be an impossible one for a declaration of war. The text of the Note would have to be most carefully formulated, and he must lay importance on the necessity of seeing the Note before its despatch. He must further stress the necessity, as regards his own person, of taking the obvious action contingent on having had his point of view rejected.

The meeting was now adjourned till the afternoon.

On the reassembly of the Ministerial Council, the Chief of the General Staff, and the Representative of the Navy Command [Admiral Kailer] were also present.

By request of the President, the Minister for War addressed the meeting and put the following three questions to the Chief of the General Staff [Von Hoetzendorff]:

(1) Whether it would be possible to mobilize against

Serbia first, and only subsequently against Russia as well, if this should become necessary?

(2)   Whether large bodies of troops could be retained in Transylvania to overawe Rumania?

(3)   At which point the war against Russia would be begun?

The Chief of the General Staff, in response to these inquiries, supplies information which is confidential, and therefore requests that it be omitted from the Minutes.

A discussion of some length develops out of these explanations as to the relation of forces and the probable course of a European war, which, on account of its confidential character, could not be entered on the Minutes.

At the end of this discussion the Hungarian Premier repeats his views on the question of war, and once more appeals to all present to weigh their decisions with care.

A discussion followed on the points to be included in the demands to be put in the Note to Serbia. The Ministerial Council took no definite decision as to these points; suggestions were simply made with a view to obtaining an idea of what demands might be put.

The President sums up to the effect that though there still existed a divergence of view between all members and Count Tisza, yet they had come nearer agreement, inasmuch as the Hungarian Premier's own proposals would in all probability lead up to that armed conflict with Serbia, which he and the others at the meeting held to be necessary.

Count Berchtold informs the meeting that he proposes to travel to Ischl on the 8th, and report to His Imperial Apostolic Majesty. The Hungarian Premier requests the President to submit also a humble memorial, which he would draw up, on his view of the situation.

After a *communiqué* had been drawn up for the Press, the President closes the meeting.

Secretary: A. Hoyos.   BERCHTOLD.
                   (Signature).   (Signature)

I have noted the contents of these Minutes.

Vienna, August 16th, 1914.

FRANZ JOSEF (Signature).

THE FIRST ULTIMATUM

AUSTRIA'S ABRUPT AND IMPOSSIBLE DEMAND TO SERBIA

JULY 23, 1914

COUNT LEOPOLD BERCHTOLD   SIR MAURICE DE BUNSEN
PRINCE ALEXANDER OF SERBIA

The ultimatum so abruptly presented to Serbia by Austria is here given in full. This vicious document of unproven accusation and tyrannical demand will always be of world interest; for it was the match wherewith the world-fire was started. Both in idea and wording the ultimatum was mainly the work of Count Leopold Berchtold, then the prime-minister and actual chief ruler of Austro-Hungary.

As to the unexpectedness of the ultimatum's presentation, its extravagance, its time limit so impossibly brief and so craftily made briefer by the moment chosen for its delivery, these and the astonishment they caused could not be better evidenced than by the official report of the British Ambassador De Bunsen, who was in Vienna at the moment. It must be remembered that at that time Britain was still indignant against Serbia, whose apparent connection with the Serajevo crime had been everywhere officially condemned. Hence De Bunsen is not at all prejudiced against Austria. He simply, as a diplomat, recognizes the Austrian note as having been deliberately worded to create a war; and he so warns his government.

The third official document here given is of particular interest. It is Serbia's own voice, showing how wholly helpless she felt herself in the face of Austria's power, and how far she was willing to go in submission so as to escape war. Even before the statesmen of other lands could speak to urge her, she voices her eagerness for conciliation and her anxious denial of the Austrian charges. King Peter of Serbia had grown very old, so the real weight of the crown rested on his son Alexander. It is also noteworthy that Serbia turned at once for aid to her great Slavic protector, Russia.

BY COUNT BERCHTOLD

Text of the Ultimatum to Serbia, July 23rd

ON the 31st of March, 1909, the Serbian Minister in Vienna, on the instructions of the Serbian Government, made the following declaration to the Imperial and Royal Government:

"Serbia recognizes that the *fait accompli* regarding Bosnia has not affected her rights and consequently she will conform to the decisions that the Powers may take in conformity with Article 25 of the Treaty of Berlin. In deference to the advice of the Great Powers, Serbia undertakes to renounce from now onwards the attitude of protest and opposition which she has adopted with regard to the annexation since last autumn. She undertakes, moreover, to modify the direction of her policy with regard to Austria-Hungary and to live in future on good neighborly terms with the latter."

The history of recent years, and in particular the painful events of the 28th of June last, have shown the existence of a subversive movement with the object of detaching a part of the territories of Austria-Hungary from the Monarchy. The movement, which had its birth under the eye of the Serbian Government, has gone so far as to make itself manifest on both sides of the Serbian frontier in the shape of acts of terrorism and a series of outrages and murders.

Far from carrying out the formal undertakings contained in the declaration of the 31st of March, 1909, the Royal Serbian Government has done nothing to repress these movements. It has permitted the criminal machinations of various societies and associations directed against the Monarchy, and has tolerated unrestrained language on the part of the press, the glorification of the perpetrators of outrages, and the participation of officers and functionaries in subversive agitation. It has permitted an unwholesome propaganda in public instruction; in short, it has permitted all manifestations of a nature to incite the Serbian population to hatred of the Monarchy and contempt of its institutions.

This culpable tolerance of the Royal Serbian Government had not ceased at the moment when the events of the 28th of June last proved its fatal consequences to the whole world.

It results from the depositions and confessions of the criminal perpetrators of the outrage of the 28th of June that the Serajevo assassinations were planned in Belgrade; that the arms and explosives with which the murderers were provided had been given to them by Serbian officers and functionaries belonging to the Narodna Odbrana; and finally, that the passage into Bosnia of the criminals and their arms was organized and effected by the chiefs of the Serbian frontier service.

The above-mentioned results of the magisterial investigation do not permit the Austro-Hungarian Government to pursue any longer the attitude of expectant forbearance which they have maintained for years in face of the machinations hatched in Belgrade, and thence propagated in the territories of the Monarchy. The results, on the contrary, impose on them the duty of putting an end to the intrigues which form a perpetual menace to the tranquillity of the Monarchy.

To achieve this end the Imperial and Royal Government see themselves compelled to demand from the Royal Serbian Government a formal assurance that they condemn this dangerous propaganda against the Monarchy; in other words, the whole series of tendencies, the ultimate aim of which is to detach from the Monarchy territories belonging to it: and that they undertake to suppress by every means this criminal and terrorist propaganda.

In order to give a formal character to this undertaking the Royal Serbian Government shall publish on the front page of their "Official Journal" of the 13-26 of July the following declaration:

"The Royal Government of Serbia condemn the propaganda directed against Austria-Hungary—*i.e.*, the general tendency of which the final aim is to detach from the Austro-Hungarian Monarchy territories belonging to it, and they sincerely deplore the fatal consequences of these criminal proceedings.

"The Royal Government regret that Serbian officers and functionaries participated in the above-mentioned propaganda and thus compromised the good neighborly relations to which the Royal Government were solemnly pledged by their declaration of the 31st of March, 1909.

"The Royal Government, who disapprove and repudiate all idea of interfering or attempting to interfere with the destinies of the inhabitants of any part whatsoever of

Austria-Hungary, consider it their duty formally to warn officers and functionaries, and the whole population of the Kingdom, that henceforward they will proceed with the utmost rigor against persons who may be guilty of such machinations, which they will use all their efforts to anticipate and suppress."

This declaration shall simultaneously be communicated to the Royal army as an order of the day by His Majesty the King and shall be published in the "Official Bulletin" of the army.

The Royal Serbian Government shall further undertake:

(1) To suppress any publication which incites to hatred and contempt of the Austro-Hungarian Monarchy and the general tendency of which is directed against its territorial integrity;

(2) To dissolve immediately the society styled "Narodna Odbrana," to confiscate all its means of propaganda, and to proceed in the same manner against other societies and their branches in Serbia which engage in propaganda against the Austro-Hungarian Monarchy. The Royal Government shall take the necessary measures to prevent the societies dissolved from continuing their activity under another name and form;

(3) To eliminate without delay from public instruction in Serbia, both as regards the teaching body and also as regards the methods of instruction, everything that serves, or might serve, to foment the propaganda against Austria-Hungary;

(4) To remove from the military service, and from the administration in general, all officers and functionaries guilty of propaganda against the Austro-Hungarian Monarchy whose names and deeds the Austro-Hungarian Government reserve to themselves the right of communicating to the Royal Government;

(5) To accept the collaboration in Serbia of representatives of the Austro-Hungarian Government for the suppression of the subversive movement directed against the territorial integrity of the Monarchy;

(6) To take judicial proceedings against accessories to

the plot of the 28th of June who are on Serbian territory; delegates of the Austro-Hungarian Government will take part in the investigation relating thereto;

(7) To proceed without delay to the arrest of Major Voija Tankositch and of the individual named Milan Ciganovitch, a Serbian State employee, who have been compromised by the results of the magisterial inquiry at Serajevo;

(8) To prevent by effective measures the coöperation of the Serbian authorities in the illicit traffic in arms and explosives across the frontier, to dismiss and punish severely the officials of the frontier service at Shabatz Loznica guilty of having assisted the perpetrators of the Serajevo crime by facilitating their passage across the frontier;

(9) To furnish the Imperial and Royal Government with explanations regarding the unjustifiable utterances of high Serbian officials, both in Serbia and abroad, who, notwithstanding their official position, have not hesitated since the crime of the 28th of June to express themselves in interviews in terms of hostility to the Austro-Hungarian Government; and, finally,

(10) To notify the Imperial and Royal Government without delay of the execution of the measures comprised under the preceding heads.

The Austro-Hungarian Government expect the reply of the Royal Government at the latest by 5 o'clock on Saturday evening the 25th of July.[1]

[1] The Austro-Hungarian Ambassador in a private letter on the 24th of July sent to the French Minister for Foreign Affairs the following correction:—

"In the copy of the dispatch which I had the honor to send to your Excellency this morning, it was said that my Government expected an answer from the Cabinet at Belgrade at latest by 5 o'clock on the evening of Saturday the 25th of this month. As our Minister at Belgrade did not deliver his note yesterday until 6 o'clock in the evening, the time allowed for the answer has in consequence been prolonged to 6 o'clock to-morrow, Saturday evening.

"I consider it my duty to inform your Excellency of this slight alteration in the termination of the period fixed for the answer to the Serbian Government."

*Letter of Explanation Transmitted with the Above to the
Various European Powers*

On the 31st of March, 1909, the Royal Serbian Government addressed to Austria-Hungary the declaration of which the text is reproduced above.

On the very day after this declaration Serbia embarked on a policy of instilling revolutionary ideas into the Serb subjects of the Austro-Hungarian Monarchy, and so preparing for the separation of the Austro-Hungarian territory on the Serbian frontier.

Serbia became the center of a criminal agitation.

No time was lost in the formation of societies and groups, whose object, either avowed or secret, was the creation of disorders on Austro-Hungarian territory. These societies and groups count among their members generals and diplomatists, Government officials and judges—in short, men at the top of official and unofficial society in the kingdom.

Serbian journalism is almost entirely at the service of this propaganda, which is directed against Austria-Hungary, and not a day passes without the organs of the Serbian press stirring up their readers to hatred or contempt for the neighboring Monarchy, or to outrages directed more or less openly against its security and integrity.

A large number of agents are employed in carrying on by every means the agitation against Austria-Hungary and corrupting the youth in the frontier provinces.

Since the recent Balkan crisis there has been a recrudescence of the spirit of conspiracy inherent in Serbian politicians, which has left such sanguinary imprints on the history of the kingdom; individuals belonging formerly to bands employed in Macedonia have come to place themselves at the disposal of the terrorist propaganda against Austria-Hungary.

In the presence of these doings, to which Austria-Hungary has been exposed for years, the Serbian Government have not thought it incumbent on them to take the slightest step. The Serbian Government have thus failed in the duty imposed on them by the solemn declaration of

the 31st of March, 1909, and acted in opposition to the
will of Europe and the undertaking given to Austria-Hungary.

The patience of the Imperial and Royal Government
in the face of the provocative attitude of Serbia was inspired
by the territorial disinterestedness of the Austro-Hungarian
Monarchy and the hope that the Serbian Government would
end in spite of everything by appreciating Austria-Hungary's
friendship at its true value. By observing a benevolent attitude towards the political interests of Serbia, the Imperial
and Royal Government hoped that the kingdom would finally
decide to follow an analogous line of conduct on its own
side. In particular, Austria-Hungary expected a development of this kind in the political ideas of Serbia, when, after
the events of 1912, the Imperial and Royal Government,
by its disinterested and ungrudging attitude, made such a
considerable aggrandizement of Serbia possible.

The benevolence which Austria-Hungary showed
towards the neighboring State had no restraining effect on
the proceedings of the kingdom, which continued to tolerate
on its territory a propaganda of which the fatal consequences were demonstrated to the whole world on the 28th
of June last, when the Heir Presumptive to the Monarchy
and his illustrious consort fell victims to a plot hatched
at Belgrade.

In the presence of this state of things the Imperial and
Royal Government have felt compelled to take new and ur-
gent steps at Belgrade with a view to inducing the Serbian
Government to stop the incendiary movement that is threat-
ening the security and integrity of the Austro-Hungarian
Monarchy.

The Imperial and Royal Government are convinced that
in taking this step they will find themselves in full agreement
with the sentiments of all civilized nations, who cannot permit regicide to become a weapon that can be employed with
impunity in political strife, and the peace of Europe to be
continually disturbed by movements emanating from
Belgrade.

OFFICIAL REPORT BY SIR MAURICE DE BUNSEN
British Ambassador in Vienna in 1914

The delivery at Belgrade on the 23rd of July of the Austrian note to Serbia was preceded by a period of absolute silence at the Ballplatz.[1] Except Herr von Tschirschky,[2] who must have been aware of the tenor, if not of the actual words of the note, none of my colleagues were allowed to see through the veil. On the 22nd and 23rd of July, M. Dumaine, French Ambassador, had long interviews with Baron Macchio, one of the Under-Secretaries of State for Foreign Affairs, by whom he was left under the impression that the words of warning he had been instructed to speak to the Austro-Hungarian Government had not been unavailing, and that the note which was being drawn up would be found to contain nothing with which a self-respecting State need hesitate to comply. At the second of these interviews he was not even informed that the note was at that very moment being presented at Belgrade, or that it would be published in Vienna on the following morning. Count Forgach, the other Under-Secretary of State, had indeed been good enough to confide to me on the same day the true character of the note, and the fact of its presentation about the time we were speaking.

So little had the Russian Ambassador been made aware of what was preparing that he actually left Vienna on a fortnight's leave of absence about the 20th of July. He had only been absent a few days when events compelled him to return. It might have been supposed that Duke Avarna, Ambassador of the allied Italian Kingdom, which was bound to be so closely affected by fresh complications in the Balkans, would have been taken fully into the confidence of Count Berchtold during this critical time. In point of fact his Excellency was left completely in the dark. As for myself, no indication was given me by Count Berchtold of the impending storm, and it was from a private source that I received on the 15th of July the forecast of what was about

[1] Office of the Austrian Ministry of State.
[2] German Ambassador at Vienna.

to happen which I telegraphed to you the following day. It is true that during all this time the *Neue Freie Presse* and other leading Viennese newspapers were using language which pointed unmistakably to war with Serbia. The official *Fremdenblatt,* however, was more cautious, and till the note was published, the prevailing opinion among my colleagues was that Austria would shrink from courses calculated to involve her in grave European complications.

On the 24th of July the note was published in the newspapers. By common consent it was at once styled an ultimatum. Its integral acceptance by Serbia was neither expected nor desired, and when, on the following afternoon, it was at first rumored in Vienna that it had been unconditionally accepted, there was a moment of keen disappointment. The mistake was quickly corrected, and as soon as it was known later in the evening that the Serbian reply had been rejected and that Baron Giesl [3] had broken off relations at Belgrade, Vienna burst into a frenzy of delight, vast crowds parading the streets and singing patriotic songs till the small hours of the morning.

The demonstrations were perfectly orderly, consisting for the most part of organized processions through the principal streets ending up at the Ministry of War. One or two attempts to make hostile manifestations against the Russian Embassy were frustrated by the strong guard of police which held the approaches to the principal embassies during those days. The demeanor of the people at Vienna and, as I was informed, in many other principal cities of the Monarchy, showed plainly the popularity of the idea of war with Serbia, and there can be no doubt that the small body of Austrian and Hungarian statesmen by whom this momentous step was adopted gauged rightly the sense, and it may even be said the determination, of the people, except presumably in portions of the provinces inhabited by the Slav races.

There had been much disappointment in many quarters at the avoidance of war with Serbia during the annexation crisis in 1908 and again in connection with the recent Balkan war. Count Berchtold's peace policy had met with little

[3] Austro-Hungarian Minister at Belgrade.

sympathy in the Delegation. Now the floodgates were opened, and the entire people and press clamored impatiently for immediate and condign punishment of the hated Serbian race. The country certainly believed that it had before it only the alternative of subduing Serbia or of submitting sooner or later to mutilation at her hands. But a peaceful solution should first have been attempted. Few seemed to reflect that the forcible intervention of a Great Power in the Balkans must inevitably call other Great Powers into the field. So just was the cause of Austria held to be, that it seemed to her people inconceivable that any country should place itself in her path, or that questions of mere policy or prestige should be regarded anywhere as superseding the necessity which had arisen to exact summary vengeance for the crime of Serajevo. The conviction had been expressed to me by the German Ambassador on the 24th of July that Russia would stand aside. This feeling, which was also held at the Ballplatz, influenced no doubt the course of events, and it is deplorable that no effort should have been made to secure by means of diplomatic negotiations the acquiescence of Russia and Europe as a whole in some peaceful compromise of the Serbian question by which Austrian fears of Serbian aggression and intrigue might have been removed for the future. Instead of adopting this course the Austro-Hungarian Government resolved upon war.

TELEGRAM FROM ALEXANDER, PRINCE REGENT OF SERBIA, TO THE CZAR OF RUSSIA

Belgrade, July 11-24, 1914.

The Austro-Hungarian Government yesterday evening handed to the Serbian Government a note concerning the *"attentat"* of Serajevo. Conscious of its international duties, *Serbia from the first days of the horrible crime declared that she condemned it, and that she was ready to open an inquiry on her territory if the complicity of certain of her subjects were proved* in the investigation begun by the Austro-Hungarian authorities. However, the demands contained in the Austro-Hungarian note are unnecessarily humiliating for Serbia and incompatible with her dignity as an independent State. Thus we are called upon in peremptory tones for a declaration of the Government in the "Official Journal," and an order from the Sovereign to the army wherein we should repress the spirit of hostility against Austria by reproaching ourselves for criminal weakness in regard to our perfidious actions. Then we have to admit Austro-Hungarian functionaries into Serbia to participate with our own in the investigation and to superintend the execution of the other conditions indicated in the note. We have received a time-limit of forty-eight hours to accept everything, in default of which the legation of Austria-Hungary will leave Belgrade. We are ready to accept the Austro-Hungarian conditions which are compatible with the position of an independent State as well as those whose acceptance shall be advised us by your Majesty. All persons whose participation in the *"attentat"* shall be proved will be severely punished by us. Certain of these demands cannot be carried out without changes in our legislation, which require time. We have been given too short a limit. *We can be attacked after the expiration of the time-limit by the Austro-Hungarian Army which is concentrating on our frontier. It is impossible for us to defend ourselves, and we supplicate your Majesty to give us your aid* as soon as possible. The highly prized good will of your Majesty, which has so often shown itself toward us, makes us hope firmly that this time again our appeal will be heard by his generous Slav heart.

In these difficult moments I voice the sentiments of the Serbian people, who supplicate your Majesty to interest himself in the lot of the Kingdom of Serbia.

ALEXANDER.

BREAKDOWN OF THE ANCIENT DIPLOMACY

EUROPE WAKING FROM ITS "FOOLS' PARADISE" FACES THE SPECTER OF WORLD WAR

JULY 24-27, 1914

BARON BEYENS   JULES CAMBON
SIR EDWARD GREY   PRINCE LICHNOWSKY
BARON TSCHIRSCHKY AND WILLIAM II

The Austrian ultimatum was followed by days of wild delirium amid the stately diplomatic offices of Europe. We know now that the German diplomats were already fixed in purpose for war; they were only waiting for Austria to become so involved that she could not draw back and desert them. Yet even they had to "play the game," the diplomatic game of appearing to be eager for peace with justice. So there was an elaborate and farcical running around in diplomatic circles, solemn official "conversations" in which nobody said the most important things they thought, the dispatching of hundreds of diplomatic notes, monarchs telegraphing to monarchs, prime-ministers communing with ambassadors, and spies volubly confidential to everybody —all to restore a peace which Austria had made impossible by her first body blow. The German authorities were indeed the most hard pressed of all, finding it increasingly difficult to make their polite platitudes of peace half decently convincing, while they kept the helm of Europe pointing steadily toward war.

The hour of trial brought out the complete breakdown of the old "diplomacy," founded as that had ever been on a publicly voiced pretense of pompous "honor," upheld by secret treachery and falsehood. Under the old system a knave had always the upper hand, as Germany well knew. For twenty years she had encouraged the Peace Conferences, first inaugurated by the unhappy Czar of Russia. Most men had taken these seriously, had really believed that the noble Peace Palace at the Hague was leading the world onward to a truly Christian era, or at least was so improving International Law that future war would be a restrained and uplifting struggle between high souled and generous adversaries.

Crash! Now came the downfall of the entire structure. The men of western Europe wakened from their "Fools' Paradise," in which they had erected happy homes and reared their laughing children as thinkers and toilers rather than as soldiers.

For the wild confusion of those days we cannot do better than cull the diplomatic reports, and let the fairest and best of the old style statesmen tell of the tumult, as they saw it for themselves. Baron Beyens was perhaps the most anxious among representatives of the smaller nations. As Belgium's Ambassador at Berlin, he foresaw the possible disaster to his own little land. His ability is emphasized by the fact that during the War he was raised to be Belgium's Minister of Foreign Affairs. The French Ambassador Cambon, shrewd, strong and understanding, we have already met in his earlier report on German conditions. Sir Edward Grey, Britain's Minister of Foreign Affairs, stands out as the earnest central figure of his country's determined effort at peace. Prince Lichnowsky, the German Ambassador in Britain at the time, is perhaps the most interesting figure of the four. He is so typically the old style diplomat, so blind to the great moving forces of the universe, so convinced that the world is ordered by the petty interplay of personal motives among a few aristocrats. He has written an entire book upon his experiences and annoyances in London, and he almost manages to say that the War was fought so that his personal rivals in Germany might throw discredit on his ambassadorial ability.

As for the remarkable comments by the Kaiser which close this article, they are chiefly valuable as revealing his personal attitude. It was his custom to comment thus in notes on the margins of state papers; and after the War these papers were published by the German Republican government. Most of the Kaiser's notes are tedious in their repetition and narrowness of view, but those here presented throw vivid light upon his bewilderment in the tumult he had himself created.   C. F. H.

OFFICIAL REPORTS BY BARON BEYENS

Berlin, July 24, 1914.

THE publication of the ultimatum addressed yesterday by the Cabinet of Vienna to that of Belgrade goes far beyond anything that the most pessimistic anticipations of which I informed you in my report of the 16th of this month had anticipated. Evidently Count Berchtold and Count Tisza, the responsible authors of this sudden blow, have come under the influence of the military party and the Austro-Hungarian General Staff. The result of such a lack of moderation and discretion will inevitably be to attract the sympathies of the great mass of European public opinion to Serbia, in spite of the horror caused by the murders of Serajevo. Even at Berlin, to judge by the Liberal papers, one has the impression that the Austro-Hungarian demands are considered excessive. "Austro-Hungary," says the *Vossische Zeitung* this morning, "will have to prove the grave accusations which she brings against Serbia and her Government by publishing the results of the judicial inquiry held at Serajevo."

Her von Jagow and Herr Zimmermann[1] had assured

[1] The German Secretary of State and Under-Secretary.

us last week that they did not know the decisions taken by
the Vienna Cabinet, nor the extent of the Austro-Hungarian
demands.   How can we believe in this ignorance to-day?
It is improbable that the Austro-Hungarian statesmen should
have made up their minds to such a step, the most dangerous
stroke which their diplomacy has ever ventured against a
Balkan State, without having consulted their colleagues at
Berlin, and without having obtained the assent of the Emperor William.   The fact that the Emperor has given a free
hand to his allies in spite of the risk of bringing on a European conflict, is explained by the fear and horror which he
has of regicides.

"What is Serbia going to do?" was the question which
the majority of my colleagues were asking this morning;
"Will she turn to Russia and beg for her support by telegram?"   If she does so, she cannot receive any reply before
the expiration of the time limit in the Austrian ultimatum.
Russia will be obliged as a preliminary to concert measures
with France and, very astutely, the Cabinet of Vienna has
postponed the outbreak of the storm until the moment when
M. Poincaré and M. Viviani [3] are on their voyage between
St. Petersburg and Stockholm.   The threatening tone in
which the Austro-Hungarian note is couched is all the more
unfortunate because the Russian Ambassador at Vienna, I
learn, had recently informed Count Berchtold that his
Government would support the Austro-Hungarian demands
with the Pashitch Cabinet if those demands were moderate.

To-day a new crisis has begun, recalling the crisis of
1909 after the annexation of Bosnia and Herzegovina.   The
best we can hope is that it will not develop in a more tragic
manner, in spite of the bellicose wishes of the Austrian General Staff, which are perhaps shared by that at Berlin.   The
best advice to give to Serbia would be to invite the mediation
and intervention of the Great Powers.

Berlin, July 25, 1914.
The situation has grown no worse since yesterday, but
this does not mean that it has grown any better.

[3] The French President and Prime Minister.

As unfavorable symptoms, mention must first be made of the language used at the Wilhelmstrasse to the members of the diplomatic body: The Imperial Government approves the *demarche* made by the Austro-Hungarian Government at Belgrade, and does not consider it excessive in form. An end must be made of the murder plots and revolutionary intrigues which are hatched in Serbia. Herr von Jagow and Herr Zimmermann would not talk in this way if they had not received orders to this effect from the Emperor, who has determined in the interests of dynastic friendship to support Austria-Hungary to the last, and who is susceptible to the very legitimate fears inspired by outrages against Royal personages.

It should, further, be remarked that the German press, with the exception of course of the socialist papers, appears to have recovered from the first astonishment caused by the Austro-Hungarian note. It plays the part of chorus to the press of Vienna and Budapest, and contemplates coolly the contingency of war while expressing the hope that it will remain localized.

Finally, the view gains ground more and more among my colleagues—and I believe it to be well founded—that it is not so much a desire to avenge the death of the Hereditary Archduke and to put an end to the pan-Serbian propaganda, as an anxiety for a personal rehabilitation as a statesman which has induced Count Berchtold to send to Belgrade this incredible and unprecedented note. From the moment when his personal feelings and reputation are at stake it will be very difficult for him to draw back, to temporize and not to put his threats into execution.

The favorable signs are less evident. However, they deserve to be pointed out. Not to mention European public opinion, which would not understand the necessity for taking up arms to determine a dispute whose settlement is undoubtedly within the sphere of diplomacy, it appears impossible not to notice the general movement of reaction and disapproval which manifests itself outside Germany and Austro-Hungary against the terms of Count Berchtold's ultimatum. The Vienna Cabinet, which was right in substance, is wrong in form. The demand for satisfaction is just; the procedure employed to obtain it is indefensible.

Although Count Berchtold has skillfully chosen his moment to act—the British Cabinet being absorbed in the question of Home Rule and Ulster, the head of the French State and his Prime Minister being on a journey, and the Russian Government being obliged to put down important strikes—the fact that the Austrian Minister has thought himself bound to send to the Great Powers an explanatory memorandum, gives to those Powers, and particularly those of the Triple Entente, the right to reply, that is to say, to open a discussion and intervene in favor of Serbia, and enter into negotiation with the Cabinet of Vienna. If it is done at the earliest moment possible, a great gain in favor of the maintenance of European peace will result. Even a hasty military demonstration by the Austro-Hungarian army against Belgrade, after the refusal of the Serbian Government to accept the ultimatum, might, perhaps, not produce irremediable consequences.

Lastly, the three members of the Triple Alliance are not in perfect agreement in the present dispute. It would not be surprising if the Italian Government should determine to play a separate part and seek to intervene in the interests of peace.

Berlin, July 26, 1914.

What I have to tell you on the subject of the crisis is so serious that I have decided to send you this report by special messenger. Yesterday's reports which I have committed to the post, with a fear lest they should be read by the German *cabinet noir,* necessarily contained opinions of a much more optimistic nature.

Repeated conversations, which I had yesterday with the French Ambassador, the Dutch and Greek Ministers, and the British Chargé d'Affaires, raise in my mind the presumption that the ultimatum to Serbia is a blow prepared by Vienna and Berlin, or rather designed here and executed at Vienna. It is this fact which creates the great danger. The vengeance to be taken for the murder of the hereditary Archduke, and the pan-Serbian propaganda would only serve as a pretext. The object sought, in addition to the annihilation of Serbia and of the aspirations of the Jugo-Slavs, would be to strike a mortal blow at Russia and France, in the hope that England would remain aloof from the struggle.

To justify these conclusions I must remind you of the opinion which prevails in the German General Staff that war with France and Russia is unavoidable and near—*an opinion which the Emperor has been induced to share.* Such a war, warmly desired by the military and pan-German party, might be undertaken to-day, as this party think, in circumstances which are extremely favorable to Germany, and which probably will not again present themselves for some time: "Germany has finished the strengthening of her army which was decreed by the law of 1912, and on the other hand she feels that she cannot carry on indefinitely a race in armaments with Russia and France which would end by her ruin. The *Wehrbeitrag* has been a disappointment for the Imperial Government, to whom it has demonstrated the limits of the national wealth. Russia has made the mistake of making a display of her strength before having finished her military reorganization. That strength will not be formidable for several years; at the present moment it lacks the railway lines necessary for its deployment. As to France, M. Charles Humbert has revealed her deficiency in guns of large caliber; and apparently it is this arm that will decide the fate of battles. For the rest, England, which during the last two years Germany has been trying, not without some success, to detach from France and Russia, is paralyzed by internal dissensions and her Irish quarrels.

In the eyes of my colleagues as well as in my own, the existence of a plan concerted between Berlin and Vienna is proved by the obstinacy with which the Wilhelmstrasse [4] denies having had knowledge of the tenor of the Austrian note prior to Thursday last. It was also only on Thursday last that it was known at Rome, from which circumstance arises the vexation and dissatisfaction displayed here by the

[4] Offices of the German Ministry.

Italian Ambassador. How can it be admitted that this note, which, owing to the excessive severity of its terms and the shortness of the period allowed to the Cabinet of Belgrade for their execution is destined to render war immediate and unavoidable, was drafted without consultation with and without the active collaboration of the German Government, seeing that it will involve the most serious consequences for that Government? An additional fact, which proves the intimate coöperation of the two Governments, is their simultaneous refusal to prolong the period allowed to Serbia. After the request for an extension formulated by the Russian Chargé d'Affaires at Vienna had been refused yesterday at the Ballplatz, here, at the Wilhelmstrasse, Herr von Jagow evaded similar requests presented by the Russian and English Chargés d'Affaires who, in the name of their respective Governments, claimed the support of the Berlin Cabinet for the purpose of inducing Austria to grant Serbia a longer interval in which to reply. Berlin and Vienna were at one in their desire for immediate and inevitable hostilities. The paternity of the scheme, as well as of the procedure employed, which are, on account of their very cleverness, worthy of a Bismarck, is attributed here, in the diplomatic world, to a German rather than to an Austrian brain. The secret had been well guarded, and the execution of the scheme followed with marvelous rapidity.

It should be observed that, even if the secret aim of the statesmen of the two empires is not to make the war general and force Russia and France to take part, but merely to destroy the power of Serbia and prevent her from carrying on her clandestine propaganda, the result is the same. It is impossible that that result has not been perceived by the far-seeing rulers of the German Empire. On either of these assumptions, the intervention of Russia would appear inevitable; they must have deliberately faced this complication, and prepared themselves to support their allies with vigor. The prospect of a European war has not caused them an instant's hesitation, if, indeed, the desire to evoke it has not been the motive of their actions.

Diplomatic relations between Austria and Serbia have

been broken off since yesterday evening. Events are developing rapidly. It is expected here that the Serbian King, together with his Government and the Army, will withdraw to the newly-annexed territories, and allow the Austrian troops to occupy Belgrade and the country abutting on the Danube, without offering any resistance. Then, however, arises the painfully acute question: what will Russia do?

We too must put this disquieting question to ourselves, and hold ourselves in readiness for the worst eventualities, for the European war, *of which people were always talking on the agreeable assumption that it would never break out,* has now become a threatening reality.

The tone of the semi-official German press is more moderate this morning and suggests the possibility of a localization of the war, only however at the cost of the *désintéressement* of Russia, who is to content herself with the assurance that the territorial integrity of Serbia will be respected. Is not the aim of this language to give some satisfaction to England and also to German public opinion which, in spite of yesterday's Austrophile demonstrations in the streets of Berlin, is still pacific and alarmed? In any event, the *dénouement* of the crisis, whatever it may be, is apparently to be expected soon.

OFFICIAL REPORT BY JULES CAMBON
French Ambassador at Berlin in 1914

Berlin, July 27, 1914.
I had a conversation yesterday with the Secretary of State and gave support to the *démarche* which Sir E. Goschen [5] had just made.

Herr von Jagow replied to me, as he had to the English Ambassador, that he could not accept the proposal that the Italian, French and German Ambassadors should be instructed to endeavor to find with Sir Edward Grey a method of resolving the present difficulties, because that would be to set up a real conference to deal with the affairs of Austria and Russia.

I replied to Herr von Jagow that I regretted his an-

[5] The British Ambassador in Berlin.

swer, but that the great object which Sir Edward Grey had in view went beyond any question of form; that what was important was the coöperation of England and France with Germany and Italy in a work of peace; that this coöperation could take effect through common *démarches* at St. Petersburg and at Vienna; that he had often expressed to me his regret at seeing the two allied groups always opposed to one another in Europe; that there was here an opportunity of proving that there was a European spirit, by showing four Powers belonging to the two groups acting in common agreement to prevent a conflict.

Herr von Jagow evaded the point by saying that Germany had engagements with Austria. I observed to him that the relations of Germany with Vienna were no closer than those of France with Russia, and that it was he himself who actually was putting the two groups of allies in opposition.

The Secretary of State then said to me that he was not refusing to act so as to keep off an Austro-Russian dispute, but that he could not intervene in the Austro-Serbian dispute. "The one is the consequence of the other," I said, "and it is a question of preventing the appearance of a new factor of such a nature as to lead to intervention by Russia."

As the Secretary of State persisted in saying that he was obliged to keep his engagements towards Austria, I asked him if he was bound to follow her everywhere with his eyes blindfolded, and if he had taken note of the reply of Serbia to Austria which the Serbian Chargé d'Affaires had delivered to him this morning. "I have not yet had time," he said. "I regret it. You would see that except on some points of detail Serbia has yielded entirely. It appears then, that, since Austria has obtained the satisfaction which your support has procured for her, you might to-day advise her to be content or to examine with Serbia the terms of her reply."

As Herr von Jagow gave me no clear reply, I asked him whether Germany wished for war. He protested energetically, saying that he knew what was in my mind, but that it was wholly incorrect. "You must then," I replied, "act consistently. When you read the Serbian reply, I entreat you in the name of humanity to weigh the terms in your conscience, and do not personally assume a part of the responsibility for the catastrophe which you are allowing to be prepared." Herr von Jagow protested anew, adding that he was ready to join England and France in a common effort, but that it was necessary to find a form for this intervention which he could accept, and that the Cabinets must come to an understanding on this point.

"For the rest," he added, "direct conversations between Vienna and St. Petersburg have been entered upon and are in progress. I expect very good results from them and I am hopeful."

As I was leaving I told him that this morning I had had the impression that the hour of *détente* [6] had struck, but I now saw clearly that there was nothing in it. He replied that I was mistaken; that he hoped that matters were on the right road and would perhaps rapidly reach a favorable conclusion. I asked him to take such action in Vienna as would hasten the progress of events, because it was a matter of importance not to allow time for the development in Russia of one of those currents of opinion which carry all before them.

In my opinion it would be well to ask Sir Edward Grey, who must have been warned by Sir Edward Goschen of the refusal to his proposal in the form in which it was made, to renew it under another form, so that Germany would have no pretext for refusing to associate herself with it, and would have to assume the responsibilities that belong to her in the eyes of England.

OFFICIAL STATEMENT BY SIR EDWARD GREY
British Secretary of State for Foreign Affairs in 1914

Foreign Office, July 27, 1914.

Count Mensdorff [7] told me by instruction to-day that the Serbian Government had not accepted the demands which the Austrian Government were obliged to address to them

[6] Escape from danger.
[7] Austro-Hungarian Ambassador in London.

in order to secure permanently the most vital Austrian interests. Serbia showed that she did not intend to abandon her subversive aims, tending towards continuous disorder in the Austrian frontier territories and their final disruption from the Austrian Monarchy. Very reluctantly, and against their wish, the Austrian Government were compelled to take more severe measures to enforce a fundamental change of the attitude of enmity pursued up to now by Serbia. As the British Government knew, the Austrian Government had for many years endeavored to find a way to get on with their turbulent neighbor, though this had been made very difficult for them by the continuous provocations of Serbia. The Serajevo murder had made clear to every one what appalling consequences the Serbian propaganda had already produced and what a permanent threat to Austria it involved. We would understand that the Austrian Government must consider that the moment had arrived to obtain, by means of the strongest pressure, guarantees for the definite suppression of the Serbian aspirations and for the security of peace and order on the southeastern frontier of Austria. As the peaceable means to this effect were exhausted, the Austrian Government must at last appeal to force. They had not taken this decision without reluctance. Their action, which had no sort of aggressive tendency, could not be represented otherwise than as an act of self-defense. Also they thought that they would serve a European interest if they prevented Serbia from being henceforth an element of general unrest such as she had been for the last ten years. The high sense of justice of the British nation and of British statesmen could not blame the Austrian Government if the latter defended by the sword what was theirs, and cleared up their position with a country whose hostile policy had forced upon them for years measures so costly as to have gravely injured Austrian national prosperity. Finally, the Austrian Government, confiding in their amicable relations with us, felt that they could count on our sympathy in a fight that was forced on them. and on our assistance in localizing the fight, if necessary.

Count Mensdorff added on his own account that, as long

as Serbia was confronted with Turkey, Austria never took very severe measures because of her adherence to the policy of the free development of the Balkan States. Now that Serbia had doubled her territory and population without any Austrian interference, the repression of Serbian subversive aims was a matter of self-defense and self-preservation on Austria's part. He reiterated that Austria had no intention of taking Serbian territory or aggressive designs against' Serbian territory.

I said that I could not understand the construction put by the Austrian Government upon the Serbian reply, and I told Count Mensdorff the substance of the conversation that I had had with the German Ambassador this morning about that reply.

Count Mensdorff admitted that, on paper, the Serbian reply might seem to be satisfactory; but the Serbians had refused the one thing—the coöperation of Austrian officials and police—which would be a real guarantee that in practice the Serbians would not carry on their subversive campaign against Austria.

I said that it seemed to me as if the Austrian Government believed that, even after the Serbian reply, they could make war upon Serbia anyhow, without risk of bringing Russia into the dispute. If they could make war on Serbia and at the same time satisfy Russia, well and good; but, if not, the consequences would be incalculable. I pointed out to him that I quoted this phrase from an expression of the views of the German Government. I feared that it would be expected in St. Petersburg that the Serbian reply would diminish the tension, and now, when Russia found that there was increased tension, the situation would become increasingly serious. Already the effect on Europe was one of anxiety. I pointed out that our fleet was to have dispersed to-day, but we had felt unable to let it disperse. We should not think of calling up reserves at this moment, and there was no menace in what we had done about our fleet; but, owing to the possibility of a European conflagration, it was impossible for us to disperse our forces at this moment. I gave this as an illustration of the anxiety that was felt. It seemed to me that the Serbian reply already involved the greatest humiliation to Serbia that I had ever seen a country undergo, and it was very disappointing to me that the reply was treated by the Austrian Government as if it were as unsatisfactory as a blank negative.

STATEMENT BY PRINCE LICHNOWSKY
German Ambassador to London in 1914

In September, 1912, Baron Marschall died after he had only been at his post in London for a few months. His appointment, which no doubt was principally due to his age and the desire of his junior officer to go to London, was one of the many mistakes of our policy.

In spite of his striking personality and great reputation, he was too old and too tired to adjust himself to the Anglo-Saxon world, which was completely alien to him; he was rather an official and a lawyer than a diplomat and statesman. From the very beginning he was at great pains to convince the English of the harmlessness of our fleet, and naturally this only produced the contrary effect.

Much to my surprise, I was offered the post in October. I had retired to the country as a "Personalreferent" after many years of activity, there being then no suitable post available for me. I passed my time between flax and turnips, among horses and meadows, read extensively, and occasionally published political essays.

Thus I had spent eight years, and it was thirteen since I had left the Embassy at Vienna with the rank of Envoy. That had been my last real sphere of political activity, as in those days such activity was impossible unless one was prepared to help a half-crazy chief in drafting his crotchety orders with their crabbed instructions.

I do not know who was responsible for my being appointed to London. It was certainly not due to H.M. alone —I was not one of his intimates, though he was at all times gracious to me. I also know by experience that his nominees generally met with successful opposition. Herr von Kiderlen had really wanted to send Herr von Stumm to London! He immediately manifested unmistakable ill-will towards me, and endeavored to intimidate me by his incivility. Herr von Bethmann-Hollweg was at that time kindly disposed towards me, and had paid me a visit at Grätz only a short time before. I am therefore inclined to think that they all agreed on me because no other candidate was available at the moment. But for Baron Marschall's unexpected death, I should no more have been called out of retirement then than at any other time during all those previous years.

It was certainly the right moment for a new effort to establish better relations with England. Our enigmatic Morocco policy had repeatedly shaken confidence in our pacific intentions. At the very least, it had given rise to the suspicion that we did not quite know what we wanted, or that it was our object to keep Europe on the *qui vive,* and, when opportunity offered, to humiliate France. An Austrian colleague, who had been in Paris for a long time, said to me: "Whenever the French begin to forget about *revanche,* you always remind them of it with a jack-boot."

After we had repulsed M. Delcassé's efforts to arrive at an understanding with us about Morocco, and prior to that had formally declared that we had no political interests there —which conformed to the traditions of the Bismarckian policy—we suddenly discovered a second Krüger in Abdul Aziz. We assured him also, like the Boers, of the protection of the mighty German Empire, with the same display and the same result; both demonstrations terminated with our retreat, as they were bound to do, if we had not already made up our minds to embark on the world-war. The distressing congress at Algeciras could not change this in any way, still less the fall of M. Delcassé.

Our attitude promoted the Russo-Japanese and later the Anglo-Japanese *rapprochement.* In face of "the German Peril" all other differences faded into the background. The possibility of a new Franco-German war had become apparent, and such a war could not, as in 1870, leave either Russia or England unaffected.

The uselessness of the Triple Alliance had been shown at Algeciras, while that of the agreements arrived at there was demonstrated shortly afterwards by the collapse of the

Sultanate, which, of course, could not be prevented. Among the German people, however, the belief gained ground that our foreign policy was feeble and was giving way before the "Encirclement"—that high-sounding phrases were succeeded by pusillanimous surrender.

It is to the credit of Herr von Kiderlen, who is otherwise overrated as a statesman, that he wound up our Moroccan inheritance and accepted as they were the facts that could no longer be altered. Whether, indeed, it was necessary to alarm the world by the Agadir incident I will leave others to say. It was jubilantly acclaimed in Germany, but it had caused all the more disquiet in England because the Government were kept waiting for three weeks for an explanation of our intentions. Lloyd George's speech, which was meant as a warning to us, was the consequence. Before Delcassé's fall, and before Algeciras, we might have had a harbor and territory on the West Coast, but after those events it was impossible.

When I came to London in November, 1912, the excitement over Morocco had subsided, as an agreement with France had been reached in Berlin. It is true that Haldane's mission had failed, as we had required the assurance of neutrality, instead of being content with a treaty securing us against British attacks and attacks with British support. Yet Sir Edward Grey had not relinquished the idea of arriving at an agreement with us, and in the first place tried to do this in colonial and economic questions. Conversations were in progress with the capable and business-like Envoy von Kühlmann concerning the renewal of the Portuguese colonial agreement and Mesopotamia (Bagdad Railway), the unavowed object of which was to divide both the colonies and Asia Minor into spheres of influence.

The British statesman, after having settled all outstanding points of difference with France and Russia, wished to make similar agreements with us. It was not his object to isolate us, but to the best of his power to make us partners in the existing association. As he had succeeded in overcoming Anglo-French and Anglo-Russian differences, so he also wished to do his best to eliminate the Anglo-German,

and by a network of treaties, which would in the end no
doubt have led to an agreement about the troublesome question of naval armaments, to ensure the peace of the world,
after our previous policy had led to an association—the
Entente—which represented a mutual insurance against the
risk of war.

This was Sir E. Grey's plan. In his own words: Without interfering with our existing friendship with France and
Russia, which has no aggressive aims and does not entail
any binding obligations on England, to arrive at a friendly
rapprochement and understanding with Germany, "to bring
the two groups nearer."

. . . Nothing can describe the rage of certain gentlemen
at my London successes and the position which I had managed to make for myself in a short time. They devised
vexatious instructions to render my office more difficult. I
was left in complete ignorance of the most important matters, and was restricted to the communication of dull and unimportant reports. Secret agents' reports, on matters about
which I could not learn without espionage and the necessary funds, were never available to me; and it was not till
the last days of July, 1914, that I learnt, quite by chance,
from the Naval Attaché of the secret Anglo-French agreement concerning the coöperation of the two fleets in case of
war. The knowledge of other important events which had
been known to the Office for a long time, like the correspondence between Grey and Cambon, was kept from me.

Soon after my arrival I obtained the conviction that
under *no* circumstances had we to fear a British attack or
British support for any foreign attack, but that *under any
circumstances England would protect the French.* I expressed this view in repeated dispatches, with minute proof
and great emphasis, but did not obtain any credence, although Lord Haldane's refusal to assent to the neutrality
formula and England's attitude during the Morocco crisis
had been pretty obvious indications. In addition there were
the secret agreements which I have referred to, and which
were known to the Office.

I always pointed out that in the event of a war between

European Powers, England as a commercial state would suffer enormously, and would therefore do her best to prevent a conflict; but, on the other hand, she would never tolerate a weakening or annihilation of France; because of the necessity of maintaining the European balance of power and of preventing a German superiority of force. Lord Haldane had told me this shortly after my arrival, and all the leading people had expressed themselves in the same sense.

At the end of June I went to Kiel by command of the Emperor. A few weeks prior to this I had been made an honorary D.C.L. of Oxford, an honor which had not been conferred on any German Ambassador since Herr von Bunsen. On board the *Meteor* we learned of the death of the Archduke. H.M.[8] regretted that his efforts to win him over to his way of thinking had thus been rendered vain. I do not know whether the plan of an active policy against Serbia had already been decided on at Konopischt.[9]

As I was not instructed about views and events in Vienna, I did not attach very great importance to this occurrence. Later on I could only remark that amongst Austrian aristocrats a feeling of relief outweighed other sentiments. On board the *Meteor* there was also an Austrian guest of the Emperor's, Count Felix Thun. He had remained in his cabin all the time suffering from seasickness, in spite of the splendid weather; but on receiving the news he was well. The fright or joy had cured him.

On my arrival in Berlin I saw the Chancellor and told him that I considered the state of our foreign relations very satisfactory, as we were on better terms with England than we had been for a long time, whilst in France also the government was in the hands of a pacifist Ministry.

Herr von Bethmann-Hollweg did not appear to share my optimism, and complained about Russian armaments. I sought to reassure him, emphasizing the fact that Russia had no interest in attacking us, and that such an attack would never receive Anglo-French support, as both countries wanted peace. Thereupon I went to Dr. Zimmermann, who

[8] Emperor William II.
[9] The Residence of the Archduke Franz Ferdinand.

was acting for Herr von Jagow, and he told me that Russia was about to raise 900,000 additional troops. His language betrayed unmistakable annoyance with Russia, which was "everywhere in our way." There were also difficulties in economic policy. Of course, I was not told that General von Moltke was pressing for war; but I learned that Herr von Tschirschky had been reprimanded because he reported that he had counseled moderation towards Serbia in Vienna.

On my return from Silesia to London I stopped only a few hours in Berlin, where I heard that Austria intended to take steps against Serbia in order to put an end to an impossible situation.

I regret that at the moment I underestimated the importance of the news. I thought that nothing would come of it this time either, and that matters could easily be settled, even if Russia became threatening. I now regret that I did not stay in Berlin and at once declare that I would not coöperate in a policy of this kind.

Subsequently I ascertained that, *at the decisive conference at Potsdam on July 5th, the Vienna inquiry received the unqualified assent of all the leading people, and with the rider that no harm would be done if a war with Russia should result.* Thus it was expressed, at any rate, in the Austrian protocol which Count Mensdorff received in London. Soon afterwards Herr von Jagow was in Vienna to consult Count Berchtold about all these matters.

At that time I received instructions to induce the British Press to adopt a friendly attitude should Austria administer the *coup de grâce* to the "Great Serbia" movement, and to exert my personal influence to prevent public opinion from becoming inimical to Austria. If one remembered England's attitude during the annexation crisis, when public opinion showed sympathy for the Serbian rights in Bosnia, as well as her benevolent furtherance of national movements in the days of Lord Byron and Garibaldi, the probability that she would support the intended punitive expedition against the murderers of the prince happened so remote, that I found myself obliged to give an urgent warning. But I also warned them against the whole plan, which I characterized as ad-

venturous and dangerous, and advised them to counsel the
Austrians to *moderation*, as I did not believe that the conflict
could be localized.

Herr von Jagow replied to me that Russia was not ready;
there would probably be some fuss, but the more firmly we
took sides with Austria, the more would Russia give way.
As it was, Austria was accusing us of weakness and therefore we dare not leave her in the lurch. Public opinion in
Russia, on the other hand, was becoming more and more
anti-German, so we must just risk it.

In view of this attitude, which, as I found later, was
based on reports from Count Pourtalès that Russia would
not move under any circumstances, and which caused us to
spur Count Berchtold on to the utmost energy, I hoped for
salvation through British mediation, as I knew that Sir E.
Grey's great influence in Petrograd could be used in the
direction of peace. I therefore availed myself of my friendly
relations with the Minister to request him in confidence to
advise moderation in Russia in case Austria, as seemed likely,
demanded satisfaction from Serbia.

At first the English Press preserved calm and was
friendly to Austria, because the murder was generally condemned. But gradually more and more voices were heard
insisting emphatically that, however much the crime merited
punishment, its exploitation for political purposes could not
be justified. Austria was strongly exhorted to use moderation.

When the ultimatum was published, all the papers, with
the exception of the *Standard*—the ever-necessitous, which
had apparently been bought by Austria—were unanimous in
condemnation. The whole world, excepting Berlin and Vienna, realized that it meant war—indeed, "the world-war."
The British Fleet, which happened to have assembled for a
naval review, was not demobilized.

My efforts were in the first place directed towards obtaining as conciliatory a reply from Serbia as was possible,
since the attitude of the Russian Government left room for
no doubts about the gravity of the situation.

Serbia responded favorably to the British efforts, as

M. Pashitch had really agreed to everything, excepting two points, about which, however, he declared his willingness to negotiate. If Russia and England had wanted the war, in order to attack us, a hint to Belgrade would have been enough, and the unprecedented Note would not have been answered.

Sir E. Grey went through the Serbian reply with me, and pointed out the conciliatory attitude of the Government of Belgrade. Thereupon we discussed his proposal of mediation, which was to include a formula acceptable to both parties for clearing up the two points. His proposal was that a committee, consisting of M. Cambon, the Marquis Imperiali, and myself, should assemble under his presidency, and it would have been an easy matter for us to find an acceptable formula for the points at issue, which mainly concerned the collaboration of Austrian Imperial officials at the investigations in Belgrade. Given goodwill, everything could have been settled at one or two sittings, and the mere acceptance of the British proposal would have brought about a relaxation of the tension, and would have further improved our relations with England. I therefore strongly backed the proposal, on the ground that otherwise there was danger of the world-war, through which we stood to gain nothing and lose all; but in vain. It was derogatory to the dignity of Austria—we did not intend to interfere in Serbian matters—we left these to our ally. I was to work for "the localization of the conflict."

Needless to say a mere hint from Berlin would have decided Count Berchtold to content himself with a diplomatic success, and to accept the Serbian reply. This hint was not given; on the contrary, they urged in the direction of war. It would have been such a splendid success.

After our refusal Sir Edward requested us to submit a proposal. We insisted on war. I could not obtain any reply but that Austria had shown an exceedingly "accommodating spirit" by not demanding an extension of territory.

Sir Edward rightly pointed out that even without an extension of territory it is possible to reduce a state to a condition of vassalage, and that Russia would see a humiliation in this, and would not suffer it.

The impression grew stronger and stronger that we wanted war under any circumstances. It was impossible to interpret our attitude, on a question which did not directly concern us, in any other way. The urgent requests and definite assurances of M. Sazonof, followed by the Czar's positively humble telegrams, the repeated proposals of Sir E. Grey, the warnings of the Marquis San Giuliano and Signor Bollati, my urgent counsels, all were of no avail. Berlin persisted; Serbia must be massacred.

The more I pressed the less were they inclined to come round, if only that I might not have the success of averting war in conjunction with Sir Edward Grey.

Finally, on the 29th, the latter decided on the famous warning. I replied that I had invariably reported that we should have to reckon with English opposition if it came to a war with France. Repeatedly the Minister said to me: "If war breaks out, it will be the greatest catastrophe the world has ever seen."

After that, events followed each other rapidly. . . . Sir Edward was still looking for new ways of avoiding the catastrophe. Sir W. Tyrrell called on me on the morning of August 1st to tell me that his chief still hoped to find a way out. Would we remain neutral if France did? I understood that we should then agree to spare France, but he had meant that we should remain altogether neutral— towards Russia also. That was the well-known "misunderstanding." Sir Edward had asked me to call in the afternoon. As he was at a meeting of the Cabinet, he called me up on the telephone, Sir W. Tyrrell having hurried to him at once. In the afternoon, however, he talked only about Belgian neutrality and the possibility that we and France might face one another in arms without attacking.

Thus this was not a proposal at all, but a question without any guarantee, as our interview, which I have mentioned before, was to take place soon afterwards. Berlin, however, without waiting for the interview, made this report the foundation for far-reaching measures. Then there came

M. Poincaré's letter, Bonar Law's letter, King Albert's telegram. The waverers in the Cabinet—excepting three members who resigned—were converted.

Till the very last moment I had hoped that England would adopt a waiting attitude. Nor did my French colleague feel at all confident, as I heard from a private source. Even on the 1st of August the King had given the President an evasive reply. But England was already mentioned as an opponent in the telegram from Berlin announcing the imminent danger of war. Berlin was therefore already reckoning on war with England.

Before my departure Sir E. Grey received me, on the 5th, at his house. I had called at his request. He was deeply moved. He told me he would always be prepared to mediate. "We don't want to crush Germany." Unfortunately this confidential interview was made public, and Herr von Bethmann-Hollweg thus destroyed the last chance of gaining peace through England.

The arrangements for our departure were perfectly dignified and calm. The King had previously sent his equerry, Sir E. Ponsonby, to express his regrets at my departure and that he could not see me himself. Princess Louise wrote to me that the whole family were sorry we were leaving. Mrs. Asquith and other friends came to the Embassy to take leave.

A special train took us to Harwich, where a guard of honor was drawn up for me. I was treated like a departing Sovereign. Such was the end of my London mission. It was wrecked, not by the wiles of the British, but by the wiles of our policy.

Count Mensdorff and his staff had come to the station in London. He was cheerful, and gave me to understand that perhaps he would remain there, but *he told the English that we, and not Austria, had wanted the war.*

Looking back after two years, I come to the conclusion that I realized too late that there was no room for me in a system that for years had lived on routine and traditions alone, and that only tolerated representatives who reported what their superiors wished to read. Absence of prejudice and an independent judgment are resented. Lack of ability and want of character are praised and esteemed, while successes meet with disfavor and excite alarm.

I had given up my opposition to the insane Triple Alliance policy, as I realized that it was useless, and that my warnings were attributed to "Austrophobia," to my *idée fixe*. In politics, which are neither acrobatics nor a game, but the main business of the firm, there is no "phil" or "phobe," but only the interest of the community. A policy, however, that is based only on Austrians, Magyars, and Turks must come into conflict with Russia, and finally lead to a catastrophe.

In spite of former mistakes, all might still have been put right in July, 1914. An agreement with England had been arrived at. We ought to have sent a representative to Petrograd who was at least of average political capacity, and to have convinced Russia that we wished neither to control the straits nor to strangle Serbia. *"Lâchez l'Autriche et nous lâcherons les Français"* ("Drop Austria and we will drop the French"), M. Sazonof said to us. And M. Cambon told Herr von Jagow, *"Vous n'avez pas besoin de suivre l'Autriche partout"* ("You need not follow Austria everywhere").

We wanted *neither wars nor alliances;* we wanted only treaties that would safeguard us and others, and secure our economic development, which was without its like in history. If Russia had been freed in the West, she could again turn to the East, and the Anglo-Russian rivalry would have been reëstablished automatically.

We could also have considered the question of the reduction of armaments, and need no longer have troubled ourselves about Austrian complications. Then Austria would have become the vassal of the German Empire, without any alliance—and especially without our seeking her good graces, a proceeding ultimately leading to war for the liberation of Poland and the destruction of Serbia, although German interest demanded the exact contrary.

I had to support in London a policy the heresy of which I recognized. That brought down vengeance on me, because it was a sin against the Holy Ghost.

BARON TSCHIRSCHKY AND WILLIAM II.

[These were telegrams sent from Vienna by the German Ambassador there, Tschirschky. The comments printed in italics are by Kaiser William, expressing his opinion on each point as it was presented to him.]

June 30th.

Count Berchtold told me to-day there was every indication that the threads of the conspiracy of which the Archduke was the victim centre at Belgrade. The affair was so cleverly designed that very young persons had been expressly selected to execute the crime, since they could not be sentenced to more than secondary penalties. (*I certainly hope this is not the case.*) The Minister spoke with intense bitterness of the Serbian plots.

I have heard even people of moderation and responsible judgment express a desire to settle once for all Austria's account with the Serbs. (*Now or never!*) They think one should submit to the Serbs a series of conditions, and in case they do not accept them, should take vigorous measures. I am seizing every opportunity to dissuade people quietly but seriously from precipitate measures. (*Who has authorized that? Utterly stupid! It's none of his business! It is for Austria alone to decide what she considers it necessary to do. If things go wrong later, they will say: Germany opposed! Let Tschirschky do me the favor to drop such foolishness. The Serbs must be settled with as soon as possible. That is self-evident. It is something that requires no argument.*)

First of all, it is important for people to know precisely what they wish. Up to the present, I have heard nothing but very vague and confused impressions. It would be well to weigh carefully the possible results of any act, and to bear in mind that Austria-Hungary is not the only country in the world; that she must show due consideration for her allies and keep in view the European situation as a whole; especially that she should not lose sight of Italy's and Rumania's attitude in matters concerning Serbia.

July 10.

Berchtold is complaining of Count Tisza's attitude,

which makes it difficult to proceed vigorously against Serbia. Tisza pretends that they should act "like gentlemen." (*With assassins! After all that has happened! Stupidity!*)

July 14.

During the discussion to-day it was unanimously decided that it was advisable to wait until Poincaré had left Russia before taking up matters with Belgrade. (*Too bad!*) For it is important, so far as is possible, to prevent the relations of those two Powers from being influenced, and perhaps determined, at St. Petersburg during the exhilaration of champagne dinners and demonstrations of fraternity by Poincaré, Iswolsky, and the Grand Dukes. It would be better to have the toast over before the Ultimatum is sent. We shall be able to go ahead on July 25.

July 14 (later).

Count Tisza called on me to-day after seeing Count Berchtold. He told me that he was a man who always counseled prudence, but that every day strengthened his opinion that the Monarchy must make up its mind to act energetically (*Certainly!*) in order to prove its vigor and to end once for all the deplorable situation on its southeastern border. The language of the Serbian press and of Serbian diplomats is insupportably arrogant. Tisza told me: "It has been disagreeable for me to advise war; but I am now fully convinced that it is necessary, and I shall exert myself to the utmost in behalf of the Monarchy."

The final text of the note to be delivered to Serbia is not yet drafted. It will be ready Sunday (July 19). It has been decided that it will be better to wait until Poincaré leaves St. Petersburg, that is, until July 25, before delivering it to Serbia. (*What a pity!*) But as soon as the period allowed Serbia to reply has elapsed, or in case she does not accept all the conditions without reservations, mobilization will be ordered. The note has been drafted in such a way that it will be practically impossible for Serbia to accept it. (*William II underlined this sentence twice.*)

[Tschirschky then explained that Berchtold was considering what demands had best be put forward to make Serbia's acceptance wholly impossible. To this the Kaiser noted] :

Evacuate the Sandjak (certain Turkish territory previously ceded by Austria to Serbia) *then the row will begin. Austria must without fail get it back so as to stop the unification of Serbia and Montenegro and the Serbs reaching the sea.*

Ambassador Lichnowsky's report to Berlin, summarized by J. W. Gordon, so as to indicate the purport of the Kaiser's comments. These are given in italics.

The Austrian ultimatum to Serbia, couched in terms of studied extravagance, had been delivered and communicated to the Powers and the maintenance of peace had become manifestly impossible. Upon receipt of it Sir Edward Grey told the German Ambassador that it had produced a very serious situation and, after discussing it, he added that he desired to make a friendly and private communication at this point. The British Government desired, as heretofore, to continue in friendly relation with the German Government and would be able, so long as the conflict was confined to Austria and Russia, to stand aside. But if France became involved the position would be altered and the British Government compelled to take a prompt decision, it would not in those circumstances be possible to stand long aside and wait. It was far from his thoughts to suggest any sort of threat, but he did desire to prevent misunderstanding on the part of the Ambassador and to protect himself against the reproach at any later date of having been wanting in candor. He, therefore, had recourse to the form of a private conversation. All this was duly reported by the Ambassador to Berlin and his dispatch bears the Kaiser's marginal annotations. Against the observation that the British Government would be able to stand aside so long as the conflict was confined to Austria and Russia the Kaiser wrote: *"That is to say, we are to abandon Austria. Utterly mean and mephistophelean! But truly English."* Opposite to the remark that if France became involved the British Government would have to take a prompt decision, he wrote: *"They are already bound."*

He pointed Sir Edward Grey's diplomatic phrase that we could not wait long in that case by the blunt comment:

"They will attack us," and opposite Sir Edward Grey's remark that he wished to avoid the reproach of wanting candor the monarch wrote: *"That will not succeed. All these years he has been uncandid right down to his latest communication."* To the dispatch there is appended a long Imperial screed which begins thus: *"At this moment England reveals herself, the idea is that we are fixed up and so to speak powerless; the base hucksters have tried to gull us with dinners and discourse. The grossest mystification is the King's word conveyed to me by Henry, 'We shall remain neutral and keep out of this as long as possible.'"* The Imperial comment finishes with the reflection: *"Grey knows well enough that if he spoke a single, earnest, sharp, persuasive word in Paris and Petersburg and took his stand upon neutrality both France and Russia would remain at peace. But he refrains from speaking that word and threatens us instead. Low hound! On England alone falls the responsibility for peace or war, not on us. That must be made clear to the public."*

It is horrible to think that the issues of peace and war hung, in those days, on decisions taken by a mind so disordered as stands here revealed. When it is suggested that in the interests of general peace Germany should leave Austria to fight her own battles the suggestion is denounced as "mephistophelean"; but because the English Foreign Minister will not promise to leave France in the lurch if wantonly attacked he is a "mean hound." These are the utterances of mere hysteria; but it is one of the momentous facts of history that this distracted man was at that particular time invested with more power than any other person in the world over the dread decision for peace or war.

AUSTRIA OPENS THE WAR

SERBIA BECOMES THE CHAMPION AND MARTYR OF NATIONALITY

JULY 28, 1914

COUNT ALBERT APPONYI   LAZARE MARCOVITCH

For a moment we must look to the Great War as though it had really been what Austria supposed it, a drama in which she was the leading and directing figure. She saw herself, and perhaps quite honestly, as a mighty punishing force, protected indeed by the still mightier power of Germany, but with that convenient ally as a mere shadow in the background. She was eager to take a decisive step before diplomacy could stop her; so on July 28th, she somewhat hurriedly declared war on Serbia.

Her ultimatum of the 23d had demanded, and had received, a reply on the 25th. The judgment of the whole outside world has been that this reply was as conciliatory and as submissive as Serbia could possibly make it. But Austria in great haste published a document finding fault with the Serbian reply; and then realizing that discussion of the matter could only emphasize the fact that she was wholly determined upon attack, she proclaimed herself wickedly insulted and aggrieved, and declared war. This first declaration of war is given here. It is as abrupt and brief, as her ultimatum had been elaborate and complex.

Following the declaration comes the official explanation of it which was offered to the American public by Count Apponyi, well known to the Western world as the Speaker of the Hungarian Parliament, a noted statesman, and a former leader of the International Arbitration or peace movement. Count Apponyi cannot see Serbia at all except as a pawn in the great game between Austria and Russia, as to which could grab most territory in the Balkans. His is the thoroughly characteristic Austrian attitude, which knows nothing of any right to existence in any race other than the Austrian and Hungarian. He talks wholly in terms of property right. Hungary *owns* these Slavic lands and these Slavic people, because Austria gave them to her. That is the basis of the Apponyi universe.

In contradiction to this rings the sharply awakened "Nationalism" of the Serbs. It is voiced here by a Serbian statesman and scholar, a professor from the University of Belgrade. Count Apponyi wasted his time when he tried to tell well-informed thinkers that men such as Lazarre Marcovitch ought to remain the permanent serfs of Hungary. We are too wholly confirmed in our Democracy. We deny the existence of any right of some one "super-race" to rule a lesser people

323

—unless indeed that lesser people attacks Democracy and Civilization, as Germany did, by recklessly devoting itself to wars of conquest.

C. F. H.

THE AUSTRIAN DECLARATION OF WAR

(Telegraphic.)   Vienna, July 28, 1914.

The Royal Serbian Government not having answered in a satisfactory manner the note of July 23rd presented by the Austro-Hungarian Minister at Belgrade, the Imperial and Royal Government are themselves compelled to see to the safeguarding of their rights and interests, and, with this object, to have recourse to force of arms.

Austria-Hungary consequently considers herself henceforward in a state of war with Serbia.

BY COUNT ALBERT APPONYI

I CONSIDER it highly important that the case for Austria-Hungary, in the present conflict of nations, should be put before the American public with minute precision.

We are all agreed in abhorring war and in deploring the outbreak of a catastrophe the like of which history has never witnessed. Those who are responsible for it will forever remain branded with a stigma of infamy which no amount of military or political success can wipe off their foreheads. Feeling as strongly as I do on that point, devoted as I am to the peace ideal, I consider myself qualified to proclaim before the whole world that my country is free from guilt in the horrible contest which has been forced upon her, and that she can face it with all the moral power of a pure conscience.

The direct cause of the outbreak is Serbia's insane ambition to extend her dominion over those southern provinces of Austria-Hungary, Bosnia and Herzegovina to begin with, Croatia and the Slovene countries to follow, where South Slavs live in great numbers. Never could a small country like Serbia nourish such designs against a great Power unless it felt sure of being supported by some other great Power. Recent developments have shown that Serbia had good reasons to expect such support. On behalf of the mad ambitions, not warranted even by the claims of racial kinship, since the Roman Catholic Croats generally abhor Serbia,[1] a constant agitation was organized in the aforementioned parts of Austria and Hungary. The origin of this agitation can be traced as far back as the accession of the Karageorgevich dynasty to the Serbian throne. Under the Obrenovitch rule, Serbia cultivated friendly relations with Austria-Hungary, to whom she was largely indebted for the recognition of her independence by the Berlin treaty of 1878. Things took a different shape when the last Obrenovitch king and his wife were murdered by military conspirators, and the present King, Peter Karageorgevich, unhesitatingly accepted the crown from the blood-stained hands of their murderers. For a short time the conscience of Europe seemed to wake, or at least a feeling of nausea prevailed among the civilized nations. King Peter found it difficult to enter into diplomatic relations with the governments of Europe. Russia alone did not scruple to take him for granted. The other Powers had to follow, England last of all. Finally recognition became universal.

From that time, Serbia has been the seat of a permanent conspiracy against Austria-Hungary. Associations were formed for the "liberation of the South Slavonic brethren" in Austria-Hungary; agents were sent to undermine among our fellow citizens of South Slavonic race the feelings of allegiance to their country; wherever a traitor could be found among them, his services were enlisted; Bosnia and Herzegovina were almost openly claimed. These two Turkish provinces had been intrusted to Austria-Hungary's care by the Berlin treaty of 1878, because only the impartial rule of a Western Power could secure peace and liberty in a country inhabited by Mohammedans, Greek Orthodox, and Roman Catholic Christians. As a matter of fact, they throve and developed under the enlightened government of Austria-Hungary to a degree of welfare unknown in any other part of the Balkan peninsula.[2] Nevertheless, Serbia took hardly

[1] All of these Croats rejoicingly united with the Serbs after the War.

[2] Austria laid these provinces waste like an enemy's country during the War.

any pains to hide her covetousness concerning these provinces, where, under her rule, two-thirds of the population
would be submitted to the same tyranny of racial and religious intolerance which the unhappy Bulgarians of Macedonia are experiencing at her hands. It was this covetousness which brought us to the verge of war in 1908, when
Bosnia and Herzegovina were formally annexed to Austria-
Hungary.

That was done precisely to shut the door against intrigues feeding on their ambiguous juridical status, which
maintained the Sultan's nominal sovereignty over them,
while the whole power and the responsibilities of sovereignty
belonged to Austria-Hungary. From the standpoint of international law, the annexation was certainly not excep-
tionable.

Turkey, whose nominal rights were set aside, had a right
to protest, and so had the signatory powers of the Berlin
treaty, but Serbia had absolutely no voice in the matter.
No right of hers was invaded, no legitimate interest of hers
impaired; only mad pretensions were thwarted and unfair
opportunities lessened. Still, it was Serbia whose outcries,
echoed by Russia, endangered the peace of Europe. Everybody knows how that first outbreak ended. Russia, Serbia's
patron and inspirer, recoiled at that time from the conflict
with Germany which aggression against Austria-Hungary
would have implied. So Serbia had to declare herself disinterested in the arrangements concerning Bosnia, and willing properly to fulfill toward Austria-Hungary the duties
of good neighborship. It was largely due to the exertions
of the Hungarian Government, to which I belonged at that
time, that Austria-Hungary accepted these verbal apologies
and pledges, and that peace, or rather the semblance of peace,
was preserved for some years more. I now almost regret
this decision of ours. Had Serbia's impudent behavior been
chastised then, as it deserved to be, the present general conflict might have been averted. On the other hand, Austria-
Hungary would not have shown that almost superhuman forbearance in which lies her clearest vindication. Anyhow, it
is important to bear in mind that Serbia's pretensions and

designs brought matters to a crisis six years ago, and that she escaped punishment only through a solemn promise of correct behavior.

How was that promise kept? By doing worse from year to year, by developing with more energy still the propaganda of high treason among Austria and Hungary's South Slavonic citizens. Still more, since the results of such merely political work ripened too slowly, the pace was mended by setting up an additional organization for political assassination, headed by military and non-military officials of the Serbian Kingdom. The thing would seem almost incredible but for the fact that the present Serbian king's rule is based on murder, and that murderers are, or were, among his chief advisers. A government boasting of an origin like this must be expected to take a lenient view of political assassination. The matter was brought to light by Archduke Franz Ferdinand's assassination. This dreadful crime, as has been established by the judicial inquiry, was not the work of a single fanatic. It was the carefully prepared result of a widespread conspiracy, centered in a great Serbian national organization, the "Narodna Obrana," whose chairman is a general in active service, and whose rules contain a paragraph of dark meaning, bidding young men to prepare for "some big deed on behalf of the national cause." Well, Archduke Franz Ferdinand's murderers, all of them affiliated with the aforesaid organization, were prepared for the "big deed," and they performed it successfully. All the implements for the murder came from Serbian army stores; bombs of the same origin were found hidden in many places; not a single accomplice of the crime could be laid hands upon on Serbian ground; they found protection there instead of prosecution.

If circumstantial evidence has any meaning, the case against official Serbia seems to be made out by these facts. But, what is more, the lamented Archduke's assassination was not the first, but, within two years, the fourth, attempt organized by the same gang of murderers against the lives of faithful public servants in the southern parts of Austria and Hungary.

Now, in the name of all that is human and just and fair,
for how many years more should we have submitted to this?
How many assassinations more should we have left unpre-
vented, unpunished? What nation, big or small, can tolerate the setting up in her neighborhood of a whole machinery of treason and destruction, the organization of a
permanent conspiracy against her moral cohesion, with murder lurking at every street corner, threatening the individual
safety of her most valued citizens? Austria-Hungary had
tolerated it long enough to feel her strength shaken, to see
her power questioned, her destruction discounted, and her
future ruler murdered. A little more of this and our fellow citizens of the South Slavonic race would have learned
to doubt the Monarchy's capacity for defending the loyal
and punishing the traitors; for making itself respected, even
by small neighbors. In the face of such weakness on one
side and such unscrupulous daring on the other, they might
have wavered in their allegiance to a State unable to protect
them.

It was high time to drag out treacherous assailants from
the dark recesses of conspiracy into the broad daylight of
plain speaking and open doing. We had to exact from official Serbia, whose moral complicity was established beyond
doubt, efficient pledges, not words—which, in the case of
confirmed liars, are valueless—but measures guaranteeing
our tranquillity as a nation and the individual safety of our
faithful public servants. Such pledges Serbia would not
give. She evaded the summons in her habitual manner of
double dealing, granting a profusion of words, professions,
and promises, whose mendacity was proved by experience,
but recoiling from every measure really efficient. She was
clearly resolved to go on with her work of sneaking aggression and to cultivate further her well-tried methods of conspiracy. Austria-Hungary would have been the laughing-
stock not of her enemies only, but of her own citizens, had
she feigned to believe where bad faith was manifest. There
was no help for it. We had to set aside our extreme unwillingness to adopt violent measures. We had to strike or to
resign our right to live.

The case was not arbitrable, nor fit to be submitted to an international inquiry. Before giving my support to any warlike step, I examined with the utmost care this side of the question, and, devoted though I am to the cause of international peace and to a constant expansion of its propaganda, I had to own that its arguments were of no use in the present case. Their applicability supposes good faith and a wish to do the right thing on both sides; failing these, honesty plays the part of a dupe.

What could have been the result of international proceedings against Serbia? A verdict establishing her malpractices and bidding her to desist from them. Serbia, of course, would have professed to submit, just as she professed to be a good neighbor after the crisis of 1908. In fact, she would have persisted in her dark work, somewhat cautiously perhaps at the beginning, more daringly afterward; and, in a couple of years, maybe after another series of attempted and successful assassinations, matters would again have ripened to a crisis. Should we then again have begun that parody of an international procedure which settles nothing because the adverse party hypocritically accepts and barefacedly evades every decision running against it? Should we have gone on rotting all the while and hastening toward dissolution? Really we could not do that; international institutions must not be converted into traps where honesty is caught and dishonesty enjoys good fun; they are meant to insure justice, not to further the designs of cheats. In the face of God and man do I proclaim: If ever there was a case of lawful self-defense, here you have it.

But what about the universal war which grew out of a local conflict? Who is responsible for its horrors, for its calamities? The answer to this question is perfectly clear. Since Austria-Hungary was in a state of lawful self-defense against Serbian aggression, those are responsible for the greater evil who espoused the cause of that aggression. And this is what Russia did. She is the great culprit. Her policy is the main fountain whence torrents of blood and of tears will flow. Her allies have been drawn by her into the concern. Not that I wish to extenuate the guilt and the disgrace of highly cultured nations like France and England, who became in some way the patrons and the associates of a gang of Serbian murderers. But on Russia rests the chief responsibility; on her head falls the great sin against humanity implied in this war. From her face the mask has fallen, unveiling the lust of power and expansion which inspires her policy and which is the real source of every unrest in Europe.

In her war manifesto, Russia tries to pose as the chivalrous defender of a weak country against a strong one. That may appeal to the ignorant; in truth, it is barefaced humbugging. When Austria-Hungary had to coerce Serbia, she solemnly declared that her only aim was to win those guarantees of her own tranquillity which Serbia would not grant, but that neither Serbia's territory nor Serbia's independence would suffer any permanent mutilation. After that solemn declaration, made in the most binding form by a Power whose word is as good as any deed, there remained not the smallest pretext for honest interference.[3]

Still, Russia did interfere. On whose behalf? On Serbia's? After the pledges freely given by Austria-Hungary, Serbia as a nation needed no protection; Austria-Hungary's coercive action was not directed against Serbia, but only against the system of treacherous conspiracies and murderous attempts fostered by her present rulers. It is these dark forces alone that were threatened by our action in Serbia. It is therefore on behalf of these, not of the weaker nation, which was perfectly safe, that Russia interfered. Russia does not wish Serbia to become a decent country and a loyal neighbor; Russia drew her sword to make it possible that the conspiracies against Austria-Hungary's safety and the plots of murder implied in them should go on undisturbed; Russia stands behind that dark work with all her might and power; it is part of her policy; through it should Austria-Hungary be kept in a state of constant unrest, economic difficulties and moral decomposition, till she became ripe for receiving the final blow! Because Austria-Hungary

---

[3] This highly honorable "Power" had made a similar pledge about Bosnia and Herzegovina, and annexed them in spite of it.

must disappear to make room for the program now openly proclaimed by the Czar—the union of all Slavs under Russian rule.

So the mask has fallen. Serbia is a simple outpost; behind her stands the policy of Russia, supporting those treacherous and abominable acts which compelled unwilling Austria-Hungary to make a stand for her dignity and safety. Before the tribunal of human conscience stands Russianism, unveiled, as responsible for the horrors of universal war and for the permanent unrest that hereafter will consume Europe's forces. The power of Russianism must be broken before peace can be enjoyed with any amount of safety, before peace institutions can work with any degree of efficiency.

Well, since Providence puts its burden on our shoulders, that work will be done, with God's help, thoroughly. The greatness of the task is felt by every soul throughout Germany and Austria-Hungary, and absolute confidence reigns everywhere that our joined forces will be able to fulfill it. Even in Germany, there is no particular animosity against France. There is more of it against England, whose intervention is considered as a piece of revolting cynicism; but the chief object of popular resentment is Russia, which only shows the unerring instinct of the masses. And what I hear at home from simple-minded but honest and straightforward people like the day laborers on my own estate is a passionate desire to have it out once for all with Russia.

It is clear, not from facts only, but from the Czar's explicit confession, that the policy of Russia pursues aims which can be attained only through universal war. The union of all Slavs under Russian dominion can be effected only after the disintegration of existing political bodies, Austria-Hungary to begin with, and by subjecting the non-Slav races encompassed by Slavs, such as the Hungarians and the Rumanians. Does that not mean war, horrible war, universal war, since neither the political bodies concerned will submit to destruction without making a desperate stand, nor the threatened races to subjection without fighting to the last? And doesn't it imply another confession of complicity with Serbia's conspiracies and crimes, which now appear quite distinctly for what they are, pioneer work on behalf of Russia?

But what would Russia's dominion over the whole mass of Slavs, the so-called pan-Slavist ideals, mean from the standpoint of the great principles and ideals of progressive humanity? What would it mean to the Slavs themselves? It would mean, if a bad pun is to be allowed here, their transformation into slaves; it would mean to those among them who are now enjoying the bliss of civilized Western government and liberty a rolling down into the abyss of darkest tyranny; religious oppression for all those who do not conform to the Orthodox creed; a wiping out of racial differences as wide as the difference between German and Dutch, Italian and Spaniard; loss of every guarantee of individual and political liberty; arbitrary police rule which makes every man and woman liable to be arrested and transported without a trial, without a judicial verdict.

These and other similar blessings does Russia offer to those who are so happy as to fall into her loving embrace. And to all mankind, the grouping of all the forces of Slavdom under Russia's despotic power would mean the most horrible menace to enlightenment, progress, liberty, and democracy: A peril of cultural retrogression, a moral and social catastrophe.

BY LAZARE MARCOVITCH [4]

When at Serajevo, on the twenty-eighth of June, 1914, a young Serbian of Bosnian origin and an Austrian subject, a fanatic patriot, Gavrilo Princip, assassinated the Austrian Archduke Franz Ferdinand and his wife, the crime caused widespread consternation, especially in the Jugo-Slav provinces of the Dual Monarchy. The Austro-Hungarian press, following a signal from the Ballplatz,[5] proclaimed Serbia and the Serbian people culpable of the crime, and notwithstanding the absurdity of such an accusation, it was maintained and developed in an alarming manner. But the

[4] Reprinted by permission from the *Yale Review*.
[5] The Austrian Ministry of State.

official circles of Vienna showed an unaccustomed reserve; and their attitude made optimists believe, for the moment, that the press accusations against Serbia would terminate as soon as the result of the official investigation was known. In the meantime the Serbian Government maintained a strictly correct attitude and expressed to the Austrian minister at Belgrade its indignation at the crime, while awaiting communications about the inquiry which might, or might not, reveal the complicity of Serbian subjects.

The Austrian authorities did not publish anything about the result of the inquiry; and the Serbian public, occupied with the elections in the country, had nearly ceased to speak of the Serajevo crime, supposing that the culprits and their accomplices would be condemned by the proper tribunals. The Austro-German diplomats made reassuring declarations which produced a favorable impression and calmed public opinion in Europe; the German Emperor was cruising in Norwegian waters; the majority of the foreign ministers were already in the country,—when, on the twenty-third of July, came the telegram from Vienna, sent to the four quarters of the globe, announcing that Austria-Hungary had delivered an ultimatum to Serbia containing ten demands which must be granted within forty-eight hours.

By this ultimatum, as is well known, the Austro-Hungarian Government made official and unofficial Serbia responsible for the crime at Serajevo and demanded from the Serbian Government a solemn declaration that it disapproved and repudiated all idea of interference in the destinies of the inhabitants of the Austro-Hungarian monarchy. The time for considering the ultimatum, between its delivery on Thursday at five o'clock in the afternoon and the limit set for the reply, six o'clock on Saturday afternoon, was shortened by the fact, known to the Austrians, that the Serbian Prime Minister, Pashitch, was in the interior of the country occupied with the elections, and could not reach Belgrade until Friday about midday. Hence the Serbian Government had hardly more than a day to reply to the Austrian note, which was so humiliating to the whole Serbian nation and which contained no proofs whatever of the alleged facts. The menace was therefore very clear, and it was evident that Austria wanted the conflict.

Although no one believed that an independent state, a free people, mindful of its present and future responsibilities, could accept such a note, the Serbian Government nevertheless had the moral courage to make the greatest sacrifices in the interests of peace, and to accept the Austrian ultimatum on all points with only two unimportant reservations. Moreover, the Serbian Government added that if Austria-Hungary was not satisfied with this answer, it proposed to submit the whole question to the decision of the Hague International Tribunal or to the arbitration of the great powers. These proposals the Austrian Government refused to accept. On the twenty-eighth of July it declared war on Serbia and began hostilities; and in a few days, in spite of the pacific efforts of the Entente Powers, the whole of Europe was in flames.

Thus it is clear that Serbia is in no way responsible for the European War. Accused unjustly and menaced arrogantly by the Austrian ultimatum, Serbia yielded despite all the humiliation and injury that it threatened. The Serbian reply constitutes, indeed, the gravest ground for accusation against the Germanic Empires and is the best proof that they wished for war at any price. Though the aggression was to precipitate a general war, the Hapsburg monarchy did not hesitate to cross the Serbian frontier and to render impossible, by its irreconcilable attitude, the pacific solution of a conflict which it had itself intentionally provoked. Even the most complete submission of Serbia to this malevolent power could not save the little people from the lot which Vienna and Berlin had prepared for them. It is necessary to recall these events and to explain at the same time the reasons for this great rage against a small country, and this firm resolution on the part of Austria to risk even a general war.

It has now become clear why Serbia had to be crushed and exposed to cruel sufferings. The reasons, known to Serbia for a long while, may be divided into two groups, according as they affect Austria-Hungary or Germany. First, the purely German reasons must be examined. To the casual observer Serbia would not seem to have for Germany any particular interest. To those who have followed closely the development of German power and the successive steps in the Germanic plans for world domination, the question appears in a different light. In the history of the relations of modern Germany with Austria, the German design may be traced. After having established a solid base in the North in 1864 through the conquest of Schleswig-Holstein, Prussia made war on Austria in 1866 and by a *coup de force* succeeded in eliminating this power from Germanic affairs and pushing it towards the East. With the desire of completely setting herself free from Austria, Prussia gave her support to the formation of the Dual Monarchy, and it was under her auspices that the Austro-Magyar agreement of 1867 was concluded. By this agreement, the character of Austria was changed; from a Germanic and centralized state, it became a dual government.

In this new form the Hapsburg monarchy could not seriously pretend to the succession of the old German Empire, and Prussia was now free to undertake the task of achieving German unity and of accomplishing the Germanic mission. After 1870, under Bismarck, who gave to the newly formed federal German state an organization which assured predomination for all time to militarist and anti-parliamentarist Prussia, the German Empire initiated its world-policy. Having developed a formidable industry and an imposing commerce, it was not contented with its actual possessions and planned new acquisitions. These were projected in two directions.

On the one hand, Germany wished to become a sea-power of the first order, so as to impose her will on England. On the other hand, she sought to extend her continental possessions, turning, for this purpose, towards the East. The famous German *Drang nach Osten* is not a mere phrase, for it expresses the essence of recent German foreign policy. Among the European powers Germany had to choose between Russia and Austria-Hungary for her alliance, and an alliance with the latter against the former best suited her plans of conquest and of domination. If Germany had contracted an alliance with Russia, Austria-Hungary, as a superannuated historical formation, would have been dismembered in the interest of Europe; her peoples would have been liberated and would have grouped themselves into small nationalistic states.

If Germany had had a true conception of civilization and a real desire to promote its best interests, she would have facilitated this realignment of states grouped according to the desires of the peoples concerned. Moreover, by such a combination she would have gained economic advantages and probably a commercial outlet on the Adriatic at Trieste. Turkey would have been driven out of Europe, her Christian subjects liberated from a most odious régime; and all nations might to-day be living in peace and quiet.

But Germany preferred the alliance with Austria-Hungary, the maintenance and the preservation of this anachronous state, the subjection of the Slav peoples, and a vigorous pushing movement towards the East. In maintaining this monarchy, the German Empire reserved for itself the fifty million inhabitants of Austria-Hungary, who could contribute five million bayonets, amongst them three million Slav soldiers. After having secured Austria, Germany passed on to the Balkans and monopolized Bulgaria and Turkey. In Turkey, it sought at first only economic concessions, such as the Bagdad Railway, believing that after the economic pledges, the political acquisitions would naturally follow. But the route to Constantinople and Bagdad was barred by Serbia. Serbia was not willing to assist in the German plans of expansion towards the East, and that is the reason why it was decided by Germany that she must be crushed.

To Austria-Hungary, Serbia presented an equally serious obstacle in her separate plans for expansion. After the annexation of Bosnia-Herzegovina, the Hapsburg monarchy proposed to descend by the Vardar valley to Salonika. Germany by Constantinople to Bagdad, and Austria-Hungary by the Vardar valley to Salonika—these were the two principal ambitions of the Central Powers. The German leaders, who used the Dual Monarchy to forward their plans, could not refuse her some small gains, especially as the desire of Austria to establish herself at Salonika was not in opposition to the German policy of territorial expansion.

But Austria-Hungary had still another motive for wishing to annihilate Serbia. In Austria-Hungary there were eight million Jugo-Slavs (Serbs, Croats and Slovenes) who speak the same language and have the same aspirations. These Jugo-Slavs regarded Serbia as their Piedmont; and it is to the free and democratic Serbian kingdom that they looked for their deliverance from the Austro-Magyar yoke. Until the Balkan wars, Austria considered Serbia a state without vitality and destined to remain powerless. The credit of Serbia was especially low during the reigns of the two last Obrenovitches; and Austria then hoped to surmount the Serbian obstacle without difficulty. But after the accession of King Peter Karageorgevitch, after the restoration of the democratic constitution of 1888 and the introduction of a parliamentary régime in its purest form, Serbian credit rose again, and the country showed astonishing progress in many directions. Then came the wars with Turkey in 1912 and with Bulgaria in 1913. They revealed an extraordinary vitality in Serbia and ended in a brilliant victory and a still greater increase of strength for the little kingdom.

The Serbian victories found a formidable echo in the Slav provinces of the Hapsburg monarchy. Indeed, they were celebrated there more than in Serbia itself. They revived the hopes of an approaching liberation and put an end to the Austrian plans of taking advantage of Serbia's weakness to annex her as Herzegovina had been annexed. The Serbian or Jugo-Slav question suddenly appeared in all its fullness. Instead of descending to Salonika by the Morava and Vardar valleys, the Hapsburg monarchy found itself obliged to direct its efforts towards crushing the movement of its Slav population for liberty. Austrian rage against Serbia is therefore quite comprehensible.

THE SECOND ULTIMATUM

GERMANY DECLARES WAR AGAINST RUSSIA

July 31, Aug. 1, 1914

GERMAN OFFICIAL GOVERNMENT STATEMENT
BRITISH OFFICIAL GOVERNMENT STATEMENT
COUNT VON REVENTLOW and THE GERMAN COMMITTEE
MAXIMILIEN HARDEN   ALEX MARKOFF

When the Great War had begun the German Government issued the following official statement both for its own people and, in a slightly differing translation, for other nations, explaining how the War started. In this statement, as its title shows, Germany blamed Russia for the War. Later she shifted her view, and blamed France; and finally she recast the entire story, and made Britain the villain of the tale. Of course the repeated falsehoods proclaimed by the German Government throughout the War have left its official statements with- out any standing whatever as to veracity. Nevertheless it is well to know exactly what case she put before her own people on the moment, in summoning them to the miseries of war.

In essence the plea is that Russia compelled war by gathering her armies. In other words, while Austria openly and Germany only half secretly were mobilizing all their forces, Russia should have sat with folded hands and waited idly till the Teuton colossus struck—either at Serbia's heart, or perhaps at Russia's own. In that case, it is true that Russia would not have brought on war, but only suicide or murder.

The large outward facts that happened were as follows. When on July 28th Austria declared war on Serbia, she immediately began her military attack by bombarding Belgrade, the Serbian capital. Russia had always announced that she would protect Serbia from actual inva- sion, and she now began her slow and cumbrous task of gathering her scattered forces for Serbia's defense. France indicated positively that she would support Russia; and Britain, while refusing to take so ex- treme a stand, urged upon Austria with increasing vigor that she should consent to some form of arbitration. Slowly the Austrian Gov- ernment realized what it had before believed impossible, that Russia and France were refusing to submit to the German dictate. That if Austria persisted in her warlike advance, even her mighty ally could not protect her from having to face the risk and endure the suffering of a real and deadly war. This was very different from the easy task she had set for herself in trampling upon Serbia. The Austro-Hun- garian medley with its many discontented peoples might not survive a long or heavy conflict. Perhaps a first chilling suspicion whispered to the Hapsburgs that Germany did not intend them to survive. At any rate they reopened argument with Russia, and by July 31st both France and Britain were voicing a renewed hope of peace.

Then Germany used the weapon of the ultimatum with which Austria had before smashed through the diplomatic card-house. Only Germany struck a blow yet more wholly unescapable. She demanded not merely words but deeds, and not in two days but in half a day. She insisted that Russia must demobilize her armies within twelve hours, or Germany would at once not only gather her troops, but strike. To make such a sudden and extreme step seem a necessary move of self-defense, required a considerable amount of explaining. Germany attempts it here.

Britain published this German statement with a brief official comment, which perhaps takes too seriously what Germany had not expected to be seriously discussed—except by Germans. When you have read both arguments, you will surely feel that never was war begun on a more shallow excuse. So too with the appeal which follows! It is an address to Americans by a large committee of the very ablest Germans. Count Ernst von Reventlow, the leading writer of the ambitious Pan-Germans, was among its editors; and men who must actually have attended the Potsdam conference of July 5th were on its directing board. Yet it asks Americans to believe that "NOT ONE HUMAN BEING AMONG US DREAMED OF WAR." There is something truly comic—and the more truly hideous for that—in such colossal and official and universal mendacity. Did the signing of such a statement bring no shame to either the former Chancellor, Von Bülow, or the great director of steamship traffic with America, Herr Ballin, or the potent leader in the Reichstag, Herr Erzberger, or the famous general, Von der Goltz, or all the long list of Princes and Counts, or the great bankers, or the distinguished Professors Francke, and Lamprecht, and Harnack, and Wundt? One's soul sickens at the list of them. Not one human being in Germany had even dreamed of war! And their war books were on every side of us! Did they really think that Americans were such silly dupes as that? Or had they wholly ceased to be capable of thinking? To clear your mind of such ponderous sentimentality and stupidity, turn to the keen and honest statement of Max Harden, a true German patriot and great radical leader, and read the witty and yet earnest presentation of Russia's case by the well-known Russian author Markoff.   C. F. H.

OFFICIAL STATEMENT OF THE GERMAN GOVERNMENT

How Russia Betrayed Germany's Confidence

ON June 28th the Austro-Hungarian successor to the throne, Archduke Franz Ferdinand, and his wife, the Duchess of Hohenberg, were assassinated by a member of a band of Serbian conspirators. The investigation of the crime through the Austro-Hungarian authorities has yielded the fact that the conspiracy against the life of the Archduke and successor to the throne was prepared and abetted in Belgrade with the coöperation of Serbian officials, and executed with arms from the Serbian State arsenal. This crime must have opened the eyes of the entire civilized world, not only in regard to the aims of the Serbian policies directed against the conservation and integrity of the Austro-Hungarian monarchy, but also concerning the criminal means which the pan-Serb propaganda in Serbia had no hesitation in employing for the achievement of these aims.

The goal of these policies was the gradual revolutionizing and final separation of the southeasterly districts from the Austro-Hungarian monarchy and their union with Serbia. This direction of Serbia's policy has not been altered in the least in spite of the repeated and solemn declarations of Serbia in which it vouchsafed a change in these policies towards Austria-Hungary as well as the cultivation of good and neighborly relations.

In this manner for the third time in the course of the last six years Serbia has led Europe to the brink of a world-war.[1]

It could only do this because it believed itself supported in its intentions by Russia.

Russia, soon after the events brought about by the Turkish revolution of 1908, endeavored to found a union of the Balkan states under Russian patronage and directed against the existence of Turkey. This union, which succeeded in 1911 in driving out Turkey from a greater part of her European possessions, collapsed over the question of the distribution of spoils. The Russian policies were not dismayed over this failure. According to the idea of the Russian statesmen a new Balkan union under Russian patronage should be called into existence, headed no longer against Turkey, now dislodged from the Balkans, but against the existence of the Austro-Hungarian monarchy. It was the idea that Serbia should cede to Bulgaria those parts of Macedonia which it had received during the last Balkan war, in exchange for Bosnia and the Herzegovina which were to

---

[1] Contrast these statements with those of both Serbia and Austria in the preceding sections.

be taken from Austria. To oblige Bulgaria to fall in with this plan it was to be isolated, Rumania attached to Russia with the aid of French propaganda, and Serbia promised Bosnia and the Herzegovina.[2]

Under these circumstances it was clear to Austria that it was not compatible with the dignity and the spirit of self-preservation of the monarchy to view idly any longer this agitation across the border. The Imperial and Royal Government apprised Germany of this conception and asked for our opinion. With all our heart we were able to agree with our ally's estimate of the situation, and assure him that any action considered necessary to end the movement in Serbia directed against the conservation of the monarchy would meet with our approval.

We were perfectly aware that a possible warlike attitude of Austria-Hungary against Serbia might bring Russia upon the field, and that it might therefore involve us in a war, in accordance with our duty as allies. We could not, however, in these vital interests of Austria-Hungary, which were at stake, advise our ally to take a yielding attitude not compatible with his dignity, nor deny him our assistance in these trying days. We could do this all the less as our own interests were menaced through the continued Serb agitation. If the Serbs continued with the aid of Russia and France to menace the existence of Austria-Hungary, the gradual collapse of Austria and the subjection of all the Slavs under one Russian scepter would be the consequence, thus making untenable the position of the Teutonic race in Central Europe. A morally weakened Austria under the pressure of Russian pan-Slavism would be no longer an ally on whom we could count and in whom we could have confidence, as we must be able to have, in view of the ever more menacing attitude of our easterly and westerly neighbors. We, therefore, permitted Austria a completely free hand in her action towards Serbia, but have not participated in her preparations.

Austria chose the method of presenting to the Serbian Government a note, in which the direct connection between the murder at Serajevo and the pan-Serb movement, as not

[2] No evidence is offered to establish these loose charges.

only countenanced but actively supported by the Serbian Government, was explained, and in which a complete cessation of this agitation, as well as a punishment of the guilty, was requested. At the same time Austria-Hungary demanded as necessary guarantee for the accomplishment of her desire the participation of some Austrian officials in the preliminary examination of Serbian territory and the final dissolution of the pan-Serb societies agitating against Austria-Hungary. The Imperial and Royal Government gave a period of 48 hours for the unconditional acceptance of its demands.

The Serbian Government started the mobilization of its army one day after the transmission of the Austro-Hungarian note.

As after the stipulated date the Serbian Government rendered a reply which, though complying in some points with the conditions of Austria-Hungary, yet showed in all essentials the endeavor through procrastination and new negotiations to escape from the just demands of the monarchy, the latter discontinued her diplomatic relations with Serbia without indulging in further negotiations or accepting further Serbian assurances, whose value, to her loss, she had sufficiently experienced.

From this moment Austria was in fact in a state of war with Serbia, which it proclaimed officially on the 28th of July by declaring war.

From the beginning of the conflict we assumed the position that there were here concerned the affairs of Austria *alone*, which it would have to settle with Serbia. We therefore directed our efforts toward the localizing of the war, and toward convincing the other powers that Austria-Hungary had to appeal to arms in justifiable self-defense, forced upon her by the conditions. We emphatically took the position that no civilized country possessed the right to stay the arm of Austria in this struggle with barbarism and political crime, and to shield the Serbians against their just punishment. In this sense we instructed our representatives with the foreign powers.

Simultaneously the Austro-Hungarian Government

communicated to the Russian Government that the step undertaken against Serbia implied merely a defensive measure against the Serb agitation, but that Austria-Hungary must of necessity demand guarantees for a continued friendly behavior of Serbia towards the monarchy. Austria-Hungary had no intention whatsoever to shift the balance of power in the Balkan.

In answer to our declaration that the German Government desired, and aimed at, a localization of the conflict, both the French and the English Governments promised an action in the same direction. But these endeavors did not succeed in preventing the interposition of Russia in the Austro-Serbian disagreement.

The Russian Government submitted an official communiqué on July 24th, according to which Russia could not possibly remain indifferent in the Serbo-Austrian conflict. The same was declared by the Russian Secretary of Foreign Affairs, M. Sazonof, to the German Ambassador, Count Pourtalès, in the afternoon of July 26th. The German Government declared again, through its Ambassador at St. Petersburg, that Austria-Hungary had no desire for conquest and only wished peace at her frontiers. After the official explanation by Austria-Hungary to Russia that it did not claim territorial gain in Serbia, the decision concerning the peace of the world rested exclusively with St. Petersburg.

The same day the first news of Russian mobilization reached Berlin in the evening.

The German Ambassadors at London, Paris, and St. Petersburg were instructed to point out energetically the danger of this Russian mobilization. The Imperial Ambassador at St. Petersburg was also directed to make the following declaration to the Russian Government:

"Preparatory military measures by Russia will force us to counter-measures which must consist in mobilizing the army.

"But mobilization means war.

"As we know the obligations of France towards Russia, this mobilization would be directed against both Russia and France. We cannot assume that Russia desires to unchain such a European war. Since Austria-Hungary will not touch the existence of the Serbian kingdom, we are of the opinion that Russia can afford to assume an attitude of waiting. We can all the more support the desire of Russia to protect the integrity of Serbia as Austria-Hungary does not intend to question the latter. It will be easy in the further development of the affair to find a basis for an understanding."

On July 27th the Russian Secretary of War, M. Suchomlinof, gave the German military attaché his word of honor that no order to mobilize had been issued, merely preparations were being made, but not a horse mustered, nor reserves called in. If Austria-Hungary crossed the Serbian frontier, the military districts directed towards Austria, *i.e.,* Kiev, Odessa, Moscow, Kazan, would be mobilized, under no circumstances those situated on the German frontier, *i.e.,* St. Petersburg, Vilna, and Warsaw. Upon inquiry into the object of the mobilization against Austria-Hungary, the Russian Minister of War replied by shrugging his shoulders and referring to the diplomats. The military attaché then pointed to these mobilization measures against Austria-Hungary as extremely menacing also for Germany.

In the succeeding days news concerning Russian mobilization came at a rapid rate. Among it was also news about preparations on the German-Russian frontier, as for instance the announcement of the state of war in Kovno, the departure of the Warsaw garrison, and the strengthening of the Alexandrovo garrison.

On July 27th, the first information was received concerning preparatory measures taken by France: the 14th Corps discontinued the maneuvers and returned to its garrison.

In the meantime we had endeavored to localize the conflict by most emphatic steps.

On July 26th, Sir Edward Grey had made the proposal to submit the differences between Austria-Hungary and Serbia to a conference of the Ambassadors of Germany, France, and Italy under his chairmanship. We declared in regard to this proposal that we could not, however much we approved the idea, participate in such a conference, as we could not call Austria in her dispute with Serbia before a European tribunal.

France consented to the proposal of Sir Edward Grey, but it foundered upon Austria's declining it, as was to be expected.

Faithful to our principle that mediation should not extend to the Austro-Serbian conflict, which is to be considered as a purely Austro-Hungarian affair, but merely to the relations between Austria-Hungary and Russia, we continued our endeavors to bring about an understanding between these two powers.

We further declared ourselves ready, after failure of the conference idea, to transmit a second proposal of Sir Edward Grey's to Vienna in which he suggested Austria-Hungary should decide that either the Serbian reply was sufficient, or that it be used as a basis for further negotiations. The Austro-Hungarian Government remarked with full appreciation of our action that it had come too late, the hostilities having already been opened.

In spite of this we continued our attempts to the utmost, and we advised Vienna to show every possible advance compatible with the dignity of the monarchy.

Unfortunately, all these proposals were overtaken by the military preparations of Russia and France.

On July 29th, the Russian Government made the official notification in Berlin that four army districts had been mobilized. At the same time further news was received concerning rapidly progressing military preparations of France, both on water and on land.

On the same day the Imperial Ambassador in St. Petersburg had an interview with the Russian Foreign Secretary, in regard to which he reported by telegraph, as follows: "The Secretary tried to persuade me that I should urge my Government to participate in a quadruple conference to find means to induce Austria-Hungary to give up those demands which touch upon the sovereignty of Serbia. I could merely promise to report the conversation and took the position that, after Russia had decided upon the baneful step of mobilization, every exchange of ideas appeared now extremely difficult, if not impossible. Besides, Russia now was demanding from us in regard to Austria-Hungary the same which Austria-Hungary was being blamed for with regard to Serbia, *i.e.,* an infraction of sovereignty. Austria-Hungary having promised to consider the Russian interests by disclaiming any territorial aspiration—a great concession on the part of a state engaged in war—should therefore be permitted to attend to its affairs with Serbia alone. There would be time at the peace conference to return to the matter of forbearance towards the sovereignty of Serbia.

"I added very solemnly that at this moment the entire Austro-Serbian affair was eclipsed by the danger of a general European conflagration, and I endeavored to present to the Secretary the magnitude of this danger.

"It was impossible to dissuade Sazonof from the idea that Serbia could not now be deserted by Russia."

In reply to various inquiries concerning reasons for its threatening attitude, the Russian Government repeatedly pointed out that Austria-Hungary had commenced no conversation in St. Petersburg. The Austro-Hungarian Ambassador in St. Petersburg was therefore instructed on July 29th, at our suggestion, to enter into such conversation with Sazonof. Count Szapary was empowered to explain to the Russian minister the note to Serbia, though it had been overtaken by the state of war, and to accept any suggestion on the part of Russia as well as to discuss with Sazonof all questions touching directly upon the Austro-Russian relations.

Shoulder to shoulder with England we labored incessantly and supported every proposal in Vienna from which we hoped to gain the possibility of a peaceable solution of the conflict. We even as late as the 30th of July forwarded the English proposal to Vienna, as basis for negotiations, that Austria-Hungary should dictate her conditions in Serbia, *i.e.,* after her march into Serbia. We thought that Russia would accept this basis.

During the interval from July 29th to July 31st [3] there appeared renewed and cumulative news concerning Russian measures of mobilization. Accumulation of troops on the East Prussian frontier and the declaration of the state of war over all important parts of the Russian west frontier allowed no further doubt that the Russian mobilization was in full swing against us, while simultaneously all such measures were denied to our representative in St. Petersburg on word of honor.

Nay, even before the reply from Vienna regarding the Anglo-German mediation whose tendencies °and basis must have been known in St. Petersburg, could possibly have been received in Berlin, Russia ordered a general mobilization.

During the same days, there took place between His Majesty the Kaiser and Czar Nicholas an exchange of telegrams in which His Majesty called the attention of the Czar to the menacing character of the Russian mobilization during the continuance of his own mediating activities.

On July 31st, the Czar directed the following telegram to His Majesty the Kaiser: "I thank You cordially for Your mediation which permits the hope that everything may yet end peaceably. It is technically impossible to discontinue our military preparations which have been made necessary by the Austrian mobilization. It is far from us to want war. As long as the negotiations between Austria and Serbia continue, my troops will undertake no provocative action. I give You my solemn word thereon. I confide with all my faith in the grace of God, and I hope for the success of Your mediation in Vienna for the welfare of our countries and the peace of Europe.

"Your cordially devoted
"NICHOLAS."

This telegram of the Czar crossed with the following, sent by H.M. the Kaiser, also on July 31st, at 2 p. m.: "Upon

---

[3] NOTE.—The following words appear here in the German text but not in the version sent officially to other States: *während diese unsere Bemühungen um Vermittelung, von der englischen Diplomatie unterstützt, mit steigender Dringlichkeit fortgeführt wurden* ("whilst these endeavors of ours for mediation were being continued with increasing energy, supported by English diplomacy").

Your appeal to my friendship and Your request for my aid I have engaged in mediation between Your Government and the Government of Austria-Hungary. While this action was taking place, Your troops were being mobilized against my ally Austria-Hungary, whereby, as I have already communicated to You, my mediation has become almost illusory. In spite of this, I have continued it, and now I receive reliable news that serious preparations for war are going on on my eastern frontier. The responsibility for the security of my country forces me to measures of defense. I have gone to the extreme limit of the possible in my efforts for the preservation of the peace of the world. It is not I who bear the responsibility for the misfortune which now threatens the entire civilized world. It rests in your hand to avert it. No one threatens the honor and peace of Russia which might well have awaited the success of my mediation. The friendship for You and Your country, bequeathed to me by my grandfather on his deathbed, has always been sacred to me, and I have stood faithfully by Russia while it was in serious affliction, especially during its last war. The peace of Europe can still be preserved by You if Russia decides to discontinue those military preparations which menace Germany and Austria-Hungary."

Before this telegram reached its destination, the mobilization of all the Russian forces, obviously directed against us and already ordered during the afternoon of the 31st of July, was in full swing. Notwithstanding, the telegram of the Czar was sent at 2 o'clock that same afternoon.

After the Russian general mobilization became known in Berlin, the Imperial Ambassador at St. Petersburg was instructed on the afternoon of July 31st to explain to the Russian Government that Germany declared the state of war as counter-measure against the general mobilization of the Russian army and navy which must be followed by mobilization if Russia did not cease its military measures against Germany and Austria-Hungary within 12 hours, and notified Germany thereof.

At the same time the Imperial Ambassador in Paris was instructed to demand from the French Government a declaration within 18 hours, whether it would remain neutral in a Russo-German war.

The Russian Government destroyed through its mobilization, menacing the security of our country, the laborious action at mediation of the European cabinets.[4] The Russian mobilization in regard to the seriousness of which the Russian Government was never allowed by us to entertain a doubt, in connection with its continued denial, shows clearly that Russia wanted war.

The Imperial Ambassador at St. Petersburg delivered his note to M. Sazonof on July 31st at 12 o'clock midnight.

The reply of the Russian Government has *never* reached us.

Two hours after the expiration of the time limit the Czar telegraphed to H.M. the Kaiser, as follows: "I have received Your telegram. I comprehend that You are forced to mobilize, but I should like to have from You the same guarantee which I have given You, viz., that these measures do not mean war, and that we shall continue to negotiate for the welfare of our two countries and the universal peace which is so dear to our hearts. With the aid of God it must be possible to our long tried friendship to prevent the shedding of blood. I expect with full confidence Your urgent reply."

To this H.M. the Kaiser replied: "I thank You for Your telegram. I have shown yesterday to Your Government the way through which alone war may yet be averted. Although I asked for a reply by to-day noon, no telegram from my Ambassador has reached me with the reply of Your Government. I therefore have been forced to mobilize my army. An immediate, clear and unmistakable reply of Your Government is the sole way to avoid endless misery. Until I receive this reply I am unable, to my great grief, to enter upon the subject of Your telegram. I must ask most earnestly that You, without delay, order Your troops to com-

[4] The text issued in Germany for German reading adds here, "just as it was on the point of succeeding." This of course intensified the public anger against Russia.

mit, under no circumstances, the slightest violation of our frontiers."

As the time limit given to Russia had expired without the receipt of a reply to our inquiry, H.M. the Kaiser ordered the mobilization of the entire German Army and Navy on August 1st at 5 p. m.

The German Ambassador at St. Petersburg was instructed that, in the event of the Russian Government not giving a satisfactory reply within the stipulated time, he should declare that we considered ourselves in a state of war after the refusal of our demands. However, before a confirmation of the execution of this order had been received, that is to say, already in the afternoon of August 1st, *i.e.,* the same afternoon on which the telegram of the Czar, cited above, was sent, Russian troops crossed our frontier and marched into German territory.

Thus Russia began the war against us.

Meanwhile the Imperial Ambassador in Paris put our question to the French Cabinet on July 31st at 7 p. m.

The French Prime Minister gave an equivocal and unsatisfactory reply on August 1st at 1 p. m., which gave no clear idea of the position of France, as he limited himself to the explanation that France would do that which her interests demanded. A few hours later, at 5 p. m., the mobilization of the entire French Army and Navy was ordered.

On the morning of the next day France opened hostilities.

OFFICIAL BRITISH COMMENTARY ON THE ABOVE

View of the Negotiations Implied by the Title of the German Book: "How Russia Betrayed Germany's Confidence"

The ground of the charge thus made by Germany against Russia is a little difficult to fix. Russia's attitude was entirely open throughout the negotiations, and the German Chancellor's telegrams to the German Ambassadors at London, Paris and Petrograd of July 26th (German Book, Nos. 10, 10A, and 10B, p. 428) show that, on the day following the rupture between Austria and Serbia, that attitude was already clearly understood in Germany. In fact, there is not a sign in the whole correspondence that any statesman in the whole of Europe ever doubted that Russia would regard an actual armed attack on Serbia under the circumstances as an attack upon herself. . . .

The German Book rests almost its whole case on the priority of mobilization measures. The way in which that case was carefully built up during the negotiations is shown by British Book No. 71, where the German Chancellor declares on July 28th that the Russian mobilization in the south endangered the efforts of the German Government to encourage direct communications between Vienna and Petrograd. It will be seen that at the moment the Chancellor was speaking, Austria had already refused both direct discussions with Petrograd and Sir E. Grey's mediation proposals, *before* she heard of the Russian mobilization, and on the sole ground that she had herself declared war on Serbia. It was *after* she heard of the Russian preparations that she resumed conversations on July 29th-30th. It will be observed that on July 28th Russia believed that the general Austrian mobilization had been ordered. As a matter of fact, in sifting any case based on mobilization reports there are several points to be remembered.

Mobilization measures as preliminaries to war are a German tradition. If any one will refer to the account of the negotiations between Prussia and Austria from March 31 to May 8, 1866, before the Prusso-Austrian war, given in Sybel's "Foundation of the German Empire," he will see the example in this line set by Bismarck. But a case based on priority of mobilization measures is never a strong one for several reasons. First, it is difficult enough to tell "who began it" when the negotiations are spread over months, but it is practically impossible to do so when, as here, it is a question of hours. The actual mobilization measures are taken in the midst of a cloud of accusations and threats, and it is impossible to separate cause from effect. Secondly, in any attempt to state the facts, the minor accusations and innuendoes must be discarded as of slight importance, except as a guide to the psychology of the moment. The same may be said of rumors of violations of frontier. They have their value, but to put them forward, as does the German and Austrian correspondence, as the actual ground for the commencement of hostilities is to assume the impossible position that the fate of nations is subject to the reported action of a roving patrol. A marked insistence on such reports, as in the German Book, shows a poor appreciation of the value of the evidence. Thirdly, mobilization "orders" are not mobilization. The mobilization systems of different countries are radically different; the precise nature of those systems, the lines of the railways and a hundred other points must be taken into consideration in judging mobilization measures, and any statement which ignores these factors is a mere bid for uninformed public opinion.

The hard fact that though Germany only proclaimed *"Kriegsgefahrzustand"* on July 31st and mobilization on August 1st, to take effect on August 2nd, the German troops were across the Luxemburg frontier at dawn on August 2nd, will probably be judged to be historical evidence of far more value than any isolated reports received during the crisis. As to Russian mobilization, it was fully realized in Germany that the Russian system was so complicated as to make it difficult to distinguish the localities really affected by mobilization. Germany accuses Russia of mobilizing against Germany, not Austria, because she is reported to be mobilizing at Vilna and Warsaw, but both those towns are nearer to the Galician frontier than Prague is to the Serbian frontier, and Austria was reported to be mobilizing at Prague four days before she declared to Russia that she was only mobilizing against Serbia. The bare facts are of very slight value as evidence without a knowledge of the points already mentioned.

If the charges as to the priority of Russian mobilization are examined in the light of these considerations, it will be admitted that the evidence for those charges is remarkably slight, and that, given the admitted extreme slowness of Russian, and the extreme rapidity of German, mobilization, a fact which is frequently alluded to in the correspondence, there is no indication in favor of, and an overwhelming presumption against, the theory that the Russian measures were further advanced than the German when war was declared on August 1st.

The charge that the Czar's telegram of July 31st was misleading, and that the mobilization orders issued about the time of its dispatch destroyed the effect of sincere efforts then being made by Germany to mediate between Russia and Austria, is also unestablished.

In the first place, a glance at the Czar's telegram is sufficient to show that this charge is, to put it frankly, of the flimsiest character. His Majesty gave his "solemn word" that, while it was "technically impossible to discontinue our military preparations," the Russian troops would "undertake no provocative action" "as long as the negotiations between Austria and Serbia continue." There was no promise not to mobilize; there was nothing but a statement which is almost word for word the same as that contained in the German Emperor's telegram to King George twenty-four hours later—the statement that, under certain circumstances, mobilization would not be converted into hostilities.

As a matter of fact, a somewhat unscrupulous use, in effect though perhaps not in intention, has been made of the Czar's telegrams to substantiate the theory of "betrayal." Take for instance the German Chancellor's statement on July 31st (British Book, No. 108), that "the news of the active preparations on the Russo-German frontier had reached him just when the Czar had appealed to the Emperor, in the name of their old friendship, to mediate at Vienna, and when the Emperor was actually conforming to that request." The telegram referred to must be that of July 29th (German Book, No. 21), since this is the only one which mentions "old friendship"; but this telegram, though it asks the Emperor to restrain Austria, also says in so many words that popular opinion in Russia would soon force measures which would lead to war.

THE GERMAN APPEAL TO AMERICANS

ISSUED BY AN IMPOSING COMMITTEE OF LEADING GERMAN
STATESMEN, SCHOLARS, BANKERS AND MERCHANTS, IN-
CLUDING PRINCE VON BÜLOW, MARSHAL VON DER GOLTZ,
MATTHIAS ERZBERGER, HERR BALLIN, COUNT VON RE-
VENTLOW, AND THE HEAD OF THE IMPERIAL BANK.

Listen, All Ye People!

Try to realize, every one of you, what we are going
through! Only a few weeks ago all of us were peacefully
following our several vocations. The peasant was gathering
in this summer's plentiful crop, the factory hand was working with accustomed vigor. Not one human being among us
dreamed of war. We are a nation that wishes to lead a
quiet and industrious life. This need hardly be stated to
you Americans. You, of all others, know the temper of
the German who lives within your gates. Our love of peace
is so strong that it is not regarded by us in the light of a virtue, we simply know it to be an inborn and integral portion
of ourselves. Since the foundation of the German Empire in
the year 1871, we, living in the center of Europe, have given
an example of tranquillity and peace, never once seeking to
profit by any momentary difficulties of our neighbors. Our
commercial extension, our financial rise in the world, are far
removed from any love of adventure, they are the fruit of
painstaking and plodding labor.

We are not credited with this temper, because we are
insufficiently known. Our situation and our way of thinking
are not easily grasped.

Every one is aware that we have produced great philosophers and poets, we have preached the gospel of humanity
with impassioned zeal. America fully appreciates Goethe
and Kant, looks upon them as corner-stones of elevated culture. Do you really believe that we have changed our na-
tures, that our souls can be satisfied with military drill and
servile obedience? We are soldiers because we have to be
soldiers, because otherwise Germany and German civilization would be swept away from the face of the earth. It has
cost us long and weary struggles to attain our independence,

and we know full well that, in order to preserve it, we must
not content ourselves with building schools and factories,
we must look to our garrisons and forts. We and all our
soldiers have remained, however, the same lovers of music
and lovers of exalted thought. We have retained our old
devotion to all peaceable sciences and arts; as all the world
knows, we work in the foremost rank of all those who strive
to advance the exchange of commodities, who further useful,
technical knowledge. But we have been forced to become a
nation of soldiers, in order to be free. And we are bound
to follow our Kaiser, because he symbolizes and represents
the unity of our nation. To-day, knowing no distinction of
party, no difference of opinion, we rally around him, willing
to shed the last drop of our blood. For though it takes a
great deal to rouse us Germans, when once aroused, our
feelings run deep and strong. Every one is filled with this
passion, with the soldier's ardor. But when the waters of
the deluge shall have subsided, gladly will we return to the
plow and to the anvil.

It deeply distresses us to see two highly civilized nations, England and France, joining the onslaught of autocratic Russia. That this could happen, will remain one of
the anomalies of history. It is not our fault: we firmly
believed in the desirability of the great nations working together, we peaceably came to terms with France and England
in sundry difficult African questions. There was no cause
for war between Western Europe and us, no reason why
Western Europe should feel itself constrained to further
the power of the Czar.

The Czar, as an individual, is most certainly not the
instigator of the unspeakable horrors that are now inun-
dating Europe. But he bears before God and Posterity the
responsibility of having allowed himself to be terrorized by
an unscrupulous military clique.

Ever since the weight of the crown has pressed upon him,
he has been the tool of others. He did not desire the brutalities in Finland, he did not approve of the iniquities of the
Jewish Pogroms, but his hand was too weak to stop the fury
of the reactionary party. Why would he not permit Austria

to pacify her southern frontier? It was inconceivable that
Austria should calmly see her heir apparent murdered. How
could she? All the nationalities under her rule realized the
impossibility of tamely allowing Serbia's only too evident
and successful intrigues to be carried on under her very eyes.
The Austrians could not allow their venerable and sorely
stricken monarch to be wounded and insulted any longer.
This reasonable and honorable sentiment on the part of
Austria has caused Russia to put itself forward as the patron
of Serbia, as the enemy of European thought and civilization.

Russia has an important mission to fulfill in its own country and in Asia. It would do better in its own interest to
leave the rest of the world in peace. But the die is cast, and
all nations must decide whether they wish to further us by
sentiments and by deeds, or the government of the Czar.
This is the real significance of this appalling struggle, all the
rest is immaterial. Russia's attitude alone has forced us to
go to war with France and with their great ally.

The German nation is serious and conscientious. Never
would a German Government dare to contemplate a war
for the sake of dynastic interest, or for the sake of glory.
This would be against the entire bent of our character.
Firmly believing in the justice of our cause, all parties,
the conservatives and the clericals, the liberals and the socialists, have joined hands. All disputes are forgotten, one
duty exists for all, the duty of defending our country and
vanquishing the enemy.

Will not this calm, self-reliant and unanimous readiness
to sacrifice all, to die or to win, appeal to other nations and
force them to understand our real character and the situation in which we are placed?

The war has severed us from the rest of the world, all
our cable communications are destroyed. But the winds
will carry the mighty voice of justice even across the ocean.
We trust in God, we have confidence in the judgment of
right-minded men. And through the roar of battle, we call
to you all. Do not believe the mischievous lies that our
enemies are spreading about! We do not know if victory

will be ours, the Lord alone knows. We have not chosen our path, we must continue doing our duty, even to the very end. We bear the misery of war, the death of our sons, believing in Germany, believing in duty. And we know that Germany cannot be wiped from the face of the earth.

BY MAXIMILIEN HARDEN.[1]

In the beginning there was a misunderstanding out of which sprang the most terrible tragedy in history.

Three decades of unfertile melodramatic political feints, the errors of which, smaller and greater sins, the high conjuncture of German management ever and again conceals from the nation; the facts that the Kaiser spoke foolishly, acted thoughtlessly and let himself be impelled by vanity and a craving for sensation, that he was better fitted to be an actor than a ruler—of these things millions of people here are aware. But nearly all of them thought and said: "This can do no harm. Nobody would take seriously this quick-change artist with his crown and his rattling sabre. We work with more perseverance than most other people; we are advancing speedily in all fields; and with our well-trained workers, our technique and industry, and with our social policy which provides for the aged and the sick, we shall in twenty years be the richest nation in Europe. It is true that our Government is bad; but this does not hinder our development. The Deutsche Bank, Krupps (which firm devoted much more work for the uses of peace than for the production of military weapons, but was much less often mentioned in that connection), our coal syndicates, iron works, steel works, *Badische Anilinfabrik, Allgemeine Elektricitats-Gesellschaft,* Hamburg-America Line, chemicals, textiles—nobody on our continent can imitate these."

The unpolitical, and therefore most easily ruled, people honestly believed this and worked unceasingly. Too unceasingly; for other peoples with greater riches and an older civilization were forced to make an inconvenient alteration in their standard of living because of the insistent offer of

[1] Reprinted by permission from The World's Work, Copyright, 1922.

cheap German goods prepared for every demand of the market. Too unceasingly; for the resulting immensely quick increase in prosperity—"American," we called it here with pride—resulted in a blind worship of success, of the power that Mammon procured, and this cast off every shred of shame and became a national danger.

Twenty years of the Kaiser's rule altered the face of Europe entirely. Instead of trying by sensible and modest negotiations to seek to secure for German thrift and technical-industrial apparatus a somewhat broader sphere, perhaps in South-Eastern Europe, unrest was started everywhere and political affairs disturbed.

The Kaiser tried to stay the decline of the sterile Turkish rule, a decline which was apparent in every sphere, and to forge an efficient weapon against England out of the Califate. He egged on the Boers, the Russians, the French, even the Americans, against England, turned the Bagdad railroad into a political thing, and called it boastfully the "dry road to India," strove to seduce Mr. Roosevelt by low flattery into anti-British and pro-German sentiments, withal (in the *Daily Telegraph* interview) prided himself on being England's only friend in Germany, and had with all his untruthfulness and feminine love of intrigue achieved only this, that nobody trusted him any longer; that the old antipathies between England and France, and England and Russia, were bridged over, and that his wise uncle, Edward VII, who knew his nephew as well as possible, tried a West-East union to guard against the eternal enemies of peace and trade.

King Edward knew that for "Willy" (of whom Bismarck had said to me long ago, "The Emperor would like to celebrate his birthday every day") the army and fleet were only the toys for his pose as warrior, the "sharp sword," the dry powder and all the rest only acting, a product of his stagey craving for applause. After Edward's death, the Kaiser's activities were taken in earnest. That was the first misunderstanding.

The second was that incapable politicians and chauvinist demagogues succeeded in persuading the German people, intoxicated with "business" and unconcerned with politics, that the Triple Entente were planning attack, not defence. With sorrow London, Petersburg, and Paris looked upon the plans of a new Tamerlane, Attila, Bonaparte. The Germans believed that the hate and envy of an inimical world threatened the prosperity achieved by their iron thrift. All this merely because a coquettish actor, His Majesty by the Grace of God, was hunting for a star part to win applause by a constant succession of costumes. His mediocre and unpopular ministers wanted to renew their prestige by repeating the role which had brought success to Prince Bülow in the Austro-Russian conflict about Bosnia. His capable generals wanted to exploit what in their opinion was the last opportunity to remove with the sword the difficulties which had been brought about by an appallingly bad policy.

The ministers wanted bluff; the generals wanted a preventive war before the superiority of the "enemy" became invincible. The Kaiser himself, outshone by his son in popularity with the people, at the call of grandiloquent cowardice, and yet the slave of his long-standing heroics, urged by his "dynastic feeling" and his fear of assassination, was pleased to take upon himself the duty of avenging the murder at Serajevo as the executant of the solidarity of monarchs. He dared not appear a coward, and, falling, as ever, on the side of the strongest alarm, he declared war.

The Germans went into the war with the deep-seated dogmatic conviction that they were being assaulted by spiteful envy, and that they were fighting for their lives and the existence of the German. nation.

BY ALEX MARKOFF

Why Russia Has Gone to War with Germany

Once upon a time there was a Man who made friends with a great, big Bear, and built around that drowsy Bear a cage. And the iron bars of that cage were diplomatically tempered. Then he put a ring in the Bear's nose, and to that ring many links, made of the old scrap iron of tradition, were attached and formed a chain. And the Man

called that chain the *"Drei Kaiser Bund,"* and told the Bear
that it bound them together in inseparable friendship. Thus,
whenever the Bear seemed inclined to object, did the Man
calm his feelings and explain things to him. Many came
and saw the Bear, and the Man told him how the bars
protected him from the ferocious people. He also told the
Bear that he would speak to the people for him and quiet
them and keep them off lest they should fall on him. And
the Man told the people in a very loud voice that it was a
very good Bear and very "candid," but that he must look
well after him lest they should get into trouble, which was,
alas! only too likely. The Bear, who was very, very reasonable, understood that one way. But the people who saw
the Man wink his eye understood it the other way, and
trembled. And when they were not obliging to the Man
and displeased him, he made as if he would let loose the
Bear. Then the people generally became obliging and accommodating. So the Man prospered greatly, for timid
people thought it wise to be generous to him, and the Bear
liked him because of the honey which the inseparable, holy
friendship seemed to bring. And the Bear believed in the
Man.

The Man was very strong, and carried a great big stick,
besides many other weapons, and it happened that on several occasions he struck the Bear over his hind legs with
the stick. The Bear, of course, felt that keenly, both in
his heart and on his legs, all the more because it always
happened just when he felt most inclined to enjoy himself
and stretch his limbs. However, the Man, in a very
friendly way, hastened to explain to him that there was a
horrid Pan-Slav cussedness about those hind legs of his,
and if the stick did not come down on them now and then
at the proper moment, they would rise against the other
members and with their great claws lacerate and wound
even his—the Bear's own head. And the Bear wondered,
understood and was mollified, for he was a very, very reasonable Bear.

But the Bear recovered his strength whilst the Man, who
had become arrogant and overconfident, went to sleep, and

the links of the chain became rusty. There was in the same town a young man who was jealous of the fame of the wise Magician—now an old man. He took the Bear away from the old Magician because he was young and strong, but forgot to put on the Magician's diplomatic boots. As this Man had an Eagle-head, a shining mail-coat and a mailed fist, he was able to hypnotize the Bear at first. However, as soon as the latter perceived that the Man had no boots on, he did not fear the Man any more, for he had never seen an eagle with goose feet. He broke the chain, began to enjoy his freedom, and met the Sailor Chap, who was quite friendly with him. The Man, seeing this, took his big stick, hit the Bear repeatedly, and let his Dalmatian dog loose, who showed his teeth. Then the Bear got furious, and decided to seize and crush them both.

"What a silly story!" "What an idiot of a bear!" I hear you exclaim. Nay, nay, you must not say so. That bear's wisdom was fully equal to the concentrated wisdom of Russian diplomacy, and the story is very true, and a story of many, many days. The above little fable will illustrate why Russia has, after so many provocations, gone to war with Germany. And it is a popular war. Has not every Russian suffered from Germans throughout centuries, and especially during the reign of the High Priest of Militarism, William II., Emperor of Germany? The whole of Russia has been waiting for the Czar to call them to the fight with the enemy of Russia and mankind. All party strife ceased, historical enmities between Poles, Finns and Russians were forgotten when our beloved Lord Emperor repeated the words of Alexander I. directed against Napoleon I. when the latter invaded Russia in 1812.

As in Napoleon's time, Russia has received the news of the declaration of war with calm and dignity, and will conduct the war to its end, however long it may be, and whatever sacrifices will have to be made. It has become a national war, and on such occasions Russia has always been united and victorious in the end, although many times nearly the whole country was overrun by the enemy. The

Russian people, men and women, rose against the enemy, and did not rest until the invader was vanquished.

How is it that Russia, who always helped Prussia in her hour of need, is now at war with Germany? Germany has been found out, and it has become impossible to live and breathe, because the strain of militarism has become unbearable. The arrogance of the Prussians and their allies, the Austrians, had become boundless, and their contempt for all Slavs, and especially Russians, had become offensive. Their constant threats, first to form a coalition against England, and when they found this impossible, to occupy Poland, had become too much even for the long-suffering Russians, and thus came it about that when, a few months ago, the German Press, guided by the German Foreign Office, started its usual periodical campaign of intimidation against Russia, the Russian Minister of War took the unusual step for an official of issuing a manifesto through the Russian Press, which up to the present had never been taken into the confidence of the Russian bureaucracy. In the interview which took place the Minister of War declared that Russia was ready, and that this time the Russians would not wait for Russia to be invaded, but would take the offensive if necessary. The whole of Russia was thankful to its Minister of War for having said openly and fearlessly what every Russian felt. This was a surprise to Germany, who had got accustomed to dictate to Russia, and who did not expect that Russia would refuse to carry out the orders of their War Lord. Russia's long-suffering patience had come to an end, and her manhood began to assert itself, seeing that Germany took for weakness what was Russian politeness, love of peace and want of self-assertion.

Up to the present the Germans have been called "Kulturtraeger" (bearers of culture) in Russia, and everything German was copied. If Russians pointed out that this would not do for Russia, they were told by the Government: "But this is so in the country of the greatest cultured nation in Europe." But our Bureaucracy and Police, shaped according to their brutal Prussian prototype, from which it was simply copied, did not represent our Russian people, who knew the brutality of the Prussians, and had not forgotten how they had suffered under the inhuman yoke of those German adventurers who overran Russia in the eighteenth century to become the rulers of the Russian people, and who pressed them into the army, whose officers they became. Having been trained by the father of Frederick the Great, they introduced the same brutal system into the Russian army, where the soldiers were treated inhumanly. The Russian people have not forgotten this, and therefore they have risen round our Lord Emperor when he called them to the war against our arch enemy, with whom we have never been in open war, but who has during two centuries misrepresented us, vilifying and slandering us at every possible opportunity, ascribing to us, a peace-loving people, those warlike designs which he harbored, being able, through clever diplomacy, to make all Europe believe that Russia was the enemy of mankind and especially of England.

During my boyhood and youth most professors of history in the Russian schools were Germans or Czechs. They taught us to hate England, who was always called "Perfidious Albion," and to look upon Germany as the modern Greece, the representative of freedom, whose greatest enemy was England. I remember very well my teacher of history who, like most of them, was a very able man. He used to speak about the evolution in the history of nations, who after rising to their greatest height had to go down to make room for a new, stronger nation. He said that Germany would remain a military power, having learned from history that only military nations could dominate, and her destiny would be to become the heir of the English Colonies, and she would strive with all her might to achieve this aim. He also taught me to love Germans, and pointed out to me how popular Emperor William I. was in Russia, where he was called "Uncle Vassily," the great friend of Alexander II. and of Russia. He introduced me to the works of Schiller, Goethe and Heine, and of Shakespeare in the German translation, telling me that the German translation was better than the original. He succeeded in making me love German literature, but not love the Germans, because I used to spend my vacations either on the estates of the Baltic German nobles or in the Baltic watering-places so much frequented by Russians from St. Petersburg. There I saw how Russians were treated by the Russian Germans, who looked with contempt on us Russians, calling us barbarians, devoid of all civilization. There I also saw how the local population hated the ruling German class. I saw very soon that my German teacher of history had not told me the whole truth about the Germans, and I revolted against them the more, as he had repeatedly attempted to instill into me hatred against England. I had often seen American and English people in my parents' house, and rather liked them. I could not reconcile hatred with culture and civilization. It was only afterwards that I was taught Russian history, and then I found out why the Germans were not liked by the people in the country: because they had not forgotten how awful the Germans' rule in our country had been.

Peter the Great invited foreigners to come to Russia in order to introduce European reforms in Russia. After his death the throne came under different empresses, and there began an epoch of ruling favorites who secured their own interests first and considered those of the nation of secondary importance. Court intrigues and cabals developed, instigated by the numerous German officers, who denounced the Russian nobles, exiled them to Siberia, which at that time they made a place of banishment, and obtained one-half of the Russian nobles' estates, where they lived as tyrants, treating the Russian serfs as slaves, and introducing the "jus primæ noctis" into Russia, forcing a girl to pay for the right to marry. The frequent palace revolutions which took place at that time required the services of the army, and as Germany produced most officers, Russia became the "happy hunting ground" wherein any impoverished German noble might glean the livelihood denied to him in his own country.

All the important offices of State and army passed into their hands. The "German party," who had developed into a powerful body, succeeded in having the surviving nobles and companions of Peter the Great cast into prison or sent to Siberia, and a general plundering of Russia by its greedy German masters began. Russia's power was crippled, and Turkey took advantage of the favorable situation, made war against Russia, forcing her to sign a treaty which secured all the substantial gains to Turkey, leaving Russia covered with glory but nothing else.

The whole country then rose against the tyrannical rule of the Germans, and Elizabeth, the daughter of Peter the Great, restricted the German rule. But it was only restricted, for the German nobles from the Baltic provinces had become too powerful in St. Petersburg. As the Russian Emperors were always married to German princesses, the rule of the Germans continued until Alexander III. came to the throne, when the German party was banished, as he had chosen as wife a Danish Princess, the sister of Queen Alexandra, who had not forgotten the treatment Denmark received from Prussia in 1864 in the Schleswig-Holstein war.

A general revulsion against Germany took place in Russia, and the portraits of "Uncle Vassily" and Bismarck gradually disappeared from Russian houses. The great master mind of diplomacy, who had been able to represent the French as enemies of Russia, and had brought England and Russia to the verge of war, laid at the Berlin Congress itself the foundation of the downfall of Germany by giving Austria the occupation of Bosnia and Herzegovina. Austria, whom Russia had saved from destruction during the time of Napoleon and the Hungarian Revolution, had left Russia in the lurch during the Crimean and the Turkish wars, and was now rewarded by Germany with two Slavic provinces. Bismarck knew very well that this would lead to eventual trouble between Russia and Austria.

After the Berlin Congress Austria began to "occupy" Bosnia and Herzegovina, and Germany prepared for another war against France. Bismarck's diplomacy was based on friendly relations with Russia, and the Emperor William I. counseled his successors to remain on good terms with

Russia. When Bismarck, the great pilot of the German Empire, was dropped by William II., whose autocratic nature could not stand any interference in foreign politics, the relations between Germany and Russia became strained, the more so as Alexander III. would not hear of another war against France. Bad diplomacy on the part of Germany led to the formation of an Alliance between Russia and France; and Germany, being prevented from attacking and conquering France, started the campaign against Russia wherever she could do her harm.

When Germany saw that Russia declined to enter into an alliance with her against England during the Boer War, she started to bring about a war between the two countries on every possible occasion, in order to weaken both. She began to build her fleet and to increase her army, to prepare for "the day" when she could fall upon us, one after the other. Two years ago she was ready to strike, when the Balkan War upset all her calculations. Turkey was beaten, and the balance of power in the Balkan peninsula destroyed. Austrian diplomacy, usually so successful, had made a miscalculation. They were ready, having annexed Bosnia and Herzegovina, and thus broken the Berlin Treaty, to annex Salonika in order to form a wedge between the Slavic nations of the Balkan Peninsula. Greece, who had also aspirations for the same port, upset all the plans so carefully worked out by German and Austrian diplomacy. The Slavs had gained a victory. Russia, who had not yet sufficiently recovered from the Japanese War, was therefore constantly checked by Germany whenever Austria made a move in the Balkans.

The traditional protector of the Christian Balkan Powers could not prevent Serbia from being systematically maltreated by Austria and excluded from the Adriatic, notwithstanding a successful war with Turkey. To create further trouble, and to allow Austria room for future intrigues, a kingdom of Albania was created which had never existed before. When Russia protested, the German Emperor again put on his shining armor and shook his mailed fist. Russia had again to give way, but resolved now to be prepared against a further German onslaught. She had not to wait long, as Austria took the first opportunity to use pressure on Serbia, this time quite openly and cynically demanding in her Note such terms as an independent State could never accept.

Still Russia counseled Serbia to accept the impossible demands and to submit two of them to arbitration. Then it became apparent that the Concert of Europe had only been created by Bismarck in order to put Russia under European tutelage; but if questions arose as regards Austria and Germany, the European Powers were not to be consulted. Russia, a great European Power, was treated by Germany as if she were the War Lord's vassal, and asked to stop her mobilization, although it was not directed against Germany. And thus Germany declared war against Russia, throwing off her mask and making Russia responsible for a war which Russia was not seeking. She has never yet had a war with either Austria or Germany, both of whom she has repeatedly saved from destruction. With a light heart William II. has started the great European war, never dreaming that it meant a war of the whole of Europe and Japan against Germany.

Posing as the bearers of European culture, the Germans are defying laws and treaties. Militarism they have preached since their existence, forcing all nations to impoverish themselves and make Germany rich. Through militarism they may perish. Like brigands they have fallen upon a small, brave nation, which had no quarrel with them. Like brigands they are burning and plundering the villages and towns through which their armies march. What a price will have to be paid for the peace to which our Emperor Nicholas II. invited all nations to The Hague!

Let us hope the outcome of this war will be that universal peace towards which all civilized nations have been striving, and that all nations will unite in the future to better the life of the people by works of peace, banishing forever those weapons of destruction which the inventors of all nations have lately done their utmost to produce in order to exterminate each other.

FRANCE ACCEPTS THE STRUGGLE TO THE DEATH

THE CLIMAX OF FORTY YEARS OF FEAR

AUGUST 3, 1914

RAYMOND POINCARÉ   RENÉ VIVIANI

BARON SCHOEN

Of all the countries involved in Germany's schemes of world-conquest, France was the only one which seems from the outset to have grasped the full meaning of the contest, the summoning of Democracy to a death-struggle. For years the shrewd French diplomats had, as the earlier sections of this volume have shown, been watching Germany with such anxiety and such accuracy that they foresaw her full purpose, and prepared against it that splendid army which saved the world.

Ever since 1871, France had been anticipating a renewal of the German attack. She was not now to be deceived by any platitudes about Serbia. She knew that any German mobilization would be primarily directed against her, the one foe truly ready against the German attack. Once the alert French army was destroyed, Germany could sweep with ease over each new unready opponent. Hence as Germany took each step toward mobilization, France promptly did the same. The French leaders, however, were fully resolved that all the world should see who were the real aggressors. All the French forces were held back more than six miles (ten kilometers) from the frontier, leaving an unprotected strip of French land along all the border. With both armies on the actual frontier, local clashes would have been inevitable, and each side would have accused the other. France wisely and temperately abandoned this six-mile strip so that no clash could come except by an obvious German crossing of the border. The favorite German trick of crying "He struck first" was thus made very difficult; and the actual declaration of war against France was delayed two days beyond that against Russia.

The publication of some of the German state papers since the War shows how perplexing the German leaders found it to manufacture any diplomatic reason for that prompt hurling of their armies against France which was part of their scheme of battle. When on July 31st they sent their ultimatum to Russia, they sent to France at the same time a formal demand to know what action France would take if this ultimatum led to war with Russia. The German ambassador at Paris, Baron Schoen, was instructed to present this demand to the French government and, if the answer was that France would support Russia, then the ambassador was prepared with a second document, which was to be presented and which declared immediate war against France. If on the other hand the answer was that France

368

would remain neutral, then the ambassador held ready a third document to be used in its turn. This third document made the extraordinary demand upon France that as pledge of her neutrality she should immediately surrender to the Germans the control of her chief frontier fortresses, Toul and Verdun.

Submission to this ultimatum would have been as suicidal for France as submission to the ultimatum of July 31st would have been to Russia. It would have meant that the French army surrendered without the formality of a battle, and handed the land over to Germany's military control. Yet rejection of the ultimatum would mean, as it did in Russia's case, immediate war, with the German leaders crying to their people, "We had to strike because France rejected our honorable and well-intended ultimatum." The French government, however, escaped this snare by responding to Ambassador Schoen's first document in a third fashion, different from either alternative for which the Germans were prepared. Instead of saying either that France would or would not remain neutral, the government responded that France "would do what her interests required." In other words, she would make no decision in advance of the facts; perhaps the ultimatum to Russia might have other results than Germany expected. This mild answer left the German ambassador unable to present either of his prepared documents, and he began telegraphing to Berlin for further instructions. How could they declare a "defensive" war against a people who insisted on doing nothing!

It must be noted that this was the essential point of the whole German movement. The leaders must absolutely convince their people that the war was "defensive," that Germany was attacked, and not attacking. Hence, after hurried communication with Ambassador Schoen, the Germans fell back upon their previous plan. The French soldiers simply *must* be invading Germany. The French precaution of keeping the soldiers so far behind the frontier was evaded by asserting that the invasion had been made by aviators, and especially that a French aviator had dropped bombs on the city of Nuremberg. This the Nuremberg mayor afterward explicitly denied. Yet on this empty pretext Germany declared war, on August 3d.

France immediately accepted the challenge. Her president, Raymond Poincaré, spoke for her the ringing words which are here reprinted. The prime-minister Viviani then went into details, and explained to the French parliament just how the situation had come about. His full, clear and mathematically exact official statement of the position of France is also given. It incorporates the German "Declaration of War" by Baron Schoen, and also the British promise of protection.   C. F. H.

PRESIDENT POINCARÉ'S ADDRESS TO THE FRENCH PARLIA-
MENT

August 4, 1914

Gentlemen,

FRANCE has just been the object of a violent and pre-
meditated attack, which is an insolent defiance of the
law of nations. Before any declaration of war had been
sent to us, even before the German Ambassador had asked
for his passports, our territory has been violated. The
German Empire has waited till yesterday evening to give at
this late stage the true name to a state of things which it had
already created.

For more than forty years the French, in sincere love of
peace, have buried at the bottom of their heart the desire
for legitimate reparation.

They have given to the world the example of a great nation which, definitely raised from defeat by the exercise of
will, patience and labor, has only used its renewed and rejuvenated strength in the interest of progress and for the
good of humanity.

Since the ultimatum of Austria opened a crisis which
threatened the whole of Europe, France has persisted in following and in recommending on all sides a policy of prudence, wisdom and moderation.

To her there can be imputed no act, no movement, no
word, which has not been peaceful and conciliatory.

At the hour when the struggle is beginning, she has the
right, in justice to herself, of solemnly declaring that she has
made, up to the last moment, supreme efforts to avert the
war now about to break out, the crushing responsibility for
which the German Empire will have to bear before history.

On the very morrow of the day when we and our allies
were publicly expressing our hope of seeing negotiations
which had been begun under the auspices of the London
Cabinet carried to a peaceful conclusion, Germany suddenly
declared war upon Russia, she has invaded the territory of
Luxemburg, she has outrageously insulted the noble Belgian nation, our neighbor and our friend, and attempted

treacherously to fall upon us while we were in the midst of diplomatic conversation.

But France was watching. As alert as she was peaceful, she was prepared; and our enemies will meet on their path our valiant covering troops, who are at their post and will provide the screen behind which the mobilization of our national forces will be methodically completed.

Our fine and courageous army, which France to-day accompanies with her maternal thought, has risen eager to defend the honor of the flag and the soil of the country.

The President of the Republic, interpreting the unanimous feeling of the country, expresses to our troops by land and sea the admiration and confidence of every Frenchman.

Closely united in a common feeling, the nation will persevere with the cool self-restraint of which, since the beginning of the crisis, she has given daily proof. Now, as always, she will know how to harmonize the most noble daring and most ardent enthusiasm with that self-control which is the sign of enduring energy and is the best guarantee of victory.

In the war which is beginning France will have Right on her side, the eternal power of which cannot with impunity be disregarded by nations any more than by individuals.

She will be heroically defended by all her sons; nothing will break their sacred union before the enemy; to-day they are joined together as brothers in a common indignation against the aggressor, and in a common patriotic faith.

She is faithfully helped by Russia, her ally; she is supported by the loyal friendship of England.

And already from every part of the civilized world sympathy and good wishes are coming to her. For to-day once again she stands before the universe for Liberty, Justice and Reason. *"Haut les cœurs et vive la France!"*

OFFICIAL STATEMENT OF PRIME-MINISTER VIVIANI
August 4, 1914

The German Ambassador yesterday left Paris after notifying us of the existence of a state of war.

The Government owe to Parliament a true account of

the events which, in less than ten days, have unloosed a
European war and compelled France, peaceful and valiant,
to defend her frontier against an attack, the hateful injustice
of which is emphasized by its calculated unexpectedness.

This attack, which has no excuse, and which began before we were notified of any declaration of war, is the last
act of a plan, whose origin and object I propose to declare
before our own Democracy and before the opinion of the
civilized world.

As a consequence of the abominable crime which cost
the Austro-Hungarian Heir-Apparent and the Duchess of
Hohenburg their lives, difficulties arose between the Cabinets
of Vienna and Belgrade.

The majority of the Powers were only semi-officially informed of these difficulties up till Friday, July 24th, the
date on which the Austro-Hungarian Ambassadors communicated to them a circular which the press has published.

The object of this circular was to explain and justify
an ultimatum delivered the evening before to Serbia by
the Austro-Hungarian Minister at Belgrade.

This ultimatum, in alleging the complicity of numerous
Serbian subjects and associations in the Serajevo crime,
hinted that the official Serbian authorities themselves were
no strangers to it. It demanded a reply from Serbia by
6 o'clock on the evening of Saturday, July 25th.

The Austrian demands, or at any rate many of them,
without doubt struck a blow at the rights of a sovereign
State. Notwithstanding their excessive character, Serbia,
on July 25th, declared that she submitted to them almost
without reserve.

This submission, which constituted a success for Austria-Hungary, a guarantee for the peace of Europe, was not
unconnected with the advice tendered to Belgrade from the
first moment by France, Russia and Great Britain.

The value of this advice was all the greater since the
Austro-Hungarian demands had been concealed from the
Chanceries of the Triple Entente, to whom in the three pre-
ceding weeks the Austro-Hungarian Government had on sev-

eral occasions given an assurance that their claims would be extremely moderate.

It was, therefore, with natural astonishment that the Cabinets of Paris, St. Petersburg and London learned on July 26th that the Austrian Minister at Belgrade, after a few minutes' examination, declared that the Serbian reply was inacceptable, and broke off diplomatic relations.

This astonishment was increased by the fact that on Friday, the 24th, the German Ambassador came and read to the French Minister for Foreign Affairs a *note verbale* asserting that the Austro-Serbian dispute must remain localized, without intervention by the great Powers, or otherwise "incalculable consequences" were to be feared. A similar *démarche* was made on Saturday, the 25th, at London and at St. Petersburg.

Need I, gentlemen, point out to you the contrast between the threatening expressions used by the German Ambassador at Paris and the conciliatory sentiments which the Powers of the Triple Entente had just manifested by the advice which they gave to Serbia to submit?

Nevertheless, in spite of the extraordinary character of the German *démarche*, we immediately, in agreement with our Allies and our friends, took a conciliatory course and invited Germany to join in it.

We have had from the first moment regretfully to recognize that our intentions and our efforts met with no response at Berlin.

Not only did Germany appear wholly unwilling to give to Austria-Hungary the friendly advice which her position gave her the right to offer, but from this moment and still more in the following days, she seemed to intervene between the Cabinet at Vienna and the compromises suggested by the other Powers.

On Tuesday, July 28th, Austria-Hungary declared war on Serbia. This declaration of war, with its aggravation of the state of affairs brought about by the rupture of diplomatic relations three days before, gave ground for believing that there was a deliberate desire for war, and a systematic program for the enslavement of Serbia.

Thus there was now involved in the dispute not only the independence of a brave people, but the balance of power in the Balkan, embodied in the Treaty of Bucharest of 1913, and consecrated by the moral support of all the great Powers.

However, at the suggestion of the British Government with its constant and firm attachment to the maintenance of the peace of Europe, the negotiations were continued, or, to speak more accurately, the Powers of the Triple Entente tried to continue them.

From this common desire sprang the proposal for action by the four Powers, England, France, Germany and Italy, which was intended, by assuring to Austria all legitimate satisfaction, to bring about an equitable adjustment of the dispute.

On Wednesday, the 29th, the Russian Government, noting the persistent failure of these efforts and faced by the Austrian mobilization and declaration of war, fearing the military destruction of Serbia, decided as a precautionary measure to mobilize the troops of four military districts, that is to say, the formations echeloned along the Austro-Hungarian frontier exclusively.

In taking this step, the Russian Government were careful to inform the German Government that their measures, restricted as they were and without any offensive character towards Austria, were not in any degree directed against Germany.

In a conversation with the Russian Ambassador at Berlin, the German Secretary of State for Foreign Affairs acknowledged this without demur.

On the other hand, all the efforts made by Great Britain with the adherence of Russia and the support of France, to bring Austria and Serbia into touch under the moral patronage of Europe, were encountered at Berlin with a predetermined negative of which the diplomatic dispatches afford the clearest proof.

This was a disquieting situation which made it probable that there existed at Berlin intentions which had not been disclosed. Some hours afterwards this alarming suspicion was destined to become a certainty.

In fact, Germany's negative attitude gave place thirty-six hours later to positive steps which were truly alarming. On July 31st, Germany, by proclaiming "a state of danger of war, cut the communications between herself and the rest of Europe, and obtained for herself complete freedom to pursue against France in absolute secrecy military preparations which, as you have seen, nothing could justify.

Already for some days, and in circumstances difficult to explain, Germany had prepared for the transition of her army from a peace footing to a war footing.

From the morning of July 25th, that is to say, even before the expiration of the time limit given to Serbia by Austria, she had confined to barracks the garrisons of Alsace-Lorraine. The same day she had placed the frontier-works in a complete state of defense. On the 26th, she had indicated to the railways the measures preparatory for concentration. On the 27th, she had completed requisitions and placed her covering troops in position. On the 28th, the summons of individual reservists had begun and units which were distant from the frontier had been brought up to it.

Could all these measures, pursued with implacable method, leave us in doubt of Germany's intentions?

Such was the situation when, on the evening of July 31st, the German Government, which since the 24th had not participated by any active step in the conciliatory efforts of the Triple Entente, addressed an ultimatum to the Russian Government under the pretext that Russia had ordered a general mobilization of her armies, and demanded that this mobilization should be stopped within twelve hours.

This demand, which was all the more insulting in form because a few hours earlier the Emperor Nicholas II., with a movement at once confiding and spontaneous, had asked the German Emperor for his mediation, was put forward at a moment when, on the request of England and with the knowledge of Germany, the Russian Government was accepting a formula of such a nature as to lay the foundation for a friendly settlement of the Austro-Serbian dispute and of the Austro-Russian difficulties by the simultaneous arrest of military operations and of military preparations.

The same day this unfriendly *démarche* towards Russia was supplemented by acts which were frankly hostile towards France; the rupture of communications by road, railway, telegraph and telephone, the seizure of French locomotives on their arrival at the frontier, the placing of machine guns in the middle of the permanent way which had been cut, and the concentration of troops on this frontier.

From this moment we were no longer justified in believing in the sincerity of the pacific declaration which the German representative continued to shower upon us.

We knew that Germany was mobilizing under the shelter of the "state of danger of war."

We learnt that six classes of reservists had been called up, and that transport was being collected even for those army corps which were stationed a considerable distance from the frontier.

As these events unfolded themselves, our government, watchful and vigilant, took from day to day, and even from hour to hour, the measures of precaution which the situation required; the general mobilization of our forces on land and sea was ordered.

The same evening, at 7.30, Germany, without waiting for the acceptance by the Cabinet of St. Petersburg of the English proposal, which I have already mentioned, declared war on Russia.

The next day, Sunday, August 2nd, without regard for the extreme moderation of France, in contradiction to the peaceful declarations of the German Ambassador at Paris, and in defiance of the rules of international law, German troops crossed our frontier at three different points.

At the same time, in violation of the Treaty of 1867, which guaranteed with the signature of Prussia the neutrality of Luxemburg, they invaded the territory of the Grand Duchy and so gave cause for a protest by the Luxemburg Government.

Finally, the neutrality of Belgium also was threatened. The German Minister, on the evening of August 2nd, presented to the Belgian Government an ultimatum requesting facilities in Belgium for military operations against France, under the lying pretext that Belgian neutrality was threatened by us; the Belgian Government refused, and declared that they were resolved to defend with vigor their neutrality, which was respected by France and guaranteed by treaties, and in particular by the King of Prussia.

Since then, gentlemen, the German attacks have been renewed, multiplied, and accentuated. At more than fifteen points our frontier has been violated. Shots have been fired at our soldiers and Customs officers. Men have been killed and wounded. Yesterday a German military aviator dropped three bombs on Lunéville.

The German Ambassador, to whom as well as to all the great Powers, we communicated these facts, did not deny them or express his regrets for them. On the contrary, he came yesterday evening to ask me for his passports, and to notify us of the existence of a state of war, giving as his reason, in the teeth of all the facts, hostile acts committed by French aviators in German territory in the Eifel district, and even on the railway near Carlsruhe and near Nuremberg. This is the letter which he handed to me on the subject:—

LETTER OF BARON SCHOEN DECLARING WAR

"M. Le President,

"The German administrative and military authorities have established a certain number of flagrantly hostile acts committed on German territory by French military aviators. Several of these have openly violated the neutrality of Belgium by flying over the territory of that country; one has attempted to destroy buildings near Wesel; others have been seen in the district of the Eifel; one has thrown bombs on the railway near Carlsruhe and Nuremberg.

"I am instructed, and I have the honor to inform your Excellency, that in the presence of these acts of aggression the German Empire considers itself in a state of war with France in consequence of the acts of this latter Power.

"At the same time, I have the honor to bring to the knowledge of your Excellency that the German authorities will retain French mercantile vessels in German ports, but they will release them if, within forty-eight hours, they are assured of complete reciprocity.

"My diplomatic mission having thus come to an end, it only remains for me to request your Excellency to be good enough to furnish me with my passports, and to take the steps you consider suitable to assure my return to Germany, with the staff of the Embassy, as well as with the Staff of the Bavarian Legation and of the German Consulate General in Paris.

"Be good enough, M. le Président, to receive the assurances of my deepest respect.

"(Signed) SCHOEN."

Need I, gentlemen, lay stress on the absurdities of these pretexts which they put forward as grievances? At no time has any French aviator penetrated into Belgium, nor has any French aviator committed either in Bavaria or any other part of Germany any hostile act. The opinion of Europe has already done justice to these wretched inventions.

Against these attacks, which violate all the laws of justice and all the principles of public law, we have now taken all the necessary steps; they are being carried out strictly, regularly, and with calmness.

The mobilization of the Russian army also continues with remarkable vigor and unrestrained enthusiasm. The Belgian army, mobilized with 250,000 men, prepares with a splendid passion and magnificent ardor to defend the neutrality and independence of their country.

The entire English fleet is mobilized and orders have been given to mobilize the land forces.

Since 1912 *pourparlers* had taken place between English and French General Staffs and were concluded by an exchange of letters between Sir Edward Grey and M. Paul Cambon. The Secretary of State for Foreign Affairs yesterday evening communicated these letters to the House of

Commons, and spoke of France amidst the applause of the members in a noble and warm-hearted manner. His language has already found an echo deep in the hearts of all Frenchmen. I wish in the name of the Government of the Republic to thank the English Government from this tribune for their cordial words and the Parliament of France will associate itself in this sentiment.

The Secretary of State for Foreign Affairs made in particular the following declaration: "In case the German fleet came into the Channel or entered the North Sea in order to go round the British Isles with the object of attacking the French coasts or the French navy and of harassing French merchant shipping, the English fleet would intervene in order to give to French shipping its complete protection in such a way that from that moment England and Germany would be in a state of war."

From now onwards, the English fleet protects our northern and western coasts against a German attack. Gentlemen, these are the facts. I believe that the simple recital of them is sufficient to justify the acts of the Government of the Republic. I wish, however, to make clear the conclusion to be drawn from my story and to give its true meaning to the unheard-of attack of which France is the victim.

The victors of 1870 have, at different times, as you know, desired to repeat the blows which they dealt us then. In 1875, the war which was intended to complete the destruction of conquered France was only prevented by the intervention of the two Powers to whom we were to become united at a later date by ties of alliance and of friendship, by the intervention of Russia and of Great Britain.

Since then the French Republic, by the restoration of her national forces and the conclusion of diplomatic agreements unswervingly adhered to, has succeeded in liberating herself from the yoke which even in a period of profound peace Bismarck was able to impose upon Europe.

She has reëstablished the balance of power in Europe, a guarantee of the liberty and dignity of all.

Gentlemen, I do not know if I am mistaken, but it seems to me that this work of peaceful reparation, of liberation and honor finally ratified in 1904 and 1907, with the genial coöperation of King Edward VII. of England and the Government of the Crown, this is what the German Empire wishes to destroy to-day by one daring stroke.

Germany can reproach us with nothing.

Bearing in silence in our bosom for half a century the wound which Germany dealt us, we have offered to peace an unprecedented sacrifice.

We have offered other sacrifices in all the discussions which since 1904 German diplomacy has systematically provoked, whether in Morocco or elsewhere in 1905, in 1906, in 1908, in 1911.

Russia also has given proof of great moderation at the time of the events of 1908, as she has done in the present crisis.

She observed the same moderation, and the Triple Entente with her, when in the Eastern crisis of 1912 Austria and Germany formulated demands, whether against Serbia or against Greece, which still were, as the event proved, capable of settlement by discussion.

Useless sacrifices, barren negotiations, empty efforts, since to-day in the very act of conciliation we, our allies and ourselves, are attacked by surprise.

No one can honestly believe that we are the aggressors. Vain is the desire to overthrow the sacred principles of right and of liberty to which nations, as well as individuals, are subject; Italy with that clarity of insight possessed by the Latin intellect, has notified us that she proposes to preserve neutrality.

This decision has found in all France an echo of sincerest joy. I made myself the interpreter of this feeling to the Italian *Chargé d'Affaires* when I told him how much I congratulated myself that the two Latin sisters, who have the same origin and the same ideal, a common and glorious past, are not now opposed to one another.

Gentlemen, we proclaim loudly the object of their attack—it is the independence, the honor, the safety, which the Triple Entente has regained in the balance of power for the service of peace. The object of attack is the liberties of

Europe, which France, her allies, and her friends, are proud to defend.

We are going to defend these liberties, for it is they that are in dispute, and all the rest is but a pretext.

France, unjustly provoked, did not desire war, she has done everything to avert it. Since it is forced upon her, she will defend herself against Germany and against every Power which has not yet declared its intentions, but joins with the latter in a conflict between the two countries.

A free and valiant people that sustains an eternal ideal, and is wholly united to defend its existence; a Democracy which knows how to discipline its military strength, and was not afraid a year ago to increase its burden as an answer to the armaments of its neighbor; a nation armed, struggling for its own life and for the independence of Europe—here is a sight which we are proud to offer to the onlookers in this desperate struggle, that has for some days been preparing with the greatest calmness and method. We are without reproach. We shall be without fear. France has often proved in less favorable circumstances that she is a most formidable adversary when she fights, as she does to-day, for liberty and for right.

In submitting our actions to you, gentlemen, who are our judges, we have, to help us in bearing the burden of our heavy responsibility, the comfort of a clear conscience and the conviction that we have done our duty.

BELGIUM RESISTS FOR HONOR

GERMAN MATERIALISM MEETS THE IMPONDERABLE FORCES OF THE SPIRIT

AUGUST 3, 1914

GERMANY'S ULTIMATUM   BELGIUM'S REPLY
COMMANDANT DE GERLACHE DE GOMERY
BARON BEYENS   KING ALBERT OF BELGIUM

When we approach the last moments of diplomatic maneuver which preceded the actual fighting of the Great War, it becomes obvious that Germany was wholly dominated by the military demand for speed. So long as she could mature her world-plot in secret, she could move with slow security. But once France was awake, once the world was awake, to the certainty that this dreaded Colossus of militarism was about to strike, then Germany's success must to a considerable extent be dependent on her ability to drive home her attack before the world's defense could be coördinated and matured. This accounts for her swift dropping of the mask as Austria's protector, and her rush with all her strength upon France, the one alert opponent.

But wary France had built along her German border such an array of forts as made even Germany doubtful of overcoming them. Had her war been really for Austria's sake, she would of course have stood on the defensive in the West behind her own row of impregnable fortifications, and would have marched to a sure victory over unwieldy Russia in the East. That game was easily in her hands. But as we now know, she was resolved from the beginning to seize Belgium for permanent annexation, to seize the neighboring districts of northern France with their immeasurably valuable mines, and to crush France so completely that the land of Napoleon would never again be more than a mere German dependency, such as Austria.

Hence came the sudden ultimatum to Belgium, the tragic, world-famed document which is here reproduced. It bases invasion on the same sort of trivial pretenses, utterly inadequate excuses, and uninvestigated charges, as were made the pretext for attacking France. No one to-day believes that French troops were preparing to invade Belgium, as the ultimatum states; all the evidence is to the contrary. No one believes, as you may here read that the German authorities afterward stated, that a French cavalry patrol had overstepped the frontier; and no one cares. Germany herself abandoned these subterfuges almost at once. Such excuses for such a harrying of a peaceful people are as criminal as they are contemptible. The road through Belgium offered the swiftest, surest attack on France; and so the Imperial Military Staff had always meant to use it. Belgian officials may have

382

imagined that by submission to Germany's invasion they could ultimately regain their freedom—we give here the interesting report of the Belgian Minister in Berlin, Baron Beyens, which suggests this alternative—but we now know that King Albert of Belgium was right in his belief, that the German wolf never intended to disgorge the rich and helpless region it was snatching with bared teeth.

To Belgium therefore came the agony of decision, and the opportunity of heroism. Should she yield in servitude, or fight a hopeless fight for freedom and for honor? To the eternal glory of her people, to the glory of the whole human race, she chose her martyrdom.

Thereby Belgium took a mighty part in the saving of the world. Read her dignified, heroic reply to the German ultimatum. Read also the account by one of her staunchest officials, Commandant De Gerlache, of the grave and earnest way in which her people and her king faced the terrible occasion. Read King Albert's speech, which De Gerlache reports; and realize the high spirit in which these despairing Belgians made their solemn choice of a resistance which they knew must mean suffering unspeakable and unimaginable. The voice of the nation echoes in the words of its minister of war, "EVEN IF WE ARE DEFEATED, WE SHALL NEVER BE CONQUERED." The eternal verities of the spirit are founded upon such strength as this.

All honor to the Belgians!   C. F. H.

THE GERMAN ULTIMATUM

Delivered by the German Minister in Belgium, Von Below Saleske

Brussels, August 2, 1914.

(Very Confidential.)

RELIABLE information has been received by the German Government to the effect that French forces intend to march on the line of the Meuse by Givet and Namur. This information leaves no doubt as to the intention of France to march through Belgian territory against Germany.

The German Government cannot but fear that Belgium, in spite of the utmost goodwill, will be unable, without assistance, to repel so considerable a French invasion with sufficient prospect of success to afford an adequate guarantee against danger to Germany. It is essential for the self-defense of Germany that she should anticipate any such hostile attack. The German Government would, however, feel the deepest regret if Belgium regarded as an act of hostility against herself the fact that the measures of Germany's opponents force Germany, for her own protection, to enter Belgian territory.

In order to exclude any possibility of misunderstanding, the German Government make the following declaration:—

1. Germany has in view no act of hostility against Belgium. In the event of Belgium being prepared in the coming war to maintain an attitude of friendly neutrality towards Germany, the German Government bind themselves, at the conclusion of peace, to guarantee the possessions and independence of the Belgian Kingdom in full.

2. Germany undertakes, under the above-mentioned condition, to evacuate Belgian territory on the conclusion of peace.

3. If Belgium adopts a friendly attitude, Germany is prepared, in coöperation with the Belgian authorities, to purchase all necessaries for her troops against a cash payment, and to pay an indemnity for any damage that may have been caused by German troops.

4. Should Belgium oppose the German troops, and in particular should she throw difficulties in the way of their march by a resistance of the fortresses on the Meuse, or by destroying railways, roads, tunnels, or other similar works, Germany will, to her regret, be compelled to consider Belgium as an enemy.

In this event, Germany can undertake no obligations towards Belgium, but the eventual adjustment of the relations between the two States must be left to the decision of arms.

The German Government, however, entertain the distinct hope that this eventuality will not occur, and that the Belgian Government will know how to take the necessary measures to prevent the occurrence of incidents such as those mentioned. In this case the friendly ties which bind the two neighboring States will grow stronger and more enduring.

THE BELGIAN REPLY

Delivered by Monsieur Davignon, Belgian Minister for Foreign Affairs

Brussels, August 3, 1914 (7 A. M.).

The German Government stated in their note of the end of August, 1914, that according to reliable information

French forces intended to march on the Meuse viâ Givet and Namur, and that Belgium, in spite of the best intentions, would not be in a position to repulse, without assistance, an advance of French troops.

The German Government, therefore, considered themselves compelled to anticipate this attack and to violate Belgian territory. In these circumstances, Germany proposed to the Belgian Government to adopt a friendly attitude towards her, and undertook, on the conclusion of peace, to guarantee the integrity of the Kingdom and its possessions to their full extent. The note added that if Belgium put difficulties in the way of the advance of German troops, Germany would be compelled to consider her as an enemy, and to leave the ultimate adjustment of the relations between the two States to the decision of arms.

This note has made a deep and painful impression upon the Belgian Government.

The intentions attributed to France by Germany are in contradiction to the formal declarations made to us on August 1st, in the name of the French Government.

Moreover, if, contrary to our expectation, Belgian neutrality should be violated by France, Belgium intends to fulfill her international obligations and the Belgian army would offer the most vigorous resistance to the invader.

The treaties of 1839, confirmed by the treaties of 1870, vouch for the independence and neutrality of Belgium under the guarantee of the Powers, and notably of the Government of His Majesty the King of Prussia.

Belgium has always been faithful to her international obligations, she has carried out her duties in a spirit of loyal impartiality, and she has left nothing undone to maintain and enforce respect for her neutrality.

The attack upon her independence with which the German Government threaten her constitutes a flagrant violation of international law. No strategic interest justifies such a violation of law.

The Belgian Government, if they were to accept the proposals submitted to them, would sacrifice the honor of the nation and betray their duty towards Europe.

Conscious of the part which Belgium has played for more than eighty years in the civilization of the world, they refuse to believe that the independence of Belgium can only be preserved at the price of the violation of her neutrality.

If this hope is disappointed the Belgian Government are firmly resolved to repel, by all the means in their power, every attack upon their rights.

BY BARON BEYENS
Official Report of the Belgian Minister at Berlin as to how the German Government received the Belgian Defiance

Your telegram was brought to me on the 3rd of August towards 8 p. m. By the time I had deciphered it, it was too late for me to go to Wilhelmstrasse. I resolved to postpone until the following morning the verbal explanations which it was my duty to demand from Herr von Jagow on the subject of the German Government's unjustifiable action. Early the next day I telephoned to him asking him to receive me as soon as possible. He replied, asking me to go immediately. At 9 o'clock I was shown into his room. The Ministry was still empty.

"Well, what have you to say to me?" These were his first words as he hurried to meet me.

"I have to ask you for explanations in regard to the ultimatum which the German Minister handed on Sunday evening to my Government. I suppose you have some reason to give in explanation of such action."

"An absolute necessity forced us to present that demand to you. It is with mortal grief that the Emperor and his Government have had to resign themselves to doing so. To myself it is the most painful resolution and the most cruel thing I have had to do throughout my career. But the passage through Belgium is for Germany a question of life and death. She must be finished with France as quickly as possible, crush her completely so as then to be able to turn against Russia, otherwise she herself will be caught between the hammer and the anvil. We have learnt that the French army was preparing to pass through Belgium and to attack us on our flank. We must forestall her."

"But," I answered, "you are in direct contact with France on a frontier of 200 kilometers; why in order to settle your quarrel did you need to turn aside and pass through our country."

"The French frontier is too strongly fortified, and we are obliged," he repeated, "to act very quickly before Russia has had time to mobilize her army."

"Contrary to what you think, France has given us a formal promise to respect our neutrality, provided that you respect it too. What would you have said if, instead of making us this promise of her own accord, she had presented to us the same summons before you, if she had demanded a passage through our country, and if we had yielded to her threats? That we were cowards, incapable of defending our neutrality and unworthy of an independent existence?"

Herr von Jagow did not reply to this question.

"Have you," I continued, "anything with which to reproach us? Have we not always correctly and scrupulously fulfilled the duties which the neutrality of Belgium imposed upon us with regard to Germany as well as the other guarantee Powers? Since the foundation of our kingdom have we not been loyal and trustworthy neighbors to you?"

"Germany has nothing with which to reproach Belgium, whose attitude has always been correct."

"And so, in recognition of our loyalty, you wish to make of our country the battlefield for your struggle with France, the battlefield of Europe; and we know what devastation modern warfare brings with it! Have you thought of that?"

"If the Belgian army," the Secretary of State replied, "allows us to pass freely, without destroying the railways, without blowing up the bridges and tunnels, and if it retires on Antwerp without attempting to defend Liége, we promise not only to respect the independence of Belgium, the lives and property of the inhabitants, but also to indemnify you for the loss incurred."

"Sir," I replied, "the Belgian Government, conscious of its duties towards all the guarantors of its neutrality, can make no reply to such a proposal other than the reply which it has made without hesitation. The whole nation will support its King and its Government. You must recognize yourself that no other reply was possible."

As I urged him to speak, Herr von Jagow, in the face of my persistence, ended by saying: "I recognize it. I understand your reply. I understand it as private individual, but as Secretary of State I have no opinion to express." And then he repeated the expression of his grief at having come to such a point after so many years of friendly relationship. But a rapid march through Belgium was for Germany a question of life or death. We in our turn should understand that.

I answered immediately: "Belgium would have lost her honor if she had listened to you, and no nation, any more than an individual, can live without honor. Europe will be our judge. And besides," I added, "you will not take Liége as easily as you think, and you will have to meet England, the faithful guarantor of our neutrality."

At these words Herr Jagow shrugged his shoulders, an action which could be interpreted in two ways. It signified: "What an idea! It is impossible!" Or, perhaps: "The lot is cast, we cannot go back."

I added, before retiring, that I was ready to leave Berlin with my staff and to ask for my passports. "But I cannot break my relations with you in this way," cried the Secretary of State; "perhaps there will still be something for us to talk over." "It is for my Government to take a decision about that," I replied; "it does not depend upon you or me. I will wait for their orders to ask for my passports."

As I left Herr von Jagow after this painful interview, which was to be our last, I carried away the impression that he had expected something else when I had asked to see him, some unforeseen proposal, perhaps the request to allow the Belgian army to retire in security to Antwerp after having made a show of resistance on the Meuse and having, on the invasion of the country, formally defended the principle of her neutrality. After my first words, the face of the speaker seemed to me to betray a feeling of disappointment, and his persistence in telling me not to break our relations yet strengthened this idea which I had had from the start of our conversation.

BY DE GERLACHE DE GOMERY

When, towards the end of July, 1914, gloomy clouds, which grew more and more threatening, began to pile themselves up on the political horizon of Europe, Belgium became alarmed, and her uneasiness increased from hour to hour.

Germany, however, down to the very eve of hostilities, endeavored to conceal her intentions.

On the 1st of August, war being imminent, M. Klobukowski, the French Minister in Brussels, officially declared to M. Davignon, our Minister of Foreign Affairs, that France would respect the neutrality of Belgium.

Informed of this declaration by M. Davignon, Herr von Below-Saleske, the German Minister to Belgium, replied that he had not been instructed to make a similar declaration to the Belgian Government, but that the latter was aware of "his personal opinion as to the security with which Belgium was justified in regarding her Eastern neighbors."

Moreover, on the preceding day Baron van der Elst, the Secretary-General to the Ministry of Foreign Affairs, had had a long conversation with Herr von Below, and had reminded him of the remarks made by Herr Bethmann-Hollweg in 1911, and the public declarations made by Herr von Jagow in 1913. Von Below not only admitted the accuracy of these statements, but added that he was "certain that the sentiments then expressed had not been modified."

Again, on the 1st of August the Military Attaché to the German Legation spontaneously congratulated the departmental head of the Ministry of War upon the rapid and remarkable progress of our mobilization. For we had, as a special precaution, just mobilized our army, as Holland had done, for that matter.

On the 2nd of August, the newspaper *Soir* gave a report, in a prominent position, of an interview which a member of its staff had had that morning with the German Minister himself. The latter had given the Belgian journalist the most definite assurance as to the eventual attitude of Germany toward Belgium, and he concluded with the words: "We have never dreamed of violating your neutrality. You may perhaps see your neighbor's house on fire, but your own home will be untouched."

These reassuring declarations assuaged the prevailing anxiety.

Now at 7.00 p. m. Herr von Below handed to M. Davignon, in the name of the Imperial German Government, an insulting ultimatum, and he demanded a reply within twelve hours—within the space of a night!

What a night it was H. Hymans, the Minister of State, has told us. What a night—what a tragic night! How could it ever be forgotten?

"The Ministers with portfolios and the Ministers of State met in the Palace, the King presiding.

"We deliberated.

"There were two solutions: one, to grant passage to the German armies marching upon France, and to obtain heavy indemnities for the loss and injury suffered. . . . This would be to tear up the statute of the Belgian nation, to violate, of our own accord, the neutrality decreed by Europe and accepted by Belgium; to betray the obligations which this neutrality imposes upon us.

"The other solution was to risk war and invasion; to affront the most formidable military Power in the world; but honor would be saved, the Belgian Statute maintained, and the treaties respected.

"There was hardly any discussion. The decision forced itself upon us. It was formed immediately: we should protest, and we should resist.

"The reply was drafted in the Department of Foreign Affairs. It was taken to the Palace, and approved unanimously by the King and Council."

It had been necessary to translate the ultimatum, the original text being in German. On the other hand, the Minister of the Interior, M. Berryer, who had lately gone to Liége, there to confer with the Military Governor and various civil officials, could not rejoin his colleagues until an advanced hour of the night, so that the day was beginning to dawn when the Ministers took leave of the King. Great clouds were gliding across the sky. "It is a gloomy day, indeed, that is dawning!" said the King, who had approached a window. "Yet," he added, after a moment's pause, "it has begun as though it was to be brilliant!"

While this meeting was being held in the Palace, the German Minister, about half-past one in the morning, visited the Secretary-General for Foreign Affairs. He stated that he was instructed by his Government to inform the Belgian Government that French dirigibles had thrown bombs, and that a French cavalry patrol had crossed the frontier, thereby violating the law of nations, as war had not been declared.

Baron van der Elst inquired of Herr von Below where these incidents had occurred.

"In Germany."

"In that case I do not understand the object of your communication."

Herr von Below replied, in substance, that these actions, being contrary to the law of nations, were of a nature to lead one to suppose that France would not hesitate to infringe international conventions in other ways.

At seven o'clock in the morning the Belgian reply to the German proposition was handed to Herr von Below.

During the morning of the 3rd of August there was a meeting of the members of the Government, when they discussed, in particular, the expediency of an appeal to the Powers which, with Prussia, had guaranteed our independence and neutrality. But as our territory had not as yet been invaded, it was decided that this appeal would be premature.

On the same day the King of the Belgians dispatched the following appealing telegram to the King of England: "Recalling to my mind the numerous marks of friendship vouchsafed by your Majesty and his predecessors, of the friendly attitude of England in 1870, and of the proof of sympathy which she now again gives us, I make a supreme

appeal to the diplomatic intervention of your Majesty's
Government to safeguard the neutrality of Belgium.

"ALBERT."

But it was too late. Diplomatically, England could do
no more; Germany wanted war, that war for which she had
so long been preparing.

. . . .

The Belgian people approved unreservedly of the proud
and dignified reply which its rulers had made to the German
proposals.

Immediately and unanimously it felt that it represented
justice, that its mission was a holy one, and that it could
not fail to accomplish it.

So, on the morning of the 4th of August, when the King,
in campaigning kit, visited Parliament, where all the representatives of the nation were awaiting him, there were frantic acclamations all along his route.

Never had our handsome monarch appeared to greater
advantage. On horseback, riding with a firm seat, he tow-
ered above the crowd, giving it the military salute, identi-
fying himself, by that martial gesture, with the feelings of
all. And it was our sole voice, the voice of an entire people,
which rose, vibrating, in a single impulse of patriotism, hail-
ing him who, in that solemn moment, symbolized it with
unexampled majesty.

In Parliament the session was unforgettable. The great
white hall had been arranged and decorated with great restraint, the effect being at once simple and impressive. In
the place of the desk the royal throne had been installed—a
large gilt armchair, upholstered in red velvet, on the back
of which is embroidered, in letters of gold, the national
motto: *L'Union fait la Force*. Above the throne was an
escutcheon with the national coat of arms, surrounded by
the folds of the Belgian flag—black, yellow, and red—and
the colonial flag—blue with golden stars.

On either side of the steps leading to the throne was a
Belgian flag.

The President and his assessors sat at the table which is generally used by the reporters.

An extraordinary animation prevailed in the semi-circle of benches; the tribunes were overflowing.

At ten o'clock the Queen arrived, accompanied by the little Princes.

Greeted by an enthusiastic acclamation, she took her place in an armchair to the right of the throne; her children were beside her. Then the King entered, and the cheering broke out again, prolonged and vibrating.

But the President rapped with his mallet. Silence ensued, and the King, standing upright before the throne, deeply moved, delivered this speech:—

BY KING ALBERT

"Gentlemen:

"Never, since 1830, has a more solemn hour struck for Belgium: the integrity of our territory is threatened.

"The very force of our righteous cause, the sympathy which Belgium, proud of her free institutions and her moral victories, has always received from other nations, and the necessity of our autonomous existence in respect of the equilibrium of Europe, make us still hopeful that the dreaded emergency will not be realized.

"But if our hopes are betrayed, if we are forced to resist the invasion of our soil, and to defend our threatened homes, this duty, however hard it may be, will find us armed and resolved upon the greatest sacrifices.

"Even now, in readiness for any eventuality, our valiant youth is up in arms, firmly resolved, with the traditional tenacity and composure of the Belgians, to defend our threatened country.

"In the name of the nation, I give it a brotherly greeting. Everywhere in Flanders and Wallonia, in the towns and in the countryside, one single feeling binds all hearts together: the sense of patriotism. One single vision fills all minds: that of our independence endangered. One single duty imposes itself upon our wills: the duty of stubborn resistance.

"In these solemn circumstances two virtues are indispensable: a calm but unshaken courage, and the close union of all Belgians.

"Both virtues have already asserted themselves, in a brilliant fashion, before the eyes of a nation full of enthusiasm.

"The irreproachable mobilization of our army, the multitude of voluntary enlistments, the devotion of the civil population, the abnegation of our soldiers' families, have revealed in an unquestionable manner the reassuring courage which inspires the Belgian people.

"It is the moment for action.

"I have called you together, gentlemen, in order to enable the Legislative Chambers to associate themselves with the impulse of the people in one and the same sentiment of sacrifice.

"You will understand, gentlemen, how to take all those immediate measures which the situation requires, in respect both of the war and of public order.

"No one in this country will fail in his duty.

"If the foreigner, in defiance of that neutrality whose demands we have always scrupulously observed, violates our territory, he will find all the Belgians gathered about their sovereign, who will never betray his constitutional oath, and their Government, invested with the absolute confidence of the entire nation.

"I have faith in our destinies; a country which is defending itself conquers the respect of all; such a country does not perish!"

. . . .

This speech, need we say, was frequently interrupted by the cheers of the whole Assembly, and the peroration was greeted by a stirring acclamation, such as had never before been heard within those walls.

After the King had withdrawn with the Queen and the Princes, Baron de Broqueville, President of the Council and Minister of War, acquainted the Chambers with the events which had occurred during the last few days. He also read a Note which the German Minister had forwarded at six o'clock that very morning to the Belgian Government, in which Germany declared her determination to cross our territory *by force of arms.*

This was war!

"We shall defend ourselves," said M. de Broqueville finally, *"and even if we are defeated we shall never be conquered."*

Various legislative proposals, inspired by the circumstances, were adopted immediately without debate.

In particular the Chamber voted unanimously a credit of 200 million francs with which to meet the first expenses. Then, about eleven o'clock, the President of the Council, with tears in his eyes, announced that the national territory had just been invaded. He further announced, amid indescribable enthusiasm, that "the King, wishing to recognize the patriotic assistance which the Opposition had afforded the Government, had decided to appoint M. Émile Vandervelde Minister of State." [1]

This historic session was terminated shortly before noon.

A few hours later words were spoken in Berlin which had less nobility than those which had rung through the Belgian Parliament.

The Chancellor of the Empire, in short, made the following declaration from the tribune of the Reichstag:—

"Our troops have occupied Luxemburg and it may be (*sic*) that they have already entered Belgium. This is contrary to the prescriptions of international law. France, it is true, assured Brussels that she was determined to respect the neutrality of Belgium as long as her adversary did so. But we knew that France was holding herself in readiness to invade Belgium. . . . In this way we have been forced to override the justified protests of the Belgian and Luxemburg Governments.

"We shall repair the injustice which we are committing as soon as our military object is attained."

---

[1] In Belgium, the Ministers of State have no portfolio; selected from among those statesmen who have been of eminent service to the country, they form, so to speak, a Privy Council of the Crown.

BRITAIN ENTERS THE WAR

THE ILLUMINATING INCIDENTS OF THE "SCRAP OF PAPER" AND THE "HYMN OF HATE"

AUGUST 4, 1914

HERBERT ASQUITH   SIR EDWARD GOSCHEN
VON BETHMANN-HOLLWEG   DAVID LLOYD GEORGE
ERNST LISSAUER

Russia had entered the Great War partly out of race sympathy with the Serbians, and partly as a matter of foreign policy, because her aristocratic leaders would not yield their plans of expansion in surrender to the similar plans of world-gambling aristocrats in Germany and Austria. Of Serbia and Belgium we can scarce say that they entered the War at all. They were agonized victims able to do no more than resist a crafty, murderous assault. Of France it is almost equally clear that she fought only because she must, that she too could already feel that coldly calculating grip outreaching for her throat. The cause of Britain's entry is not so glaringly obvious. She cared only vaguely about Serbia or even about Russia. She had been frequently at quarrel with France until only a few years before. As to fear of Germany's world-dominion, of autocracy throttling democracy, or of Britain's being herself attacked by Germany in a later war—there is no clear evidence that the British Parliament acted on, or even was fully awake to, any of these dangers.

The German Chancellor in his official statement to his countrymen, here reprinted, attributes to Britain motives of world conquest like his own. But his charges rest wholly on his own assumptions; and he is hopelessly incapable of understanding Britain, because he persists in regarding her as an autocracy like Imperial Germany. Hence he attributes to Britain all the casuistry and the evasion, the ambition and the cruelty which he knows to actuate his own government. Yet even Bethmann-Hollweg, as a climax, is able to establish no more against Britain than one of those characteristic German arguments of such obstinate onesidedness. His plea is that had Britain positively warned Russia and France that she would abandon them if they fought for Serbia, they would have been afraid to fight. That is, if Britain had not only herself abandoned Serbia to destruction, but also compelled everybody else to, then Germany and Austria would have made a meal of Serbia in bloody comfort and there would have been no war. Since Britain had neglected thus to bind her friends, and lay them helpless at the feet of her enemies, she had caused the War.

In sharpest contrast to this rambling accusation is the clear statement to the British Parliament by Prime Minister Asquith, as also the briefer resumé by that later British Prime Minister, Lloyd George, who took over the work of Asquith and carried the War to a successful end.

As a matter of straightforward fact, Britain's calm attitude at the opening of the War stands out magnificently. For a dozen years before, her ministers, and especially her Foreign Minister Sir Edward Grey, had been acting on the principle that world-peace was a necessity for Britain's prosperity. They had smoothed over almost every antagonism which an earlier British arrogance had fostered. Even the opposition of Germany's increasing commerce they expected to meet by improving their own methods of trade rather than by the uncertain arbitrament of war. So even with Germany they essayed the impossible task of trying to make harmonious arrangements toward an equal peace. Across all these British efforts at good will, the Great War came as with the slash of a knife. It was not of Britain's seeking.

Her Ministers saw all their efforts swept away; they saw the Balkans in chaos; they saw France in deadly danger. For Serbia they contented themselves with diplomatic protest; for France they marshaled their fleet and might have fought. But when Germany took the further step, when she as it were struck Britain flatly in the face by attacking Belgium, which both Prussia and Britain had pledged themselves to protect, then Britons could have no further doubt. As clearly as the alternative had been put to Belgium, so clearly was it put to them. They must sacrifice their honor, must bow to German dictate, or they must fight. Quite simply they chose as Belgium had chosen.

The oft-told incident of the "Scrap of Paper," the discussion between the German Chancellor and the British Ambassador about that treaty pledging support of Belgium's neutrality, is here given in its original version, as the Ambassador, Sir Edward Goschen, told of it in his official report. We give also the Chancellor's explanation of the phrase when, months later, after he had seen its influence, he endeavored to explain it away.

Then at the close, as a fitting summary to our volume, we give the notorious "Hymn of Hate." No words could better convey the "mass hypnotism" of Germany, the readiness with which the people shifted their hatred at command. They had been told first that Russia, and then that France was their true antagonist. Now England was accused; and this poem was the people's answer. It was sung everywhere and by all classes. By 1917, however, the German leaders wished to give a new direction to their people's anger. America had entered the war. The Chancellors who succeeded Bethmann-Hollweg discarded all his charges against Britain. They announced officially and repeatedly that these charges were mistaken. Britain had not at all been guilty of these secret machinations. The United States was now the one true foe. So a new stanza was added to the "Hymn of Hate" in which Uncle Sam was raged at in his turn, and named as the secret villain of the plot.

C. F. H.

BY HERBERT ASQUITH

Prime Minister of Britain, His Address to Parliament Announcing
the War on August 6, 1914

WITH the utmost reluctance and with infinite regret,
His Majesty's Government have been compelled to
put this country in a state of war with what for many years
and indeed generations past has been a friendly Power. The
Papers which have since been presented to Parliament will,
I think, show how strenuous, how unremitting, how persistent, even when the last glimmer of hope seemed to have
faded away, were the efforts of my right hon. Friend the
Foreign Secretary [1] to secure for Europe an honorable and
a lasting peace.

Every one knows in the great crisis which occurred last
year in the East of Europe, it was largely, if not mainly, by
the acknowledgment of all Europe, due to the steps taken
by my right hon. Friend that the area of the conflict was
limited, and that so far as the great Powers are concerned,
peace was maintained. If his efforts upon this ocasion have,
unhappily, been less successful, I am certain that this House
and the country—and I will add posterity and history—will
accord to him what is, after all, the best tribute that can be
paid to any statesman : that, never derogating for an instant
or by an inch from the honor and interests of his own country, he has striven, as few men have striven, to maintain
and preserve the greatest interest of all countries—universal
peace.

The Papers, which are now in the hands of hon. Members, show something more than that. They show what were
the terms which were offered to us in exchange for our
neutrality. I trust that not only the Members of this House,
but all our fellow-subjects everywhere will read the communications—will read, learn and mark the communications
which passed only a week ago to-day between Berlin and
London in this matter. The terms by which it was sought to
buy our neutrality are contained in the communication
made by the German Chancellor to Sir Edward Goschen on

[1] Sir Edward Grey.

the 29th July. I think I must refer to them for a moment. After alluding to the state of things as between Austria and Russia, Sir Edward Goschen goes on:—

"He [the German Chancellor] then proceeded to make the following strong bid for British neutrality. He said that it was clear, so far as he was able to judge the main principle which governed British policy, that Great Britain would never stand by and allow France to be crushed in any conflict there might be. That, however, was not the object at which Germany aimed. Provided that neutrality of Great Britain were certain, every assurance would be given to the British Government that the Imperial Government"——

Let the Committee observe these words—

"aimed at no territorial acquisition at the expense of France should they prove victorious in any war that might ensue."

Sir Edward Goschen proceeded to put a very pertinent question:—"I questioned His Excellency about the French colonies"—— What are the French colonies? They mean every part of the dominions and possessions of France outside the geographical area of Europe—"and he said that he was unable to give a similar undertaking in that respect."

Let me come to what, in my mind, personally has always been the crucial and almost the governing consideration, namely, the position of the small States:—"As regards Holland, however, His Excellency said that so long as Germany's adversaries respected the integrity and neutrality of the Netherlands, Germany was ready to give His Majesty's Government an assurance that she would do likewise."

Then we come to Belgium:—"It depended upon the action of France what operations Germany might be forced to enter upon in Belgium, but, when the war was over, Belgian integrity would be respected if she had not sided against Germany."

Let the Committee observe the distinction between those two cases. In regard to Holland it was not only independence and integrity, but also neutrality; but in regard to Belgium, there was no mention of neutrality at all, nothing but an assurance that after the war came to an end the integrity of Belgium would be respected. Then His Excellency added:—"Ever since he had been Chancellor the object of his policy had been to bring about an understanding with England. He trusted that these assurances"—the assurances I have read out to the House—"might form the basis of that understanding which he so much desired."

What does that amount to? Let me just ask the Committee. I do so, not with the object of inflaming passion, certainly not with the object of exciting feeling against Germany, but I do so to vindicate and make clear the position of the British Government in this matter. What did that proposal amount to? In the first place, it meant this: That behind the back of France—they were not made a party to these communications—we should have given, if we had assented to that, a free license to Germany to annex, in the event of a successful war, the whole of the extra European dominions and possessions of France. What did it mean as regards Belgium? When she addressed, as she has addressed in these last few days, her moving appeal to us to fulfill our solemn guarantee of her neutrality, what reply should we have given? What reply should we have given to that Belgian appeal? We should have been obliged to say that, without her knowledge, we had bartered away to the Power threatening her our obligation to keep our plighted word. The House has read, and the country has read, of course, in the last few hours, the most pathetic appeal addressed by the King of Belgium, and I do not envy the man who can read that appeal with an unmoved heart. Belgians are fighting and losing their lives. What would have been the position of Great Britain to-day, in the face of that spectacle, if we had assented to this infamous proposal?

Yes, and what are we to get in return for the betrayal of our friends and the dishonor of our obligations? What are we to get in return? A promise—nothing more; a promise as to what Germany would do in certain eventualities; a promise, be it observed—I am sorry to have to say it, but it must be put upon record—given by a Power which was at that very moment announcing its intention to violate its own treaty and inviting us to do the same. I can only say, if we had dallied or temporized, we, as a Government, should have covered ourselves with dishonor, and we should have betrayed the interests of this country, of which we are trustees. I am glad, and I think the country will be glad, to turn to the reply which my right hon. Friend made, and of which I will read to the Committee two of the more salient passages. This document, No. 101 of the Papers, puts on record a week ago the attitude of the British Government, and, as I believe, of the British people. My right hon. Friend says:—

"His Majesty's Government cannot for a moment entertain the Chancellor's proposal that they should bind themselves to neutrality on such terms. What he asks us in effect is to engage to stand by while French Colonies are taken if France is beaten, so long as Germany does not take French territory as distinct from the Colonies. From the material point of view"—— My right hon. Friend, as he always does, used very temperate language—"Such a proposal is unacceptable, for France, without further territory in Europe being taken from her, could be so crushed as to lose her position as a Great Power, and become subordinate to German policy."

That is the material aspect. But he proceeded:—"Altogether, apart from that, it would be a disgrace for us to make this bargain with Germany at the expense of France, a disgrace from which the good name of this country would never recover. The Chancellor also in effect asks us to bargain away whatever obligation or interest we have as regards the neutrality of Belgium. We could not entertain that bargain either."

He then says:—"We must preserve our full freedom to act, as circumstances may seem to us to require."

And he added, I think in sentences which the Committee must appreciate:—"You should . . . add most earnestly that the one way of maintaining the good relations between England and Germany is that they should continue to work together to preserve the peace of Europe. . . . For that object this Government will work in that way with all sincerity and goodwill.

"If the peace of Europe can be preserved and the present crisis safely passed, my own endeavor will be to promote some arrangement to which Germany could be a party, by which she could be assured that no aggressive or hostile policy would be pursued against her or her allies by France, Russia, and ourselves, jointly or separately. I have desired this and worked for it"—the statement was never more true—"as far as I could, through the last Balkan crisis, and Germany having a corresponding object, our relations sensibly improved. The idea has hitherto been too Utopian to form the subject of definite proposals, but if this present crisis, so much more acute than any that Europe has gone through for generations, be safely passed, I am hopeful that the relief and reaction which will follow may make possible some more definite rapprochement between the Powers than has been possible hitherto."

That document, in my opinion, states clearly, in temperate and convincing language, the attitude of this Government. Can any one who reads it fail to appreciate the tone of obvious sincerity and earnestness which underlies it; can any one honestly doubt that the Government of this country in spite of great provocation—and I regard the proposals made to us as proposals which we might have thrown aside without consideration and almost without answer— can any one doubt that in spite of great provocation the right hon. Gentleman, who had already earned the title— and no one ever more deserved it—of "Peace Maker of Europe," persisted to the very last moment of the last hour in that beneficent but unhappily frustrated purpose?

I am entitled to say, and I do so on behalf of this country—I speak not for a party, I speak for the country as a whole—that we made every effort any Government could possibly make for peace. But this war has been forced upon us. What is it we are fighting for? Every one knows, and no one knows better than the Government, the terrible, incalculable suffering, economic, social, personal and political, which war, and especially a war between the Great Powers of the world, must entail. There is no man amongst us sitting upon this bench in these trying days—more trying perhaps than any body of statesmen for a hundred years have had to pass through—there is not a man amongst us who has not, during the whole of that time, had clearly before his vision the almost unequaled suffering which war, even in a just cause, must bring about, not only to the people who are for the moment living in this country and in the other countries of the world, but to posterity and to the whole prospects of European civilization. Every step we took we took with that vision before our eyes, and with a sense of responsibility which it is impossible to describe. Unhappily, if in spite of all our efforts to keep the peace, and with that full and overpowering consciousness of the result, if the issue be decided in favor of war, we have, nevertheless, thought it to be the duty as well as the interest of this country to go to war, the House may be well assured it was because we believe, and I am certain the country will believe, that we are unsheathing our sword in a just cause.

If I am asked what we are fighting for I reply in two sentences: *In the first place, to fulfill a solemn international obligation,* an obligation which, if it had been entered into between private persons in the ordinary concerns of life, would have been regarded as an obligation not only of law but of honor, which no self-respecting man could possibly have repudiated. I say, *secondly, we are fighting to vindicate the principle* which, in these days when force, material force, sometimes seems to be the dominant influence and factor in the development of mankind, we are fighting to vindicate the principle *that small nationalities are not to be crushed,* in defiance of international good faith, by the arbitrary will of a strong and overmastering Power.

I do not believe any nation ever entered into a great controversy—and this is one of the greatest history will ever know—with a clearer conscience and a stronger conviction that it is fighting, not for aggression, not for the maintenance even of its own selfish interest, but that it is fighting in defense of principles the maintenance of which is vital to the civilization of the world. With a full conviction, not only of the wisdom and justice, but of the obligations which lay upon us to challenge this great issue, we are entering into the struggle. Let us now make sure that all the resources, not only of this United Kingdom, but of the vast Empire of which it is the center, shall be thrown into the scale.

BY SIR EDWARD GOSCHEN
British Ambassador at Berlin, His Official Report of the Breaking of Diplomatic Relations and of the "Scrap of Paper"

In accordance with the instructions contained in your telegram of the 4th instant, I called upon the Secretary of State that afternoon and inquired, in the name of His Majesty's Government, whether the Imperial Government would refrain from violating Belgian neutrality. Herr von Jagow at once replied that he was sorry to say that his answer must be "No," as, in consequence of the German troops having crossed the frontier that morning, Belgian neutrality had been already violated. Herr von Jagow again went into the reasons why the Imperial Government had been obliged to take this step, namely, that they had to advance into France by the quickest and easiest way, so as to be able to get well ahead with their operations and endeavor to strike some decisive blow as early as possible. It was a matter of life and death for them, as if they had gone by the more southern route they could not have hoped, in view of the paucity of roads and the strength of the fortresses, to have got through without formidable opposition entailing great loss of time. This loss of time would have meant time gained by the Russians for bringing up their troops to the German frontier. Rapidity of action was the great German asset, while that of Russia was an inexhaustible supply of troops. I pointed out to Herr von Jagow that this *fait accompli* of the violation of the Belgian frontier rendered, as he would readily understand, the situation exceedingly grave, and I asked him whether there was not still time to draw back and avoid possible consequences, which both he and I would deplore. He replied that, for the reasons he had given me, it was now impossible for them to draw back.

During the afternoon I received your further telegram

of the same date, and, in compliance with the instructions
therein contained, I again proceeded to the Imperial Foreign Office and informed the Secretary of State that unless
the Imperial Government could give the assurance by 12
o'clock that night that they would proceed no further with
their violation of the Belgian frontier and stop their advance, I had been instructed to demand my passports and
inform the Imperial Government that His Majesty's Government would have to take all steps in their power to uphold the neutrality of Belgium and the observance of a
treaty to which Germany was as much a party as themselves.

Herr von Jagow replied that to his great regret he could
give no other answer than that which he had given me
earlier in the day, namely, that the safety of the Empire
rendered it absolutely necessary that the Imperial troops
should advance through Belgium. I gave his Excellency a
written summary of your telegram and, pointing out that
you had mentioned 12 o'clock as the time when His Majesty's Government would expect an answer, asked him
whether, in view of the terrible consequences which would
necessarily ensue, it were not possible even at the last moment that their answer should be reconsidered. He replied
that if the time given were even twenty-four hours or more,
his answer must be the same. I said that in that case I
should have to demand my passports. This interview took
place at about 7 o'clock. In a short conversation which ensued Herr von Jagow expressed his poignant regret at the
crumbling of his entire policy and that of the Chancellor,
which had been to make friends with Great Britain, and
then, through Great Britain, to get closer to France. I said
that this sudden end to my work in Berlin was to me also
a matter of deep regret and disappointment, but that he
must understand that under the circumstances and in view
of our engagements, His Majesty's Government could not
possibly have acted otherwise than they had done.

I then said that I should like to go and see the Chancellor,
as it might be, perhaps, the last time I should have an opportunity of seeing him. He begged me to do so. I found

the Chancellor very agitated. His Excellency at once began a harangue, which lasted for about twenty minutes. He said that the step taken by His Majesty's Government was terrible to a degree; *just for a word—"neutrality," a word which in war time had so often been disregarded—just for a scrap of paper Great Britain was going to make war on a kindred nation* who desired nothing better than to be friends with her. All his efforts in that direction had been rendered useless by this last terrible step, and the policy to which, as I knew, he had devoted himself since his accession to office had tumbled down like a house of cards. What we had done was unthinkable; it was like striking a man from behind while he was fighting for his life against two assailants. He held Great Britain responsible for all the terrible events that might happen. I protested strongly against that statement, and said that, in the same way as he and Herr von Jagow wished me to understand that for strategical reasons it was a matter of life and death to Germany to advance through Belgium and violate the latter's neutrality, so I would wish him to understand that it was, so to speak, a matter of "life and death" for the honor of Great Britain that she should keep her solemn engagement to do her utmost to defend Belgium's neutrality if attacked. That solemn compact simply had to be kept, or what confidence could any one have in engagements given by Great Britain in the future? *The Chancellor said, "But at what price will that compact have been kept. Has the British Government thought of that?"* I hinted to his Excellency as plainly as I could that fear of consequences could hardly be regarded as an excuse for breaking solemn engagements, but his Excellency was so excited, so evidently overcome by the news of our action, and so little disposed to hear reason that I refrained from adding fuel to the flame by further argument. As I was leaving he said that the blow of Great Britain joining Germany's enemies was all the greater that almost up to the last moment he and his Government had been working with us and supporting our efforts to maintain peace between Austria and Russia. I said that this was part of the tragedy which saw the two nations fall apart just at the moment when the relations between them had been more friendly and cordial than they had been for years. Unfortunately, notwithstanding our efforts to maintain peace between Russia and Austria, the war had spread and had brought us face to face with a situation which, if we held to our engagements, we could not possibly avoid, and which unfortunately entailed our separation from our late fellow-workers. He would readily understand that no one regretted this more than I.

After this somewhat painful interview I returned to the embassy and drew up a telegraphic report of what had passed. This telegram was handed in at the Central Telegraph Office a little before 9 p. m. It was accepted by that office, but apparently never dispatched.

At about 9.30 p. m. Herr von Zimmermann, the Under-Secretary of State, came to see me. After expressing his deep regret that the very friendly official and personal relations between us were about to cease, he asked me casually whether a demand for passports was equivalent to a declaration of war. I said that such an authority on international law as he was known to be must know as well or better than I what was usual in such cases. I added that there were many cases where diplomatic relations had been broken off, and, nevertheless, war had not ensued; but that in this case he would have seen from my instructions, of which I had given Herr von Jagow a written summary, that His Majesty's Government expected an answer to a definite question by 12 o'clock that night and that in default of a satisfactory answer they would be forced to take such steps as their engagements required. Herr Zimmermann said that that was, in fact, a declaration of war, as the Imperial Government could not possibly give the assurance required either that night or any other night.

BY CHANCELLOR BETHMANN-HOLLWEG

A Published Interview Explaining the "Scrap of Paper" Phrase

My conversation with Sir E. Goschen occurred on the 4th of August. I had just declared in the Reichstag that only dire necessity, only the struggle for existence, compelled Germany to march through Belgium, but that Germany was ready to make compensation for the wrong committed. When I spoke I already had certain indications, but no absolute proof, on which to base a public accusation that Belgium had long before abandoned its neutrality in its relations with England. Nevertheless, I took Germany's responsibilities towards neutral States so seriously that I spoke frankly on the wrong committed by Germany. What was the British attitude on the same question? The day before my conversation with the British Ambassador, Sir Edward Grey had delivered his well-known speech in Parliament, wherein, while he did not state expressly that England would take part in the war, he left the matter in little doubt. One needs only to read this speech through carefully to learn the reason of England's intervention in the war. Amid all his beautiful phrases about England's honor and England's obligations we find it over and over again expressed that England's interests—its own interests—called for participation in war, for it was not in England's interests that a victorious, and therefore stronger, Germany should emerge from the war. This old principle of England's policy—to take as the sole criterion of its actions its private interests regardless of right, reason, or considerations of humanity—is expressed in that speech of Gladstone's in 1870 on Belgian neutrality from which Sir Edward quoted. Mr. Gladstone then declared that he was unable to subscribe to the doctrine that the simple fact of the existence of a guarantee is binding upon every party thereto, irrespective altogether of the particular position in which it may find itself at the time when the occasion for action on the guarantee arrives, and he referred to such English statesmen as Aberdeen and Palmerston as supporters of his views.

England drew the sword only because she believed her own interests demanded it. Just for Belgian neutrality she would never have entered the war. That is what I meant when I told Sir E. Goschen, in that last interview when we sat down to talk the matter over privately man to man, that among the reasons which had impelled England into war the Belgian neutrality treaty had for her only the value of a scrap of paper. I may have been a bit excited and aroused. Who would not have been at seeing the hopes and work of the whole period of my Chancellorship going for naught? I recalled to the Ambassador my efforts for years to bring about an understanding between England and Germany, an understanding which, I reminded him, would have made a general European war impossible, and have absolutely guaranteed the peace of Europe. Such understanding would have formed the basis on which we could have approached the United States as a third partner. But England had not taken up this plan, and through its entry into the war had destroyed forever the hope of its fulfillment. In comparison with such momentous consequences, was the treaty not a scrap of paper?

Speech of the Chancellor Before the Reichstag

Where the responsibility in this greatest of all wars lies is quite evident to us. Outwardly responsible are the men in Russia who planned and carried into effect the general mobilization of the Russian army. But in reality and truth the British Government is responsible. The London Cabinet could have made war impossible if they had unequivocally told Petersburg that England was not willing to let a continental war of the Great Powers result from the Austro-Hungarian conflict with Serbia. Such words would have compelled France to use all her energy to keep Russia away from every warlike measure. Then our good offices and mediation between Vienna and Petersburg would have been successful, and there would have been no war! But England has chosen to act otherwise. She knew that the clique of powerful and partly irresponsible men surrounding the Czar were spoiling for war and intriguing to bring it about. England saw that the wheel was set a-rolling, but she did not think of stopping it. While openly professing sentiments of peace, London secretly gave St. Petersburg to understand that England stood by France and therefore by Russia too. This has been clearly and irrefutably shown by the official publications which in the meantime have come out, more particularly by the Blue Book edited by the British Government. Then St. Petersburg could no longer be restrained. In proof of this we possess the testimony of the Belgian Chargé d'Affaires at St. Petersburg, a witness who is surely beyond every suspicion. He reported (you know his words, but I will repeat them now), he reported to his Government on July 30th that "England commenced by making it understood that she would not let herself be drawn into a conflict. Sir George Buchanan said this openly. To-day, however, everybody in St. Petersburg is quite convinced,— one has actually received the assurance—that England will stand by France. This support is of enormous weight and has contributed largely toward giving the war-party the upper hand." Up to this summer English statesmen have assured their Parliament that no treaty or agreement existed influencing England's independence of action, should a war break out, England was free to decide whether she would participate in a European war or not. Hence, there was no treaty obligation, no compulsion, no menace of the homeland which induced the English statesmen to originate the war and then at once to take part in it. The only conclusion left is that the London Cabinet allowed this European war, this monstrous world war, because they thought it was an opportune moment with the aid of England's political confederates, to destroy the vital nerve of her greatest European competitors in the markets of the world. Therefore, England, together with Russia (I have spoken about Russia on the 4th of August), is answerable before God and man for this catastrophe which has come over Europe and over mankind.

The Belgian neutrality which England pretended she was bound to shield, is but a mask. On the 2nd of August, 7 p. m., we informed Brussels that France's plan of campaign was known to us and that it compelled us, for reasons of self-preservation, to march through Belgium, but as early as the afternoon of the same day, August 2nd, that is to say, before anything was known and could be known of this step, the British Government promised unconditional aid to France in case the German navy attacked the French coastline. Not a word was said of Belgian neutrality. This fact is established by the declaration made by Sir Edward Grey in the House of Commons on the 3rd of August. The declaration was communicated to me on August 4th, but not in full, because of the difficulties experienced at that time in the transmission of telegrams. Besides the very Blue Book issued by the British Government confirms that fact. How, then, can England allege that she drew the sword because we violated Belgian neutrality? How could British statesmen, who accurately knew the past, talk at all of Belgian neutrality? When on the 4th of August I referred to the wrong which we were doing in marching through Belgium, it was not yet known for certain whether the Brussels Government in the hour of need would not decide after all to spare the country and to retire to Antwerp under protest. You remember that, after the occupation of Liége, at the request of our army leaders, I repeated the offer to the Belgian Government. For military reasons it was absolutely imperative that at the time, about the 4th of August, the possibility for such a development was being kept open. Even then the guilt of the Belgian Government was apparent from many a sign, although I had not yet any positive documentary proofs at my disposal. But the English statesmen were perfectly familiar with these proofs. The documents which in the meantime have been found in Brussels, and which have been given publicity by me, prove and establish in what way and to what degree Belgium has surrendered her neutrality to England.[2]

[2] The charges against Belgium, here and elsewhere referred to, form but another example of the falsehoods by which Germany long managed to keep neutral nations and especially the American public in doubt as to the real nature of the War. The falsehood here given such solemn weight and official sanction by a Chancellor who knew its falsity, was based on two documents extracted from the refuse left behind by the Belgian Government when it abandoned Brussels. These really worthless documents were of a type such as exists in every State office in Europe. Two military attachés of different countries hold a military "conversation" beginning "*If* my country and yours should ever be allied in war against this and that other one, what could we do to aid each other?" And they vary their imaginary antagonists at will, and get much military practice at no expense. Occasionally the attachés in such a conversation report its substance to their governments, so proving their professional industry. But no authority or State

The whole world is now acquainted with two outstanding facts: (1) In the night from the 3rd to the 4th of August, when our troops entered Belgian territory, they were not on neutral soil, but on the soil of a state that had long abandoned its neutrality. (2) England has declared war on us, not for the sake of Belgian neutrality, which she herself had helped to undermine, but because she believed that she could overcome and master us with the help of two great military powers on the Continent. Ever since the 2nd of August when England promised to back up the French in this war, she was no longer neutral, but actually in a state of war with us. On the 4th of August she declared war, the alleged reason being our violation of Belgian neutrality. But that was only a sham motive and a spectacular scene intended to conceal the true war motive and thus to mislead both the English people and foreign neutral countries.

The military plans which England and Belgium had worked out to the minutest details now being unveiled, the policy of English statesmen is branded for all times of history to come. But English diplomacy still added to this: At its call, Japan snatched from us Kiautschau, so bravely defended, and thus violated Chinese neutrality. Has England interfered with that breach of neutrality? Has she shown in this instance her scrupulous anxiety about the neutral states?

When, in 1910, I became Chancellor, the Triple Alliance had to reckon with a solid counter-combination of Powers. England had created the Triple Entente and knitted it firmly for the purpose of maintaining the "balance of power." For

agreement goes with these "conversations" which exist by hundreds, and never acquire any meaning unless the initial *if* is some day removed by Fate.

The two documents plucked from the Belgian waste baskets were of such conversations between Britons and Belgians. So far as they proved anything, they proved not that Belgium had surrendered her neutrality but that she meant to defend it against any and all invaders. The German Government deliberately misrepresented these commonplace reports of under-officers as being the text of a secret treaty between Belgium and Britain. They are even hinted at as causing the Belgian invasion, the Chancellor forgetting that it was a French intrusion he then officially announced.

centuries it had been a fundamental tenet of British policy to turn against that Continental Power which was strongest, and this principle was to find its most efficient instrument in the Triple Entente. Thus, whilst the Triple Alliance was of a strictly defensive character, the nature of the Triple Entente was offensive from the beginning. In this lay all the elements of a terrific explosion. A nation as great and efficient as the Germans are does not allow its free and pacific development to be thwarted. In the face of this aggressive combination the course of German policy was clear. We had to try to come to a separate understanding with each member of the Triple Entente in order to dispel the clouds of war, and at the same time we had to increase our armaments so as to be ready if war actually broke out. Gentlemen, you know that have done both. In France we encountered, again and again, sentiments of revenge. These sentiments being fed and fostered by ambitious politicians proved stronger than the wish, undoubtedly cherished by a part of the French people, to live with us, as neighbors should, on friendly terms. We made, indeed, some specific agreements with Russia, but her close alliance with France, her opposition to our Austro-Hungarian ally and an anti-German feeling, born and bred of the Panslavistic craving for power, made agreements impossible which would have averted all dangers of war in the case of a political crisis. Freer than France and Russia was England. I have already reminded you how British statesmen in parliament, again and again, proudly affirmed Great Britain's absolutely unrestricted right to steer her own course. The attempt to come to an understanding, which would have safeguarded the peace of the world, was easiest to make with England.

On these lines I had to act and I did act. I well knew that it was a narrow road, not easy to tread. In the course of centuries, the English insular way of thinking had evolved the political maxim that England had a right to an "arbitrium mundi," which she could only uphold by an unrivaled supremacy on sea and by the maintenance of the balance of power on the Continent. I never had any hopes that my persuasion could break that old English maxim.

What I did hope and thought possible was that the growth of German power and the increase of the risks of a war might open England's eyes to the fact that her old-fashioned maxim had become untenable and impracticable, and that an amicable settlement with Germany was preferable. But that old doctrine of hers more than once stood in the way of a peaceful understanding. The crisis of 1911 gave a new impetus to the negotiations. The English people suddenly realized that they had stood at the brink of a European war. Popular sentiment forced the British Government to a rapprochement with Germany. After long and arduous negotiations we finally arrived at an understanding on various disputed questions of an economic character, regarding Africa and Asia Minor. This understanding was to lessen every possible political friction. The world is wide. There is room enough for both nations to measure their strength in peaceful rivalry as long as our national strength is allowed free scope for development. German policy always stood up for that principle. But during the negotiations England was indefatigable in her endeavors to enter into ever closer relations with France and Russia. The decisive point was that beyond the political sphere of action one military agreement after the other was made in view of a possible continental war. England kept these negotiations as secret as possible. When something about them would percolate, it was declared, both in the press and in Parliament, to be perfectly harmless. But things could not be concealed, as you know from the official papers that were published by me. The general situation was this: England was indeed ready to come to an understanding on single items, but the first and foremost principle of her policy was the "balance of power" as a means of checking German strength in its free development.

This forms the border-line of England's amicable relations with Germany; and the purpose was the utmost strengthening of the Triple Entente. When the Allies demanded military assurances in return, England was at once ready to give them. The circle was closed. The English were sure of the following of France and hence of Russia.

But they, too, had to abandon their free-will. As the jingoes of France and Russia found their strongest support in the military accommodation promised by her, England, as soon as either of the two Allies began the war, was morally bound to support them. And all this was done to what purpose? Because Germany was to be kept down. We have not been remiss in warning the British Government. As late as the beginning of last July I gave them to understand that their secret negotiations with Russia about a naval agreement were well known to me. I called their attention to the grave danger which such policy implied for the peace of the world. As soon as a fortnight afterward my predictions came true.

We have taken the consequences of the general situation. In quick succession I have laid before you the hugest war bill which history ever recorded, and you, gentlemen, fully recognizing the country's danger, have gladly made the sacrifice and have granted what was necessary for our national self-defense. And when war broke out, England dropped the mask of hypocrisy. Loudly and openly she declares her determination to fight until Germany is laid prostrate both in an economic and military sense. Anti-German Panslavism joins its jubilant notes, France with the full strength of an old warlike nation hopes to redeem the humiliation inflicted on her in 1870. Our only answer to our enemies is: Germany does not allow herself to be crushed!

BY DAVID LLOYD GEORGE

An Address Delivered in June, 1917

It is a satisfaction for Britain in these terrible times that no share of the responsibility for these events rests on her. She is not the Jonah in this storm. The part taken by our country in this conflict, in its origin, and in its conduct, has been as honorable and chivalrous as any part ever taken in any country in any operation. We might imagine from declarations which were made by the Germans, aye! and even by a few people in this country, who are constantly referring to our German comrades, that this terrible war was wantonly and wickedly provoked by England—never Scotland—never

Wales—and never Ireland. Wantonly provoked by England to increase her possessions, and to destroy the influence, the power, and the prosperity of a dangerous rival.

There never was a more foolish travesty of the actual facts. It happened three years ago, or less, but there have been so many bewildering events crowded into those intervening years that some people might have forgotten, perhaps, some of the essential facts, and it is essential that we should now and again restate them, not merely to refute the calumniators of our native land, but in order to sustain the hearts of her people by the unswerving conviction that no part of the guilt of this terrible bloodshed rests on the conscience of their native land. What are the main facts? There were six countries which entered the war at the beginning. Britain was last, and not the first. Before she entered the war Britain made every effort to avoid it; begged, supplicated, and entreated that there should be no conflict. I was a member of the Cabinet at the time, and I remember the earnest endeavors we made to persuade Germany and Austria not to precipitate Europe into this welter of blood. We begged them to summon a European conference to consider. Had that conference met arguments against provoking such a catastrophe were so overwhelming that there would never have been a war. Germany knew that, so she rejected the conference, although Austria was prepared to accept it. She suddenly declared war, and yet we are the people who wantonly provoked this war, in order to attack Germany. We begged Germany not to attack Belgium, and produced a treaty, signed by the King of Prussia, as well as the King of England, pledging himself to protect Belgium against an invader, and we said, "If you invade Belgium we shall have no alternative but to defend it." The enemy invaded Belgium, and now they say, "Why, forsooth, you, England, provoked this war."

It is not quite the story of the wolf and the lamb. I will tell you why—because Germany expected to find a lamb and found a lion.

BY ERNST LISSAUER [3]

The Hymn of Hate

French and Russian, they matter not,
A blow for a blow and a shot for a shot!
We love them not, we hate them not,
We hold the Weichsel and Vosges gate.
We have but one, one only hate,
We love as one, we hate as one,
We have one foe and one alone.
He is known to you all, he is known to you all,
He crouches behind the dark gray flood,
Full of envy, of rage, of craft, of gall,
Cut off by waves that are thicker than blood.
Come, let us stand at the Judgment Place,
An oath to swear to, face to face,
An oath of bronze no wind can shake,
An oath for our sons and their sons to take.
Come, hear the word, repeat the word,
Throughout the Fatherland make it heard.
We will never forego our hate,
We have all but a single hate,
We love as one, we hate as one,
We have one foe and one alone—
ENGLAND!

In the Captain's Mess, in the banquet hall,
Sat feasting the officers, one and all,
Like a saber blow, like the swing of a sail,
One seized his glass and held high to hail;
Sharp-snapped like the stroke of a rudder's play,
Spoke three words only: "To the Day!"
Whose glass this fate?
They had all but a single hate.
Who was thus known?
They had one foe and one alone—
ENGLAND!

[3] Dr. Lissauer afterward spoke half apologetically of this poem, saying it was only the expression of a momentary mood. Presumably he regards the War and all its massacres in the same kindly light.

Take you the folk of the Earth in pay,
With bars of gold your ramparts lay,
Bedeck the ocean with bow on bow,
Ye reckon well, but not well enough now.
French and Russian, they matter not,
A blow for a blow, a shot for a shot,
We fight the battle with bronze and steel,
And the time that is coming Peace will seal.
You we will hate with a lasting hate,
We will never forego our hate,
Hate by water and hate by land,
Hate of the head and hate of the hand,
Hate of the hammer and hate of the crown,
Hate of seventy millions choking down.
We love as one, we hate as one,
We have one foe and one alone—
              ENGLAND!